African Literatures as World Literature

LITERATURES AS WORLD LITERATURE

Can the literature of a specific country, author, or genre be used to approach the elusive concept of 'world literature'? **Literatures as World Literature** takes a novel approach to world literature by analyzing specific constellations – according to language, nation, form, or theme – of literary texts and authors in their own world-literary dimensions.

World literature is obviously so vast that any view of it cannot help but be partial; the question then becomes how to reduce the complex task of understanding and describing world literature. Most treatments of world literature so far either have been theoretical and thus abstract, or else have made broad use of exemplary texts from a variety of languages and epochs. The majority of critical work, the filling in of what has been traced, lies ahead of us. **Literatures as World Literature** fills in the devilish details by allowing scholars to move outward from their own areas of specialization, fostering scholarly writing that approaches more closely the polyphonic, multiperspectival nature of world literature.

Series Editor
Thomas O. Beebee

Editorial Board
Eduardo Coutinho, Federal University of Rio de Janeiro, Brazil
Hsinya Huang, National Sun-yat Sen University, Taiwan
Meg Samuelson, University of Adelaide, Australia
Ken Seigneurie, Simon Fraser University, Canada
Galin Tihanov, Queen Mary University of London, UK
Mads Rosendahl Thomsen, Aarhus University, Denmark

Volumes in the Series

German Literature as World Literature, edited by Thomas O. Beebee

Roberto Bolaño as World Literature, edited by Nicholas Birns and Juan E. De Castro

Crime Fiction as World Literature, edited by David Damrosch, Theo D'haen and Louise Nilsson

Danish Literature as World Literature, edited by Dan Ringgaard and Mads Rosendahl Thomsen

From Paris to Tlön: Surrealism as World Literature, by Delia Ungureanu

American Literature as World Literature, edited by Jeffrey R. Di Leo

Romanian Literature as World Literature, edited by Mircea Martin, Christian Moraru and Andrei Terian

Brazilian Literature as World Literature, edited by Eduardo F. Coutinho

Dutch and Flemish Literature as World Literature, edited by Theo D'haen

Afropolitan Literature as World Literature, edited by James Hodapp

Francophone Literature as World Literature, edited by Christian Moraru, Nicole Simek and Bertrand Westphal

Bulgarian Literature as World Literature, edited by Mihaela P. Harper and Dimitar Kambourov

Philosophy as World Literature, edited by Jeffrey R. Di Leo

Turkish Literature as World Literature, edited by Burcu Alkan and Çimen Günay-Erkol

Elena Ferrante as World Literature, by Stiliana Milkova

Multilingual Literature as World Literature, edited by Jane Hiddleston and Wen-chin Ouyang

Persian Literature as World Literature, edited by Mostafa Abedinifard, Omid Azadibougar and Amirhossein Vafa

Mexican Literature as World Literature, edited by Ignacio M. Sánchez Prado

Beyond English: World Literature and India, by Bhavya Tiwari

Graphic Novels and Comics as World Literature, edited by James Hodapp

African Literatures as World Literature, edited by Alexander Fyfe and Madhu Krishnan

Feminism as World Literature, edited by Robin Truth Goodman
Polish Literature as World Literature, edited by Piotr Florczyk and K. A. Wisniewski (forthcoming)
Taiwanese Literature as World Literature, edited by Pei-yin Lin and Wen-chi Li (forthcoming)
Pacific Literatures as World Literature, edited by Hsinya Huang and Chia-hua Yvonne Lin (forthcoming)
Central American Literature as World Literature, edited by Sophie Esch (forthcoming)
Kazuo Ishiguro as World Literature, by Chris Holmes (forthcoming)

African Literatures as World Literature

Edited by

*Alexander Fyfe and
Madhu Krishnan*

BLOOMSBURY ACADEMIC
NEW YORK • LONDON • OXFORD • NEW DELHI • SYDNEY

BLOOMSBURY ACADEMIC
Bloomsbury Publishing Inc
1385 Broadway, New York, NY 10018, USA
50 Bedford Square, London, WC1B 3DP, UK
29 Earlsfort Terrace, Dublin 2, Ireland

BLOOMSBURY, BLOOMSBURY ACADEMIC and the Diana logo are trademarks of
Bloomsbury Publishing Plc

First published in the United States of America 2023
Paperback edition published 2024

Volume Editor's Part of the Work © Alexander Fyfe and Madhu Krishnan, 2023
Each chapter © Contributors, 2023

Cover design and illustration © Simon Levy Associates

All rights reserved. No part of this publication may be reproduced or transmitted in any form or by any means, electronic or mechanical, including photocopying, recording, or any information storage or retrieval system, without prior permission in writing from the publishers.

Bloomsbury Publishing Inc does not have any control over, or responsibility for, any third-party websites referred to or in this book. All internet addresses given in this book were correct at the time of going to press. The author and publisher regret any inconvenience caused if addresses have changed or sites have ceased to exist, but can accept no responsibility for any such changes.

Library of Congress Cataloging-in-Publication Data
Names: Fyfe, Alexander, editor. | Krishnan, Madhu, 1981– editor.
Title: African literatures as world literature / edited by Alexander Fyfe and Madhu Krishnan.
Other titles: Literatures as world literature.
Description: New York : Bloomsbury Academic, 2022. | Series: Literatures as world literature | Includes bibliographical references and index. |
Summary: "A consideration of the theoretical, conceptual, and material connections between African literatures and "the world." " – Provided by publisher.
Identifiers: LCCN 2022018283 (print) | LCCN 2022018284 (ebook) |
ISBN 9781501379956 (hardback) | ISBN 9781501379994 (paperback) |
ISBN 9781501379963 (epub) | ISBN 9781501379970 (pdf) | ISBN 9781501379987
Subjects: LCSH: African literature–History and criticism. | African literature–Appreciation.
Classification: LCC PL8010 .A35456 2022 (print) | LCC PL8010 (ebook) |
DDC 809.896--dc23/eng/20220415
LC record available at https://lccn.loc.gov/2022018283
LC ebook record available at https://lccn.loc.gov/2022018284

ISBN: HB: 978-1-5013-7995-6
PB: 978-1-5013-7999-4
ePDF: 978-1-5013-7997-0
eBook: 978-1-5013-7996-3

Series: Literatures as World Literature

Typeset by Newgen KnowledgeWorks Pvt. Ltd., Chennai, India

To find out more about our authors and books visit www.bloomsbury.com and sign up for our newsletters.

CONTENTS

List of Figures ix
Notes on Contributors x

1 Introduction: African literatures and the problem of 'the world' 1
   Alexander Fyfe and Madhu Krishnan

2 'African borders are unnatural': Nairobi and the rise of a world literature 17
   Bhakti Shringarpure

3 Can Nairobi 'world' without the 'great Kenyan novel'? 37
   Billy Kahora

4 The problem with French and the world: Imagining the province and the global in francophone African fiction 47
   Sarah Arens

5 The first Ethiopian novel in Amharic (1908) and the world: Critical and theoretical legacies 71
   Sara Marzagora

6 The Kaiser, Angoche and the world at large: Swahili poetry from Mozambique as world (war) literature 91
   Clarissa Vierke and Chapane Mutiua

7 Early Sesotho, isiXhosa and isiZulu novels as world literature 115
   Ashleigh Harris

8   African multilingualism as an asset in world literature: A case against cultural conformity and uniformity 139
    Munyao Kilolo

9   New cartographies for world literary space: Locating pan-African publishing and prizing 153
    Zamda R. Geuza and Kate Wallis

10 Aké Festival and the African world stage 183
    Lola Shoneyin

11 Contemporary African literature and celebrity capital 189
    Doseline Kiguru

12 Reversing the global media lens: Colonial spectacularization in the writing of Binyavanga Wainaina 213
    Penny Cartwright

13 The facts at the heart of the matter: Character and objectivity in the making of the Fante Intelligentsia 233
    Jeanne-Marie Jackson

Index 255

FIGURES

6.1	Page 3 of the Kaisa written by Fundi Halide 95
6.2	Fundi Halide holding the register 96
9.1	Tweet from the Kiswahili Prize celebrating the 2018 award ceremony 154
9.2	*Mmeza Fupa* by Ali Hilal Ali 166
9.3 and 9.4	*Mwanangu Rudi Nyumbani* by Dotto Rangimoto 167
9.5	Mkuki na Nyota's Kiswahili Prize–winning authors on the African Books Collective website 169

CONTRIBUTORS

Sarah Arens is a British Academy postdoctoral fellow and lecturer in French at the University of Liverpool, UK. Sarah's research focuses on fictional and scientific texts, and visual culture, produced during and in the aftermath of Belgian and French colonialism, as well as science and speculative fiction in French.

Penny Cartwright is a lecturer in English at the University of Oxford, UK. She completed her PhD at the University of Bristol in 2020, examining representations of 'global space' versus 'global orientations' in contemporary Anglophone African literature, including Ngũgĩ wa Thiong'o, Binyavanga Wainaina and Igoni Barrett. She is currently working on her first monograph, developed from this work. Her broader research interests include world and comparative literature theory, literatures of neoliberalism, narrative theory (especially ideas of 'worlding') and Global South epistemologies.

Alexander Fyfe is Assistant Professor of Comparative Literature and African Studies at the University of Georgia, United States. His articles have appeared in *Interventions: International Journal of Postcolonial Studies*, *Research in African Literatures* and *Critique: Studies in Contemporary Fiction*, among other venues. He has guest-edited special issues of *African Identities* and (with Rosemary Jolly) *The Cambridge Journal of Postcolonial Literary Inquiry*.

Zamda R. Geuza is an assistant lecturer in the Centre for Communication Studies at the University of Dar es Salaam, Tanzania. She is currently pursuing her PhD at the University of Exeter exploring feminist publishing in Tanzania. She holds a MSc in Publishing Studies from Moi University. Her research interests are in the areas of publishing, African literature and women's studies.

Ashleigh Harris is Professor of English at Uppsala University, Sweden. Her recent publications include *Afropolitanism and the Novel: De-Realizing Africa* (2020); 'African street literature: A method for emergent form beyond world literature' (with Nicklas Hållén) in *Research in African Literatures*; '"The Diary of a Country in Crisis": Zimbabwean Censorship and Adaptive Cultural Forms', *Journal of Southern African Studies* (2021) and 'African literature as indigenous history in South Africa's "Decolonize-the-Curriculum" movement', in *The Routledge Companion to Indigenous Global History* (2021). She is currently writing a monograph entitled *Literary Form Beyond the Book in Southern Africa*.

Jeanne-Marie Jackson is Associate Professor of English at Johns Hopkins University, United States, and the author of two books: *The African Novel of Ideas* (2021) and *South African Literature's Russian Soul* (2015).

Billy Kahora is a writer, editor and lecturer in Creative and Professional Writing at the University of Bristol, UK. His short fiction and creative non-fiction have appeared in *Chimurenga*, *McSweeney's*, *Granta Online*, *Internazionale*, *Vanity Fair* and *Kwani?* He has written a short story collection titled *The Cape Cod Bicycle War and Other Youthful Follies*, released in 2019, and a non-fiction book titled *The True Story of David Munyakei* in 2012. His story 'Urban Zoning' was shortlisted for the Caine Prize for African Literature in 2012, as was 'The Gorilla's Apprentice' in 2014. He wrote the screenplay for the film *Soul Boy* and co-wrote *Nairobi Half Life*, which each won the Kalasha award and were shown on the European film festival circuit. He has finished a novel titled *The Applications*.

Doseline Kiguru is a researcher with an interest in literary texts and their production mechanisms. Her research engages with cultural and literary production in Africa with a focus on different literary platforms such as publishing and prize industries, book fairs and festivals, literary magazines and writers' organizations, exploring the networks they create and the effects that they have on contemporary African literary production. She is currently a research associate at the University of Bristol, UK.

Munyao Kilolo is the projects officer at the Ngũgĩ wa Thiong'o Foundation and the administrator of the Mabati Cornell Kiswahili Prize. He previously served as the managing editor of *Jalada Africa*, where he conceived and led their inaugural translation project. The project saw one story, originally written in Gikuyu, translated into one hundred languages. In 2021, he founded Ituĩka, a literary platform devoted to African languages and translation. The platform has created a comprehensive database of African languages teachers and is engaged in other projects that promote African languages. His writing in his mother tongue, Kiikamba, has been published in the 26th issue of *Absinthe: World Literature in Translation*. He has also appeared in the *Routledge Handbook of Translation and Activism*, *Saraba Magazine* and *Jalada Africa*, among others.

Madhu Krishnan is Professor of African, World and Comparative Literatures in the Department of English at the University of Bristol, UK. She is the author of three books: *Contemporary African Literature in English: Global Locations, Postcolonial Identifications* (2014), *Writing Spatiality in West Africa: Colonial Legacies in the Anglophone/Francophone Novel* (2018) and *Contingent Canons: African Literature and the Politics of Location* (2018).

Sara Marzagora is a lecturer in Comparative Literature at King's College London, UK. Sara has published single-authored and jointly authored articles on world literature theory, proposing methodologies that counter the teleological and modernist biases of canonical accounts of world literature. She has edited a special issue of the *Journal of African Cultural Studies* charting new disciplinary approaches to the study of literatures in African languages, and co-edited (with Francesca Orsini and Karima Laachir) a special issue of *Comparative Studies of South Asia, Africa and the Middle East* on multilingual literary cultures in the precolonial period. Her work on Ethiopian nationalisms and Ethiopian conceptions of history has been published in the *Journal of African History* and in *Global Intellectual History*.

Chapane Mutiua holds a degree in History from the Faculty of Humanities and Social Sciences of Eduardo Mondlane University and a masters in Historical Studies from the History Department of the University of Cape Town. He is a PhD candidate in African Studies at the Centre for the Study of Manuscript Cultures of the University of Hamburg, Germany, and a full-time researcher at the Centre for African Studies of the University of Eduardo Mondlane, Mozambique. His research interests include local knowledge in the context of the discourse of modernity and development, as well as Swahili and Islamic culture in northern Mozambique.

Lola Shoneyin is a novelist, poet and educator. She is founder/director of the Aké Arts and Book Festival. Her third novel, *The Secret Lives of Baba Segi's Wives*, was published in 2010 and won the 2011 PEN Oakland/Josephine Miles Literary Award and two Association of Nigerian Authors Awards. In addition to her work with the Aké festival, she is also director of the Lagos-based publishing house Ouida Books.

Bhakti Shringarpure is Associate Professor at the University of Connecticut, United States, jointly appointed in English and women's, gender and sexuality studies. She is the author of *Cold War Assemblages: Decolonization to Digital* (2019), the founding editor of *Warscapes* magazine and creative director of the Radical Books Collective. Her writing has also appeared in *The Guardian*, *The Funambulist*, *Los Angeles Review of Books*, *Literary Hub* and *Africa Is a Country*, among others. She was awarded the Fulbright US Scholar fellowship to teach and research in Kenya in 2019–20.

Clarissa Vierke is Professor of Literatures in African Languages at the University of Bayreuth, Germany. She is an expert on Swahili poetry, manuscript cultures and has been working on travelling texts in East Africa – both in Anglophone Kenya and Tanzania and Lusophone Mozambique. Together with colleagues working on Francophone and Lusophone literature, she is currently running a research project on literary entanglements in the Indian Ocean across boundaries of nations, languages and media. At the University of Bayreuth, she is principal investigator of the Cluster of excellence 'Africa Multiple: Reconfiguring African Studies'.

Kate Wallis is Senior Lecturer in World Literatures in the Department of English and Film at the University of Exeter, UK. She is currently working on a monograph exploring pan-African literary networks post-2000, building on her doctoral research on Kwani Trust, Farafina and Cassava Republic Press. Her work has been published in *Wasafiri*, *Research in African Literatures*, *Eastern African Literary and Cultural Studies* and *The Routledge Handbook of African Literature*. She is a director for Kigali-based publishing company Huza Press, a co-founder of www.africainwords.com and co-producer of Africa Writes – Bristol and Exeter literary festivals.

1

Introduction: African literatures and the problem of 'the world'

Alexander Fyfe and Madhu Krishnan

In the preface to his essay collection, *You're Not a Country, Africa*, Pius Adesanmi writes, 'The question of what Africa means has exercised the minds of some of the continent's best thinkers in the twentieth and twenty-first centuries. It stands unanswered at the ideological core of pan-Africanism, Negritude, nationalism, decolonisation, and all other projects through which Africans have sought to understand and restore their violated humanity'.[1] Adesanmi's comments here point to a fundamental question that has been at the heart of debates around African literary production throughout the long twentieth century: what is this 'Africa' of which we speak when we speak of African literature? Can there be a unified geography that we consider under the sign of Africa when its referent is the second-largest continent in the world, one of unparalleled geographic, ecological, cultural and demographic diversity? Who decides what Africa admits, and against what parameters are its contours constituted? Implicit in these questions is the larger tension that inheres when one considers the question of Africa and the world, Africa in the world and, of course, Africa as the world. Who speaks the 'African world' and what, precisely, determines the image of this world? In what languages is this world articulated and through which epistemological frameworks, ideologies and discourses? How can one reconcile the persistence of colonial boundaries that, along with imperial policies oriented towards accumulation by dispossession in the name of

---

[1] Pius Adesanmi, *You're Not a Country, Africa* (London: Penguin, 2011), p. x.

expropriation, simultaneously elide a longer history of extraversion,[2] on the one hand, and, on the other, Africa's own invisibilized centrality to a world-system dependent on its resources, labour and wealth? This volume seeks to address these questions through a range of contributions that consider how African literature does and has always registered a sense of worldliness, not in the common-sense definition of cosmopolitanism or its cognates but through its own function as a site of world-building, world-fashioning and world-projection. At the same time, as the essays collected here show, world-projection is not a metaphor: the world(s) of African literature arise from specifically constituted material contexts and themselves contribute to the structuration of the world in which we live.

In this regard, it is important to remember that the increased production of written African literatures from the late nineteenth and into the twentieth century was accompanied by a variety of implicit claims about what constituted the 'African world'. There was, for instance, pressure from the missionary education system to represent a continent governed by Christian moral principles, a world view often subtly undermined by the very writers whom the missions sponsored.[3] Meanwhile, British and French publishing houses often tended to favour texts that provided anthropological constructions of the African world. Indeed, works like Chinua Achebe's *Things Fall Apart* (1958) and Onuora Nzekwu's *Wand of Noble Wood* (1961), while not reducible to their anthropological content, nevertheless explained and translated African worlds in ways that made them comprehensible to a metropolitan readership. Several decades earlier, the Negritude movement (at least in its Senghorian version) used the lyric form to produce an African world governed by its own rhythmic principles.

Despite (and indeed influenced by) these competing pressures to represent the African world according to certain codes, numerous African writers achieved through their work what Wole Soyinka has influentially described as 'a reinstatement of values authentic to [a particular African] society, modified only by the demands of a contemporary world'.[4] What Soyinka discerns in the work of certain African writers with a 'secular social vision' is the ability to articulate African worlds in terms of their own deep mythologies, separate from prevailing ideologies, colonial, anti-colonial or otherwise.[5] This 'self-apprehension' of African worlds is itself a highly political and decolonial act insofar as it reconstitutes the self-referential

---

[2]Jean-François Bayart, 'Africa in the World: A History of Extraversion', *African Affairs*, vol. 99, no. 395 (2000): 217–67.
[3]See, for instance, Thomas Mofolo's (1925) Sesotho language novel *Chaka*, which caused consternation among its missionary sponsors because of its validation of an African world view.
[4]Wole Soyinka, *Myth, Literature, and the African World* (Cambridge: Cambridge University Press, 1986), p. x.
[5]Ibid., p. xii.

dynamism and deep interconnectivity of *being* in a particular African society.⁶ Crucially, such texts do not attempt to merely invoke an idea of a lost pre-colonial African world (as does Negritude, in Soyinka's reading) but instead demonstrate how the terms of such a world continue to operate in the present day. The process of apprehending the African world is therefore engaged with a plurality of influences and is never simply a validation of 'tradition' over modernity. The deeply affirmative and generative possibilities of African literary world-making have generally been absent from attempts to think about African literature *as* world literature. By way of approaching the questions that this volume raises, it will be instructive to interrogate some of the assumptions that underlie existing studies of this relationship.

At the heart of discussions of African literatures and the world – or, perhaps more specifically, African literatures *as* world literature – lies the question of what we mean by 'African literature'. As noted above, the very term is subject to contestation, riven by divisions across genre, form, language and circulation. In the wider context of the global literary market and its attendant critical-intellectual apparatuses, few analyses of African literature have been as influential as Eileen Julien's (2006) essay 'The Extroverted African Novel'. Julien proposes that the kinds of African novels that tend to circulate internationally – that is, novels that we might broadly consider to be 'worldly' in the common-sense usage of the term – share a set of common features, notably their 'intertextuality with hegemonic or global discourses and … appeal across borders'.⁷ Since the publication of that essay, Julien has clarified that her diagnosis of the extroverted African novel was intended to excavate how both the circulation, marketing and publishing of texts on the one hand, and their formal parameters on the other, combine to determine its status as 'African literature' in the global market. The extroverted African novel, then, 'is a sub-genre of novel, marked by its themes and formal qualities',⁸ a sub-genre that is 'one form among many',⁹ albeit one form made particularly visible on a global scale, turning outwards and seemingly 'born translated', in Rebecca L. Walkowitz's sense. Yet, many discussions of African literary writing and world literature tend to overwhelmingly focus on the extroverted African novel, usually written in English (sometimes in French or, more rarely, Portuguese), equating its intertextuality with global discourses and processes with its hegemonic globality.

There is, therefore, a sense in which the very notion of 'the world' as understood in extant discussions of African literature can only be coextensive

---

⁶Ibid., p. viii.
⁷Eileen Julien, 'The Extroverted African Novel', in *The Novel*, ed. Franco Moretti (Princeton, NJ: Princeton University Press, 2006), pp. 667–702, 681.
⁸Eileen Julien, 'The Extroverted African Novel, Revisited: African Novels at Home, in the World', *Journal of African Cultural Studies*, vol. 30, no. 3 (2 September 2018): 371–81, 376.
⁹Ibid., 686.

with 'the global', seen, for instance, in the reliance on concepts such as the global literary market, global aesthetics, the global novel and similar as indexes through which the literary comes into view. As Karima Laachir, Sara Marzagora and Francesca Orsini note when proposing their concept of 'significant geographies', in discussions of 'literary production, circulation and reception across the world beyond Europe',

> The complexity of the literary world gets reduced to economic or political frames such as the 'global capitalist system' or 'empire' that inevitably encourage models of 'diffusion' and 'assimilation' of non-Western literatures into Western categories (Mufti) and direct attention to some literary forms (the novel, principally, or the travelogue) and away from others which, however worldly they may be, become 'not-world'.[10]

While in this volume we maintain the belief that there remains value in the concept of the 'world' and 'world literatures', we share with Laachir, Marzagora and Orsini a concern that extant discussions of African literature and world literature have become overdetermined by the extroverted African novel, to the detriment of a more nuanced understanding of the plurality of world-making processes that obtain in African literary writing. These discussions, broadly, neglect Julien's disclaimer that the extroverted African novel is one amongst many manifestations of African literature, foregrounding a particular genre and mode of circulation – one increasingly congruent with those of Afropolitanism, as we will return to below – to the critical neglect or invisibilization of other modes of literary world-making and world-formation. Indeed, in her contribution to this volume, Bhakti Shringarpure demonstrates how the future of world literature might well rest elsewhere, arguing for the potential of the digital short form writing as able to project models of world-formation more in line with contemporary life. Centring her argument on Nairobi as a space inherently produced through the intersection of migration, humanitarianism and digital innovation, Shringarpure argues that the mobility of the digital enables it to capture the complex dynamics of worlding, which extant models of world literature have failed to fully account for. And yet, as Billy Kahora notes in his response to Shringarpure, there remains something particularly important about the novel within the landscape of world literatures. For Kahora, the move to digital forms and literary activism operates as a consequence of the lack of structural support for sustained writing and creation in Nairobi. The Great Kenyan Novel, something once dreamed of by Kahora's colleague and *Kwani?* founder Binyavanga Wainaina, seems less and less likely in a

---

[10]Karima Laachir, Sara Marzagora and Francesca Orsini, 'Significant Geographies: In Lieu of World Literature', *Journal of World Literature*, vol. 3, no. 3 (10 August 2018): 290–310, 292.

context where the lack of sustainable avenues for funding and creation has led writers and artists to move elsewhere.

Indeed, as Moradewun Adejunmobi notes in her 2021 essay on Abiola Irele and the publicness of African letters, it is important to emphasize that different levels of visibility – what we might think of as different intensities of being and circulating in the public – accrue to different types of literary and critical discourse and, as Kahora's essay makes clear, different forms of writing.[11] Questions of where and how, for instance, modes of world-projection or interactions with varying and plural conceptualizations of the world, as such, occur in literary writing are themselves inevitably mediated through these differential intensities. In this volume, we attempt to make visible circulatory effects and aesthetic encounters with and projections of the world that have perhaps received less critical visibility, in Adejunmobi's term, than the more globally dominant form of the extroverted or Afropolitan novel. For these reasons, the essays gathered here consider a plurality of literary forms and languages, as well as texts from a broad range of time periods. In some cases, the world of the text, like the world of the extroverted novel, might be said to be coextensive with the globe. In other cases, the world might be a region, a location or an ambulatory path that extant scalar models cannot quite capture. In all cases, however, the primary interest of this volume is less to justify or explain *whether* texts count as world literature and more to explore and examine *how* texts engage with different conceptions of world, of literature, of scale and of circulation.

Literature, as Stefan Helgesson and Mads Rosendahl Thomsen note, is a 'cluster concept', a term they borrow from Wittgenstein. That is, it is 'a thing consisting of many things – a composite entity'.[12] It is in this sense, then, that *world* literature, specifically, bifurcates around two interrelated modes: the affirmative and the critical.[13] Helgesson and Rosendahl Thomsen make a strong argument for the need to keep both versions of world literature in view, arguing that it is through this nexus that ' "world literature" becomes … not an add-on or an epiphenomenon, but rather an aesthetic outlook that regards the boundaries between people, languages and cultures as epiphenomena'.[14] World literature, put more simply, is '*a practice*',[15] intricately bound not only to the circuits of production, circulation and consecration through which 'a literature' as such is produced but also through its inextricable ties with the external world – what we might think about as 'world' in its normative

---

[11] See Moradewun Adejunmobi, 'Abiola Irele and the Publicness of African Letters', *Journal of the African Literature Association*, vol. 14, no. 1 (2020): 72–89.
[12] Stefan Helgesson and Mads Rosendahl Thomsen, *Literature and the World* (Abingdon: Routledge, 2019), p. 1.
[13] Ibid., pp. 3–4.
[14] Ibid., p. 10.
[15] Ibid., p. 17.

sense – from which it arises and through which it moves. As Eric Hayot notes, '"World" is thus both a philosophical concept and an example of that concept; a concept that is in the deepest possible way an instance of itself. ... What we idealize when we speak of "world" as a ground is *the* world's material role as a ground.'[16] He continues,

> For this reason the philosophical concept of the world cannot alone govern the history of the world of the work of art. While the work is, in the Heideggerian sense, a world, it also shows a world, just as the world itself shows a world. Both work and world show both world and its worlding. To focus exclusively on the worlding – as does Heidegger in 'The Origin of the Work of Art' – entails passing over the action of the world that is worlded by the work, the world whose practical being-in-the-world acts as both the ground and the expression of a philosophical concept of the world. There is no world-form without world content.[17]

This dual appearance and interconnection of world-form and world-content is of particular salience in the realm of African literary writing. As a category operating in the global literary marketplace, African literature has always been concerned with its ability to project a world and, with it, an assertion of a place in the world. For Simon Gikandi, the rise of the African novel (largely in English, though this remains unspoken in his formulation) is inextricably tied to the need to assert a kind of cultural nationalism or culturally inflected sense of world and place in the world in the era of political decolonization.[18] The literary, in this sense, is neither neutral nor disinterested but deeply vested in the struggle to ascertain the limits and strictures of the newly emerging nation state and, with it, the place of the continent in a re-ordering world-system. If, as Jean-Luc Nancy suggests, worlds exist only insofar as they are lived, operating as a projection for a desired unity or future (a sentiment captured in a similar vein by Souleymane Bachir Diagne in his work on translation and language in an African context as the projection of a desired future that has yet to come),[19] this world of desire or projection of a lateral world cannot be decoupled from the material realities, structures and ideologies that mediate its possibilities.

---

[16]Eric Hayot, *On Literary Worlds* (Oxford: Oxford University Press, 2012), p. 25.
[17]Ibid.
[18]Simon Gikandi, 'Introduction', in *The Novel in Africa and the Caribbean since 1950*, ed. Simon Gikandi (Oxford: Oxford University Press, 2016), pp. xv–xxvii, xx.
[19]Jean-Luc Nancy, *The Creation of the World, or Globalization*, trans. François Raffoul and David Pettigrew (Albany: State University of New York Press, 2007), pp. 42–3; Souleymane Bachir Diagne and Jean-Loup Amselle, *In Search of Africa(s): Universalism and Decolonial Thought* (Cambridge: Polity Press, 2020), p. 66.

The essays in this volume all attempt to move beyond the assumptions that often underlie discussions about the world-literariness of African writing by asking how different constructions of the world inform and influence the production of literary forms and how literary world-making occurs in different African contexts. In this sense, we aim to pursue several of the questions raised by Orsini and Zecchini in their recent introduction to a special issue of the *Journal of World Literature*:

> How do … writers work through, use, challenge, or re-invent the macro categories (region, nation, sub-continent, continent, world) with which literary histories are written and literary cartographies are constituted? What is the relevance of these geographical categories to them, and how do they reallocate or realign them? What worlds do these literatures simultaneously inhabit and create? What networks – often transnational or multilingual, but rendered invisible or underground in singular views of the world literary space – do writers and institutions, specific genres and works of literature, but also circuits of readership, translation and publishing, produce? And what are the imagined, alternative, or discrepant geographies, the different cosmopolitanisms, that may be invented in the process?[20]

What is particularly valuable about this formulation is that no term or category is assumed to be fixed prior to the analysis. Cosmopolitanism, for instance, is not a status that is simply achieved but rather a diverse and highly specific set of practices with very different valences. World literary studies here becomes less an exercise of determining literature's relation to a predetermined 'world' and more one of considering how the constantly shifting positionings of writers across numerous spheres and networks constitute a highly intersectional process of worlding. In examining the multi-nodal and self-reflexive nature of African literary world-making, we seek to identify some of the specific ways in which this process occurs on the continent and in its diasporas. Furthermore, rather than placing the onus of theorizing the 'world' on any particular theory of world literature, we are concerned with how literature itself stages questions of worldliness in ways that may be irreducible to the conflation of the 'world' and the 'global'. While this involves asking materialist questions about the kinds of economic, political and cultural networks in which individual works participate, it is also to focus intensively on the question of literary form.

---

[20] Francesca Orsini and Laetitia Zecchini, 'The Locations of (World) Literature: Perspectives from Africa and South Asia: Introduction', *Journal of World Literature*, vol. 4, no. 1 (6 March 2019): 1–12, 2–3.

This work of world-projection, then, is anything but disinterested in the external world against which it appears. A key example of the ways in which tensions inhere between the desire to re-script or re-draw a concept of 'world' and the larger structures against and through which that comes appears in the drawn-out controversy over a 2007 manifesto calling for a world literatures in French, discussed in greater length in Sarah Arens's contribution to this volume. In the 15 March 2007 issue of *Le Monde des livres*, a group of forty-four prominent Francophone writers, JMG Clézio, Tahar Ben Jelloun, Maryse Condé and Alain Mabanckou amongst them, published their now-famous manifesto, 'Pour une "littérature-monde" en français'. In this manifesto, the authors point to the then-recent success of so-called peripheral writers in the landscape of prize culture as one of many indicators of the topographies of literary production in French, which they identify as central to the pressing need to re-shape literary imaginaries:

> Simple hasard d'une rentrée éditoriale concentrant par exception les talents venus de la 'périphérie', simple détour vagabond avant que le fleuve revienne dans son lit? Nous pensons, au contraire: révolution copernicienne. Copernicienne, parce qu'elle révèle ce que le milieu littéraire savait déjà sans l'admettre: le centre, ce point depuis lequel était supposée rayonner une littérature franco-française, n'est plus le centre. Le centre jusqu'ici, même si de moins en moins, avait eu cette capacité d'absorption qui contraignait les auteurs venus d'ailleurs à se dépouiller de leurs bagages avant de se fondre dans le creuset de la langue et de son histoire nationale: le centre, nous disent les prix d'automne, est désormais partout, aux quatre coins du monde. Fin de la francophonie. Et naissance d'une littérature-monde en français.[21]

> [The simple coincidence of an editorial exceptionally based on concentrating on talented writers from the 'periphery', a simple, meandering detour before the course of things returns to its path? We think, to the contrary: a Copernican revolution. Copernican because it reveals what the literary world has known without admitting it: the centre, the point from which a Francophone-French literature was meant to radiate, is no longer the centre. The centre until now, even if less and less so, has had a capacity to absorb which forced authors from elsewhere to strip themselves of their baggage (culture) before melting into the crucible of the national language and history. The centre, as the prizes

---

[21]'Pour une "littérature-monde" en français', *Le Monde*, 15 March 2007, https://www.lemonde.fr/livres/article/2007/03/15/des-ecrivains-plaident-pour-un-roman-en-francais-ouvert-sur-le-monde_883572_3260.html. Accessed 8 July 2019. See also the edited volume that followed: *Pour une littérature-monde*. Sous le direction de Michel Le Bris et Jean Rouaud (Paris: Gallimard, 2007).

awarded this autumn tell us, is now everywhere, in the four corners of the world. The end of la Francophonie, and the birth of a world literature in French.]

Their call for a wider and more expansive notion of 'litterature-monde en français' in place of the continued dominance of 'la Francophonie' was not, however, without its detractors. In a response published in the same paper on 30 March 2007, for instance, the Lebanese lawyer and writer Alexandre Najjar argued that the mere concept of 'litterature-monde en français' is little more than a 'periphrase' of la Francophonie, nothing new and certainly nothing meriting a 'Copernican revolution' as the authors of the manifesto so claim: 'Car qu'est-ce que la francophonie sinon la langue française «ouverte sur le monde et transnationale», c'est-à-dire la définition même qu'on veut donner à la «littérature-monde en français»?'[22] At the core of Najjir's disagreement with the manifesto appears to be a larger conflict over the topographical mapping of 'the world' and where – if anywhere – its centre might hold. These arguments, in turn, gesture towards France's larger imperial history and, particularly, the geographies of power that underwrote efforts to create a concept of 'greater France' and that persist into the present day under the auspices of la Francophonie.[23] Literature and indeed the contours of a world literature are anything but disinterested, deeply rooted instead in the lived realities of imperial cartographies whose legacies persist under new names in the present day. As Swamy notes, the controversy around the manifesto might be attributed to the author's assertion that 'the term francophone is based on the claim that it evokes a relationship that is unduly weighted towards the Hexagon, and more specifically, the ghost of a colonial France', enacting a vision of the world in which the imperial centre remains unmoved and immutable.[24]

At the same time, as the manifesto makes clear, the hexagon has never been the sole fulcrum for the production of literary worlds in French. Echoing an editorial published in *Le Monde* a year earlier, in which acclaimed Congolese writer Alain Mabanckou calls for French literature to open beyond its borders, coming to the Francophone, rather than the other

---

[22] Alexandre Najjar, 'Contre le manifeste «Pour une littérature-monde en français» Expliquer l'eau par l'eau', *Le Monde*, 20 March 2007, http://archive.wikiwix.com/cache/index2.php?url=http%3A%2F%2Fwww.najjar.org%2FlitteratureMondeEnFrancais.asp. Accessed 21 July 2019.
[23] See Gary Wilder, *The French Imperial Nation-State: Negritude and Colonial Humanism between the Two World Wars* (Chicago: University of Chicago Press, 2005).
[24] Vinay Swamy, '"Pour une littérature-monde": Tahar Ben Jelloun's *Partir*', *Contemporary French and Francophone Studies*, vol. 13, no. 4 (2009): 471–8, 472. For further reactions to the manifesto, see Lydie Moudileno, '*Francophonie*: Trash or Recycle?' in *Transnational French Studies: Postcolonialism and Littérature-Monde*, ed. Alex Hargreaves, Charles Forsdick and David Murphy (Liverpool: Liverpool University Press, 2010), pp. 109–24.

direction,[25] the manifesto and its supporters articulate a vision of literature in French that demands a shift in thinking beyond the 'world republic of letters', in Casanova's term,[26] and that might instead encompass the wider landscapes and histories of literary production that emanate from the French-speaking world. Yet, as Arens discusses in her essay in this volume there is another, more complex way in which to read the manifesto controversy and, more pertinently, its literary registrations. For Arens, this requires a perspective that centres the inherent heterogeneity of the French language and de-centres France itself and the colonial binary of which it forms a part. In the writing of Mabanckou and In Koli Jean Bofane, moreover, she sees the articulations of a range of other world-formations outside the colonialist model of the world as defined by centres and peripheries, world-formations that hearken to other kinds of temporalities, geographical assemblages and histories of solidarity.

As Arens's essay demonstrates, then, there remain multiple and distinct ways of thinking about the world-projecting properties of African literary writing, particularly when we move away from a focus on Europhone writing, as has dominated extant discussions of African literature and world literature. In this volume, we bring together contributions that seek to explore how the concept of the world – and, indeed, its contours – might shift if we take as our 'centre' different linguistic and geographical lifeworlds and scales of being. Sara Marzagora in Chapter 5 looks at 'the first Ethiopian novel in Amharic, Labb Wällād Tarik', eschewing what she terms 'top-down' models that have dominated formulations of world literature and instead seeking to develop a framework for understanding the work of worlding – and the relationship between text and world – from the work itself, emanating outwards through an exploration of its own critical vocabularies. By so doing, she extends both the temporalities and spatialities that define 'the modern' as such. Analysing how the text calls into being certain connections with the concept of the world through its themes, its formal structures and its genealogy, Marzagora offers a robust example of how decentring the universal presumptions of North American and European world literary scholarship can enable multiple topographies of the world to emerge, each of which can be seen less as a point zero and more as a horizon towards which the text strives. In their contribution, Clarissa Vierke and Chapane Mutiua also explore what insights we might derive when we unsettle the linguistic, spatial and ideological assumptions of world literary scholarship in their reading of the *Kaisa*, a long poem written in the Swahili language and told from northern Mozambique. The *Kaisa*,

---

[25] Alain Mabanckou, 'La francophonie, oui, le ghetto: non!', *Le Monde*, 18 March 2006, https://www.lemonde.fr/idees/article/2006/03/18/la-francophonie-oui-le-ghetto-non_752169_3232.html. Accessed 8 July 2019.
[26] Pascale Casanova, *La République mondiale des Lettres* (Paris: Éditions de Seuil, 2008).

they argue, offers a dynamic imaginary of the world map, highlighting its changing cartographies on the one hand, and leveraging its First World War context on the other, to produce a conceptually realized aesthetic world unto itself. In both Marzagora's and Vierke and Mutiua's contributions, moreover, we begin to see how any call to provincialize world literatures or to focus through the lens of the multiple, significant geographies it comprises demands an expansion of our understanding of the relationship between language and worlding and the (im)possibilities of translation to contain this complexity.

Harris's essay in this volume points to one of the central challenges to world literary critique, which argues for the emancipatory (liberatory?) potential of literary writing as a means of projecting other worlds. Sarah Brouillette, responding to Pheng Cheah's assertion that the literary holds a singular ability to offer a site of resistance to global capital with its unique capacity to project other worlds, asserts,

> Despite their adherence to some form of Marxism, recent accounts of world literature have preferred to highlight works with congenial political tendencies rather than grounding their analysis in the sociology of high art and the shifting fortunes of literature's social effects. Their celebrations of a critical world-literary mode imply that literature reaches a substantial audience of uninitiated readers who need to learn what writers want to teach them.[27]

Brouillette's key point, that the literary continues to operate as an elite form with a vested interest in promoting the idea of its own radical potential for its reproduction, is of crucial importance and worth engaging with at some length. As she writes with respect to recent world literary scholarship, 'We can be wholly on board with the opposition to capitalist globalization and yet still ask: To whom is literature's countering force relevant? To what audience of literary readers does it speak?'[28] The 'revelatory insights' inherent to literature's idealization, moreover, are for Brouillette 'a key part of literary socialization' that 'is fundamental to how institutions of world-literary production have sold themselves and justified their own relevance'.[29] She continues,

> Scholarship on world literature, meanwhile, has almost wholly overlooked the fact that uneven development and capitalist 'peripheralization' (Cheah 193) are more than tragic themes or occasions for formal experimentation

---

[27]Sarah Brouillette, *UNESCO and the Fate of the Literary* (Stanford: Stanford University Press, 2019), p. 3.
[28]Ibid.
[29]Ibid., pp. 3–4.

within literature. They instead infect all literary activity influencing who can write professionally and who has access to literary experiences that may or may not be affecting. Even as it takes the depredations of capitalism as one of its key targets, developed high-literary culture able to sustain professional livelihoods is an affordance of relative wealth. Writers who grow up in places that have underdeveloped economies often leave, and their target audiences, editors, agents and publishers are often elsewhere.[30]

Drawing on an extended study of UNESCO's book programmes over the second half of the twentieth century, Brouillette argues that the institution of the literary, and particularly the world literary, remains intertwined in processes that 'mask the character of the primary social relations that are necessary to its own flourishing',[31] such as the distribution of material infrastructure, wealth and robust copyright provisions. Moreover, she powerfully notes the extent to which the claim for a radical horizon implicit in the literary, available for decoding and generation by the learned reader, is itself a highly constrained and mediated claim, access to which remains deeply asymmetrical and materially mediated, all the more so, as Harris's essay demonstrates, when operating in languages outside English (or, in South Africa, Afrikaans) and when considering forms beyond that of the novel in its global manifestations.

The challenges of producing literature in non-Europhone African languages are further explored by Munyao Kilolo in Chapter 8 who, faced with the lack of literary infrastructure for writing in his mother tongue Kiikamba, pursues 'small but practical steps contributing to the visibility of African languages'. Through a discussion of the importance of translation into and between African languages (drawing on his own role in the well-known *Jalada* Translation Project); the improved publication, circulation and availability of texts; and the building of audiences beyond the continent, Kilolo in Chapter 8 outlines the preconditions for 'African languages to fully contribute to literary production and become a solid part of world literatures'. To write in a particular language, of course, is to participate in a particular kind of ecology and economy. One of the principal contributions of this volume is to trace how literature redefines and reimagines the boundaries of spheres that, in general world literature discussions, are often subsumed under the category of 'the world'. Zamda R. Geuza and Kate Wallis explore 'new cartographies of world literary space' in their analysis of the collaboration between the Tanzanian publisher Mkuki na Nyota, based in Dar es Salaam, and the Mabati Cornell Kiswahili Prize for African

---

[30]Ibid., p. 4.
[31]Ibid., p. 5.

Literature, which awards an annual prize for books written in Swahili. They argue that Mkuki na Nyota's publication of some of the winning entries of the Mabati Cornell award points to new possibilities for the continent's engagement with 'world literary space'. Over the course of this argument, they identify numerous ways in which the 'mutually beneficial collaboration' has allowed for the creation of cultural value and increased the circulation of books in the Swahili literary sphere. They also suggest that the pan-African ideals of the Kiswahili Prize create considerable opportunities for 'cross-border and global dialogue'. This leads to the important conclusion that world literature can be rethought in terms of a 'pan-African ethos', one that is 'defined in part through a commitment to Afrophone African languages, enabling collaborative relationships that can stretch across intersecting literary systems and cut through reductive hierarchies of global/local or insider/outsider' (see Chapter 9 of this volume). Transnational literary collaborations (within and beyond the continent) therefore have the capacity to create new and more equitable networks and modify the linguistic and national coordinates of world literary space.

Writing in her role as founder/director of the Aké Arts and Book Festival *and* as a writer, Lola Shoneyin in Chapter 10 argues for the importance of an 'African world stage', one 'where themes that pertain to Africa and African writers are at the core of the discourse'. She describes how her practice as a festival organizer, publisher and literary activist has enabled her to produce new ways of thinking about what literature from an African world stage might offer, particularly in terms of curation and language, as well as the need to produce platforms for literary expression that are not necessarily tethered to the institutions of the Global North. This concern with the networks that sustain the practice of literature also prompts Doseline Kiguru's essay, which argues for the importance of 'celebrity capital' (a concept she borrows from media theorist Olivier Driessens), to the contemporary African literary marketplace. Focusing on the example of Chimamanda Ngozi Adichie, as well as the LongStorySHORT collective and the literary platform *Mbogi ya Mawriters*, Kiguru in Chapter 11 illuminates the complex process of capital intra-conversion which means that 'celebrity culture facilitates and maintains a literary network of value that is simultaneously local and global'.

Penelope Cartwright's essay considers the intersections between journalism and literature in the work of Binyavanga Wainaina in Chapter 12. Whereas the Western media tends to *world* Africa through a process of 'colonial spectacularisation', 'a dominating mode of looking that claims as exclusive both the right *to look* – and so to act – upon others, and the relationship between one's look and reality as such', Wainaina's short story 'Ships in High Transit' ('SHiT') and *Beyond River Yei* constitute 'two opposing interventions into the problem of colonial spectacularization and the kinds of world-formation it instantiates'. Cartwright's essay is testament to an important aspect of the posthumous power of Wainaina's works insofar as it identifies how the author used his fictions to critique and move beyond the discursive construction and reification of African worlds by neocolonial discourse and deployed literary forms – in this case the short story and a generically heterogenous text – to recode the dynamics of *looking* at Africa and the world-making that such a gaze involves.

One of the effects of the tendency to equate the world in world literature with the global is a restrictive focus on works written between the mid-twentieth and twenty-first centuries, neglecting a long list of African writers who self-consciously used literature to examine and (re)articulate their place in the world before the era of decolonization. Jeanne-Marie Jackson's essay provides an important corrective to this tendency in its analysis of the political treatises and essays of several Fante intellectuals working in the early twentieth century: J. E. Casely Hayford, John Mensah Sarbah, S. R. B. Attoh Ahuma and J. W. de Graft Johnson. With extreme sensitivity to the complex self-positioning of these thinkers and their deployment of the intellectual legacy of the Fante Confederacy (1868–74), Jackson in Chapter 13 argues that, through their 'focused characterological exposition' of the 'literate African' and linking of facts with character (rather than simply 'reality'), these writers reclaim 'objectivity' from British colonial discourse and redeploy it as a 'uniquely African moral and political credential'. These political treatises and essays therefore constitute a world-making activity that is 'not primarily translational or oppositional, but righteous and even messianic' insofar as they reactivate the conceptual work of the Fante Confederacy to imagine new ways of existing within the world order of the early twentieth century. Jackson's essay is therefore an important reminder of the world-making potential of 'non-creative' literary genres and of the important role they have played in the histories of the African continent.

As the reader will notice, the essays in this volume do not follow a chronological or geographical approach. This is by design and intended to highlight the shared and common themes and preoccupations across contributions. Whereas theories of world literature have often appeared to reach for all-encompassing and (at least to their critics) unsatisfactory explanations for the totality of literary writing that circulates beyond its immediate point of production, the essays in this volume adopt an Afrocentric approach to the problem. They demonstrate that thinking about the plurality of African literatures in relation to the myriad and highly specific understandings of world literature requires intensive study of specific cases and a turn to new and different archives, both contemporary and historical. World literature in African contexts emerges as a hugely variegated set of practices with diverse political valences and ambitions. The study of such practices involves reading and listening closely to the texts themselves for the ways in which they construe their own worldliness.

Bibliography

Adejunmobi, Moradewun (2020), 'Abiola Irele and the Publicness of African Letters', *Journal of the African Literature Association*, vol. 14, no. 1: 72–89.
Adesanmi, Pius (2011), *You're Not a Country, Africa*, London: Penguin.
Bayart, Jean-François (2000), 'Africa in the World: A History of Extraversion', *African Affairs*, vol. 99, no. 395: 217–67.
Brouillette, Sarah (2019), *UNESCO and the Fate of the Literary*, Stanford: Stanford University Press.
Casanova, Pascale (2008), *La République mondiale des Lettres*, Paris: Éditions de Seuil.
Diagne, Souleymane Bachir, and Jean-Loup Amselle (2020), *In Search of Africa(s): Universalism and Decolonial Thought*, Cambridge: Polity Press.
Gikandi, Simon (2016), 'Introduction', in *The Novel in Africa and the Caribbean since 1950*, ed. Simon Gikandi, Oxford: Oxford University Press, pp. xv–xxvii.
Hayot, Eric (2012), *On Literary Worlds*, Oxford: Oxford University Press.
Helgesson, Stefan, and Mads Rosendahl Thomsen (2019), *Literature and the World*, Abingdon: Routledge.
Julien, Eileen (2006), 'The Extroverted African Novel', in *The Novel*, ed. Franco Moretti, Princeton, NJ: Princeton University Press, pp. 667–702.
Julien, Eileen (2018), 'The Extroverted African Novel, Revisited: African Novels at Home, in the World', *Journal of African Cultural Studies*, vol. 30, no. 3: 371–81.
Laachir, Karima, Sara Marzagora and Francesca Orsini (2018), 'Significant Geographies: In Lieu of World Literature', *Journal of World Literature*, vol. 3, no. 3: 290–310.
Le Bris, Michel, and Jean Rouaud (eds) (2007), *Pour une litterature-monde*, Paris: Gallimard.
Mabanckou, Alain (2006), 'La francophonie, oui, le ghetto: non!', *Le Monde*, 18 March, https://www.lemonde.fr/idees/article/2006/03/18/la-francophonie-oui-le-ghetto-non_752169_3232.html.
Mofolo, Thomas (1925), *Chaka*, trans. Daniel P. Kunene, Heinemann.
Moudileno, Lydie (2010), '*Francophonie*: Trash or Recycle?' in *Transnational French Studies: Postcolonialism and Littérature-Monde*, ed. Alex Hargreaves, Charles Forsdick and David Murphy, Liverpool: Liverpool University Press, pp. 109–24.
Najjar, Alexandre (2007), 'Contre le manifeste «Pour une littérature-monde en français» Expliquer l'eau par l'eau', *Le Monde*, 20 March, http://archive.wiki wix.com/cache/index2.php?url=http%3A%2F%2Fwww.najjar.org%2FlitteratureMondeEnFrancais.asp. Accessed 1 March 2022.
Nancy, Jean-Luc (2007), *The Creation of the World, or Globalization*, trans. François Raffoul and David Pettigrew, Albany: State University of New York Press.
Orsini, Francesca, and Laetitia Zecchini (2019), 'The Locations of (World) Literature: Perspectives from Africa and South Asia: Introduction', *Journal of World Literature*, vol. 4, no. 1: 1–12.
'Pour une "littérature-monde" en français' (2007), *Le Monde*, 15 March, https://www.lemonde.fr/livres/article/2007/03/15/des-ecrivains-plaident-pour-un-roman-en-francais-ouvert-sur-le-monde_883572_3260.html.

Soyinka, Wole (1986), *Myth, Literature, and the African World*, Cambridge: Cambridge University Press.
Swamy, Vinay (2009), '"Pour une littérature-monde": Tahar Ben Jelloun's *Partir*', *Contemporary French and Francophone Studies*, vol. 13, no. 4: 471–8.
Wilder, Gary (2005), *The French Imperial Nation-State: Negritude and Colonial Humanism between the Two World Wars*, Chicago: University of Chicago Press.

2

'African borders are unnatural': Nairobi and the rise of a world literature

Bhakti Shringarpure

The city of Nairobi exudes constant, extraordinary movement. Lamenting traffic jams and unbearably long commutes are just as much a part of everyday conversation as the sight of *matatus* and *bodas* whirring past at breakneck speed and masses of people walking briskly on any given day. Unique to Nairobi's culture of movement and mobility is that it is a hub of migrant journeys internal to Kenya as well as external surrounding countries. The domestic and the international cultures of mobility remain interlocked with each other due to Kenya's mammoth international non-governmental organization (INGO) and humanitarian sector, much of which is focused on assisting displaced populations. This sector does generate employment opportunities for Kenyan nationals but also tends to bring in expat appointments from various countries, which then means an increase in domestic roles in the form of drivers, housekeepers and cleaning staff. This unusual traffic between regional displacement, the sector to support the displaced, and the formal and informal economy around this sector makes Kenya in general, and Nairobi in particular, a saturated and vigorous site for these many intersecting dynamics. Furthermore, the city of Nairobi is home to a large population of migrants from neighbouring Sudan and South Sudan, Somalia, Uganda and the rest of East Africa. Additionally, both Kakuma and Dadaab are fully fledged refugee camps that are situated in Kenya. A focus on Nairobi's literary and cultural production of the past decade illustrates a core engagement with questions of mobility and migration, and the dynamics of intra-African migration call into question the paradox of fixity and flux of national borders in the Horn of Africa, and the new literary forms it engenders. Approaching African literary studies through this lens of migration and mobility generates productive questioning of existing notions of 'world literature' by allowing contemporary East African writing to breathe new life into what I view as an ossified and Eurocentric paradigm of the world literature canon. I examine Nairobi as a robust site for the emergence of innovative new literary paradigms, while also working through the history of world literature as a field, and its limitations.

The history of contemporary, post–Cold War African literature dovetails neatly into the development of the field of geography called mobility studies. This framework of mobility studies can account for the sheer numbers of people moving in and out of East Africa and beyond but also illustrates that mobility has, in a sense, come to constitute identity. Broadly speaking, African literature shows a deep engagement with migration, mobility, nomadism, exile and itinerancy. Writers such as Nuruddin Farah, William Conton, Cyprian Ekwensi and Tsitsi Dangarembga have explored movement from rural to urban areas. African literature in the twenty-first century seems unabashedly focused on migration and movement. An entire generation of contemporary writers such as Chimamanda Ngozi Adichie, Imbolo Mbue, Yaa Gyaasi, Leila Aboulela, Teju Cole, Helon Habila and Taiye Selasi can certainly be categorized as exploring movement and movement's impact on their protagonists. Relatedly, the paradigm of Afropolitanism (an ideology, identity and aesthetic that insists on African lineages of belonging in the world rather than nation) has also held immense sway in African literary studies.[1] Thus, the African continent has a much longer history with 'migrant forms': literatures that 'are structured by, feature, and textualize such processes of continuous migration.'[2] Viewing African literature through the lens of mobility allows for a reconfiguration of several entrenched and overlapping paradigms.

In a conversation between writers Yvonne Adhiambo Owuor and Jennifer Nansubuga Makumbi titled 'The Origin of Nations', borders, distances, travel, mobility, geographies and migration became the anchoring themes for a discussion about what constitutes an African literary imagination.[3]

---

[1] For a comprehensive study on Afropolitanism, see Carli Coetzee (ed.), *Afropolitanism: Reboot* (London: Routledge, 2017).
[2] Stephanie B. Santana, 'Migrant Forms: African Parade's New Literary Geographies', *Research in African Literatures*, vol. 45, no. 3 (2014): 167–87, 168. For more on migrant forms, see Bhakti Shringarpure, 'Digital Forms, Migrant Forms: Yaa Gyasi's Homegoing and Chimamanda Ngozi Adichie's Americanah', *Postcolonial Text*, vol. 15, nos 3 and 4 (2020).
[3] Yvonne Adhiambo Owuor and Jennifer Nansubuga Makumbi, A conversation on 'The Origin of Nations' hosted by *A Long House* magazine, 27 March 2021. Part 1, https://www.youtube.

Makumbi's declaration that 'African borders are unnatural' is a point of intervention for Owuor who believes that 'an intentional reimagining of African boundaries and borders' has been long overdue. For Owuor, whose recent novel *The Dragonfly Sea* engages with plural histories of the Swahili coast, African identity is constituted through migrant geographies that are fundamentally fluid and borderless. Owuor states,

> The sense of people with such long, long, long histories; histories before the idea of Africa even came into being; the idea that these are fluid identities that are not woven from the terrestrial space but from the waters ... the ease with which they can say that yes, there's family in Yemen, there's family in Gujarat, there's family in Kerala, and you speak of these families as you're speaking from the East African shores. So, these become part of place, belonging and identity formations specially through geographies.

While Owuor shares an alluring vision of a borderless and deeply interconnected world that is not tied to regional specificity or the stirrings of nationalist tethering, her vision is in fact in the service of an East African identity. A sense of place, even the notion of home, is important for Owuor: 'I love belonging to the geography of East Africa.' Thus, for Owuor, it is more of a neo-East African vision, in which Kenya can play a central role in the re-imagining of national and international identities and in which migration, flexible borders, a multicultural ethos and an intuitive topographic awareness become pivotal. Indeed, Owuor's writing and this conversation push back against the tendency to view histories of colonialism as the starting point for African studies scholarship. It also harks back to historian Frederick Cooper's claims that the

> very notion 'Africa' itself has been shaped for centuries by linkages within the continent and across oceans and deserts – by the Atlantic slave trade, by the movement of pilgrims, religious networks and ideas associated with Islam, by cultural and economic connections across the Indian Ocean.

Cooper's attempts to critique the 'fad' of globalization at the turn of the century inadvertently reflect on the much longer and deeper history of the continent, all of which emerged out of intra-continent movement across various terrains long before the coming of European colonialism.[4] Thus the formulations of Santana, Owuor and Cooper foreground a deeply

---

com/watch?v=PSCuIZjUMCY and Part 2; https://www.youtube.com/watch?v=TJtZRKFWa2Y. Accessed 20 August 2021.

[4] Frederick Cooper, 'What Is the Concept of Globalization Good For? An African Historian's Perspective', *African Affairs*, vol. 100 (2001): 189–213, 190.

mobile, migratory and flux-prone African continent. Nairobi is an exciting case study, given how the city's culture of mobility and prolific literary production interact with each other. However, it is imperative to first inquire into the framework of 'world literature' and African literature's somewhat perplexing place in it.

Where in world literature is Africa?

The concept of 'world literature' is often attributed to Goethe, who saw it as a visionary concept, and a paradigm that could transcend national borders, languages and cultures, with universality and translatability as its core values. Today, world literature has become a much theorized and debated topic, as well as an academic field, with intense argument over what or who can or cannot be included. Even though the canon of world literature now includes works from all over Asia, Eastern Europe, Middle East and Latin American, literature from the African continent remains under the radar and has particularly weak ties with the field of African literary studies.[5] However, the field of world literature, whether as phenomenon, framework, theory, field or method, is perpetually in a state of crisis. The first reason for this is that world literature has a complicated temporality: it has appeared and reappeared over the past two centuries but remains an idea projected into future time. A comprehensive volume on the subject starts by introducing world literature as having had a 'shadowy existence' for two centuries; that it remains an 'open-ended discussion'; and is imbued with an 'array of problems'.[6] Over the years, there have been revivals, resurgences and debates but editors of the volume seem certain that the concept has not necessarily become foundational nor does it claim to have a unifying identity or approach. In fact, several contributors, as well as older essays included in the volume, prove again and again that world literature has the extraordinary potential for bringing together a vast, global corpus of writing together but that this is yet to happen. This is the temporal crisis to which I refer, reinforcing my argument that world literature can only exist as a futuristic entity. It has also been attached to the question of philology due to contributions by Erich Auerbach and his enormously influential 1946 book *Mimesis*. Auerbach wrote from a place of exile during the Second World War and this furthers the impression of world literature as something idealistic and glorious from a bygone era.

---

[5]Simon Gikandi, 'African Literature in the World: Imagining a Post-Colonial Public Sphere', Keynote lecture at the ALA 2017 Annual Conference at Yale University, https://www.youtube.com/watch?v=x6g1pL0qTuE. Accessed 16 July 2018.
[6]Theo D'haen, César Domínguez and Mads Rosendahl Thomsen, *World Literature: A Reader* (New York: Routledge, 2013), pp. x–xi.

The second reason for this crisis is that the home or 'world' of world literature, whichever way we spin it, is *unheimlich* (unhomely) and 'uncanny' in the Freudian sense of the word. For some literary scholars this home is the earth; for some it has been the globe; for some it is simply motifs traced on a map; and for some, it is language. D'haen et al. argue that part of the problem is disciplinary, since world literature that is often housed in several types of literature departments has 'had difficulty living up to the ambition of being sufficiently inclusive to the literatures of the world. One reason certainly had to do with the enormity of the field. Another resided in a proven lack of interest in so-called "minor" and particularly non-Western literatures'.[7] The *unheimlich* is perfectly illustrated in this crisis of a 'home' discipline. Despite that, it is important to note that the home-world remains forever entrenched in Europe. World literature discourses have found it particularly difficult to abolish binary understandings of the world as split between core and periphery, Europe and elsewhere, Europhone languages and other languages, colonizer and colonized or, as the quotation suggests, 'minor' and 'major' literatures. Attempts to resist existing binaries can trigger and perpetuate them, as I explain below.

Thirdly, there is also a crisis around the question of method in world literature. Auerbach, whose scholarship is foundational to world literatures, has argued for *Ansatzphänomen*, wherein engaging a single point of departure facilitates the recognition and formulation of the general problem.[8] However, the rules about what constitutes a point of departure can be very stringent, making it difficult for the method to be applied and used. Franco Moretti, yet another proponent of the paradigm of world literature, advocates many different techniques and has been associated with 'distant reading', which can potentially liberate world literature scholarship from its dependency on the small and much regurgitated literary canon that close reading naturally requires, thus opening up the world itself.[9] However, the fact that ploughing through data requires vast amount of human and financial resources becomes a deterrent in terms of working with or even teaching such a method. WReC, the Warwick Research Collective, urges world literature frameworks to be done away with and instead calls for a literature of a modern capitalist world-system that will then de-link it 'from the idea of the west' and yoke it instead to the logic of a capitalist world-system.[10] Unfortunately, Moretti and WReC, while offering some radical interventions, remain in the grip of a literary system that is founded on a

---

[7] Ibid., p. x.
[8] Erich Auerbach, *Mimesis: The Representation of Reality in Western Literature*, trans. William R. Trask (Princeton, NJ: Princeton University Press, 2013), p. 14.
[9] Franco Moretti, *Distant Reading* (New York: Verso Books, 2015).
[10] WReC (Warwick Research Collective), *Combined and Uneven Development: Towards a New Theory of World-Literature* (Liverpool: Liverpool University Press, 2015), p. 14.

core and a periphery structure, thus echoing previous approaches to literary studies.

It thus appears that world literature as an idea has a sway on the academic imagination but when it comes to method, discipline and theory, it remains somewhat under-realized. However, since formulations of inclusion and exclusion in certain canons may once again force a reckoning with Eurocentric paradigms of literary studies, it is more productive to ask not how these frameworks can be shattered or reformed but how African literature can be made into the protagonist of its own story that is not merely an add-on or derivative of Euro-American literary histories. Given the above critiques of world literature, it would be more pertinent to ask if African literary studies could infuse new life into a troubled and perhaps disjointed field. It is productive to return to Moretti, who is keenly aware of the limits of his own methods and characterizes world literature thus: 'World literature is not an object, it's a problem, and a problem that asks for a new critical method: and no one has ever found a method by just reading more texts. That's not how theories come into being; they need a leap, a wager – a hypothesis, to get started.'[11] This chapter insists on engaging migration and mobility a priori for the practice of worldmaking in African literature.

Recently, postcolonial theorist Debjani Ganguly has delineated a new category called the 'world novel', which she believes emerged in the wake of three critical phenomena: war and violence in the aftermath of the Cold War; the advent of information technology; and the prevalence of a new humanitarian consciousness. The literature emerging out of these preconditions 'reformulate[s] for our times the conundrum of imagining the human condition on a world scale'.[12] Through the theoretical capaciousness afforded by Ganguly's concept of the 'world novel', it becomes possible to establish that these migrant literatures belong in a world literary system that is formed through dynamic intersections of the local and regional with the global and cosmopolitan. Indeed, migrant writers are involved in worldmaking, the cosmopolitan activity through which world literature, as Pheng Cheah states, 'enables us to imagine a world'.[13] Such worldmaking in migrant writing takes on an urgency as economic precarity, physical and psychological violence, and profound instability mark the migrant experience. Placing these new works in conversation with a longer history of East African canonical literature can offer alternative genealogies of African literary studies. For a city like Nairobi and the literature emerging

---

[11]Franco Moretti, 'Conjectures on World Literature', *New Left Review*, vol. 1 (January–February 2000): 54–68, 55.
[12]Debjani Ganguly, *This Thing Called the World: The Contemporary Novel as Global Form* (Durham, NC: Duke University Press, 2016), p. 37.
[13]Pheng Cheah, 'What Is a World? On World Literature as World-Making Activity', *Daedalus*, vol. 137, no. 3 (Summer 2008): 26–38, 26.

from it, Ganguly's three-point argument applies as follows: firstly, the post–Cold War displacement caused by internecine conflicts in the region, with Nairobi providing a safe refuge and thus forcing an active engagement with the dynamics of migration; secondly, the deep investment in technology and digitality making Nairobi the new 'silicon savannah'[14] for the African continent; and finally, the pervasive discourses of humanitarianism engendered by the powerful INGO sector housed in the city. It is imperative to look back over the last decade or so of Nairobi's cultural history, which includes many large and renowned organizations, and ask if these initiatives were able to engage, include and absorb Nairobi's identity as a site of migration and mobility and one that comprises several nationalities, histories of displacement and is undergirded by cultures of mobility. However, I depart from Ganguly with regard to the novel, since these innovative projects engage many other genres, such as story, essay, digital writing and poetry.

Nairobi and maps of exile

Nairobi has had a vibrant history of literary-cultural initiatives since the start of the new millennium, thanks largely in part due to *Kwani?*, an initiative that dominated the Kenyan and arguably the Anglophone African literary and publishing landscape for fifteen years. By the death of its prolific co-founder Binyavanga Wainana in 2019 and amid disagreements within the key members of the collective, *Kwani?* had published a roster of new writers who are now well on their way to international success, had received grants from prestigious foundations and organized all kinds of cultural festivals and conferences. Following the same timeline were other significant developments in Nairobi, such as the establishment of the GoDown Arts Centre, also founded in 2003 by architect, activist and performer Joy Mboya.[15] Though they had seemingly different goals and approaches, a key preoccupation was to boost the creative industries in Kenya. This literary and cultural renaissance was possible due to a confluence of political shifts and factors within Kenya, but both Mboya and Wainana, among several others, belonged to a group of Kenyans that returned home after educational or career stints abroad. In a sense, their world, cosmopolitan or even Afropolitan ethos pervaded the projects they founded and took on. Both organizations focused on amplifying and nourishing the local cultural scene while accessing funding from the Global North and finding a measure

---

[14] Laura Mallonee, 'The Techies Turning Kenya into a Silicon Savannah', *Wired* magazine, 8 December 2018, https://www.wired.com/story/kenya-silicon-savannah-photo-gallery/. Accessed 10 August 2021.
[15] GoDown Arts Centre, https://godowntransforms.org/. Accessed 10 August 2021.

of renown outside Kenya. GoDown Arts Centre has continued its expansion and cultural programming even during the global pandemic.

Kate Wallis highlights comments made by Billy Kahora, Kenyan writer and former managing editor of *Kwani?* who believes that *Kwani?* 'was consciously concerned with "reaching out of the borders of our national space"', rejecting solely national structures and instead creating 'a huge push for the universal' (Kahora) through dialogue with a pan-African and international space of writing, publishing and prizing.[16] Without doubt, these comments reflect the self-conscious investment of *Kwani?* investment in transnational structures and certainly their collaborations with like-minded organizations in other countries are evidence of a pluralistic identity. However, if *Kwani?* were to be retrospectively viewed from the vantage point of the many new magazines, collectives and organizations that emerged in the second decade of the twenty-first century, one might detect a neo-nationalist ethos.[17] Carey Baraka's provocative take-down of *Kwani?* hints at this nationalist narrative and Joy Mboya, the founder of GoDown, openly admits to being part of efforts to build a 'new Kenyan nation'.[18] What precisely were the cultural, literary and creative worlds that these initiatives chose to produce and maybe delimit? The last few years have seen other initiatives spring up and these illustrate a commitment to paradigms of pan-African collectives, visions of a borderless Africa, a focus on mobility between African regions. Particularly poignant for this chapter are online initiatives such as *Jalada Africa*, *Lolwe magazine* and *A Long House*; books such as the *Nairobi Noir* anthology edited by Peter Kimani, novels by Mũkoma wa Ngũgĩ and writing by Yvonne Owuor that engage a multiplicity of migrant identities in Nairobi; and event platforms such as *Pawa 254* and my own collaborative literary salons, *Nairobi: Maps or Exile*, as well as festivals such as *Macondo Literary Festival* and *Afrolit Sans Frontières*. Another synthesis point with these new projects is a long-standing blog written by James Murua that assembles and archives all the news about events, awards and publications from the African continent through a particular localized engagement with Kenya (Murua resides in Nairobi). In fact, Nairobi remains an anchoring location with events, book launches, meetings and spontaneous social events occurring frequently and ensuring that many popular venues in Nairobi remain busy.

---

[16] Kate Wallis, 'Exchanges in Nairobi and Lagos: Mapping Literary Networks and World Literary Space', *Research in African Literatures*, vol. 49, no. 1 (Spring 2018): 163–86, 166.
[17] Carey Baraka, 'Intimations of an Ending', *Johannesburg Review of Books*, 27 August 2020, https://johannesburgreviewofbooks.com/2020/08/27/intimations-of-an-ending-carey-baraka-on-the-unspoken-demise-of-kwani-and-the-death-of-a-dream/. Accessed 27 January 2022.
[18] Bhakti Shringarpure, 'What Is Our Resistance? A Conversation with Joy Mboya', *Los Angeles Review of Books*, 21 June 2021, https://lareviewofbooks.org/article/what-is-our-resistance-a-conversation-with-joy-mboya/. Accessed 27 January 2022.

An interesting, recent dimension has also been an engagement with elements of Black identity in ways that draw upon North American Afropessimist approaches.[19] Such attempts to construct affinities with African American writing and culture have slowly appeared in the past years through works like Yaa Gyasi's *Homegoing* (2017) that draws heavily from Saidiya Hartman's *Lose Your Mother* (2006), Adichie's *Americanah* (2013) and Teju Cole's *Open City* (2011). They are also visible in writings about the Black Mediterranean that refer to theories of Black Atlantic culture and compare migrants drowning in the oceans to the Middle Passage of slavery. Films like *Black Panther* and Beyoncé's use of African mythological imagery also contribute to these sympathies between the African continent and North America. Here, again, it is the history of mobilities between the continents that enlivens the connection. Incidents such as the lynching of George Floyd in 2020 deepen the ties within a Global Blackness. A poignant example of this is the call for submissions put out by *A Long House* magazine. Explaining their special issue on 'Origins', they write, 'today, two words describe most of the discourse around Africa and the black diaspora: "racism" and "colonization." But the idea of a Black self outside of external definitions requires language that exists beyond the influences of these boundaries.'[20] Another illustration was Murua's blog, which went from claiming to archive African literature to labelling itself as 'James Murua's African Literature Blog: Archiving African and Black Literature', thus significantly expanding the framework of African literature and its thematic and aesthetic preoccupations. Below, I summarize some of the particularities of the works being featured by these initiatives, arguing that the cumulative effect is that they not only centre discourses of mobility but have also fundamentally altered literary production from the continent.

The last few years in traditional book publishing have certainly proven exciting, not only in terms of the large numbers of African literary works being published but also in terms of more complex renditions of national identities, themes of migration and transnational tropes. A new generation of Kenyan writers is devoted to the project of complicating Kenyan identity. Yvonne Adhiambo Owuor's Caine Prize-winning novella *The Weight of Whispers* is set in Nairobi and tells the story of a Rwandan refugee who flees to neighbouring Kenya. Owuor's multicultural and multilingual representation of Nairobi sets a new precedent with which to think about the dynamics of intra-African migration and the violent East African histories that lead to these journeys. Owuor's two novels do similar work of subverting

---

[19] A historical overview of the term 'Afropessimism' and its importance with the current movements for Black Lives can be found in Jesse McCarthy, 'On Afropessimism', *Los Angeles Review of Books*, 20 July 2020, https://www.lareviewofbooks.org/article/on-afropessimism/. Accessed 27 January 2022.
[20] Lolwe, https://lolwe.org/. Accessed 20 August 2021.

existing Kenyan national imaginaries through very mobile protagonists. *The Dragonfly Sea* in particular deeply engages the affective geographies that come into being from relationships anchored to oceanic travel. Here, Kenya comes about through its long-standing kinship with Asia and the many Muslim characters in the book also shatter the myth of a country that tends to be associated only with Christianity. Mũkoma wa Ngũgĩ's works of detective fiction, *Nairobi Heat* (2011) and *Black Star Nairobi* (2013), both set in Nairobi, also weave Rwandan refugees and Rwandan characters in their plots and also foreground humanitarian organizations. Importantly, Mũkoma's detective protagonist, Ishmael, is a Black, African American man who must journey from the American South to Nairobi to solve the mystery. Though not deliberately, Ishmael begins to connect to his own racial identity as a Black man and interrogate his African diasporic roots. Through Ishmael, the author makes Nairobi the site for a confrontation between the histories and relationships that the violence of slavery, dispossession and colonialism brought about. Thus, the literary universe of this detective duology succeeds in creating a uniquely transnational and hitherto unexplored ethos between East Africa and the United States. Lastly, I will briefly mention *Nairobi Noir* (2020), an anthology of noir short fiction edited and put together by Peter Kimani in Kenya but published by Akashic Books in the United States. It can be argued that anthologies make worlds either through the themes that bind the collection together, or often the country that the collection is honouring. Kimani's Nairobi is primarily a place of haves and have-nots, and most stories in the volume skew towards explorations of poverty. However, despite this focus, there are two stories in the volume that specifically centre Somali refugees. Migrant experiences appear frequently in new Kenyan writing though it is the literary magazine scene that has succeeded in synthesizing this vision of Nairobi as a world where nationalities, identities and stories of exile abound.

Identifying itself as a 'pan-African' writers' collective, *Jalada* came to prominence after they published a short story by Ngũgĩ wa Thiong'o that was translated into ninety-seven languages. A third of these languages were African. Following this success, *Jalada*'s ascent was fast and remarkable with features about them in *The Guardian* and the *Times Literary Supplement* and high-profile collaborations with places like *Transition* magazine, currently based at Harvard. At the outset, *Jalada* had a mailing address in Nairobi but an origin story and editorial team that involved people from several different regions. *Jalada*'s managing editor at the time, Wanjeri Gakuru, expressed it thus: '22 writers from Kenya, Uganda, Nigeria, Zimbabwe, Botswana and South Africa dared to imagine something new.'[21]

---

[21] Wanjeri Gakuru, 'The Inventiveness and Daring of Jalada Africa', *Brittle Paper*, 26 October 2020, https://brittlepaper.com/2020/10/the-inventiveness-and-daring-of-jalada-africa/. Accessed 20 August 2021.

Their managerial structure is unique with leadership roles changing on a biannual basis, thus ensuring that the nationality of the managing editor is continually changing. While the first issue cohered their pan-African agenda, following issues and ensuing event initiatives became increasingly focused on topics that allowed an exploration of fluid African identities, diaspora connections and the fluidity of the body. Mobility, travel and movement were lyrically integrated into these agendas and the featured artwork. 'The Railway Map', a speculative map of a Somali railway network using the style and colours from the London tube map, is a key example. This tongue-in-cheek image not only draws attention to Somalia's locked-out status in the world but also projects an aspiration of unbounded movement. *Jalada* showcases an immensely diverse range of writing from across the African continent and their event ideas departed from the more traditional festivals and prizes of *Kwani?*.

Of significance to this chapter is the *Jalada* Mobile Literary and Arts Festival described by Gakuru as 'a hybrid between a traditional place-based festival and a literary/art bus tour. The goal was to celebrate cultural diversity through conversations, multilingual performances and exhibitions. Co-curated by Moses Kilolo, Richard Oduor and myself, the 28-day trip covered over 4,500 kilometres and had over 7,000 total attendees.'[22] The touring festival visited various locations in five different countries and not only synthesized a pan-African agenda but also illustrated how it could be physically and materially achieved. *Jalada's* mobile approach to programming was spatially spread out and broke the mould of Kenyan national literature very quickly. The fact that it was a collective that credited twenty-two people for its creation also emphasized its plural vision and work ethic. The chosen themes for each *Jalada* issue (such as diaspora, Afro-futures and bodies) also illustrate an openness to moving the conversation beyond the local and the national through their deceptive simplicity and breadth. Thus *Jalada* has created an opening with which to frame the literary works that they publish as constitutive of a world literature that has a more cosmopolitan, border-defying and transnational agenda.

An even more recent addition is the literary magazine *Lolwe*, founded in 2020 by Kenyan writer Troy Onyango. The word *Lolwe* derives from Nam Lolwe, the original or traditional Luo name for Lake Victoria, meaning endless lake or water body, and thus *Lolwe* suggests 'having or seeming to have no end or limit'.[23] Despite its local Luo roots, the name of the magazine already engages with notions of a world without limits, and the contents of *Lolwe* similarly aspire to a rich vision of African literature. *Lolwe* shows

---

[22]Ibid.
[23]Socrates Mbamalu, 'Kenyan Writer Troy Onyango Launches *Lolwe*, a New Literary Magazine', *This Is Africa*, 24 January 2020, https://thisisafrica.me/arts-and-culture/kenya-troy-onyango-launches-lolwe-literary-magazine/. Accessed 20 August 2021.

itself as immediately connected to a larger network of writers and poets dispersed across the continent. A recently published poem, 'At Elmina Castle, I Bleed' by Sarpong Osei Asamoah also links to the Afropessimist ethos I mentioned earlier by harking back to the history of slavery. The poet exclaims, 'I want them to hear my coming, my dead', and evokes the ancestors either taken away to the Americas or who remain buried under the Atlantic. African literature literally opens up to include the oceans, those scattered by violent histories, and harnesses the threads of diasporic Blackness across the world. Another publication (*A Long House*) also works to redefine African literature by engaging Blackness and situating the African within a historical ethos of transnational experiences of race and slavery. They hoped to hark back to a time when 'the black persona was entirely self-determined' and not determined or designed by histories of colonial contact or occupations. *A Long House* notes,

> The aim is not of course to deny racism or colonization – these are important touchpoints in our collective black experience. The goal is to consider how we might constitute ourselves today outside of these projects which have long sought to hold our imagination in chains. Is there a black self outside of these boundaries? Is there historical precedence for such a black self?[24]

Furthermore, they wish to encapsulate a world and Africa as a home for such a re-imagined and redrawn world. They insist that they and us are 'persuaded that this self-determining, self-shaping African milieu – spatial and temporal, continental and diasporic, a canopy that extends to anywhere there are black people in the world – is not situated only in the past'. The insistence here is on envisioning a new future but it is also about engaging a deeply thought-out and aesthetically experimental Blackness that originates from Africa rather than being imported from North America.

Events and festivals in Nairobi have also displayed a similar worldmaking thrust in their curatorial style and logic. In late 2019, I started monthly literary salons in Nairobi in collaboration with Somali Canadian journalist and writer Hassan Ghedi Santur who was based in Kenya, and a company called The CARROT Co., founded and run by Taye Balogun, a filmmaker who worked in the humanitarian and development sector. Santur's family had fled the war in Somalia in the early 1990s and migrated to Canada while retaining a large network of relatives and friends in the East Africa region. Both Balogun and Santur were connected to the INGO worlds and The CARROT described themselves explicitly as a 'collective of pan-African

---

[24] A Long House, https://opencountrymag.com/a-long-house-calls-for-submissions-to-first-issue-origins/. Accessed 1 March 2022.

artists – scholars and practitioners, working solely to support the development sector with creative communication bridging the gap between mass population and policy-makers'. Their interest lay in 'storytelling with emphasis on art, culture and indigenous knowledge' that came out of the African continent but the hope was that art and storytelling could amplify and engage a host of developmental problems, including gender inequality, inadequate African leadership, poor water and sanitation provision, and insufficient refugee rights.[25] Titled *Nairobi: Maps of Exile*[26] my research and scholarly impetus was to locate writers who had migrated to Nairobi from surrounding East Africa and to understand if there was an emerging corpus of writing that identified as specifically East African. Without much effort, our salons attracted writers from Somalia, Sudan, Nigeria, Rwanda, the United States and the UK, all of whom had either migrated to Nairobi as children or had recently moved to work in the INGO sector. With sudden closures from the Covid-19 pandemic, some salons had to be cancelled but the five planned salons offered a strong sense of what was brewing in Nairobi and the sheer diversity of writers in the city.

However, *Nairobi: Maps of Exile* was certainly not the first example of a fusion of art and humanitarianism. Organizations like Pawa 254 had centred 'artivism' for almost a decade. Pawa 254 described themselves as integrating 'art and activism to promote active civic participation, livelihoods and employment development for Kenyan youth'. It is interesting to note here that despite Pawa 254's adamant, neo-nationalist mission to foreground Kenyan issues, many of their events inadvertently ended up showcasing migrant and refugee literature, art and film. Their collaboration with FilmAid, an NGO that provided film and documentary education at the Dadaab and Kakuma refugee camps, led to the curation of film festivals focused on refugees in 2016[27] and 2018.[28] *Kwani?* used similar vocabulary and has explicitly aimed to imitate NGO- and development-centric models to establish a creative industries sector in Kenya. Yet another example is the Circle Art Gallery's show 'Freedom| Flight| Refuge' from 2016 that exhibited thirty-five artists working on themes of internally displaced persons after Kenya's controversial presidential elections in 2007/8. They were joined by poet Sitawa Namwalie and novelist Yvonne Owuor, who read from

---

[25] The CARROT Co., https://www.thecarrotco.org/#about-us. Accessed 20 August 2021.
[26] *Warscapes* magazine. Videos, http://www.warscapes.com/videos/nairobi-maps-exile. Accessed 20 August 2021.
[27] 'Nairobi: Celebrating Efforts to Spark Change: Film Festival to Address Migration, Radicalization, Women in Leadership', *Human Rights Watch* news, https://www.hrw.org/news/2016/10/21/nairobi-celebrating-efforts-spark-change. Accessed 20 August 2021.
[28] FilmAid Film Festival at PAWA 254, Eventbrite announcement, https://www.eventbrite.com/e/filmaid-film-festival-at-pawa254-tickets-50066953606?fbclid=IwAR1g34V BnqhR6LMTMnyWSbiZo_wt6gse3tjP70KPYwGgrkf3kVf8ZcMtw-Y. Accessed 27 January 2022.

their work on related themes.[29] Many of these events collaborate with or find funding through the powerful international agency UNHCR, whose Artists for Refugees Project[30] not only insists on art as a form of therapy for refugees but also provides a platform so that 'talented refugees can discover, explore, hone and display their talents'.[31] Ten years before Ganguly, Joseph R. Slaughter had argued that the body of emerging 'world literature' in the early twentieth century engages discourses as well as formal characteristics of human rights and law narratives. Ganguly takes these concerns further in her work. In all these examples, not only do migration, refugee experiences and mobility emerge as undergirding aspects in the curation of these events but the interconnectedness between humanitarianism, development and human rights sectors with the creative industries is strengthened. This is a literary and artistic universe where these imbrications have become inevitable, and constitute a new canon of world literature alongside other artistic and cultural production.

Two Nairobi-based literary festivals were also 'worlding' in the sense defined by Donna Haraway, whose claims about speculative fiction could easily be transposed here. Haraway's research emerged out of several workshops on the concept of 'worlding' and insists that 'storytelling and fact telling' lead to 'the patterning of possible worlds and possible times, material-semiotic worlds, gone, here, and yet to come'.[32] The *Macondo Literary Festival* and the completely digital *Afrolit Sans Frontières* festival illustrated Haraway's vision of worlding accurately. Macondo, named after the magical place in the fiction of Colombian novelist Gabriel Garcia Màrquez, sought to 'promote literature and authors of and from Africa beyond linguistic borders'.[33] Macondo launched in 2019, in Nairobi's historically and culturally rich downtown neighbourhood, which housed the Kenya National Theatre, and was located right next to the University of Nairobi. Worlding as it occurred during this festival was as much material as it was imaginative, with a programme that aimed at an exciting synergy between Anglophone and Lusophone Africa. Writers and translators from Mozambique, Angola and Guinea-Bissau were placed in generative conversations between Anglophone writers from Kenya, South Africa, Nigeria and other countries. Over the next few days, panels

---

[29] Anjellah Owino, 'Exhibition Showcases Plight of Displaced Persons and Migrants.' *Standard Digital*, Kenya, 21 February 2016, https://www.standardmedia.co.ke/article/2000192446/exhibition-showcases-plight-of-displaced-persons-and-migrants. Accessed 20 August 2021.
[30] 'Artists for Refugees Project.' The UN Refugee Agency, Kenya, https://www.unhcr.org/ke/artists-refugees-project. Accessed 20 August 2021.
[31] UNHCR, https://www.unhcr.org/ke/artists-refugees-project. Accessed 20 August 2021.
[32] Donna Haraway, *Staying with the Trouble: Making Kin in the Chthulucene* (Durham, NC: Duke University Press, 2016), p. 31.
[33] Macondo Literary Festival, https://www.macondolitfest.org/about-us. Accessed 20 August 2021.

worked through questions of home and belonging, physical and linguistic borders, and the role of literature in creating new African histories and geographies.[34] Less than a year later and in an attempt to keep the literary world united and energized, South African writer Zukiswa Wanner and blogger Murua organized a virtual literary festival on Instagram.[35] The virtual format allowed writers of African heritage from all over the world to come together and build a new cosmopolitan and global ethos that would have been impossible on a physical and material scale. The name of the festival included *sans frontières* (without boundaries), which spoke volumes about the direction in which the African literary imaginary was headed. Haraway's ominous declarations about worlds and times yet to come ring particularly true here as we await new frontiers of African literatures whose foundations have been put into place by creating new solidarities, traversing linguistic barriers and harnessing a 'world' through literature.

The future of world literature is probably digital

While Auerbach, a key figure associated with world literature, was in exile during and after the Second World War, Italian Jesuit priest Roberto Busa made an *index verborum* of all the words in the work of St Thomas Aquinas and related authors, totalling 11 million words of medieval Latin. Father Busa had heard of computers and, predicting that a machine might aid his ambitious project, solicited the help of a person at IBM in the United States. Today, he is seen as the father of Digital Humanities, a scholarly field concerned with the intersection of computing and humanities. Around the same time, in 1950, the American CIA founded the Congress for Cultural Freedom (CCF). The CCF infiltrated, funded and (directly and indirectly) managed over thirty small magazines worldwide.[36] Armed with a watered-down, apolitical high modernism that had been transformed merely into a set of formal techniques, the CCF propagated certain styles, authors and genres that successfully drove a wedge between art and politics that

---

[34]Macondo Literary Festival, program schedule, https://www.macondolitfest.org/program-2019. Accessed 1 March 2022.
[35]Afrolit Sans Frontieres Festival. *Wikipedia*, https://en.wikipedia.org/wiki/Afrolit_Sans_Frontieres_Festival. Accessed 27 January 2022.
[36]For more on this, see Frances Stonor Sanders, *Who Paid the Piper? CIA and the Cultural Cold War* (London: Granta Books, 1999); Giles Scott-Smith, *Campaigning Culture and the Global Cold War: The Journals of the Congress for Cultural Freedom* (London: Palgrave Macmillan, 2017).

continues to this day.³⁷ Not to be left out of the Cold War culture scuffle, the USSR's Afro-Asian Solidarity movement started the Afro-Asian Writer's Association in 1958 with its journal *Lotus*, which embraced socialist realism and revolutionary romanticism in literary creation.³⁸

What emerges from these events is a sense that an extraordinary surge in technology had completely radicalized the circuits of transmission, dissemination and diffusion of literature. Systems of technology are often credited with altering and reshaping the course of history. In the Euro-American academy, the 1990s were a particularly industrious time for scholars of world literature as well as for those tentatively starting out in humanities computing fields. Massive text and image archives first made their presence felt with the Women Writers Project and The William Blake Archive, for example, soon followed by The Nines and the Rossetti Archive. The coming of the internet, the World Wide Web, software developments for text-encoding and hypertext editing among other things enabled truly multimedia and cross-disciplinary work and which, for several different reasons, became situated in literary studies. In a special issue of *Modern Languages Quarterly*, Ted Underwood and James English claimed that literary studies is facing a 'crisis of largeness' as it expands uncontrollably, and echoed scholars like Moretti who were concerned about questions of method.³⁹

Oddly, the surge in technology, standardization and new global modalities has been a subject of great anguish in world literature, with scholars often expressing a sense of crisis. I urge them to consider the digital turn as an opening and not as a problem. By this, I do not mean we should embrace an uncritical cyber-utopianism with its teleological assumptions of progress and innovation. Indeed, digitality can only be an uneven enabler of worldmaking, reliant as it is on material factors and the availability of resources. Despite this, it is important to acknowledge that African literature and the discourses surrounding it have intersected with a saturated, fertile and frenetic digital moment. African literature has become the protagonist in a global new media and digital system that has altered circuits of mobility, revised our ways of reading, generated new hierarchies of power, deployed new chronotopes and foregrounded overlappings and entanglements in literary studies. These phenomena raise a variety of questions about the histories of

---

³⁷Greg Barnhiselg, *Cold War Modernists: Art, Literature, and American Cultural Diplomacy* (New York: Columbia University Press, 2015); Bhakti Shringarpure, *Cold War Assemblages: Decolonization to Digital* (London: Routledge, 2019).
³⁸Hala Halim, 'Afro-Asian Third-Worldism into Global South: The Case of Lotus Journal', *Global South Studies*, 22 November 2017, https://globalsouthstudies.as.virginia.edu/key-moments/afro-asian-third-worldism-global-south-case-lotus-journal. Accessed 20 August 2021.
³⁹Ted Underwood and James F. English (eds), 'Scale and Value: New and Digital Approaches to Literary History', *Modern Languages Quarterly*, vol. 77, no. 3 (1 September 2016): 279.

African writing, as well as forms and innovations within it. These questions also complicate origins and imaginaries, rupture the complacency around the issues of literary prestige and allow for multilingual and multimedia research to become possible.

With most places today hyper-reliant on digital modes and the global Covid-19 pandemic having only exacerbated these needs, the digital footprint is now everywhere and not just attributed to the wealthy. At the same time, masses of human populations are in flux and this non-stop movement has made technology a matter of survival for populations. Being connected is an urgent priority. More than ever, people are building worlds behind screens, boundaries are being completely remediated and time is unfolding in protean shapes. Nairobi is a key illustration of a site where all those concerns and experiences overlap and reveal themselves through a prescient and intuitive literary and cultural production, which has embraced this intersecting digital turn, as well as the mobilities turn. Owuor asks if the new generation that she laughingly calls 'cyborgs' (those who have grown up with technology) are 'already operating with new sense of borderlessness through the internet'. Furthermore, she declares, 'I have every faith that that impulse will transfer itself into their geographies … I'm hoping there will be a convergence, an intentional reimagining of borders and boundaries in the same way that the borders of Africa were unnaturally imagined'.[40] Even though Owuor may sound optimistic, perhaps even delusional to some, her cyber-utopic dreams have already been manifested, written up, represented, published and presented by a host of different books, magazines, websites and events. Nairobi is one example where these creative forces have converged but it is imperative to ask similar questions and engage these frameworks for other places. The parallel and dynamic history of Nairobi's literary circuits can completely revitalize and revolutionize current theories, approaches and methods of engaging with world literature.

Bibliography

'Artists for Refugees Project'. The UN Refugee Agency, Kenya, https://www.unhcr.org/ke/artists-refugees-project. Accessed 1 March 2022.

Auerbach, Erich (2013), *Mimesis: The Representation of Reality in Western Literature*, trans. William R. Trask, Princeton, NJ: Princeton University Press.

Baraka, Carey (2020), 'Intimations of an Ending', *Johannesburg Review of Books*, 27 August, https://johannesburgreviewofbooks.com/2020/08/27/intimations-of-an-ending-carey-baraka-on-the-unspoken-demise-of-kwani-and-the-death-of-a-dream/. Accessed 1 March 2022.

---

[40] Owuor and Makumbi, A conversation on 'The Origin of Nations'.

Barnhiselg, Greg (2015), *Cold War Modernists: Art, Literature, and American Cultural Diplomacy*, New York: Columbia University Press.

Cheah, Pheng (2008), 'What Is a World? On World Literature as World-Making Activity', *Daedalus*, vol. 137, no. 3 (Summer): 26–38.

Coetzee, Carli (ed.) (2017), *Afropolitanism: Reboot*, London: Routledge.

Cooper, Frederick (2001), 'What Is the Concept of Globalization Good For? An African Historian's Perspective', *African Affairs*, vol. 100: 189–213.

D'haen, Theo, César Domínguez and Mads Rosendahl Thomsen (2013), *World Literature: A Reader*, New York: Routledge.

FilmAid Film Festival at PAWA 254, Eventbrite Announcement, https://www.eventbrite.com/e/filmaid-film-festival-at-pawa254-tickets-50066953606?fbclid=IwAR1g34VBnqhR6LMTMnyWSbiZo_wt6gse3tjP70KPYwGgrkf3kVf8ZcMtw-Y. Accessed 1 March 2022.

Gakuru, Wanjeri (2020), 'The Inventiveness and Daring of Jalada Africa', *Brittle Paper*, 26 October, https://brittlepaper.com/2020/10/the-inventiveness-and-daring-of-jalada-africa/. Accessed 1 March 2022.

Ganguly, Debjani (2016), *This Thing Called the World: The Contemporary Novel as Global Form*, Durham, NC: Duke University Press.

Gikandi, Simon (2017), 'African Literature in the World: Imagining a Post-Colonial Public Sphere', Keynote lecture at Princeton University, at the ALA Annual Conference at Yale University, https://www.youtube.com/watch?v=x6g1pL0qTuE. Accessed 1 March 2022.

GoDown Arts Centre, https://godowntransforms.org/. Accessed 1 March 2022.

Halim, Hala (2017), 'Afro-Asian Third-Worldism into Global South: The Case of Lotus Journal', *Global South Studies*, https://globalsouthstudies.as.virginia.edu/key-moments/afro-asian-third-worldism-global-south-case-lotus-journal. Accessed 1 March 2022.

Haraway, Donna (2016), *Staying with the Trouble: Making kin in the Chthulucene*, Durham, NC: Duke University Press. Lolwe, https://lolwe.org/. Accessed 1 March 2022.

Macondo Literary Festival, https://www.macondolitfest.org/. Accessed 1 March 2022.

Mallonee, Laura (2018), 'The Techies Turning Kenya into a Silicon Savannah', *Wired* magazine, 8 December, https://www.wired.com/story/kenya-silicon-savannah-photo-gallery/. Accessed 1 March 2022.

Mbamalu, Socrates (2020), 'Kenyan Writer Troy Onyango Launches *Lolwe*, a New Literary Magazine', *This Is Africa*, 24 January, https://thisisafrica.me/arts-and-culture/kenya-troy-onyango-launches-lolwe-literary-magazine/. Accessed 1 March 2022.

McCarthy, Jesse (2020), 'On Afropessimism', *Los Angeles Review of Books*, 20 July, https://www.lareviewofbooks.org/article/on-afropessimism/. Accessed 1 March 2022.

Moretti, Franco (2000), 'Conjectures on World Literature', *New Left Review*, vol. 1 (January–February): 54–68.

Moretti, Franco (2015), *Distant Reading*, New York: Verso Books.

'Nairobi: Celebrating Efforts to Spark Change: Film Festival to Address Migration, Radicalization, Women in Leadership', *Human Rights Watch* news, https://

www.hrw.org/news/2016/10/21/nairobi-celebrating-efforts-spark-change. Accessed 1 March 2022.

Owino, Anjellah (2016), 'Exhibition Showcases Plight of Displaced Persons and Migrants'. *Standard Digital*, Kenya, 21 February, https://www.standardmedia.co.ke/article/2000192446/exhibition-showcases-plight-of-displaced-persons-and-migrants. Accessed 1 March 2022.

Owuor, Yvonne Adhiambo, and Jennifer Nansubuga Makumbi (2021), A conversation on 'The Origin of Nations' hosted by *A Long House* magazine, 27 March 2021. Part 1, https://www.youtube.com/watch?v=PSCuIZjUMCY and Part 2, https://www.youtube.com/watch?v=TJtZRKFWa2Y. Accessed 1 March 2022.

Santana, Stephanie B. (2014), 'Migrant Forms: African Parade's New Literary Geographies', *Research in African Literatures*, vol. 45, no. 3: 167–87.

Scott-Smith, Giles (2017), *Campaigning Culture and the Global Cold War: The Journals of the Congress for Cultural Freedom*, London: Palgrave Macmillan.

Shringarpure, Bhakti (2019), *Cold War Assemblages: Decolonization to Digital*, London: Routledge.

Shringarpure, Bhakti (2020), 'Digital Forms, Migrant Forms: Yaa Gyasi's Homegoing and Chimamanda Ngozi Adichie's Americanah', *Postcolonial Text*, vol. 15, nos 3 and 4.

Shringarpure, Bhakti (2021), 'What Is Our Resistance? A Conversation with Joy Mboya', *Los Angeles Review of Books*, 21 June, https://lareviewofbooks.org/article/what-is-our-resistance-a-conversation-with-joy-mboya/. Accessed 1 March 2022.

Stonor Sanders, Frances (1999), *Who Paid the Piper? CIA and the Cultural Cold War*, London: Granta Books.

The CARROT Co., https://www.thecarrotco.org/#about-us. Accessed 1 March 2022.

Underwood, Ted, and James F. English (eds) (2016), 'Scale and Value: New and Digital Approaches to Literary History', *Modern Languages Quarterly*, vol. 77, no. 3 (1 September).

Wallis, Kate (2018), 'Exchanges in Nairobi and Lagos: Mapping Literary Networks and World Literary Space', *Research in African Literatures*, vol. 49, no. 1 (Spring): 163–86.

Warscapes magazine. Videos, http://www.warscapes.com/videos/nairobi-maps-exile. Accessed 1 March 2022.

Warwick Research Collective (2015), *Combined and Uneven Development: Towards a New Theory of World-Literature*, Liverpool: Liverpool University Press.

3

Can Nairobi 'world' without the 'great Kenyan novel'?

Billy Kahora

Nairobi, like most sub-Saharan African cities, has always been tough for writers. The common refrains – *Nairobi ina wenyewe* (Nairobi has its owners – we are all visiting and one day we all have to go back to our motherlands) or *Nairobi ni shamba la mawe* (it is a garden of stone) – capture its capitalistic social history best, since its colonial days as a processing station of agricultural produce from its rich farming hinterlands in the Rift Valley. Meja Mwangi, writing in the 1960s to the 1980s, remains the greatest chronicler of the city's harsh economic realities. Ben, who describes himself as the 'horny-toed barefoot son of the rusty concrete mixer', is the protagonist of Mwangi's novel *Going Down River Road*, and undergoes all the ignominies possible as one of those at the bottom of the city's economic layers. Nothing much has changed decades later, when Yvonne Owuor's Rwandese protagonist, Kuseremane, in her 2003 short story *Weight of Whispers* observes in an epiphanic moment, 'these Kenyans and their shillings' after a series of encounters in Nairobi as a refugee. Nairobi's harsh economics might explain why fewer and fewer novels (the currency of world literature for such a long time) are emerging from the city.[1] Writing good novels requires not only a room of one's one for the writer but also

---

[1] A quick look at an annual mapping of Kenyan literary production 2005–19 in the *Commonwealth Journal of Literature* by Grace Musila reveals 340-odd works of fiction in this period. However, when novels by Kenyan writers are isolated and compared to 1968–83 (a period of similar length, mapped in the same publication), they are far fewer.

a great deal of creative time in it. In Nairobi and many other sub-Saharan African cities, such temporal and spatial possibilities are only held by the independently wealthy – those whose time is their own, with a roof of their head that is also theirs. How is that time and space to be found by those (mostly young writers) trying to write a novel? Like most in the city, they are hustling to pay rent and keep their heads above water. Nairobi has increasingly become a deterrent rather than an inspiration for the novelist. In recent years, several prominent writers and artists have been known to flee Nairobi to work in cheaper but also less frenetic spaces in Kenya.

This is why Bhakti Shringarpure's essay, 'African borders are unnatural: Nairobi and the rise of a world literature', arguing for the potential of Nairobi to become a leading space of world literature, poses some fascinating possibilities and alternatives. By providing a literary tour of present and past literary initiatives like *Kwani?* and *Jalada* as well as other forms of literary activity, Shringarpure argues that such examples form a base from which the city can become a leader in world literature. She also frames her argument through postcolonial scholar Debjani Ganguly and her articulation of the world novel as a form emerging from 'three critical phenomena: war and violence in the aftermath of the Cold War; the advent of information technology; and the prevalence of a new humanitarian consciousness', and this becomes problematic on two levels. Shringarpure is right that Nairobi is well placed in these three contexts – the city has long been a refuge for many escaping conflicts in neighbouring Ethiopia, Sudan and Somalia to the North but also Uganda, Rwanda and the Congo; it has a 'silicon savannah' in the region with its iHubs and digital start-ups; and boasts the most extensive international non-governmental organization (INGO) real estate on the continent, before Jo'burg emerged as a competitor, post-apartheid. However, all this is not without problems when one considers how it relates to literature, the arts and culture in the city. In turn, the same could be said of the dynamic existing in literary initiatives and their relationship to the production of the novel form in Nairobi – long the currency of world literature. A look at just one of the city's more prominent literary initiatives – *Jalada*, a group of writers who describe themselves as Pan-African and who Shringarpure rightly uses as an example of the city's literary dynamism – offers some insights into some of the current challenges of operating in the city, what this would mean for it as a future imaginary space for world literature and where the novel form falls into all this.

Jalada emerged in the late 2000s to organically bring together the most talented and original voices of a new generation, including Okwiri Oduor, Clifton Gachagua and Mehul Gohil in Kenya, but also reaching out to writers from Nigeria, Zimbabwe and Botswana. The group thrived as a collective, but after a while some of the original names dropped away to 'concentrate on their own writing'. Many of these writers spoke of trying to develop their own aesthetic, which they loosely defined in different ways as local and immediate to place. As a group, *Jalada* seemed to be worlding (here I borrow Shringarpure's use of the term in her essay, defined by Pheng Cheah as to 'enact the opening of a world').[2] *Jalada* worlded – opening themselves to the world – by initially highlighting their Pan-African thrust and later engaging in collaborative ventures in and outside the continent. Talk of building their own aesthetic (local and Nairobi-/Kenya-/Africa-based) seemed to be left to individual writers. These two simultaneous directions reveal the kind of tension – opening up and 'worlding' but also trying to work on one's own aesthetic imprint – that has always been prevalent in Kenyan literature. What Shringarpure calls an identity crisis has always been an attempt by the Kenyan writer to find economic opportunities while remaining true to the local and immediate.[3] Ultimately, *Jalada* became more known for another literary initiative, this time the translation of a fable by Ngũgĩ wa Thiong'o. Like their other initiatives, this seemed to point towards not only a 'worlding' but a more pragmatic approach that also involved activities that required fundraising, like their 2017 mobile festival. The actual writing seemed to become less public-facing and is yet to be fully recognized for its far-reaching implications. This includes the group's admirable attempt to reject Kenyan literary realism, shifting towards new experimental takes on what it means to be Kenyan today. Thus their work has provided fantastic imaginaries and possibilities on the fluidity of Kenyan identity, freeing Kenyan writing not only from a certain kind of nationalistic ethos but also an ethnic focus, looking at more complex ways of being through sexuality and urbanity. *Jalada* also seems to have been caught up in the struggles of operating in the city, which as a space heightens the tension between being pragmatic and remaining artistic, between 'initiatives' and 'projects' and the writing itself. This remains true of all the exciting literary things happening in Nairobi. All these now happen *despite* the city, not because of it. These initiatives talk more to the creative and entrepreneurial spirit of youth especially and their ability to hustle – no word better describes Nairobi, and that is telling. At present, only one Kenyan writer in the collective has a published novel. This is not to knock *Jalada* but to provide a perspective on the relationship between literary initiatives and the currency of world literature: the novel. It is also worth mentioning that *Jalada's* precursor *Kwani?* also struggled with producing the same.

---

[2] Shringarpure defines this through Pheng Cheah's articulation in which 'literature's formal structures ... allow for a mapping of spatiality and temporality to "enact the opening of a world"'.
[3] Shringarpure describes the tension as 'as an identity crisis trapped within an outward-facing, Western market logic on the one hand, while straddling an interest in a proudly neo-nationalist, local agenda on the other'.

In relation to Nairobi's advantages as a city of world literature based on Ganguly's criteria for the world novel at present, the same harsh economic imperatives present problems. The city's position as regional capital of the international humanitarian effort seems to have done relatively little in terms of literature, other than being part of a larger donor ecosystem that has hugely benefited arts, culture and literature. The real benefits of these institutions and bodies are, however, financial in cruder macro-economic terms – their gleaming offices in uptown Nairobi exist far from the directly observable ongoing bustle of Kenyan life that is the city-based writer's life blood. Instead, they exist in ecosystems of privilege and distance. The INGO economy that completely built Gigiri, the high-end suburb north-west of the city around the American Embassy, also continues to rent-service the city's high-end suburbs. Auxiliary NGOs that satellite this economy have driven Nairobi's real estate boom for the last two decades. While the national economy seems to be constantly in trouble, apartments and hotels continue to go up. High-end cafes, bars and gyms teem with foreigners at the upper end of the economic scale. The real work in Dadaab and Kakuma refugee camps remains a universe away from the city.

As for all the war and conflict in the region and its seriousness, I feel that any artistic and literary activities around these in the city have always felt peripheral to the mainstream. Sponsorship for UN-funded projects has arguably targeted many other initiatives, such as Kenyan slum photography or hip-hop concerts. UN funding of arts refugee projects has always felt far from the more Kenyan-oriented ongoing activities and projects, whether it is the amazing 2007 post-election violence groundswell by artists and writers or the string of events on the city's cultural calendar held in its popular venues. Pawa 254 remains better known for the subversion-through-photography art by its founder, Boniface Mwangi, than anything else. For all the humanitarian and cultural cross-pollination that has taken place, many writers have lived or passed through Nairobi, including Warsan Shire (born in Nairobi to Somali parents), Maaza Mengiste (Ethiopia), Sulaiman Addonis (Djibouti) and even world-famous artists like Faustin Linyekula from Congo. All have found their way to the Western publishing capitals of the world, with little contact with both Nairobi's literary space and the city itself, even when they've become writers of the same conflicts that have made it the regional capital of humanitarian consciousness.

Turning to Shringarpure's articulation of Ganguly's second characteristic of the world novel – its engagement with the internet – it becomes tempting to think of Nairobi as full of digital possibilities for writers and artists. There is little to challenge the advantages of the internet in opening up public discourse and public debate in Kenya like everywhere else. But in truth, the city's young and thriving digital sector, which has given Nairobi its 'silicon savannah' moniker, is not at all above the city's harsh economic realities, and has also taken a more marked neoliberal turn over the last decade with increased Western investment. The promise of digital initiatives for the public good seemed limitless when iHub Research and Ushahidi created a crowd-mapping tool that analysed SMSs sent during the 2007–8 post-election violence. That's how *Kwani?* managed to publish these revealing narratives, in addition to many of the narratives of the time, in its *Kwani 5* issue. This now seems aeons ago. There have been relatively few meaningful collaborations between digital Nairobi and literature, arts and culture, and this is purely about market forces. Following the success of that collaboration around PEV 2007, between *Kwani?* and Ushahidi, I remember meetings with Community managers at iHub trying to find digital and mobile app solutions for publishing. There were many reasons for being unable to find sustained individual collaborators, but the corporate nature of Nairobi's digital world (and its market rates for developers on the one hand and the non-profit and communal nature of the arts and writing initiatives and their scarce resources on the other) was key. Most of the denizens of the silicon savannah were looking for the highest payer – understandably so. Power to them. I also remember a well-meaning competition that the British Council set up a few years later to bring together digital entrepreneurs and artists, but nothing really came of that, at least on the literary side of things. By and by, we learned the hard way at *Kwani?* that the best way to go digital was to learn everything ourselves – even coding reader apps for our content – rather than expecting collaborations with digital Nairobi. There is simply too much money out there for digital entrepreneurs and software developers for them to be concerned with artists and writers. The relationship between the digital denizens of the silicon savannah and Nairobi's corporate industry is much closer than between other local creatives.

For most writers on the continent, the novel remains the ultimate form and the answer to Nairobi's potential as a world literature space might therefore lie in a refocusing of its literary initiatives: 'activities' and 'projects' are not ends in themselves but build towards the production of the novel as the form with most currency in world lit. Most well-known contemporary African novels are, however, mostly written by writers in the diaspora or those who have managed to tap into the mobilities and trajectories of the global writing industry to find writers' residences and sinecures. Few emerge from sub-Saharan African cities like Nairobi. More often than not, the African novel is now written in the West, or through a succession of residencies and sponsorships by Western bodies for the Africa-based writer, or through a great deal of sacrifice. Most locally produced Kenyan novels that lack those advantages – access to Western publishers or book value chains (whether agents or editors) – show great promise in terms of honesty to place and local agendas but illustrate poor production. For the writer actually based in Kenya, the best chance to finish a novel manuscript is while living at university or with their parents. That, or being lucky enough to win the Miles Morland scholarship. Without these options, Nairobi's harsh realities call.

I remember my early days at *Kwani?* and Binyavanga Wainaina talking about the need for a 'great Kenyan novel'. This obsession seemed to mean a novel that was obviously set in Kenya, understood the place and 'us', captured 'Kenyan-ness' and allowed that to mean different things at different times. Such a book also had to be recognized worldwide, which meant ideally appearing on the Booker shortlist, but at the same time capturing Nairobi's *mtaas* and streets. Binyavanga's obsession seemed to have also been fed by an astute understanding of what had come before *Kwani?* and I remember him dragging me along to meet writer Charles Mangua whose 1994 novel *Kanina and I* he always gushed about. Those meetings had a constant refrain: how new novels by local writers could be produced successfully. Yet all along Binyavanga was also clearly focused on a need to sell the same to a world republic of letters controlled by Euro-American publishing. Binyavanga was just worlding, like many before him and just like *Jalada* would after *Kwani?*. Going back before *Kwani?* it is worth noting how Ngũgĩ's eye for the local in *A Grain of Wheat* gives way to problematizing the problems of the new African nation in *Petals of Blood* and, with more than a decade in exile, switching to allegory and symbolism in *Wizard of the Crow*. A nod to recognized world literary forms at the expense of local knowledge from a long absence? Meja Mwangi seems to have shifted from detailing Nairobi's mean streets in *Going Down River Road* and *The Cockroach Dance* to more thriller-like fare in *The Bushtrackers* that hinted that he was planning to become a filmmaker in Germany. Mwangi's later work can also be seen in the more genre-like crime, erotica and romance novels of Davis Maillu, Mwangi Ruheni, John Kiriamiti and Mwangi Gicheru. The Moi era seemed to become all-encompassing for the best-known writers like Wahome Mutahi to break the worlding mould, to get back to local agendas by writing harsh political take-downs of the regime and its human rights abuses. Kenya's best-known novel of the 1990s, *The River and Source* by Margaret Ogolla, re-focused on a local agenda by skirting around the heightened and all-consuming politics of the Moi era, seeking a kind of precolonial purity in tribal ancestry to tell her story. This also seemed to echo the push towards oral literature in Kenya's literary academy at the time as a way of surviving the Moi years. These latter novels of the 1980s and the 1990s seemed to focus on the national, while those before had always attempted to world. The end of the Cold War, and subsequently Moi and his regime, seems to have freed the next literary generation through *Kwani?* and others. Once CNN came into our sitting rooms, we became global. And as *Kwani?* came to be and Binyavanga hankered after what he called the Kenyan *Things Fall Apart*, through which Kenyan writing could 'world', a few of the influential writers in the early *Kwani?* set wanted to concentrate on the 'local'. They did this either through non-fiction essays or highly 'nationalized' short stories published in the *Kwani?* journals. Outside *Kwani?* there were novels that remained clearly fixed on long-standing national traditions, from Gazemba's *Stone Hills of the Maragoli* to books by Kinyanjui Kombani, Mbugua Ngang'a and more recently Peter Kimani. The schizophrenia of *Kwani?* is quite clear in its early journals. Eventually, *Kwani?* would end up producing more short stories and non-fiction, as well as engaging in literary events and the initiatives that were a precursor to the present trend of literary initiatives. The closest answer to the great Kenyan novel that Binyavanga dreamt in those early *Kwani?* years was ultimately Yvonne Owuor's *Dust*. But for that one example, the novel remained spoken of but never really actualized. The *Kwani?* Manuscript Prize in 2012 produced novels, not just Kenyan ones. Practical questions intruded. There were immediate opportunities for 'worlding' through the short story because of the Caine Prize. More importantly, the short story as a form was also more amenable to funding possibilities, in that it could be harnessed by a collective, compared to the more individual form of the novel. In the political ecosystem of the time, collectives of writers, artists and cultural players were key to the media, arts and culture funding economy that was emerging. Collectives could be yoked to the activist ethos of the time after the end of the Moi regime. So, it was simply easier to be funded as a collective of writers working towards an anthology than as writers working on individual novels. The novel as a form was simply not suited to funding cycles and non-profit possibilities at the time, at least not for the emerging writer. That is why *Kwani?*'s Manuscript Prize was initially self-funded after the organization won the Prince Claus Prize. Even after finally producing some African novels, a large part of the legacy of *Kwani?* will always be its failure to produce more Kenyan examples of the form. *Kwani?* may have been successful in other forms (the short story, the creative non-fiction piece, literary activities and activism, festivals and workshops and panels), but these were initially always means to an end: the novel. It remains a tough literary form on the continent. Now it is the writer who can 'world' best that has often found the most success in this form. Outside that, funding still provides the best way to survive the harsh realities of a place like Nairobi as a writer. But it is also demanding. This is a world of proposals, outputs and reports. It leaves less time for literary dreams and artistic ideals. It is a world where professional managers and administrators thrive, rather than radical artists, thinkers and writers. A history of funding in East Africa is yet to be written but behind the scenes, there have always been close links with the political, social and economic hierarchies of Nairobi.[4] For *Kwani?* the only option was a balancing act between its dreams and economic

---

[4]Bethuel Ogot's autobiography *My Footprints on the Sands of Time* (2003) provides a compelling account of fights over international funding between him and political elites in the Kenyatta regime and when he set up the East African Institute of Social and Cultural

reality, and the latter would eventually prevail. Now there are fewer novels than funded projects, more arts managers and literary activists than artists and writers in the city. The last two decades have also seen a ubiquitous merging of the two roles, which usually means neither is done properly. As a result, over the last two decades there have been more festivals than ever in Nairobi, more writing workshops than ever, more panels than the writing itself. Novels require a longer game. They are also largely written far from the madding activist crowd. Short stories and non-fiction pieces can be written relatively quickly – packaged by savvy activist editors and managers for larger purposes (i.e. translation, post-election violence). Since the packaging of the anthology and the public-facing rhetoric does not necessarily compromise the literary value of the writing, the short story provides the best form for a literary economy based on donor funding. This is not to knock the short story or any other forms of literary activity, but this results in a way of being literary in the world, rather than a push for a place in world literature. Nairobi has acquired great skill at world-facing but is yet to produce a literature that can be rightly described as 'of the world'. It does great festivals and salons and workshops and symposiums, but other than Yvonne Owour there are no writers producing novels consistently recognized beyond the city and the region.

Shringarpure's observation that world literature is always in crisis therefore strikes a chord with the city as a literary space. Nairobi also means surviving crises. Financial survival for established arts and literary initiatives is an end-of-month battle with landlords. Organizations spring up and die all the time. Writers give up the hustle and get grown-up jobs and disappear from the scene. There is constant juggling between the *here* and *now* in the city, and *there* in the West and its possibilities. Even with the vibrancy and energy, there is a disturbing impermanence when the advantages of a long *durée* of literary production are so evident in other places. All this instability when permanence and time is required. *Jalada* is an outlier rather than the norm in its resilience – many literary collectives and spaces disappear so fast that they cannot even be archived by their curators. This creates a huge disadvantage for Nairobi, Kenyan and African literatures at large with all the knowledge and information increasingly found in Western archives. Nairobi's place as a leader in world literature thus becomes a perpetual possibility. So it was when *Kwani?* started and folded, and so it remains. Festivals like Storymoja have come and gone. Initiatives like Enkare Review have spluttered out. Many new spaces threaten to start and have promise on paper due to their curators – well-known writers and artists – but they never take off as artistic and cultural managers/administrators, and their

---

Affairs (EAISCA). There has always been a close relationship between international funding and political elites especially in the 1990s and multiparty politics.

art also suffers. When Shringarpure observes that world literature is always an expression of 'potential and possibility and not so much an actuality', the same can be said of Nairobi. Novels now feel few and far between in Nairobi, even as production in other places on the continent outstrips it. And yet, the novel continues to be the form to aspire to for the writer in the city. Several novels have emerged over the last few years, without any traditional links to the well-known literary spaces of Nairobi.[5] This points to a healthy demystification of the form and the need to just get on with it rather than treating it as a Holy Grail, as the early *Kwani?* writers did. But it also means that there is space beyond these dynamic and energetic literary spaces, which cannot, for all the reasons given, contribute much to the form. Until then the tension continues – to world or not to world – while we wait for the next great Kenyan novel that Binyavanga dreamt about.

---

[5]Peter Kimani's *Dance of the Jakaranda* (2017), Makena Maganjo's *South B's Finest* (2019) and Shiru Koinange's *The Havoc of Choice* (2019) are recent examples.

4

The problem with French and the world: Imagining the province and the global in francophone African fiction

Sarah Arens

'*Vous êtes dans la mondialisation, vous aussi?*'
[YOU ARE IN GLOBALIZATION TOO?][1]

Penser l'Afrique, c'est cheminer dans une aube incertaine, le long d'une voie balisée où le marcheur est sommé de hâter la cadence pour rattraper le train d'un monde semble-t-il parti il y a quelques siècles. C'est débroussailler une forêt dense et touffue. ... un lieu investi de concepts, d'injonctions censées refléter les téléologies sociales, un espace saturé de sens.
[To think about Africa is to walk in an uncertain dawn, along a marked path where the walker is summoned to hasten the pace to

---

[1] In Koli Jean Bofane, *Congo Inc.: Bismarck's Testament*, trans. Marjolijn de Jager (Bloomington: Indiana University Press, 2018), p. 43.

catch up with the train of a world that seems to have departed a few centuries ago. It is clearing a dense and thick forest. ... a place invested with concepts, with injunctions supposed to reflect social teleologies, a space saturated with meaning]*²*

In a 2018 article entitled '*Le français, notre bien commun?*' [French, our common good?], novelist Alain Mabanckou and political theorist Achille Mbembe condemn the current French president Emmanuel Macron's historical 'amnesia' regarding his announcement to make French 'the second world language', which forms part of wider criticism Macron has received for his inconsistency on France's colonial legacy. Mabanckou and Mbembe describe instead the French language's subversive potential, which they locate with cultural producers from outside the Hexagon '*parce qu'ils savent depuis fort longtemps que la langue française est plus grande que la France*' [because they have known for a very long time that the French language is bigger than France].³ They point to the asymmetrical and neocolonial power relations between France and many of its former colonies via the institution of '*la Francophonie*' – the International Organization of La Francophonie (OIF), which currently consists of eighty-eight member states. Mabanckou has been at the forefront of questioning the implicitly hierarchical division between *littérature française* [French literature] and *littérature francophone* [Francophone literature]. The latter, while also used to denote writing from other Francophone European regions, usually describes literature by writers originating from countries once colonized by France or Belgium. However, Mabanckou and Mbembe draw upon the same binaries between France and countries and territories formerly or still under French control for which the controversial 2007 *littérature-monde* manifesto was criticized.⁴ Mabanckou himself was one of the signatories, alongside forty-four well-known writers from both France and the French-speaking world, such as Tahar Ben Jelloun and Maryse Condé. The manifesto has received sustained criticism. For instance, Alec Hargreaves, Charles Forsdick and David Murphy note that it 'may decry the persistence of colonial mentalities, but its call is for the creation of an egalitarian (and utopian) world literature in French, and not for a more finely attuned historical and political engagement with the

---

²Felwine Sarr, *Afrotopia* (Paris: Éditions Philippe Rey, 2016), p. 13; my translation.
³Alain Mabanckou and Achille Mbembe, 'Le français, notre bien commun?' *BibliObs*, 12 February 2018, https://bibliobs.nouvelobs.com/idees/20180211.OBS2020/le-francais-notre-bien-commun-par-alain-mabanckou-et-achille-mbembe.html. Accessed 1 March 2022.
⁴See, for instance, Alec G. Hargreaves, Charles Forsdick and David Murphy (eds), *Transnational French Studies: Postcolonialism and Littérature-monde* (Liverpool: Liverpool University Press, 2012); Kathryn Kleppinger, 'What's Wrong with the Littérature-Monde

legacies of imperialism'.⁵ Indeed, the question of language has become central to discussions of what constitutes a world literature 'in French'. Forsdick further argues in this context that

> the manoeuvres of the ... [OIF] against the anglophone emphases of globalization are based, for instance, on advocacy for a *diversité* that is significantly *culturelle* and not explicitly *linguistique*; and even a movement hostile to the OIF that launched by the *littérature-monde* manifesto ... limits the openness of its reach by appending to 'world-literature' the restrictive, monolingualizing and seemingly oxymoronic 'en français'.⁶

However, I would argue that this act of 'monolingualizing' requires further nuance, regarding recent calls for paying greater attention to multilingualism in Francophone world literature.⁷ French, like any other language, is not a monolithic entity. It is always already in close contact with other 'minor' and 'major' languages, both within Europe and where it arrived as an instrument of two colonial powers. What is more, literature 'in French' exists across an extremely uneven global literary marketplace that still largely revolves around Paris, what Christopher Miller has termed the publishing industry's 'rigorous Francocentrism and Parisocentrism'.⁸ It is therefore important to problematize the binary opposition between 'provincial', regional or national languages versus French as 'world language'.

Likewise, the relationship between African literature and its engagement with metropolitan France has been subject to significant changes since the political end of colonialism around 1960. In 2006, Lydie Moudileno wrote that '*la France avait relativement disparu de la fiction Africaine après les*

Manifesto?' *Contemporary French and Francophone Studies*, vol. 14 (2010): 74–84, https://doi.org/10.1080/17409290903412722.

⁵Hargreaves, Forsdick and Murphy, *Transnational French Studies*, p. 3.

⁶Charles Forsdick, 'Global France, Global French: Beyond the Monolingual', *Contemporary French Civilization*, vol. 42, no. 1 (2017): 13–29, 15, https://doi.org/10.3828/cfc.2017.2.

⁷See, for instance, Forsdick, 'Global France'; Jane Hiddleston, 'Writing World Literature: Approaches from the Maghreb', *PMLA*, vol. 131, no. 5 (2016): 1386–95, https://doi.org/10.1632/pmla.2016.131.5.1386.

⁸Christopher L. Miller, 'The Theory and Pedagogy of a World Literature in French', *Yale French Studies*, vol. 120 (2011): 33–48, 47, https://www.jstor.org/stable/41337115. See also recent scholarship on literary prizes and Francophone literature such as Madeline Bedecarré, 'Prizing Francophonie into Existence: The Usurpation of World Literature by the Prix des Cinq Continents', *Journal of World Literature*, vol. 5, no. 2 (2020): 298–319, https://doi.org/10.1163/24056480-00502010. However, it is worth mentioning that some of the most well-known writers of the DRC's diaspora are publishing in locations outside the former imperial centres. See Julien Jeusette and Silvia Riva, 'Contemporary Congolese Literature as World Literature', *Journal of World Literature*, vol. 6 (2021): 123–32, 124, https://doi.org/10.1163/24056480-00602001.

indépendances, au profit d'un recentrement sur des thèmes inspirés des réalités sociopolitiques des nouvelles nations Africaines' [France had pretty much disappeared from African fiction after independence, in favour of refocusing on themes inspired by the socio-political realities of the new African nations].⁹ She went on to consider authors like Mabanckou as belonging to a new generation of African writers who reassign a central position to France within their texts by refocusing on the topos of the 'journey to the metropole' and on migration more broadly.¹⁰ More recent writing, however (including the novels of two writers discussed in this chapter, Mabanckou's 2015 *Petit Piment* [*Black Moses* (2017)] and Belgium-based Congolese author In Koli Jean Bofane's 2014 *Congo Inc.: Le testament de Bismarck* [*Congo Inc.: Bismarck's Testament* (2018)]), seems to 'displace' the former imperial centre again. They engage with the world beyond the colonial binary, and express Sanjay Krishnan's definition of 'the global' as 'a mode of thematization or a way of bringing the world into view. It does not point to the world as such but at the conditions and effects attendant upon institutionally validated modes of making legible within a single frame the diverse terrains and peoples of the world.'¹¹ Krishnan's argument 'challenges the ways in which the "global" has been uncritically assimilated, in the humanities and social sciences, to a transparent comprehension of the world'.¹² Focusing on the term's insufficient historicization, Krishnan further criticizes scholars who 'tacitly perpetuate the naturalization of a frame that was elaborated as an instrument of modern imperial expansion'.¹³ Against this background, this chapter analyses to what degree literary production then represents a reclaiming or recontextualizing of 'the global'. Bofane's and Mabanckou's texts re-engage with transnational concepts to present new intellectual, political and socio-economic relations in the postcolonial era. For Mabanckou, this is a re-engagement between African and North American literary culture, a new 'Black Atlantic', to borrow Paul Gilroy's influential concept, and referencing the 1930s *Négritude* movement:

> We have now moved, however, from a literature campaigning to recover an identity – the pioneering *Négritude* movement – to an introspective literature concerned with the condition of Black people around the world: a new generation of writers divided between 'neo-*Négritude*' on

---

⁹Lydie Moudileno, *Parades postcoloniales: La fabrications des identités dans le roman congolais* (Paris: Karthala, 2006), p. 108.
¹⁰Ibid.
¹¹Sanjay Krishnan, *Reading the Global: Troubling Perspectives on Britain's Empire in Asia* (New York: Columbia University Press, 2007), p. 4.
¹²Ibid., p. 1.
¹³Ibid.

the one hand and caustic commentary on the mores of Blacks caught up in globalization on the other.[14]

This transatlantic vision of 'moving forward' is in contrast to Bofane's global vision, which presents an ideologically very different choice and turns his reader's attention to non-Western solidarities.[15] Both writers renegotiate the status of French, by including languages spoken in both Congo states, such as Lingala and Kikongo, and languages that (neo)colonialism and capitalism have brought with them, such as English and Chinese (Mandarin).

These questions of language and globalization are also inextricably connected to issues of temporality and historiography. In his reading of Fernand Braudel, who suggested that parts of the world such as Africa could effectively remain outside what he calls 'world time' ['*le temps du monde*'], Mbembe argues for the existence of multiple, overlapping temporalities:

> In the case of Africa, long-term developments, more or less rapid deviations, and long-term temporalities are not necessarily either separate or merely juxtaposed. Fitted within one another, they relay each other; sometimes they cancel each other out, and sometimes their effects are multiplied.[16]

Mabanckou's and Bofane's representations of the two Congos' different, yet connected histories thus emerge as a particularly interesting region in which to consider African literature in French, the worlds it creates and the visions of 'the global' it produces. Jane Hiddleston criticizes the popular theories of Pascale Casanova and David Damrosch for not engaging with the concept of 'worldliness' and defines it as follows: '*Worldliness* ... connotes connectedness but not fusion, an awareness of how global history shapes national history but at the same time a commitment to challenging the inequalities produced by those histories.'[17] She notes further that 'worldliness suggests a way of thinking, an alertness to different cultures but also a worldly wisdom about the text's limits that attenuates the utopianism

---

[14] Alain Mabanckou and Donald Nicholson-Smith, 'Immigration, "Littérature-Monde," and Universality: The Strange Fate of the African Writer', *Yale French Studies*, vol. 120 (2011): 75–87, 75.

[15] See, for example, Duncan M. Yoon, 'Africa, China, and the Global South Novel: In Koli Jean Bofane's *Congo Inc.*', *Comparative Literature*, vol. 72, no. 3 (2020): 316–39, https://doi.org/10.1215/00104124-8255350.

[16] Achille Mbembe, 'At the Edge of the World: Boundaries, Territoriality, and Sovereignty in Africa', trans. Steven Rendall, *Public Culture*, vol. 12, no. 1 (2000): 259–84, muse.jhu.edu/article/26186.

[17] Hiddleston, 'Writing World Literature', p. 1389.

of some theories of world literature'.[18] She shares this insistence on connected global histories, asymmetrical power relations, anti-utopianism and resistance with Pheng Cheah, who, analysing different philosophical accounts of conceptualizing the world – curiously, predominantly Western ones, Heidegger, Arendt, Derrida – reminds us that

> the first step in reenvisioning world literature's vocation is to see the world as a dynamic process with a normative practical dimension instead of reducing worldliness to circulatory flows within a spatio-geographical whole. Flows of market exchange and their geographical mapping are certainly important material conditions of a world. But as phenomenological and deconstructive accounts of worldliness remind us, they are modes of world-making that ultimately make us worldless.[19]

Cheah highlights the importance of focusing on the subversive potential that lies in creative 'world-making' of texts that resist colonial categorization and forms of knowledge (he initially cites the imposition of Greenwich Mean Time on the 'rest of the world'). By connecting the global and the local with considerations of language(s), temporalities and histories, Bofane's and Mabanckou's novels set out to critically reinscribe their visions of 'Africa' through literature as world literature; the 'worldliness' of their texts removes their Congos from the colonial binary and presents more complex visions of postcolonial globalization. This chapter throws light on what this means for African literature written (predominantly) in French by demonstrating how the novels critically engage with questions of representation, solidarities and the circulation of knowledge and resources.

Literature, nation, globalization

Mabanckou's novel tells the story of Tokumisa Nzambe po Mose yamoyindo abotami namboka ya Bakoko (Moses), who, like his biblical namesake, is a foundling. He grows up in an orphanage in Loango, a small town outside the big city of Pointe-Noire in the Republic of the Congo, where he encounters a fellow petty criminal, who fashions himself as Robin Hood. He adopts this persona towards the end of the novel, where the reader learns that he has narrated his story from a psychiatric detention centre, where he is incarcerated for killing the mayor of Pointe-Noire. This returns us to Loango, as the facility occupies the same site as the orphanage.

---

[18] Ibid., p. 1388.
[19] Pheng Cheah, *What Is a World? Postcolonial Literature as World Literature* (Durham, NC: Duke University Press, 2016), p. 192.

Bofane's protagonist is also a young man who tries to 'make it' in the big city: Isookanga, a young member of the Ekonda clan (part of the Mongo people, a so-called Pygmy) from a small village inside Salonga National Park in what is today the Democratic Republic of the Congo (DRC). Isookanga is dissatisfied with his life in the province and decides to go to Kinshasa, the DRC's capital, as he considers himself 'an internationalist who aspires to becoming a globalizer'[20] ['*un mondialiste qui aspire à devenir mondialisateur*'].[21] In Kinshasa, Isookanga joins a group of street children called *shégués* and meets the homeless Chinese migrant labourer Zhang Xia, with whom he tries to establish a business selling fresh water branded '*Eau Pire Suisse*' ['purest/worst Swiss mineral water']. After a brief incarceration, following their dealings with the former warlord and now director of Salonga National Park Kiro Bizimungu, Zhang Xia is deported and Isookanga returns to his village.

Both protagonists are social and/or ethnic outsiders and find themselves at the very bottom layer of urban/national/global society. Both become part of the ecosystem of the city, and both return to the 'province'. This narrative arc – the young, male protagonist arriving in the city with a grand project of self-realization – is loosely reminiscent of the eighteenth-century German *Bildungsroman*. This intertextual link is used here not only to mobilize globally circulated, recognizable texts and tropes but also to create worlds in which the former imperial centres might still function as a point of reference, culturally and economically, but in which colonial binaries have broken up. The novels do not produce stories of capitalist success but alternative narratives of 'development' that complicate the old opposition between 'the centre' and 'the periphery' in the age of global capitalism. Joseph R. Slaughter writes of the concept of *Bildung*:

> A notoriously untranslatable word that denotes simultaneously image and image making, culture and cultivation, form and formation, *Bildung* names an achieved state as well as a process of humanistic socialisation that cultivates a universal force of human personality ... that is naturally inclined to express itself through the social media of the nation-state and citizenship.[22]

While both texts complicate any easy (Western) assumption of what *Bildung* constitutes, they do so by troubling notions of universality in a postcolonial context, for instance, through father figures who represent alternative models to the national and transnational regimes of power. Translation thereby

---

[20]Bofane, *Congo Inc.*, p. 11.
[21]In Koli Jean Bofane, *Congo Inc.: Le testament de Bismarck* (Arles: Actes Sud, 2014), p. 26.
[22]Joseph R. Slaughter, *Human Rights, Inc.: The World Novel, Narrative Form, and International Law* (New York: Fordham University Press, 2007), pp. 92–3.

appears as a broader language issue, showcasing the problem with French and the worlds the texts create: French has become one reference point of many. It is not the language determining hegemonic power relationships as might have been the case in earlier texts, while still connoting legacies of colonialism and the transatlantic trafficking of enslaved Africans. Both texts critically engage with foreign and domestic exploitation within the nation state and depict state power as ineffective in protecting its citizens and migrants. Notably, each text stages this not only through representations of corruption, and economic, ecological, sexual and intellectual exploitation, but also through resistance to these practices.

Petit Piment/*Black Moses*: A (new?) Black Atlantic?

Ayo A. Coly describes Mabanckou as 'the architect and entrepreneur of a world literature project that ... recalibrates the relations between literary traditions in the category of world literature'.[23] In particular, she highlights his use of intertextuality, which she describes as 'the Mabanckou-championed project of a world literature in French that would dismantle the hierarchizing boundaries between French and Francophone literatures'.[24] While Coly's argument is certainly convincing with regard to Mabanckou's 2005 breakthrough novel *Verre Cassée* [*Broken Glass*], her analysis is very much anchored in questions of identity. Referring to Michel de Certeau's influential work on walking as a way of subverting hegemonic structures, Coly considers Mabanckou's work 'tactics of infiltration of the dominant system'.[25] This is problematic for two reasons: firstly, it leaves out critiques of de Certeau's celebratory account of walking as subversive. For instance, Charles Forsdick has pointed to the problematic liberatory universalism underlying the study of walking and foregrounds the privilege that underlies certain 'nostalgic' attitudes that favour the act of walking.[26] This critical assessment then problematizes Coly's analogy to the work of Mabanckou's subversive potential within the world literary system. Secondly, Mabanckou's position within the Western academy and the global literary marketplace, for instance, as professor at UCLA and appointed to the Collège de France (France's most prestigious research institution) in 2016 grants him a

---

[23]Ayo A. Coly, 'Alain Mabanckou and the Category of World Literature', *Research in African Literatures*, vol. 51, no. 2 (2020): 27–39, 28, https://doi.org/10.2979/reseafrilite.51.2.02.
[24]Ibid., p. 30.
[25]Ibid., p. 36.
[26]Charles Forsdick, *Travel in Twentieth-Century French and Francophone Cultures: The Persistence of Diversity* (Oxford: Oxford University Press, 2005), p. 170.

privileged visibility, especially compared to other authors from the Congo and sub-Saharan Africa.

Instead, I suggest taking a closer look at more specific moments of intertextuality in Mabanckou's work to get a more nuanced understanding of his complex engagement with the category of world literature. For instance, this engagement seems to focus strongly on a transatlantic dimension. This has been an established thread throughout his oeuvre, for example, his rewriting of tropes of (true) crime fiction in *African Psycho* (2003) and his self-presentation as James Baldwin's 'translator' for French-speaking audiences in his 2007 *Lettre à Jimmy* [*Letter to Jimmy*].[27] The title of the English-language translation of *Petit Piment* continues this engagement with US-American references:

> *Black Moses* brings to mind soul [music] legend Isaac Hayes' 1971 album of the same name or, more recently, D'Angelo's *Black Messiah* (2014). Whether a stylistic choice or editorial decision to market the English translation to a US audience, … the title locates the novel and, importantly, the reader in a North American cultural context.[28]

The references to religion and Black Music call to mind Paul Gilroy's 'intercultural and transnational formation' of the Black Atlantic:[29] 'their [expressive cultural forms'] special power derives from a doubleness, their unsteady location simultaneously inside and outside the conventions, assumptions, and aesthetic rules which distinguish and periodise modernity'.[30] This ambivalence characterizes Mabanckou's use of Western literary tropes, such as the *Bildungsroman*, as well as his use of (presumably) provincial and global textual locations.

Slaughter describes the *Bildungsroman*'s historical social role as 'incorporating the problematic individual into the rights and responsibilities of citizenship, and thereby legitimating the democratic institutions of the emergent rights-based nation-state'.[31] Mabanckou locates this recognizable narrative in the establishment of the Marxist-Leninist People's Republic of the Congo in 1969 and its aftermath. This Soviet-style single-party state lasted until 1992 and was replaced by the more or less uninterrupted rule

---

[27]See Sarah Arens, 'Killer Stories: "Globalizing" the Grotesque in Alain Mabanckou's *African Psycho* and Leïla Slimani's *Chanson douce*', *Irish Journal of French Studies*, vol. 20 (2020): 143–72, https://doi.org/10.7173/164913320830841692.

[28]Sarah Arens, 'The Problem with the Prophet: Review of Alain Mabanckou's *Black Moses*', *Africa in Words* (blog), 23 October 2017, https://africainwords.com/2017/10/23/the-problem-with-the-prophet-review-of-alain-mabanckous-black-moses. Accessed 1 March 2022.

[29]Paul Gilroy, *The Black Atlantic: Modernity and Double Consciousness* (London: Verso, 1993), p. ix.

[30]Ibid., p. 73.

[31]Slaughter, *Human Rights, Inc.*, p. 94.

of President Denis Sassou Nguesso (who had already been president from 1979 until 1992). The first chapter presents the dysfunctional state system – characterized by nepotism, corruption, violence, cruelty, bureaucracy and general abuse of power – within the microcosm of the orphanage in Loango. Like the other children, Moses is at the mercy of its director, Dieudonné Ngoulmoumako. The 'godgiven' Ngoulmoumako is their dictator, the hyperbolic and repetitive quality of his speeches a satire of Cold War–era rhetoric:

> Yes, dear children, a new age is dawning, a liberating rainbow sent to us all the way from the Union of Soviet Socialist Republics! ... Also remember, dear children, the words of wisdom spoken by the President of our own Republic, for he too is a wise man, he too has a Jovian appetite for communicating and building bridges, lantern in hand, illuminating the dark labyrinth of our innermost hearts and minds.[32]

This form of rhetoric exposes itself: through hyperbole and neo-imperial imagery. The 'lantern ... illuminating the dark labyrinth of our ... hearts' is, of course, an intertextual reference to Joseph Conrad's *Heart of Darkness*, as well as to the French 'civilizing mission' bringing 'enlightenment' to its colonies. By representing Ngoulmoumako as a party functionary working for a system that superficially claims to do away with 'Imperialism and its local lackeys', but that in fact continues exploitative colonial policies, Mabanckou very much inscribes himself into the tradition of the twentieth-century African dictatorship novel.[33] He seems to reference landmark works, such as Congolese novelist Sony Labou Tansi's *La Vie et demie* [*Life and a Half*], who was also a co-founder of the Congolese Movement for Democracy and Integral Development, a liberal political party working against the Nguesso government.

The continuation of colonial-era oppression perpetrated by the postcolonial state's ruling cliques is thereby connected to Mabanckou's negotiation of 'provincial' and global spaces. For instance, the location of the orphanage itself provides an important intersection of his transnational vision of historiography and storytelling:

> Our orphanage was separate from the rest of the Congo, in fact from the whole rest of the world. Since the school was in the hinterland, we knew nothing of the neighbouring agglomerations of Mabindou, Poumba,

---

[32] Alain Mabanckou, *Black Moses*, trans. Helen Stevenson (London: Serpent's Tail, 2017), p. 19.
[33] Ibid., pp. 14, 20. See also Eline Kuenen, 'Creation through Inversion: The Carnivalesque Postcolonial State in the Novels of Alain Mabanckou and In Koli Jean Bofane', in *Fictions of African Dictatorship: Cultural Representations of Postcolonial Power*, ed. Charlotte Baker and Hannah Grayson (Oxford: Peter Lang, 2018), pp. 79–97.

Loubou, Tchiyèndi, or our own economic capital, Pointe-Noire, which was spoken of as though it was the promised land Papa Moupelo used to talk to us about.[34]

Yet despite representing a microcosm of the Congo's 'Marxist-Leninist' revolution, the orphanage's isolated location removes it from any immediate national context. Instead, the narrator positions it at the periphery of the 'economic capital' of Pointe-Noire. By calling it the proverbial 'promised land', Papa Moupelo not only foreshadows the boy's later departure to the big city but also connotates the orphanage as a place of (biblical) exile.

Papa Moupelo is a crucial, larger-than-life character in the early stages of the narrative: '"Moupelo" meant "priest" in Kikongo, and it was no coincidence that he'd become a messenger of God like his father before him.'[35] He gave Moses his full name: Tokumisa Nzambe po Mose yamoyindo abotami namboka ya Bakoko, 'which in Lingala means "Thanks be to God, the black Moses is born on the earth of our ancestors"…'.[36] While Kikongo and Lingala are spoken in both Congo states, the narrator describes the latter as 'Papa Moupelo's language', who hails from what was then Zaire under Mobutu's dictatorship.[37] The figure of a 'Black Moses', then, who leaves the exile of the orphanage behind for the 'promised land' of Pointe-Noire, is particularly recognizable to North American audiences, establishing references to Harriet Tubman, Marcus Garvey and Isaac Hayes. The historical figure of Moses the Black, however, was not a leader of enslaved people but a formerly enslaved person who joined a violent gang of robbers in the Nile Valley before converting to Christianity and becoming a hermit in the desert.[38] Mabanckou's Moses experiences a similar transition, in reverse. Before running away to join a street gang in Pointe-Noire, the gang itself being reminiscent of Jesus' disciples, Moses is instructed by a priest at the orphanage.[39] Papa Moupelo functions as a translator within Moses's education, but specifically for Lingala, Central Africa's lingua franca: 'We complained how difficult most of us found the arcane Lingala vocabulary taken from the books written by Europeans missionaries, in which they had recorded our age-old beliefs, legends, tales and songs.'[40] Mabanckou's

---

[34] Mabanckou, *Black Moses*, p. 34.
[35] Ibid., p. 7.
[36] Ibid., p. 3.
[37] Ibid., p. 6.
[38] See, for instance, Elena V. Kravchenko, 'The Matter of Race: Brotherhood of St. Moses the Black and the Retelling of African American History through Orthodox Christian Forms', *Journal of the American Academy of Religion*, vol. 89, no. 1 (2021): 298–333, https://doi.org/10.1093/jaarel/lfab025.
[39] Mabanckou, *Black Moses*, p. 110.
[40] Ibid., p. 4.

perspective on this European archivist work is complex: it is not outrightly negative (from the perspective of the young Moses, a notoriously unreliable narrator), yet there is a sense of appropriation and displacement of knowledge by these agents of European colonization. Moses's connection to Moses the Black affirms a transnational presence of the Christian faith in Africa *prior* to the arrival of Europeans. At the same time, the narrator is critical of both the regime's outright ban on religion – which signals the end to Papa Moupelo's presence at the orphanage – and other transnational but more institutionalized forms, such as Pentecostalism. The brief mention of 'the band made up of flocks from the Pentecostal churches, furious at their pastors, who had promised them mountains and miracles and had delivered neither' furthers Mabanckou's vision of a (new?) Black Atlantic:

> They maintained that the route to paradise was via the Côte Sauvage, and they went to gaze at it at four in the morning, trying, without success, to walk on the water, because their guru had drummed it into them that since Jesus had pulled off this feat, his worshippers should be able to do it standing on their heads, and let the devil burn in hell.[41]

Pentecostalism, a movement of evangelical Protestantism, arrived in Africa in the early twentieth century via missionaries from the United States and Britain. Cédric Mayrargue notes, however, that it should be distinguished from other forms of 'fundamental Christianity', due to its origins in both predominantly Black and white churches in the United States.[42] The movement, which features an expressive religious practice, including healing and miracles, has a particularly strong following in the two Congos.[43] The narrator portrays the Pentecostals' blind belief in the dogmas of their guru, depicting their quest to cross the ocean, becoming part of the Atlantic World in search of a better (after)life, as helplessly naïve and anti-scientific. Mabanckou mobilizes Pentecostal anti-intellectualism and transatlantic history as always doomed to fail and incommensurate with his own vision of a transnational literary circulation of ideas.

In the same vein, myth-making is presented as genuinely effective, if only temporarily, in the realm of storytelling, legend and folklore, for instance, by Moses's appropriation of the Robin Hood persona, a globally circulated Western text. At the same time, this blurring of boundaries between the 'real' and the fictional (or rather between the 'fictional real' and the 'fictional

---

[41]Ibid., p. 111.
[42]Cédric Mayrargue, 'The Paradoxes of Pentecostalism in Sub-Saharan Africa', *Notes de l'Ifri*, April 2008, https://www.ifri.org/sites/default/files/atoms/files/mayrargue_the_paradoxes_of_pentecostalism.pdf. Accessed 1 February 2022.
[43]Ibid.

fictional') is not limited to Moses's 'local' performance of a 'global' text. By erasing clear-cut distinctions between the global and the local, the fictional and the non-fictional, the narrator also problematizes the hierarchical difference between 'history' and 'story'. This is most obvious in the narrator's tale of the replacement of the orphanage's history teacher Monsieur Doukou Daka by Monsieur Montoir, who 'was white and taught us mostly French history, featuring none of the characters Monsieur Doukou Daka had taught us about'.[44] He includes the latter teaching transnational oral histories, such as stories of the Kongo's foundational ancestress Nzinga,[45] and depicts Loango's status as a significant port for the transatlantic trafficking of enslaved Africans.[46] While not eclipsing European responsibility and cruelty, Monsieur Doukou Daka tells a more complex story of local agency and complicity that is at odds with the new regime's vision of history:

> Monsieur Doukou Daka would turn his back, lower his voice, and look out of the window, as though worried he might be overheard, then confide in us, in aggrieved tones, that many of the rich business people in Loango had been involved in the trafficking and had sent their sons to a region of France called Brittany to study the secrets of the trade.[47]

One of the few mentions of France in the text, the former colonial metropole appears here as the destination for the very few who accumulated wealth through the trafficking of enslaved people. Importantly, it is a hinterland that generates wealth for the capital, connected to the colony through its location on the Atlantic. Monsieur Doukou Daka's history highlights the entanglement between colonizer and colonized via its provinces and problematizes the colonial differentiation between province and capital. The ocean becomes a vast repository of memories and stories – a cultural space that connects the Congolese diaspora between Africa, the Americas and France. Monsieur Doukou Daka's history lesson is presented as dissent from the postcolonial regime: those who benefitted by collaborating with the enslaving colonizer, the ethnic group of Vili, to which the orphanage's director and his nephews belong, remain in power post-independence. This vision of history is not new: Mabanckou explored a similar perspective in his 2012 essay *Le Sanglot de l'homme noir* [*The Tears of the Black Man*, 2018] and its critique of a falsely essentializing Black universalism and orientation towards the future moves him closer towards the Francophone Caribbean *Créolité* of, for example, Edouard Glissant and Patrick Chamoiseau. Mabanckou's vision of African, more specifically Congolese, literature, as

---

[44]Mabanckou, *Black Moses*, p. 37.
[45]Nzinga Mbande, the queen of the Anbundu Kingdoms of Ndongo and Matamba.
[46]Mabanckou, *Black Moses*, p. 34.
[47]Ibid., pp. 34–5.

world literature, thus remains very much inscribed within the framework of the Black Atlantic and its literary traditions. Bofane's *Congo Inc.*, however, presents a radically different approach to 'worldliness' and engaging with shared histories of violence and oppression that move away from traditional ties and towards world literature's relationship with (and, implicitly, responsibility for) critically engaging European historiography.

Congo Inc.: Le testament de Bismarck: Rethinking global histories in the age of digital capitalism

Towards the end of Bofane's novel, the narrator explains its title, which describes the colonization of what is today the DRC as an algorithm:

> The algorithm Congo Inc. had been created at the moment that Africa was being chopped up in Berlin ... Under Leopold II's sharecropping, they had hastily developed it so they could supply the whole world with rubber from the equator, without which the industrial era wouldn't have expanded as rapidly as it needed to at the time. Subsequently, its contribution to the First World War effort had been crucial ... The involvement of Congo Inc. in the Second World War proved decisive.[48]

Interestingly, Bofane only mentions King Leopold II's appropriation of what would become the infamous so-called Congo Free State at the 1884–5 Berlin Conference in passing and resists engaging with its well-documented atrocities. Instead, he attends to the conference's organizer Otto von Bismarck, then chancellor of the German Reich (1871–90), who was instrumental in building the German colonial project. The narrator goes on to conclude,

> Loyal to Bismarck's testament, Congo Inc. had been appointed as the accredited supplier of internationalism, responsible for the delivery of strategic minerals for the conquest of space, the manufacturing of sophisticated armaments, the oil industry, and the production of high-tech telecommunications.[49]

Crucially, by discussing the Congo's exploitation by foreign powers and multinational corporations, the narrator assumes a 'transcolonial'

---

[48] Bofane, *Congo Inc.*, p. 174.
[49] Ibid., p. 175.

perspective, to use Olivia Harrison's term, and describes what Dominic Thomas calls 'the unquenchable transgenerational thirst for Congo's natural resources'.[50] Instead of positioning the narrative within the colonial binary, they extend it by highlighting the involvement of other actors, such as the United States, and their use of Congolese resources, as well as Western and African protagonists of the Cold War. Like Monsieur Doukou Daka in *Black Moses*, by designating 'Congo Inc.' as Bismarck's legacy, which is conventionally discussed within the context of German unification, Bofane provides an alternative historiography thereof. While the nationalism and militarism Bismarck fuelled had disastrous consequences for Europe, his architecture of the so-called 'Scramble for Africa', including organizing the Berlin Conference and therefore the almost entire colonization of Africa it 'legitimatized', has obviously had a more urgent significance for the Congo.

Another crucial aspect of this alternative historiography is the narrator's description of the colonial state's exploitation as an algorithm that presents colonialism as an artificially generated temporality.[51] Thinking of an algorithm – in a simplified way – as a sequence of programmed instructions suggests an indefinite repeatability, as well as a core principle of what Daniel Schiller calls 'digital capitalism'.[52] It presents the fundamental role that the exploitation of resources played for the benefit of European powers, their industrialization and their global wars as a sequence, reproducing the same basic mechanism. This indefinite repeatability, reminiscent of Cheah's discussion of the colonial imposition of standardized time, also presumably locks those affected by it into a constant state of contemporaneity, as Éloïse Brezault argues in her reading of the novel.[53] I suggest, however, that the novel presents its reader with a complex reckoning with colonial exploitation and, in particular, its epistemological violence via its negotiation of different 'global' and 'provincial' spaces through (mis)communication, which, in turn, produces a vision of 'worldliness' rooted in solidarity and resistance of globalized oppression.

The novel opens with its protagonist, Isookanga, seeking invertebrates in the rainforest for his uncle Lomama. The third-person narrator describes the forest as a complex ecosystem which, while functional and seemingly

---

[50]Dominic Thomas, 'In Koli Jean Bofane's Congo Inc.: Bismarck's Testament: The Limits of Empathy and the Postcolonial Scramble for Africa', Foreword to *Congo Inc.: Bismarck's Testament*, by In Koli Jean Bofane, trans. Marjolijn de Jager (Bloomington: Indiana University Press, 2018), p. xiii; Olivia C. Harrison, *Transcolonial Maghreb: Imagining Palestine in the Era of Decolonization* (Stanford: Stanford University Press, 2015).
[51]See, for example, Pie Tshibanda, *Un fou Noir au pays des Blancs* (Brussels: Le grand miroir, 1999).
[52]See Daniel Schiller, *Digital Capitalism: Networking the Global Market System* (Cambridge, MA: MIT Press, 2000).
[53]Éloïse Brezault, 'Mondialisation et "Afrocontemporanéité" dans *Congo Inc.* ou comment repenser la mémoire coloniale et la modernité?' *Francofonia*, vol. 76 (2019): 67–82, 69.

undisturbed by Isookanga's presence, not unlike contemporary society, is governed by competition, territorial demarcation, decay, waste and death.[54] However, Isookanga is merely enraged by what he perceives as his uncle's and the rest of the clan's resistance to 'modernity', embodied by their opposition to the cell tower the company China Network has installed in their village. While this tower provides Isookanga with access to the internet, and therefore opportunities for online gaming, his surroundings, even including the caterpillars in the forest, perceive the installation as a threat to their way of life: 'For Isookanga it was blatant proof that those blasted little beasts had no more common sense than the members of his clan, for he had indeed been forced to walk many kilometers to find them. Such had not been the case before.'[55] The opening pages establish the initial binary opposition between Isookanga, his uncle and the wider local community: modernity versus tradition, the Congolese village versus the wider world connected through the internet and global trade. Indeed, the Ekonda village is initially portrayed as intellectually, socially and geographically isolated, even from the rest of Équateur Province.[56] The narrator describes the setting sun as 'going off to illuminate other worlds', while the delegation from the DRC's capital, there for the tower's inauguration, seems like other-worldly beings to Isookanga:

> You might have thought they came not from the capital but from much farther away – from another planet perhaps. Everything about them was different. ... the Kinshasans remained reclined in their seats, impassive to the intense heat in spite of their suits and tightly knotted ties, ... as if air conditioning had become one of the options of their organism. Isookanga ... wanted to collect every bit of information necessary for his Kinshasan future.[57]

Not only do they come from far away, but the delegation appears as a different species: in Isookanga's imagination, their bodies have become 'optimized' to deal with adverse conditions; just a little later he notices that 'behind their smoky glasses it seemed they couldn't see a thing, as if by having different means of discernment they didn't need to'.[58] They are 'further developed' than the 'normal' bodies of the local notables, who 'persisted in constantly wiping their foreheads and waving their handkerchiefs around like fly swatters'.[59] When Isookanga experiences this event as formative to

---

[54] Bofane, *Congo Inc.*, p. 1.
[55] Ibid., p. 6.
[56] Ibid., pp. 7–8.
[57] Ibid., p. 10.
[58] Ibid.
[59] Ibid.

prepare him for his 'Kinshasan future', the delegation appears as visitors from this very future, that already exists in a place far away from the village where he feels stuck – turning the DRC into a space of multiple temporalities, rather than existing in one all-encompassing presence. The English-language translation of the novel loses the almost-homonyms of the French original: 'kinois' [Kinshasan] and 'chinois' [Chinese], locating the capital city as far from the village as China Network's headquarters.

However, while this is similar to the *Bildungsroman*-like representation of the big city as the 'promised land' in Mabanckou's novel – an imagined space of opportunity and future-oriented optimism that never materializes – these initial assumptions are rendered more complex throughout *Congo Inc.*'s narrative. For instance, Isookanga's encounter with the white Belgian academic Aude Martin, who introduces herself as an 'Africanist with a speciality in social anthropology', an academic field whose inception in Belgium is inextricably tied to colonialism and pro-imperial propaganda.[60] Aude proceeds to interview Isookanga and, despite the fact that they both speak French, she is incapable of engaging with his 'views of modernity' and can only perceive him as an exoticized research object:

> The way Isookanga had of accentuating his words, of being unambiguous in his opinions, or of sometimes taking his time when uttering a syllable to better emphasize the meaning of the word instilled Aude's body with an energy she was unable to identify or locate. After the interview she went back to her seat, moved not so much by what Isookanga had revealed to her as by the encounter she knew was exceptional, worthy of a different universe.[61]

Aude, attending to *how* Isookanga expresses himself but not to what he is saying, stands paradigmatically for the epistemological violence perpetrated by Western academics before, during and after the colonial period. Her unwillingness to engage with him in any meaningful way translates into her description of the encounter as 'worthy of a different universe'; he remains as alien to her as the Kinshasan delegation remains to him. Isookanga, aware of this asymmetrical power relationship, decides to appropriate her laptop as postcolonial retribution, as he explains to his best friend Bwale:

> My act counts as a refund for the colonial debt! ... Besides, Mongo tradition demands that a future spouse steal a chicken from his own village to prove to the *bokilo* [parents in law] that he will always find a

---

[60]See, for instance, Marc Poncelet, *L'invention des sciences coloniales belges* (Paris: Karthala, 2008).
[61]Bofane, *Congo Inc.*, p. 13.

way to provide for the needs of his betrothed! For me, my betrothed is high technology. And my test for a union with the universe goes by way of stealing the computer you see here.[62]

While otherwise dismissive of tradition, here Isookanga employs it humorously to justify stealing Aude's laptop. More importantly, however, he frames the appropriation of this device that provides him with access to the internet – note how there is no mention of the world or the 'global' but the universe – as a challenge to (re-)gain what he has historically been deprived of: taking part in globalization and benefitting from it.

Breakdowns of communication and the failure to overcome them are not limited to globalization and neo-imperial research practices but extend to culture and religion. Like Mabanckou's scathing dismissal of Pentecostal anti-intellectualism, Bofane depicts the 'Church of Divine Multiplication' as a scam that only serves to enrich Reverend Jonas Monkaya.[63] Moreover, Modogo, one of Isookanga's fellow *shégué*, who memorizes lines from English-language horror films and is cast out by his parents who cannot understand him, highlights what is at stake when the ability to speak the language(s) of globalization is replaced with religious dogma:

> The deacons and deaconesses all wanted to be present to observe this child who was probably an unadulterated product of the satanic world. What came out of his mouth was neither Latin nor the speech of any Pentecostal language, nor did it sound like any idiom a simple Christian could understand.[64]

Ironically, the followers of a religious movement from the United States cannot understand the language of its founders, thereby creating what Russell West-Pavlov calls 'the force field between Euro-American globalism and African localism, ... between participatory promise and a politics of exclusion whose tenor is scatological ... even abject'.[65] Indeed, despite Isookanga's position at the bottom of the social hierarchy, he clings to the 'participatory promise' of global capitalism.

This impossible position eventually results in this 'refund of the colonial debt', reproducing violence during Aude's and Isookanga's final meeting in

---

[62]Ibid., p. 14. See, for instance, Patience Kabamba, 'External Economic Exploitation in the DRC: 1990–2005', *African Studies Review*, vol. 55, no. 1 (2012): 123–30, https://www.jstor.org/stable/41804133. *La dette coloniale* is also the title of Maguy Kabamba's 1995 novel.
[63]Bofane, *Congo Inc.*, p. 89.
[64]Ibid., p. 52.
[65]Russell West-Pavlov, 'Participatory Cultures and Biopolitics in the Global South in In Koli Jean Bofane's *Congo Inc.*', *Research in African Literatures*, vol. 48, no. 4 (2017): 105–21, 105–6, https://doi.org/10.2979/reseafrilite.48.4.08.

Kinshasa. While this chapter's framework does not allow for an adequate analysis of the sexual assault that brings together several of the novel's main themes – epistemological violence and violence specifically against women (rape as war crime, sexual exploitation of minors by 'expats') – it is portrayed as the result of Isookanga's 'loathing of the Africanist's condescension' and their inability to communicate.[66] His attack is framed within a wider history of violence and exploitation; from the atrocities of the so-called Congo Free State to 'the salvos fired off by vicious neocolonialists ... the diktats of the International Monetary Fund ... the resolutions of the UN ... a reprint of *Tintin au Congo* ... the speech of an ill-informed French president in Dakar ... the propaganda of racist sentiments on Twitter'.[67] In 2007, then French president Nicolas Sarkozy proclaimed in Dakar, Senegal,

> *Le drame de l'Afrique, c'est que l'homme africain n'est pas assez entré dans l'histoire. ... Dans cet imaginaire où tout recommence toujours, il n'y a de place ni pour l'aventure humaine, ni pour l'idée de progrès. ... Jamais l'homme ne s'élance vers l'avenir.*
>
> [The tragedy of Africa is that the African has not fully entered history. In this imaginary where everything starts over and over again, there is no place for human adventure or the idea of progress. This man ['the African'] has never launched himself towards the future.][68]

Sarkozy's comments testify to a European hegemonic historiography that denies African agency and places Africa outside world time. However, Bofane also proposes a more hopeful alternative to the perpetual reproduction of violence: through Isookanga's friendship and exchange with the Chinese migrant worker Zhang Xia, towards the end of the novel, he is confronted with the importance of critical thinking and questioning regimes of power – be they Mao's Great Leap Forward or actors of globalized capitalism, from a multinational pharma company to a local warlord.[69] Bofane's vision of 'worldliness' thus suggests a 'bottom-up' approach to world literature, rooted in global and local/'provincial' solidarity. This 'prosaic worldliness' then gestures towards an idea of world literature that moves away from all-encompassing and totalizing definitions, one that is decentralized, multilingual

---

[66]Bofane, *Congo Inc.*, p. 124.
[67]Ibid., p. 125.
[68]'Le discours de Dakar de Nicolas Sarkozy: L'intégralité du discours du président de la République, prononcé le 26 juillet 2007', *Le Monde*, 9 November 2007, https://www.lemonde.fr/afrique/article/2007/11/09/le-discours-de-dakar_976786_3212.html. Accessed 1 February 2022.
[69]See Bofane, *Congo Inc.*, pp. 141–2.

and questions, as Karima Laachir, Sara Marzagora and Francesca Orsini put it, 'linear and teleological historical narratives that inevitably begin with Goethe'.[70] Mabanckou's and Bofane's novels present different visions of African intellectual and literary engagements with the world not only in terms of their orientation towards the Atlantic and China, respectively, but also through their different intertextual engagement with the *Bildungsroman* genre since *Wilhelm Meister's Apprenticeship* more broadly.

In lieu of a conclusion: Re-engaging history for dissent or solidarity

In *Human Rights Inc.*, Slaughter writes,

> The implicit *Bildungsroman* narrative of personality development codified in international law unfolds ... a plot for keeping the broken promise of the Enlightenment with the individual's reabsorption into universal humanity through the 'natural' medium of the nation-state.[71]

Both novels adhere superficially to the classic *Bildungsroman* narrative and focus on young, male protagonists, whose 'rebellion' consists in their departure from the province where they feel stuck to the urban space that allegedly promises freedom and self-realization through connection to the world. For them, however, as postcolonial subjects in dysfunctional nation states, the 'broken promise of Enlightenment' has never been one at all: the French and Belgian 'civilizing missions', under the pretext of Enlightenment zeal, brought physical, epistemological and environmental violence. In the post-independence era of Cold War politics (in *Black Moses*) and global capitalism (in *Congo Inc.*), these different forms of violence change (sometimes) form and perpetrator, and all characters across the two texts are caught up in this reproduction of destruction. Importantly, part of *Congo Inc.*'s representation of globalization, neo-colonialism and extractivism is a nuanced engagement with radical politics, as Duncan M. Yoon notes: 'the paradox that is the transition of the Chinese state from a locus of radical Third Worldism to the world's factory, and now as foreign direct investor

---

[70] Karima Laachir, Sara Marzagora and Francesca Orsini, 'Multilingual Locals and Significant Geographies: For a Ground-Up and Located Approach to World Literature', *Modern Languages Open*, vol. 19, no. 1 (2018): 1–8, 1, http://doi.org/10.3828/mlo.v0i0.190. See also Francesca Orsini, 'The Multilingual Local in World Literature', *Comparative Literature*, vol. 67, no. 4 (2015): 345–74, https://doi.org/10.1215/00104124-3327481; Julien Jeusette and Silvia Riva, 'Contemporary Congolese Literature as World Literature', *Journal of World Literature*, vol. 6 (2021): 123–32, https://doi.org/10.1163/24056480-00602001.
[71] Slaughter, *Human Rights, Inc.*, p. 92.

in the Congolese economy'.[72] Despite describing graphic violence, Bofane departs from the grotesque aesthetics of the postcolonial dictatorship novel – still visible in Mabanckou's text – to represent a transnational history from below that provides at least temporary communal survival for those who don't benefit from being implicated in global capitalism. The novels' mobilization of alternative historiographies that either subvert official state versions (in *Black Moses*) or testify to a 'worldliness' that, in Hiddleston's words, demonstrates the inextricability of global and national – and, I would add, local – histories that displace the old colonial binaries demonstrates the multifacetedness of African literature in French as world literature.

Bibliography

Arens, Sarah (2017), 'The Problem with the Prophet: Review of Alain Mabanckou's *Black Moses*', *Africa in Words* (blog), 23 October, https://africainwords.com/2017/10/23/the-problem-with-the-prophet-review-of-alain-mabanckous-black-moses. Accessed 21 November 2021.

Arens, Sarah (2020), 'Killer Stories: "Globalizing" the Grotesque in Alain Mabanckou's *African Psycho* and Leïla Slimani's *Chanson douce*', *Irish Journal of French Studies*, vol. 20: 143–72, https://doi.org/10.7173/164913320830841692.

Bedecarré, Madeline (2020), 'Prizing Francophonie into Existence: The Usurpation of World Literature by the Prix des Cinq Continents', *Journal of World Literature*, vol. 5, no. 2: 298–319, https://doi.org/10.1163/24056480-00502010.

Bofane, In Koli Jean (2014), *Congo Inc.: Le testament de Bismarck*, Arles: Actes Sud.

Bofane, In Koli Jean (2018), *Congo Inc.: Bismarck's Testament*, trans. Marjolijn de Jager, Bloomington: Indiana University Press.

Brezault, Éloïse (2019), 'Mondialisation et "Afrocontemporanéité" dans *Congo Inc.* ou comment repenser la mémoire coloniale et la modernité?' *Francofonia*, vol. 76: 67–82.

Cheah, Pheng (2016), *What Is a World? Postcolonial Literature as World Literature*, Durham, NC: Duke University Press.

Coly, Ayo A. (2020), 'Alain Mabanckou and the Category of World Literature', *Research in African Literatures*, vol. 51, no. 2: 27–39, https://doi.org/10.2979/reseafrilite.51.2.02.

Forsdick, Charles (2005), *Travel in Twentieth-Century French and Francophone Cultures: The Persistence of Diversity*, Oxford: Oxford University Press.

Forsdick, Charles (2017), 'Global France, Global French: Beyond the Monolingual', *Contemporary French Civilization*, vol. 42, no. 1: 13–29, https://doi.org/10.3828/cfc.2017.2.

---

[72]Duncan M. Yoon, 'Figuring Africa and China: Congolese Literary Imaginaries of the PRC', *Journal of World Literature*, vol. 6 (2021): 167–96, 189–90, https://doi.org/10.1163/24056480-00602004.

Gilroy, Paul (1993), *The Black Atlantic: Modernity and Double Consciousness*, London: Verso.
Hargreaves, Alec G., Charles Forsdick and David Murphy (eds) (2012), *Transnational French Studies: Postcolonialism and Littérature-monde*, Liverpool: Liverpool University Press.
Harrison, Olivia C. (2015), *Transcolonial Maghreb: Imagining Palestine in the Era of Decolonization*, Stanford: Stanford University Press.
Hiddleston, Jane (2016), 'Writing World Literature: Approaches from the Maghreb', *PMLA*, vol. 131, no. 5: 1386–95, https://doi.org/10.1632/pmla.2016.131.5.1386.
Jeusette, Julien, and Silvia Riva (2021), 'Contemporary Congolese Literature as World Literature', *Journal of World Literature*, vol. 6: 123–32, https://doi.org/10.1163/24056480-00602001.
Kabamba, Patience (2012), 'External Economic Exploitation in the DRC: 1990–2005', *African Studies Review*, vol. 55, no. 1: 123–30, https://www.jstor.org/stable/41804133.
Kleppinger, Kathryn (2010), 'What's Wrong with the Littérature-Monde Manifesto?' *Contemporary French and Francophone Studies*, vol. 14: 74–84, https://doi.org/10.1080/17409290903412722.
Kravchenko, Elena V. (2021), 'The Matter of Race: Brotherhood of St. Moses the Black and the Retelling of African American History through Orthodox Christian Forms', *Journal of the American Academy of Religion*, vol. 89, no. 1: 298–333, https://doi.org/10.1093/jaarel/lfab025.
Krishnan, Sanjay (2007), *Reading the Global: Troubling Perspectives on Britain's Empire in Asia*, New York: Columbia University Press.
Kuenen, Eline (2018), 'Creation through Inversion: The Carnivalesque Postcolonial State in the Novels of Alain Mabanckou and In Koli Jean Bofane', in *Fictions of African Dictatorship: Cultural Representations of Postcolonial Power*, ed. Charlotte Baker and Hannah Grayson, Oxford: Peter Lang, pp. 79–97.
Laachir, Karima, Sara Marzagora and Francesca Orsini (2018), 'Multilingual Locals and Significant Geographies: For a Ground-Up and Located Approach to World Literature', *Modern Languages Open*, vol. 19, no. 1: 1–8, http://doi.org/10.3828/mlo.v0i0.190.
'Le discours de Dakar de Nicolas Sarkozy: L'intégralité du discours du président de la République, prononcé le 26 juillet 2007' (2007), *Le Monde*, 9 November, https://www.lemonde.fr/afrique/article/2007/11/09/le-discours-de-dakar_976786_3212.html. Accessed 1 December 2021.
Mabanckou, Alain (2017), *Black Moses*, trans. Helen Stevenson, London: Serpent's Tail.
Mabanckou, Alain, and Achille Mbembe (2018), 'Le français, notre bien commun?' *BibliObs*, 12 February, https://bibliobs.nouvelobs.com/idees/20180211.OBS2020/le-francais-notre-bien-commun-par-alain-mabanckou-et-achille-mbembe.html. Accessed 1 February 2022.
Mabanckou, Alain, and Donald Nicholson-Smith (2011), 'Immigration, "Littérature-Monde," and Universality: The Strange Fate of the African Writer', *Yale French Studies*, vol. 120: 75–87.

Mayrargue, Cédric (2008), 'The Paradoxes of Pentecostalism in Sub-Saharan Africa', *Notes de l'Ifri*, April, https://www.ifri.org/sites/default/files/atoms/files/mayrargue_the_paradoxes_of_pentecostalism.pdf. Accessed 1 February 2022.

Mbembe, Achille (2000), 'At the Edge of the World: Boundaries, Territoriality, and Sovereignty in Africa', trans. Steven Rendall, *Public Culture*, vol. 12, no. 1: 259–84, muse.jhu.edu/article/26186.

Miller, Christopher L. (2011), 'The Theory and Pedagogy of a World Literature in French', *Yale French Studies*, vol. 120: 33–48, https://www.jstor.org/stable/41337115.

Moudileno, Lydie (2006), *Parades postcoloniales: La fabrications des identités dans le roman congolais*, Paris: Karthala.

Orsini, Francesca (2015), 'The Multilingual Local in World Literature', *Comparative Literature*, vol. 67, no. 4: 345–74, https://doi.org/10.1215/00104124-3327481.

Poncelet, Marc (2008), *L'invention des sciences coloniales belges*, Paris: Karthala.

Sarr, Felwine (2016), *Afrotopia*, Paris: Éditions Philippe Rey.

Schiller, Daniel (2000), *Digital Capitalism: Networking the Global Market System*, Cambridge, MA: MIT Press.

Slaughter, Joseph R. (2007), *Human Rights, Inc.: The World Novel, Narrative Form, and International Law*, New York: Fordham University Press.

Thomas, Dominic (2018), 'In Koli Jean Bofane's Congo Inc.: Bismarck's Testament: The Limits of Empathy and the Postcolonial Scramble for Africa', Foreword to *Congo Inc.: Bismarck's Testament*, by In Koli Jean Bofane, trans. Marjolijn de Jager, Bloomington: Indiana University Press.

Tshibanda, Pie (1999), *Un fou Noir au pays des Blancs*, Brussels: Le grand miroir.

West-Pavlov, Russel (2017), 'Participatory Cultures and Biopolitics in the Global South in In Koli Jean Bofane's *Congo Inc.*', *Research in African Literatures*, vol. 48, no. 4: 105–21, https://doi.org/10.2979/reseafrilite.48.4.08.

Yoon, Duncan M. (2020), 'Africa, China, and the Global South Novel: In Koli Jean Bofane's *Congo Inc.*', *Comparative Literature*, vol. 72, no. 3: 316–39, https://doi.org/10.1215/00104124-8255350.

Yoon, Duncan M. (2021), 'Figuring Africa and China: Congolese Literary Imaginaries of the PRC', *Journal of World Literature*, vol. 6: 167–96, https://doi.org/10.1163/24056480-00602004.

5

The first Ethiopian novel in Amharic (1908) and the world: Critical and theoretical legacies

Sara Marzagora

Introduction

The discipline of world literature emerged in the early 2000s out of the consideration that national criticism had become insufficient to capture the global character of contemporary literature. Since its inception, scholars of world literature have debated which methodologies best capture the relationship between literary production and socio-economic globalization. Some proponents of world literature have reproposed some of the critical paradigms of postcolonial studies, such as the distinction between a world 'centre' and world 'peripheries' and the appraisal of 'peripheral' literature in terms of how it relates to the 'centre'. This chapter takes Franco Moretti's early work as an example of this type of scholarship. Scholars like Moretti, as we shall see, understand the relationship between 'centres' and 'peripheries' of world literature according to a unilinear developmental timeline, in which Western literatures are generally considered to pave the way for modern literary production.

In this chapter, I look at the first Ethiopian novel in Amharic, Lǝbb Wälläd Tarik ('story born out of the heart', later published in Amharic under the title Tobbya) by Afäwärq Gäbrä-Iyäsus, not through unified top-down models that all too easily assume the universal validity of Western critical terminology but through a context-specific approach that employs the text's own conceptual categories to analyse its relationship with the 'world'. When analysed through its own critical and aesthetic vocabulary, *Ləbb Wälläd Tarik* clearly resists being classified as either 'peripheral' or developmentally 'behind' the European novel. Afäwärq's novel is instead fully modern in its content (section 1), in its genre features (section 2) and for the type of historical processes that led to its publication (section 3). The novel is self-conscious and assertive about its engagement with modern processes of global political and economic integration, and in no way understands itself as 'peripheral' or derivative. Following on from the critical insights of Yonas Admassu and Taye Assefa, the chapter ultimately argues for a reconceptualization of the goals of world literature as a discipline. Instead of taking the categories of 'world' and 'literature' for granted, a context-specific and bottom-up approach to the discipline forces us to account for the many meanings of 'the world', the many meanings of 'literature' and the different ways in which historical agents, from their own specific geopolitical and aesthetic positions, have found textual and aesthetic solutions to the questions posed by global modernity.

Ləbb Wälläd Tarik and the world: Thematic links

Afäwärq Gäbrä-Iyäsus published *Ləbb Wälläd Tarik* in 1908. The text opens with an epigraph, which Taddesse Tamrat translates as, 'Much is due to those who are generous towards others / Much is lost to those who do evil onto others / The generous person never gives, but lends.'[1] The story is set in a mythical time in an unnamed place.[2] The opening paragraphs explain that the land has been ravaged by two opposing armies, one led by a Christian king and one by an 'infidel' king. The latter, stronger in numbers, have the upper hand in the war, and the Christians are in retreat. The story now zooms in on a Christian general, who is taken prisoner by his enemies. His enslavers ask his family for a hefty ransom, which the family cannot afford. The general's son Wahəd decides to leave the family home in search of money. He offers his services to a merchant, explaining his personal circumstances, but the merchant refuses to hire him on account of his youth. Wahəd returns home, and the future of the family seems bleak,

---

[1] See Taddesse Tamrat, 'Tobbya', *Ethiopian Observer*, vol. 8, no. 3 (1964): 242–67, 258.
[2] Taye Assefa, 'The Form and Content of the First Amharic Novel', in *Silence Is Not Golden: A Critical Anthology of Ethiopian Literature*, ed. Taddesse Adera and Ali Jimale Ahmed (Lawrenceville, NJ: Red Sea Press, 1995), pp. 61–92, 76.

until one night the general unexpectedly appears at the door. The merchant was moved by Wahəd's story and paid the ransom himself. The family feels indebted, and immediately Wahəd decides to set out again, this time with the objective of finding the merchant and thanking him. Things do not go according to plan, and Wahəd is taken into slavery during his travels. His father, mother and twin sister Ṭobbya wait for him, and when he does not return, it is the father's turn to go in search of him. Ṭobbya insists on accompanying her father, disguised as a boy for safety. They fail to find Wahəd and are discovered by the army of the infidel king, who mercifully takes them under his protection. Impressed by the virtues of Ṭobbya and her father, the king resolves to help them and manages to locate Wahəd. Seeing the misfortunes that have befallen Ṭobbya's family as a result of the war, the king decides to put an end to hostilities. The denouement of the plot is a royal marriage: once it is revealed that Ṭobbya is a girl, the king asks her to marry him, but she is firm in her religious principles and initially refuses, on the grounds that she would only marry another Christian. The king converts to Christianity, and the marriage can finally be celebrated. Wahəd marries the king's cousin, but the real heroine is clearly Ṭobbya, as highlighted by the coda that closes the text: 'Because of one merchant everybody was saved / Because of one woman everybody believed / By the word of one king Ethiopia was established.'[3]

The coda makes it clear that, regardless of when the story is set, Afäwärq is inspired by recent historical events. The story of a country ridden by wars and religious factionalism that becomes politically united under a single Christian king loosely reproduces the process of political centralization that the Ethiopian empire underwent from the mid-nineteenth century onwards. If we unpack the historical referents of the text, the initial conflict in the plot likely might allude to the *Zämänä Mäsafənt* (conventionally dated 1769–1855), a century of political fragmentation marked by the weakening of the central authority of the emperor and persistent power struggles between regional leaders. The final pacification of the country refers to the reign of Emperor Mənilək, who, in conventional Ethiopian history, consolidated the process of imperial centralization started by Emperors Tewodros and Yohannəs before him.[4]

Afäwärq's other publications from 1908 and 1909 are all concerned with Mənilək's reign, which shows that corresponding events in Ethiopia were high on his list of intellectual preoccupations. In 1909, most notably, Afäwärq published *Dagmawi Mənilək Nəgusä Nägäst Zältyoṗya* ('Mənilək

---

[3]Adapted from Yonas Admassu, 'The First-Born of Amharic Fiction', in *Silence Is Not Golden: A Critical Anthology of Ethiopian Literature*, ed. Taddesse Adera and Ali Jimale Ahmed (Lawrenceville, NJ: Red Sea Press, 1995), pp. 93–112, 100.
[4]Teshale Tibebu, *The Making of Modern Ethiopia 1896–1974* (Lawrenceville, NJ: Red Sea Press, 1995), p. 31.

II, King of Kings of Ethiopia'), a historical volume that celebrates Mənilək's reign and political standing. Afäwärq's argument in *Dagmawi Mənilək* is that Ethiopia has been held back economically and politically by greedy, self-aggrandizing, power-thirsty leaders who prioritized their own wealth and status over the people's welfare. In Mənilək, however, Ethiopia has finally found a leader who will rule according to the principles of Christian morality, and who therefore has the credentials to lead Ethiopia towards progress and modernization. It is hard not to see parallels between Afäwärq's historical assessment of Mənilək's reign and the ending of *Ləbb Wälläd Tarik*. In both *Ləbb Wälläd Tarik* and *Dagmawi Mənilək*, peace and justice are restored by an enlightened leader whose rule marks a new beginning for the country. Similarly, in both cases the restoration of peace is not merely presented as a welcome political development but is understood theologically as the restoration of the 'light' of virtue over the 'darkness' of vice. In this sense, the two texts are inspired by the same political philosophy which sees the need for political power to be firmly rooted in a Christian religious world view.

Afäwärq's preoccupation with the role of religion in Mənilək's Ethiopia should be seen as a response to the global power system of the time. On the one hand, stressing the Christian character of the Ethiopian monarchy allowed Ethiopian elites to pitch Ethiopia as part of the same civilization as its European counterparts, thus leveraging Christian ecumenicalism against European notions of African and Black 'otherness'. A peaceful, Christian Ethiopia united under a pious monarch could easily disprove the European characterization of Africans as primitive and barbaric. At the same time, the way in which Afäwärq defends the public role of Christianity prefigures the widespread opposition to secularism in subsequent Ethiopian political thought. While Europeans propagandized the notion that secularism was a more 'modern' form of political organization, Afäwärq and his successors considered it a sign of the spiritual regression of Europeans. Strong in its Christian public morality, Ethiopia would instead be able to achieve an even more advanced modernization, able to combine the politico-economic, scientific and technological advances that Europe had achieved with the spiritual advances that Europe had foolishly abandoned. The denouement of the plot is, in this sense, an ideological intervention against European imperialism in the Horn of Africa.

Christianity is also Afäwärq's answer to other crucial questions: in the new Ethiopian nation state, how would people come together? What kind of political community would the new nation state represent? How would Ethiopian rulers forge a sense of belonging to the nation state? Afäwärq rules out the possibility of a civic type of nationalism, structured around citizenship and civil rights. He opts instead for a religious type, in which the new national community would be bound together by Christian values of fraternal and neighbourly love. The consequence of erecting Christianity as a pillar of Ethiopia's national identity, however, is the exclusion of non-Christians. It is clear from *Ləbb Wällåd Tarik* that non-Christians would be tolerated in the ideal state created by the marriage between Ṭobbya and the king. In the proclamation with which he ends the war, the king clearly states, 'Let everyone live according to their own religion. We have had enough of the old religious conflicts and we all must respect each other's religion. ... Though I am not a Christian myself, it is my duty to rule everyone equally irrespective of their religion'.[5] However, the values of religious tolerance promoted by the king are not enough to mark a new era. The plot requires the king to convert to Christianity for the ideal state to be ushered in. Yonas Admassu makes the incisive point that only with conversion can the king's power marry virtue, as true virtue is only to be found in faith. The end of religious conflict in Ethiopia does not lie in the public balance between different religions but rather in the assimilation of the whole community to the one true faith.

The novel gives one straightforward answer to questions of who Ethiopia's ideal ruler might be, and what kind of national community the Ethiopian state should represent: the ideal ruler should be the caretaker and protector of the Christian faith, and rule according to the moral principles of Christianity. The national community is envisioned as a community of believers, whose social unity and social harmony would be regulated by Christian values of generosity and tolerance. And if non-Christians are tolerated, it will be nevertheless clear that they are not fully virtuous and therefore not full citizens of a Christian state. The themes treated in the novel and the questions it addresses, then, are eminently modern in character, as they respond to the political imperatives of the time about the forging of new nation states and the assertion of political sovereignty in the global arena. The plot, structured around the theme of the quest and ending with a royal marriage, can strike the reader as folktale-like, but *Ləbb Wällåd Tarik* is in fact deeply grounded, politically and ideologically, in its historical milieu – not timeless but profoundly modern.

Ləbb Wällåd Tarik and the world: Formal links

The second way to think about the links between *Ləbb Wällåd Tarik* and the world is by looking at literary form and genre. The global transformations of the modern era were supported by, and in turn supported, shifts in epistemology. For Ethiopian intellectuals, as for intellectuals around the world, processes of political and cultural internationalization made

---

[5]Taddesse, 'Tobbya', p. 258.

available new types of knowledge and new truths. The new debates in political thought went hand in hand with the exploration of forms of textuality able to speak about the world and articulate a new social identity for Ethiopian intellectuals. *Ləbb Wälläd Tarik* is a prime example of these textual innovations. Up until now, we have called the book a novel, but as we shall see, critics have spent decades debating this label.

Afäwärq is aware that *Ləbb Wälläd Tarik* constitutes an innovation in the landscape of Ethiopian genres of the time, and helps the reader situate the text vis-à-vis more established genres. His choice of title explains it all: *tarik* means 'history', and this history is qualified as born out (*wälläd*) of the heart (*ləbb*). The heart was considered the place in the body where imagination originates. Hence, the title translates as 'invented' or 'imagined' history. The book is therefore a *tarik*, which was a very familiar genre for Afäwärq's Ethiopian readers, but with a twist: it is not a history of real events but events that never happened. The story was not born (*wälläd*) in reality but birthed by the writer. This is how Afäwärq defines the fictional nature of his literary creation. Fictional, however, does not mean false in this context. Afäwärq would have likely had a strong reaction against the insinuation that, because the story is invented, it is somehow untrue. The whole story is, on the contrary, designed to celebrate the one superior truth of the Christian God. Further, the whole argument of the story is precisely that the revealed truth of Christianity should be at the very forefront of the Ethiopian state. In other words, this is still somehow a *tarik*, albeit a subgenre of it, with its own peculiarities. Certainly the characters have never existed, but Afäwärq still narrates the history of Ethiopia. The fact that he does so through invented characters differentiates his book from the *tarik* tradition; while remaining in line with it Afäwärq intends to celebrate the truth of God and empire. *Tarik*, after all, appeared for the most part in the form of *tarikä nägäst*, literally the 'history of kings' or royal chronicles, and what is *Ləbb Wälläd Tarik* if not the coming-of-age story of a young king who gradually learns how to lead? We see here how Afäwärq carefully positions his text in relation to existing genres, defining it as a new offshoot of an existing textual tradition.

Such negotiation of genres and forms of textuality is a key feature of the Ethiopian intellectual environment of the beginning of the twentieth century. The tradition of the newspaper, for example, was initially framed as an offshoot of the *awaj*, or imperial proclamation. These were edicts or announcements on the part of the emperor or provincial rulers, recited orally by imperial heralds travelling from village to village. The intellectual generally credited with producing the first handwritten news-sheets around 1901, Gäbrä-Əgziabher Gila-Maryam, adopted some of the key textual features of the *awaj*, opening his written dispatches with expressions such as *hulaččəhu səmuň* (listen to me, everyone), as would have been the case with an imperial proclamation recited aloud by heralds.

The new genres of the *ləbb wälläd tarik* and the newspaper (*gazeṭa*) gradually became more and more established, to the point that some of the genres introduced in later decades were defined against them. *Ləbb wälläd tarik* took some decades to become the go-to translation of the word 'novel' from English, *roman* from French and *romanzo* from Italian. In a 1927 catalogue of 'books found in Ethiopia', another great intellectual of the period, Həruy Wäldä-Səlasse, classified novels using the French term *roman* (transliterated in the Amharic script). But the distinction between genres of *ləbb wälläd*, products of the author's imagination, and genres that were *not* products of the author's imagination must have been already operative in those years. In 1931, Emperor Haylä Səllase introduced Ethiopia's first constitution to the public by explaining that it was not *ləbb wälläd*, meaning it was a binding document rooted in the reality of the country, not idiosyncratically made up by him. In the 1940s, *ləbb wälläd tarik* became the Amharic translation of the English word 'novel'. Novels published in this decade used *ləbb wälläd tarik* as a subtitle to convey their genre. From identifying a single specific story published by a specific author in a specific year, the locution had come to designate a whole genre. It is therefore unsurprising that, when *Ləbb Wällä d Tarik* was republished in the 1950s, the title had to be changed to *Ṭobbya*, making it clear that the readers of that decade saw the female heroine as the real protagonist. The new title stuck, and the book is still popularly known as *Ṭobbya*.

The reorganization of Amharic genres of the beginning of the twentieth century should be framed in connection with processes of global integration. Gäbrä-Əgziabher Gila-Maryam's 1901 news dispatches addressed new figures of foreign-educated intellectuals that had started gravitating to Emperor Mənilək's court. Around the same time, Emperor Mənilək sponsored the first Amharic newspaper, *Aəmro* ('intellect' or 'intelligence'), partly as a reaction to the increased popularity among Ethiopian elites of missionary newspapers and French newspapers from Djibouti. The state-sponsored newspapers of the subsequent three decades consolidated this process of elite creation. All the main intellectuals from the 1920s and 1930s at some point contributed to the flagship newspaper *Bərhanənna Sälam*, solidifying a secular and globally oriented space of intellectual discussion. The new constitution in 1931 was seen as an essential step to reinforce Ethiopia's claim to sovereignty. All other independent states at the time had a constitution, and the Ethiopian government felt pressed to demonstrate that the Ethiopian state, too, ticked that important legal box. The legal texts that preceded the 1931 constitution did not really speak the language of sovereign statehood and were therefore seen as obsolete.

The social changes of modernity and globalization, then, constituted new audiences and created the need for new forms of textuality. The new genres were defined in relation to existing ones, sometimes as subgenres (the novel is an 'imagined history'), sometimes as antithetical genres (the constitution is not 'imagined' like the novel). The 1908 publication of *Ləbb Wällad Tarik* needs more probing, though: why did Afäwärq choose to write an 'imagined' history? What prompted him to write in a different genre? To answer these questions, we need to look outside the content and form of the novel and explore the specific historical circumstances in which the text was written and published.

Ləbb Wällad Tarik and the world: Genealogical links

Ləbb Wällad Tarik is a clear product of the global changes of the modern period. Afäwärq grew up in Zäge, on Lake Ṭana, and underwent church schooling there until he was introduced to Mənilək's court sometime after 1880. The court at this time was increasingly frequented by a wide array of foreigners in Addis Abäba either in a personal or official capacity. One such, the Italian envoy Count Pietro Antonelli, offered to arrange for Afäwärq to be educated in Italy. In 1890, Afäwärq returned to Ethiopia and soon fell out of Empress Ṭaytu's favour because of his Italian affiliations, at a time when the relationship between Ethiopia and Italy was deteriorating. Mənilək, who had a more accommodating position than his wife towards the Italians, protected Afäwärq from Ṭaytu's hostility by arranging to send him to Switzerland for further study. As the tensions between Ethiopians and Italians escalated in the first Italo-Ethiopian war of 1895–6, Afäwärq made the momentous decision to cross the border from Switzerland into Italy and seemingly offered his services to the Italians. The crushing defeat suffered by the Italians at Adwa put a temporary end to their colonial ambitions in Ethiopia, but Afäwärq could hardly come home after his betrayal. He stayed in exile in Italy and was hired as Amharic teacher at the Orientale University in Naples, where he collaborated closely with one of the most prominent Italian scholars of Ethiopia, Francesco Gallina. Gallina encouraged Afäwärq to publish what would become some of his most famous works. *Ləbb Wällad Tarik* and *Dagmawi Mənilək Nəgusä Nägäst Zältyopya* were both published in Rome under Gallina's supervision, and Afäwärq assigned *Ləbb Wällad Tarik* for his Italian students of Amharic to read at the Orientale University.

Ləbb Wällad Tarik is therefore a product of the transnationalism of the time. The end of the nineteenth century saw an intensifying of Ethiopia's interactions with the outside world, mostly due to the opening of the Suez Canal in 1859. Improved connectivity brought many more foreigners to Ethiopia, and many more Ethiopians to Europe. This growing network of diplomats, travellers, merchants, doctors, missionaries and interpreters created a new social class of Ethiopians, comfortable interfacing with foreigners, foreign languages and foreign lifestyles. Many of them had studied in Europe, mostly out of fortuitous personal connections. At the same time, this increased connectivity also exposed Ethiopia to the dangers of European colonialism, and Afäwärq was an active participant in the events that led to Italy's attempted colonization of Ethiopia. The Orientale University exemplified the colonial production of knowledge about the 'other', but it would be wrong to consider Afäwärq a mere pawn in Italy's colonial ideology and colonial designs.

Ləbb Wälläd Tarik and Dagmawi Mənilək Nəgusä Nägäst Zältyoṗya are fiercely nationalist texts with no hints of European or Italian colonial ideologies. Both texts are overwhelmingly concerned with the problems Ethiopian intellectuals were debating at home. Dagmawi Mənilək is an apologetic, if not outright sycophantic, account of Mənilək's reign. The book goes all-in to legitimize, even sanctify Mənilək's rule. This was probably a way for Afäwärq to ingratiate himself with Mənilək and seek forgiveness for his past betrayal, hoping to be allowed home. The implication is that Afäwärq is writing with an Ethiopian readership in mind, even though the text was printed in Italy and first read by Italian readers. Similarly, Ləbb Wälläd Tarik might have been written for Italian students of Amharic, but its intertextual references are all from the Ethiopian tradition.

The complex transnational history behind the publication of the text also determined Afäwärq's choice of genre. He offers a detailed explanation in Dagmawi Mənilək, which we can take as valid by extension for Ləbb Wälläd Tarik. In the case of the novel, the title immediately signals that the text is not a tarikä nägäst (royal history or royal chronicle) but an 'invented' type of history. Dagmawi Mənilək is closer to the tradition of royal chronicles, and certainly the title, centring as it does the figure of Emperor Mənilək, can easily lead the Ethiopian reader to think that this is a tarikä nägäst. Afäwärq is therefore careful to explain why, contrary to his reader's expectations, Dagmawi Mənilək is not a tarikä nägäst. Afäwärq admits that, as a writer, he does not meet the requirements to be able to write an official chronicle: 'If I wrote the official history of Mənilək's rule I would be happy and honored, but [if I do not write it] is because I do not have the means (aḳme).'[6] Afäwärq refers here to the socially defined criteria that make a tarikä nägäst valid and the mechanisms by which authorial legitimacy is built within the genre. In both cases, he does not have the means (aḳme could also signify power, capability, ability) to meet the requirements of a valid tarikä nägäst.

To write a proper tarikä nägäst, Afäwärq implies, an historian must muster an experiential kind of knowledge. The primary way to build authorial legitimacy is through the direct observation of events. The abundance

---

[6]Afäwärq Gäbrä-Iyyäsus, Dagmawi Mənilək Nəgusä Nägäst Zältyoṗya ['Mənilək II, King of Kings of Ethiopia'] (Rome, 1909), p. 8.

of precise details is what the reader expects of a good *tarikä nägäst* and being present on the ground enables the historian to meet high standards of precision and accuracy. This methodological path to the *tarikä nägäst* is barred to Afäwärq, he laments. He was not present when Mənilək's actions unfolded; the little he heard was via third parties; and he does not remember dates and details. This is all a consequence of moving abroad: 'Since my life has been spent abroad for the most part, I have forgotten everything.'[7] As a consequence, *Dagmawi Mənilək* is just a 'small history' (*tənnəš tarik*), as Afäwärq explains at the end of the volume[8] – a partial, incomplete and unassuming contribution to the histories of Mənilək's reign. While *Dagmawi Mənilək* is apologetically presented as a lower kind of *tarikä nägäst*, *Ləbb Wälläd Tarik* acknowledges its novelty with more confidence. Afäwärq may have forgotten dates and details of Mənilək's reign, but the heart (*ləbb*) will fill these gaps with invented characters and content. The very same global mobility that defined Afäwärq's life forces him to experiment with new genres. His distance from home makes him rely on creativity to supplement his lack of experiential knowledge.

Afäwärq had to wait for Emperor Mənilək to die before he could return to Ethiopia in 1916. Copies of his works had already been circulating in Ethiopia and had been read by other prominent intellectuals. For example, Gäbrä-Həywät Baykädañ's *Aṭe Məniləkənna Ityop̣ya* ('Emperor Mənilək and Ethiopia'), published in Asmara in 1912, engages at length with Afäwärq's *Dagmawi Mənilək*. When Afäwärq returned to Ethiopia, he brought more copies of his books with him, so we can assume that most Ethiopian readers accessed the texts in the 1920s and early 1930s, when Afäwärq took up important positions in Ethiopia's government. His government responsibilities did not leave much time for writing, and Afäwärq died in 1947 without publishing any other major work. All the major Amharic writers of the post–Second World War period were familiar with *Ləbb Wälläd Tarik*, so the text had a long-term impact on the subsequent development of Amharic literature. By then, however, Afäwärq's reputation had been permanently tarnished by his high-profile collaboration with the Fascists during the Italian occupation of Ethiopia (1936–41). While the circumstances of his association with the Italians during the first Italo-Ethiopian war are murky, his collaboration with the Italians in the second Italo-Ethiopian war is completely unambiguous. Afäwärq proactively defended and advanced the Italian colonial cause, to the point that the Fascists gave him the title *Afa Qesar*, the 'mouth[piece] of the Caesar' (i.e. Mussolini). It is not a surprise that the critical legacy of *Ləbb Wälläd Tarik* is very mixed, to say the least.

---

[7] Ibid., p. 8.
[8] Ibid., p. 111.

Ləbb Wällåd Tarik in world literature and Ethiopian literary criticism

For the most part, *Ləbb Wällåd Tarik* came under critical attack for its stylistic and narrative choices, rather than the political affiliation of the author. Although the expression *ləbb wällåd tarik* has come to designate the genre of the novel, critics have since paradoxically denied that Afäwärq's text can itself be classified as a novel. The major reservations have to do with *Ləbb Wällåd Tarik*'s lack of realism and Afäwärq's lack of narrative skill. This debate took place almost entirely within the self-enclosed space of Ethiopian studies and the participants were all scholars of Ethiopian literature, only discussing Amharic texts.

Yet, these debates have a close bearing on world literature. Since its rise as a discipline in the 2000s, world literature, like postcolonial studies before it, came under fire for reproposing Eurocentric models of the world. This was seen as a conspicuous methodological contradiction for a discipline that purported to create more inclusive frameworks through which to look at global literary production. Here I am going to focus on one aspect of this argument: the employment, on the part of some of the early proponents of world literature, of diffusionist interpretative frameworks. Diffusionism, as a modality of intellectual inquiry aimed at tracing the origin and lines of transmission of specific ideas, texts or cultural traits, is not per se Eurocentric, but Eurocentrism is almost always diffusionist. In the modern era, Eurocentrism is the assumption that modern ideas and innovations came from Europe, generally understood as an internally homogeneous and monolithic entity. The argument that these modern ideas and innovations originated in Europe was then used to claim that Europe was intrinsically superior in its culture and civilization. These innovations then spread to the rest of the world, often on the back of colonial conquest, where globally 'peripheral' intellectuals adopted, appropriated or reacted against them. It is this latter modality that postcolonial studies set out to study, and while the focus on the periphery's reaction against the centre sheds light on histories of antiracist activism and anticolonial resistance, it also reproduced an essentialized dichotomy between a European 'centre' and non-European 'peripheries'. Some key proponents of world literature adopted the same framework, most notably Franco Moretti, whose 2000 article 'Conjectures on world literature' is continually cited as one of the foundational critical texts of the new discipline. Moretti has revisited his argument several times since 2000, but this article remains very useful in tracing how world literature has often uncritically reproposed diffusionist frameworks of interpretation. This trend is not representative of the whole discipline, of course, and in fact critiques of diffusionism have animated world literature debates as much as diffusionist frameworks themselves.⁹ Nor should Moretti be taken as the only exponent of a diffusionist approach; Pascale Casanova, for example, describes a similar centre–periphery model in her foundational *The World Republic of Letters*.¹⁰

Moretti's argument in 'Conjectures' is well known to all world literature scholars and practitioners. He defines world literature as 'one and unequal', divided into a hegemonic Western centre and a marginalized non-Western periphery.¹¹ Western literatures 'completely ignore' the periphery, while the periphery is 'intersected and altered' by the centre.¹² A case in point is the modern novel, defined by Moretti as 'a wave' that originates in the Western centres, and which, in its movement from the centre to the periphery, 'runs into the branches of local traditions, and is always significantly transformed by them'.¹³ This is what Moretti calls 'a law of literary evolution', writing that 'in cultures that belong to the periphery of the literary system, the modern novel first arises not as an autonomous development but as a compromise between a Western formal influence (usually French or English) and local materials'.¹⁴ Moretti's approach is quintessentially diffusionist. He assumes a general homogeneity of the Western 'centre', from where the literary innovations of the novel spread to the 'peripheries' like 'a wave'. The peripheries, metaphorically compared to static and passive 'trees', receive Western literary innovations and adapted Western forms to local contexts. This diffusionist model implies a specific chronology: the advent of literary modernity in the peripheries comes *after* the advent of literary modernity in the centre. Literary peripheries enter world literature only when 'intersected' by the cultures of the centre, existing in this model only in relation to Europe. Moretti rules out the possibility of exchanges between different peripheral areas, of autonomous literary innovations in the peripheries, of the peripheries ever systemically influencing the centre, and of local hierarchies and local power relations *within* the centre or *within* the periphery. Another unexamined assumption of Moretti's argument is the definition of the novel. Did all the 'peripheral' writers he considers understand their texts as novels? Did they use other terms, and are these terms perfect translations of the term 'novel'? Moretti considers the novel as defined by literary realism, but can we really assume

---

[9] Francesca Orsini, 'The Multilingual Local in World Literature', *Comparative Literature*, vol. 67, no. 4 (2015): 345–74.
[10] Pascale Casanova, *The World Republic of Letters* (Cambridge, MA: Harvard University Press, 2004).
[11] Franco Moretti, 'Conjectures on World Literature', *New Left Review*, vol. 1 (2000): 55–67, 55.
[12] Ibid., p. 56.
[13] Ibid., p. 67.
[14] Ibid., p. 58.

a perfect global translatability of the notion of 'novel' as a genre label and 'realism' as a literary technique?

Ethiopian critics had been debating precisely the same questions in relation to Ləbb Wälläd Tarik. I am going to focus here on three critics in particular: Fikre Tolossa, Taye Assefa and Yonas Admassu. Fikre Tolossa starts his 1983 dissertation with a normative definition of literary realism. Mastering realism is necessary for Amharic writers to move onto socialist realism, which was the literary style officially endorsed by the Marxist-inspired military junta that ruled Ethiopia from 1974 to 1991. His assessment is that 'Amharic literature as a whole is not competent enough to move to socialist realism now.'[15] In his view, therefore, it is possible to give a univocal definition of literary realism, and then assess whether a writer is 'competent' enough to meet these criteria. Ləbb Wälläd Tarik for him does not pass the test: 'Even though it reflects some elements of reality, ... it is nothing but a folktale.'[16] Later he concedes that we can see it as 'a folktale with some realistic elements in it'.[17] Fikre based this uncompromising assessment on a number of considerations. First of all, 'a realistic writer has his [sic] setting in a historically defined place and time', while Ləbb Wälläd Tarik is set in an 'indefinite period of time' and 'indefinite place'.[18] Secondly, the plot is packed with implausible coincidences: 'There are too few truthful details in it.'[19] It is not believable, for example, that the infidel king invades the country a second time, when he could have subjugated after his previous victory.[20] This implausibility extends to the characters: 'The physical and psychological conditions of the characters are not portrayed in detail.'[21] For example, it is unclear in which religion the infidel king believes. If he is Muslim, Fikre argues, it is not credible that his soldiers are seen drinking alcohol.[22] Characters are just 'puppets' that 'fulfil the wish of the author' and 'do not have [their] own personality'.[23]

Fikre Tolossa exemplifies the tendency to read literary history through the lens of modernization theory. This framework assumes all literatures evolve following a unilinear pattern of development, with realism as the universally valid developmental target. As a result, Amharic literature is analysed in an evolutionistic way, from early, 'primitive' attempts to a growing command of realism as the key literary technique. This type of

---

[15]Fikre Tolossa, 'Realism and Amharic literature (1908–1981)', unpublished PhD thesis, University of Bremen, 1983, p. 37.
[16]Ibid., p. 58.
[17]Ibid., p. 65.
[18]Ibid., pp. 58–9.
[19]Ibid., p. 62.
[20]Ibid., p. 61.
[21]Ibid., p. 62.
[22]Ibid., p. 63.
[23]Ibid., p. 64.

criticism appraises Ethiopian literature in relation to the literary history and aesthetic values of the Western 'centre', and normatively judges its progress on the author's acquisition of a toolkit of literary techniques and formulae. Literary progress is then conceived as the gradual acquisition of specific literary competences and the progressive rectification of early faults and mistakes, leading to the step-by-step accomplishment of a realist style. *Labb Wällad Tarik* tries to be a novel but fails because it retains too many local, traditional narrative features. For Fikre, the ultimate goal of Amharic literary evolution is exogenous: literary modernity has already been accomplished elsewhere, and Amharic writers need to catch up. This diffusionist argument is strikingly similar to Moretti's position in 'Conjectures'. Moretti would likely understand *Labb Wällad Tarik* as an example of that 'unstable compromise' between Western form and local content, which he considers typical of the delayed beginning of the novelistic tradition in the world's literary peripheries.

Fikre Tolossa's dissertation was met with a wide degree of critical scepticism, not least on the part of Fikre's own thesis examiner Lanfranco Ricci, who published a cutting review of Fikre's work in the academic journal *Rassegna di Studi Etiopici*. Ricci takes issue with Fikre's prescriptive attitude, arguing he is 'imprisoned' in his definition of realism as 'verisimilitude' and that he normatively applies it to Amharic literature in an 'unnatural' and 'unsustainable' way.[24] The polemic was later expanded and amplified by Taye Assefa and Yonas Admassu. Both Taye and Yonas call for a context-sensitive approach to the study of Amharic literature, able to critically contextualize a text within the aesthetic parameters, sociological functions, genre and style conventions typical of its socio-historical environment.[25] The critic must understand the text from within its narrative and stylistic premises: why did the author make these narrative and stylistic choices? Literary criticism should analyse the text for what it is, not for what it ought to be.[26] The task of the critic is to explain, not to judge, the author's choices and to appraise the text as the author created it.[27] Top-down, prescriptive critical attitudes distort the interpretation of the text and risk lending support to Eurocentric literary assumptions on the cultural 'backwardness' of the peripheries.

In this sense, the arguments advanced by Yonas and Taye can be taken as *ante litteram* rejoinders to Moretti's 'law of literary evolution'. 'The significance of [*Labb Wällad Tarik*] in its social context,' Yonas laments, 'seems to have been either little understood, or simply considered not worth

---

[24]Lanfranco Ricci, 'Review of Realism and Amharic Literature (1908–1981) by Fikre Tolossa', *Rassegna di Studi Etiopici*, vol. 30 (1984–6): 202–6, 203–4.
[25]Admassu, 'The First-Born of Amharic Fiction', p. 96.
[26]Yonas Admassu, 'On the State of Amharic Literary Scholarship', *Journal of Ethiopian Studies*, vol. 34, no. 1 (2001): 25–41, 35.
[27]Ibid., p. 38.

the serious interpretative effort it really deserves. ... Isolated instances in the book have been taken out of context and subjected to "criticisms" in a rather prescriptive fashion'.[28] Taye argues that Fikre's understanding of realism as verisimilitude is in itself conceptually problematic, since there is no single, permanent and unchanging 'truth' on which authors, readers and characters can agree.[29] If we privilege the attempt to understand the *text* over the attempt to find a universally valid *law* or *model* then the whole issue of realism and genre labels suddenly appears inconsequential. Yonas brushes it off in unambiguous terms: 'The question of whether Ṭobbya is written in the "realistic" mode or not is hardly relevant to the interpretation I am trying to offer.'[30] We learn very little by admitting that the text does not meet the conventional definition of the novel: 'One may go as far as to say that, when it comes to particular texts, the attempt to freeze them in a rigid fashion into one or the other of the genres may simply be futile.'[31] Against such a prescriptive approach, we need to read *Ləbb Wällad Tarik* as a text with 'a definite moral purpose', which should direct the critic to an analysis of 'how the [narrative] details contribute to the formal structure as well as to the moral content of the work'.[32] Taye notes that the text is self-conscious about the implausibility of some of its events, and does indeed carefully instruct the readers on when and how to suspend their disbelief.[33] The story is set up so as to logically anticipate events to come. Fikre, for instance, argued that it is implausible for the infidel king to invade the land a second time, but the opening alerted the reader to the notion of the wars between Christians and infidels as cyclical. In other words, *Ləbb Wällad Tarik* is constructed according to an internal narrative rationale that remains coherent throughout. Taye and Yonas agree that this internal logic is encapsulated by the epigraph and the coda, which should be read as 'naturalising devices'[34] and 'twin codes'[35] with which to interpret the story. As is made clear when reading the epigraph and coda together, the principle behind the structural organization of the text is a religious ideology that prizes generosity and gratitude, and 'the verisimilitude of the frequent coincidences and other extraordinary events cannot be appreciated apart from this context'.[36] The plot unfolds according to the notion of divine predetermination, which is then not only the text's ultimate message but

---

[28] Yonas, 'The First-Born', p. 96.
[29] Taye, 'Form and Content', p. 72.
[30] Yonas, 'The First-Born', p. 98.
[31] Ibid., p. 111.
[32] Ibid., p. 98.
[33] Taye, 'Form and Content', p. 73.
[34] Ibid., pp. 74–5.
[35] Yonas, 'The First-Born', p. 101.
[36] Taye, 'Form and Content', p. 71.

also its narrative backbone. For the characters, 'irrespective of whether it appears to be causally motivated or merely the work of chance, ... every occurrence is equally and without distinction a manifestation of [God's] mysterious will'.[37]

A diffusionist reading of Ləbb Wällåd Tarik would be flawed on at least two major counts. Firstly, this is not a text that understands itself as 'peripheral' in any way; and secondly, this is a profoundly modern text, not a delayed response to an allegedly European literary modernity. Designed in the short term to teach Italian students about Ethiopia and its language (although with an Ethiopian audience in mind for the long term), Ləbb Wällåd Tarik does not betray any sense of global peripherality. Afäwärq makes full use of the range of linguistic possibilities of the Amharic language, creating a rich, flowery syntax that only advanced students of Amharic would have been able to penetrate lexically and grammatically. The context in which the text was composed is the opposite of the story we often hear in postcolonial studies – of the writer from the colony forced to learn the language of their colonizers, 'writing back' to their oppressors in that language. Ləbb Wällåd Tarik educates Europeans about Ethiopia, without making any attempts to appease a European readership. As a university textbook, it is written in challenging Amharic; it does not explain any of its references; and it is unapologetically nationalist in its description of Ethiopia as God's nation. Afäwärq does not make his European readers comfortable and forces them to labour to access the text. Afäwärq, of course, knew that his country was looked down upon in Europe as marginal and backwards, but does not seem to give this a second thought. This is also evident from his formal choices: Ləbb Wällåd Tarik is not a refunctionalization of the European novel inspired by 'local materials' but rather a refunctionlization of the tarikä nägäst for a global era, in which the expatriate intellectual must use their heart (i.e. their imagination) rather than their eyes (i.e. their hands-on experience) to convey moral truths of God and empire.

Afäwärq would have likely not hesitated to consider Ləbb Wällåd Tarik somehow 'realist' for the way the plot (like reality for those who believe in the Christian God) is predetermined by divine providence. The encoding of Christian teleology in the literary texture of Ləbb Wällåd Tarik is far from pre-modern either. On the contrary, it is precisely through that theology that Ethiopia, according to Afäwärq, could position itself at the forefront of modernity. This is also the political message of the text: a firm reassertion of Ethiopia's centrality to world history, from its past glories to its divinely ordained destiny of greatness. In this sense, Ləbb Wällåd Tarik helps to challenge the Eurocentric timeline that informs diffusionist models

---

[37]Ibid., p. 70.

of world literature – one that tends to equate modernity with the West. The conceptualization of modernity as a European product, achieved via a set of intrinsic cultural qualities that non-Europeans do not possess, is perhaps the quintessential definition of Eurocentrism. Both global history and global intellectual history have, in recent years, built a solid corpus of scholarship that goes against this conception, showing how modernity, both in its socio-economic and in its intellectual components, was transnationally co-constituted in its origin and subsequent trajectories. This scholarship allows us to reframe Ləbb Wällädä Tarik not as a derivative text that responds to an intrinsically Western modernity but as a part and parcel of those sociopolitical processes and ideas that co-constituted modernity transnationally.

Conclusions: Critical and theoretical legacies

The politics and ethics of literary criticism put forward by Yonas Admassu and Taye Assefa are vital contributions to current debates on world literature. These two critics push back against the uncritical assumption that the Western critical vocabulary has a universal application. They caution against Fikre Tolossa's (and by extension Moretti's) assumptions about the 'portability' and 'translatability' of texts, which risks assimilating them, and thus flattening them, to make them fit (or not) into a unified general theory of world literature. Cartographic and topological models of world literature aspire to a universalism that, under its scientific (Darwinian, for Moretti) façade, relies in fact on unexamined Eurocentric expectations about what a 'novel' is, what 'realism' is, what is 'foreign' or 'local' and what is 'stable' or 'unstable'. Some critical terminology might have easy equivalents in other intellectual traditions, but we must not assume an a priori conceptual translatability. If anything, the scholar of world literature should begin precisely by putting their own critical vocabulary under scrutiny. A text like Ləbb Wällädä Tarik should be appraised through its own internal conceptual and linguistic categories and intertextual frames of reference. Only by doing so can we avoid the 'hubris of the zero point', in the words of decolonial theorist Santiago Castro-Gomez. Comparativism is at its most rigorous and effective when it rejects this hubris and recognizes both the opacity of texts and the difficulties of the interpretative process.

Yonas Admassu and Taye Assefa also reject the normative, prescriptive and predictive models of transnational literary analysis and persuasively advocate a context-sensitive, situated and bottom-up literary criticism. Why debate whether Ləbb Wällädä Tarik is a novel or not, given that Afäwärq has clearly instructed the reader that he is writing a 'history from the heart'?

Yonas and Taye are openly uninterested in abstract, overarching models. It is unhelpful, if not outright misleading, to approach Lɔbb Wälläd Tarik with the objective of proving or disproving laws of literary evolution, teleologies of literary development or general models of global literary circulation. Moreover, the positivist search for a 'law of literary evolution' is not only unproductive but impossible. As soon as we follow literary trajectories on the ground, the pictures that emerge are too messy, partial and heterogeneous to fit neatly into universal laws. The messiness and heterogeneity of literary trajectories should be, on the contrary, embraced as evidence of the rich and complex networks of people, texts and power relations that defined literary transnationalism in the modern era. This is a plurality that actively resists being organized in a unilinear history, a single map, a single conceptual vocabulary, a predictive evolutionary law. This irreducible messiness, though, should not be considered to undermine the project of world literature, or to prevent world literature from delivering on its disciplinary promises. Far from holding the discipline back, not knowing is an ethical stance that immensely enriches the discipline.

From this point of view, then, the objectives of world literature as a discipline can be flipped on their head. Most publications that are in dialogue with the discipline nowadays tend to take both the 'world' and 'literature' for granted, and focus on developing a methodology or, as we have seen, a model, to bring the two together. However, resisting what Alessio Mattana calls the 'allure of the synthesis' allows us to reframe the 'world' and 'literature' as the end goals of world literature, not its unexamined starting points. World literature would then become a way to interrogate how certain actors, in their specific socio-historical context, imagined, conceptualized and narrated the 'world' through 'literature' and how literary production was affected by transnational political and economic phenomena. This is what I have attempted to do in this chapter by showing how Lɔbb Wälläd Tarik addresses the political imperatives of an unequal world through new genres, plots and epistemologies.

Bibliography

There are no surnames as such in the Ethiopian naming system, so Ethiopian authors are listed by their first name followed by their father's name, as common in Ethiopian studies.

Afäwärq Gäbrä-Iyyäsus (1908), *Lɔbb Wälläd Tarik*, Rome. Republished in 1958 in a new Amharic edition, Addis Ababa, Commercial Printing Press. First published in English in *Ethiopian Observer* (1964), trans. Tadesse Tamrat (see below).

Afäwärq Gäbrä-Iyyäsus (1909), *Dagmawi Mɔnilɔk Nɔgusä Nägäst Zältyopya*, Rome.

Casanova, Pascale (2004), *The World Republic of Letters*, Cambridge, MA: Harvard University Press.
Castro-Gomez, Santiago (2021), *Zero-Point Hubris: Science, Race, and Enlightenment in 18th Century Latin America*, London: Rowman & Littlefield.
Conrad, Sebastian (2012), 'Enlightenment in Global History: A Historiographical Critique', *American Historical Review*, vol. 117, no. 4: 999–1027.
Damrosch, David (2003), *What Is World Literature?* Princeton, NJ: Princeton University Press.
Fikre Tolossa (1983), 'Realism and Amharic Literature (1908–1981)', unpublished PhD thesis, University of Bremen.
Fusella, Luigi (1951), 'Il "Lebb Wållad Tārik"' ['The "Ləbb Wälläd Tarik"'], *Rassegna di Studi Etiopici*, vol. 10: 56–70.
Liu, Andrew (2020), *Tea War: A History of Capitalism in China and India*, New Haven, CT: Yale University Press.
Mattana, Alessio (2020), 'The Allure of Synthesis: Science and the Literary in Comparative and World Literature', *Comparative Critical Studies*, vol. 17, no. 3: 351–72.
Moretti, Franco (2000), 'Conjectures on World Literature', *New Left Review*, vol. 1: 55–67.
Orsini, Francesca (2015), 'The Multilingual Local in World Literature', *Comparative Literature*, vol. 67, no. 4: 345–74.
Ricci, Lanfranco (1984–6), 'Review of "Realism and Amharic Literature (1908–1981)" by Fikre Tolossa', *Rassegna di Studi Etiopici*, vol. 30: 202–6.
Tadesse Tamrat (1964), 'Tobbya', *Ethiopian Observer*, vol. 8, no. 3: 242–67.
Taye Assefa (1995), 'The Form and Content of the First Amharic Novel', in *Silence Is Not Golden: A Critical Anthology of Ethiopian Literature*, ed. Taddesse Adera and Ali Jimale Ahmed, Lawrenceville, NJ: Red Sea Press, pp. 61–92.
Teshale Tibebu (1995), *The Making of Modern Ethiopia 1896–1974*, Lawrenceville, NJ: Red Sea Press.
Warwick Research Collective (2015), *Combined and Uneven Development: Towards a New Theory of World Literature*, Liverpool: Liverpool University Press.
Yonas Admassu (1995), 'The First-Born of Amharic Fiction', in *Silence Is Not Golden: A Critical Anthology of Ethiopian Literature*, ed. Taddesse Adera and Ali Jimale Ahmed, Lawrenceville, NJ: Red Sea Press, pp. 93–112.
Yonas Admassu (2001), 'On the State of Amharic Literary Scholarship', *Journal of Ethiopian Studies*, vol. 34, no. 1: 25–41.

6

The Kaiser, Angoche and the world at large: Swahili poetry from Mozambique as world (war) literature

Clarissa Vierke and Chapane Mutiua

Introduction

Though the term 'world literature' may seem to denote a welcoming project – opening up views on literature in, from and about the world – in practice, literature has measured its 'worldliness' primarily with reference to Western modernity. Literary history has often been written in unilinear ways, mostly taking the Western novel (as written in a few European languages) as the only starting (as well as end) point of its investigation.[1] In the context of African literature, the postcolonial paradigm has imposed a similarly teleological history. It has created a rigid dichotomy between 'traditional' oral literature in African languages tied to a circumscribed community on the one hand, and 'modern' literature mostly written in the former colonial languages, on the other, as Karin Barber has pointed out. The postcolonial narrative

---

[1] For a criticism, see, for instance, Francesca Orsini, 'The Multilingual Local in World Literature', *Comparative Literature*, vols 6/7, no. 4 (2015): 345–74; Eric Hayot, *On Literary Worlds* (Oxford: Oxford University Press, 2012), pp. 1–6.

relegates the 'traditional' in African languages to a primordial past, writing it out of social and literary history.[2]

In this chapter, we suggest an alternative approach to 'world' and 'literature', concentrating on a long poem, the *Kaisa* ('Kaiser'), that narrates the wide world from a remote town in northern Mozambique. We – an historian and a scholar of African literatures – came across the poem in 2015, when we were conducting research on Swahili poetry in the area, both orally performed and preserved in deteriorating manuscripts in Arabic script. The existence of a poem in the Swahili language with a title referring to the German Kaiser and narrating world history from the outlook of contemporary northern Mozambique – cut off from the world since its disastrous civil war – surprised us. We decided to translate the poem with the help of an important local scribe and performer, the late Fundi Halide.[3] The poem aids critically rethinking some of the assumptions outlined above; as we will show, it questions the narrow dichotomy of 'traditional' and 'modern', 'local' and 'global' and the notion that a globalized world can only be narrated in newly adapted literary genres from the West. It urges us to consider many possible conceptual pathways to take, a multitude of literary histories and many ways to imagine worlds.

Not only has the 'literature' in world literature been defined too narrowly, the term 'world' has a similar problem, much like the 'world' in 'First World War'. Particularly in the last two decades, critical historians of global history have fought for a global perspective on the First World War, since the Great War was less a war of nations than of colonial empires, as Michael Pesek underlines.[4] Increasing effort has been made to recognize not only the participation of non-European (particularly Asian and African) soldiers in the horrors of the European trench battles but also battlefields outside the West, East Africa included.[5] Articulating the war's connection with imperialism and colonialism (particularly neglected in the case of

---

[2] Karin Barber, 'African-Language Literature and Postcolonial Criticism', *Research in African Literatures*, vol. 26, no. 4 (1995): 3–28.

[3] We are greatly indebted to the late Fundi Halide, with whom we collaborated on the translation of this poem, and Eugeniusz Rzewuski, who drew our attention to the *Kaisa*. Furthermore, we want to thank Chale Musa and Senhor Braimo Alfane (Ncocottoko) of Mozambique Island for also discussing the poem with us, as well as Mahmoud Mau of Lamu, who engaged with us on the notion of *dunia*. A grant from the Fritz Thyssen foundation provided us with the means to travel to Angoche in 2015, and the 'Africa Multiple' Cluster of Excellence (funded by the *Deutsche Forschungsgemeinschaft*) with the environment to work on the text. We are grateful to Kristen de Joseph for commenting on and proofreading the text.

[4] Michael Pesek, *Das Ende eines Kolonialreiches: Ostafrika im Ersten Weltkrieg* (Frankfurt: Campus, 2010), pp. 7–10; see also Sebastian Conrad, Andreas Eckert and Ulrike Freitag (eds), *Globalgeschichte: Theorien, Ansätze, Themen* (Frankfurt: Campus, 2007).

[5] See, for instance, the great volume Heike Liebau, Katrin Bromber, Katharina Lange, Dyala Hamzah and Ravi Ahuja (eds), *The World in Wars: Experiences, Perceptions and Perspectives from Africa and Asia* (Leiden: Brill, 2010).

German and Portuguese colonialism) by including African perspectives and sources on the war have become important concerns. The historian Frederick Cooper argues for a more 'searching examination', 'watching out for dynamics and ambivalences' and focusing on the 'efforts of colonized intellectuals' to work across the 'colony-metropole divide' – which also speaks to our arguments in this contribution.[6] As we will show, the *Kaisa*'s poetic agenda is not to represent the world from a local perspective, whose contours are clear, but to offer a poetic imagination of a dynamic world map of both colony and metropole.

Angoche seems to best satisfy Cooper's interest in shifting away from colonies, empires and nations as clearly delineated territories, since it has been part of both changing and overlapping world maps. Angoche – a thriving industrial harbour in the 1970s, right after independence; reduced to a village during the Mozambican civil war; and now on the margin of the Mozambican nation – used to be an important Swahili sultanate and a hub of Indian Ocean trade from the fifteenth to the early twentieth century. It also sat at the edge of several empires, as articulated in the poem. Politically situated in Portuguese East Africa but controlled by British Nyasaland at the beginning of the twentieth century, the region became a brutal war zone where a mostly British alliance fought a never-ending war against German troops. On both sides, the majority of soldiers were African.

We take the *Kaisa* not only as reflecting changing political maps but also (building on Eric Hayot's notion of 'literary worlds') as an 'aesthetic world' and hence a narrative 'approach to world'.[7] The poem relates to experiences of the First World War in East Africa, and does not merely document historical events (as no text ever does) but narrates its own 'diegetic totality' of the First World War: 'Aesthetic worlds ... are among other things always a relation to and theory of the lived world.'[8] Thus, 'world' is also an effect of the poem, which makes it perceptible through its own literary and conceptual means – largely tied, as we will argue, to the *utenzi* genre. There is a dialectic relationship – Hayot calls it an 'aesthetic worldedness' – between the poem's world and the 'extradiegetic world' outside the narrative.[9] Taking inspiration from Beecroft's notion of literary ecologies, which focuses on the link between changing polities and literary forms of 'aesthetic self-representation', we will consider the political maps that Angoche has been part of and the aesthetic world of the *Kaisa* in relation to the literary language, Swahili, and the literary genre, the *utenzi*.[10]

---

[6] Frederick Cooper, *Colonialism in Question: Theory, Knowledge, History* (Berkeley: University of California Press, 2005), pp. 6, 14, 15.
[7] Hayot, *On Literary Worlds*, p. 44.
[8] Ibid.
[9] Ibid., p. 45.
[10] Alexander Beecroft, *An Ecology of World Literature: From Antiquity to the Present Day* (New York: Verso, 2015), p. 105.

The *Kaisa*

The *Kaisa* is a Swahili poem that has been recited in northern Mozambique since the beginning of the twentieth century, passed down in manuscripts written in Arabic script; its orality and written-ness do not exclude each other. We have found three manuscripts of the *Kaisa*, two from Angoche and one, largely damaged, from Mozambique Island. The manuscript from Angoche that we worked with presumably dates from the 1970s and was written on a spare colonial administrative register, which provided the scribe with neat columns into which he could fit the metrically strict verses of the *Kaisa* (see Figures 6.1 and 6.2). It has 317 pages and 1,585 stanzas. A recitation of it – such as we witnessed parts of – would take at least three nights. On both Mozambique Island and Angoche, recitation has become rare, but it was very popular in the 1950s. The recitation of the poem by two performers, chanting it in an antiphonal style while a third performer translates the poem *ex tempore* into the local language, Ekoti (not unlike film dubbing), attracted huge audiences at that time. Swahili is a language which an Ekoti audience did not and does not easily understand. However, as Fundi Halide explained, Swahili has been a prestigious language, reserved for literary and religious recitations and writing, providing windows onto a wider world – an aspect to which we will return.

At the beginning of the narrative poem, composed in an Ekoti-inflected Swahili, the 'king of the world' (*mfalume duniani*, p. 6), the 'sultan of Istanbul' (*Sultani Rumu*, p. 10), sends a telegram to invite all the 'pagan kings' (*wafaume wakufari*, p. 6) to a banquet: the Japanese, the British, the Austrian, the Belgian, the Russian, the Bulgarian, the American, the German Kaiser, the British Kingi and Lapuliyao (Napoleon). The atmosphere is cheerful, the guests dancing and drinking, until the sultan asks *Aliyo hapa nani mweziwe kumuhofia* ('Who among you here is afraid of the other?' p. 29). They all answer that they fear only the sultan. However, the German Kaiser announces that he wants to conquer 'the country of the French' (p. 30). All the 'kings of the world tremble' (*Wafaume wa dunia / wote wakazizima*, p. 30); and everybody departs in a hurry.

Back in France, Lapuliyao consults with his ministers, prepares *manuwari*[11] ('warships') and cannons and recruits soldiers (p. 38) from various parts of Portuguese East Africa, British Central Africa, the Belgian Congo and Madagascar to come to Poripo (Bordeaux) and Marisea (Marseille). He sends a letter to the Kaiser in Hambo (Hamburg) seeking revenge (pp. 43–54). The sea battle fought in Swisi (Switzerland) is fierce: ships explode, and thousands die. With the French troops utterly defeated, the Kaiser celebrates in Hamburg. While the French assemble new troops, the Kaiser bombards

---

[11]Derived from English 'man-of-war'.

THE KAISER, ANGOCHE AND THE WORLD AT LARGE

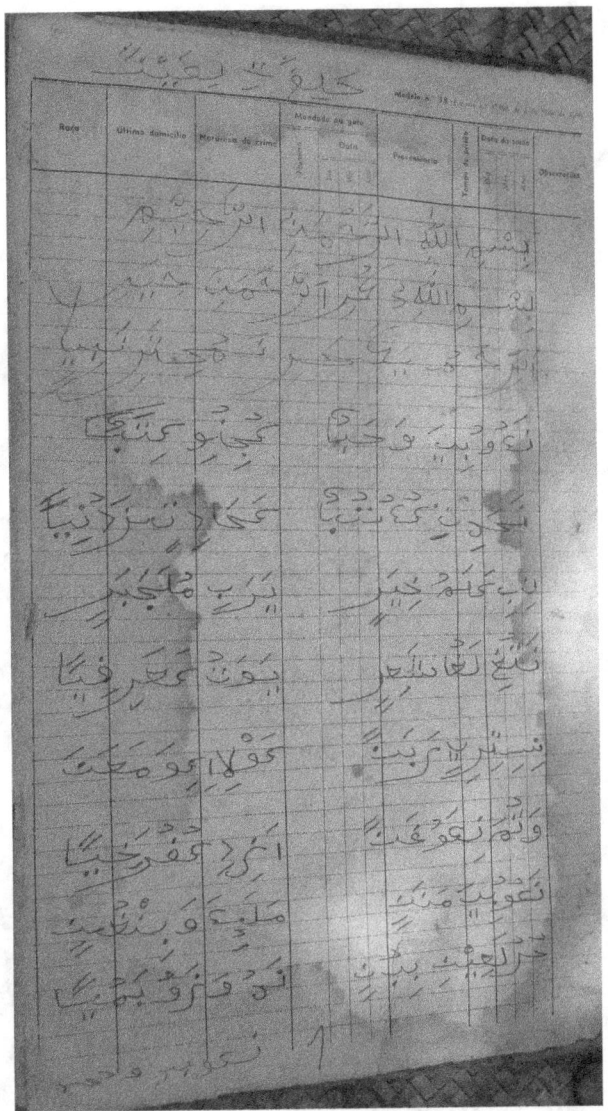

FIGURE 6.1 *Page 3 of the Kaisa written by Fundi Halide.*

Paris; thousands are wounded or die in the spreading fire. A new sea battle starts with a volley of strikes. Both sides continuously recruit new soldiers to wage increasingly large battles, and the list of fallen soldiers grows longer and longer. When Napoleon finally gives up – 'the war is over for me' (*hurubu umenishia*, p. 127), he demands that the British king (Kingi) buy him out and pay for his losses: *Munilipe marekebu aliyokwangamia* ('Pay

FIGURE 6.2 *Fundi Halide holding the register.*

me for my sunken warships', p. 131). Kingi pays 'three sacks of pounds' (*pauni junia tatu*, p. 141) to Lapuliyao in Marisea, and prepares for war, calling on troops from across British Nyasaland (now Malawi), while the Kaiser also assembles his troops (p. 165).

Another great sea battle breaks out between 'the German' (*Lamao*) and 'the British' (*Waingereza*) troops, with soldiers from 'Lake Meru up to Gorongoza' (*Mweru hata Kelengezi*, p. 176) and 'crowds from Tanganyika' (*kaumu ya Tanganyika*, p. 176) joining in. The British prevail; the German commanders escape to Austria. In Hamburg, the Kaiser's wife Lihuwara assembles an army of soldiers as 'vast as the sea' (*mitili kana bahari*), who kill many of the advancing British troops. Kingi sends a messenger to the British headquarters in Mesheke (Manchester, p. 195)[12] asking for more soldiers.

The battle resumes 'in the bush' (*mwituni*), where soldiers fall or die of hunger – since 'there is no food' (*wala chakula hapana*, p. 278) – until both sides decide to lay down their arms for a few days. The Kaiser finally gives the order to attack the queen's palace in Mesheke (p. 287). When the soldiers fail to break through the British defence, they call on the Kaiser to send General Rito (probably General Lettow-Vorbeck) with *matowpito* ('torpedoes') to set the town on fire (p. 305). The poem ends abruptly with a bitter fight between the troops led by Bwana Chande – the British army's last resort – and the Germans under Rito. With the help of new 'machine guns' (*bunduki za mariti*), Rito wipes out whole areas, so that *tamboni hapana watu, watu hata watoto wote wamangamia* ('There is no one on the battlefield; all the adults and children have perished', p. 316).

Dynamic Swahili worlds: Changing maps and literary worlds

We will first enter the Kaiser's world in Angoche through the lens of its literary language, Swahili – which reflects the changing coastal 'ecologies'[13] – and its genre, the *utenzi*, which has provided a template from which to write changing worlds' histories.

While Swahili has been the first language of many, and a second or third language of even more people on the East African coast – the so-called 'Swahili coast', which stretches from Barawa in present-day Somalia to ancient Sofala in Mozambique – since at least the end of the first millennium, it has been most broadly diffused from the nineteenth century onwards. In a seemingly paradoxical way, at the time when the Omani sultan moved his throne from Muscat to Zanzibar, and at a time of increasing European influence, neither Arabic nor the colonizer's languages (Portuguese, English or German) began to dominate. Rather, Swahili became a transregional, cosmopolitan language of trade and communication more than ever, all

---

[12]We are not absolutely sure that Mesheke is referring to Manchester.
[13]Beecroft, *An Ecology of World Literature*, p. 105.

along the Swahili coast, extending into the continent along the caravan routes and into the Indian Ocean to Madagascar, Yemen and Oman.

Swahili also became a language of Islamic learning and poetry in Arabic script in the nineteenth century. From the Lamu archipelago in northern Kenya to northern Mozambique, Swahili largely supplanted Arabic – both in poetry and religious learning – which, for an elite of well-trained scholars, had been the exclusive language of scholarly and theological exchange for centuries. The rise of Swahili as a literary and religious language and the growth of a body of Swahili poetic manuscripts are closely linked with the growing importance of Sufi brotherhoods from the eighteenth century onwards and their vision to popularize Islamic education.[14] For them, poetry was considered a particularly appealing way to reach out to different parts of the population uneducated in Arabic or the Islamic canon of learning. With ardent fervour, the most renowned scholars, well versed in Arabic, occupied themselves with written translations (or rather, creative adaptations) into Swahili.[15]

The largest body of written adaptations of Arabic source texts from the eighteenth to the nineteenth century is linked to the *Kaisa*'s poetic genre, the *utenzi* (pl. *tenzi*), which, though meant for recitation, became closely linked with manuscript writing.[16] The *utenzi*, a genre defined by strict verse prosody, either provides a catalogue of moral conduct or, like the *Kaisa*, dramatizes historical events. The earliest narrative *tenzi* typically narrated battles against opponents of Islam during the Prophet's lifetime – such as the *Utendi wa Tambuka* ('The Poem of Tambuka') dating to 1728 and sometimes considered the oldest *utenzi*, which dramatizes the struggle against the Byzantine Emperor Heraklios.[17] Providing a broad population a struggle with which they could identify and kindling a new religious zeal in them (also against Christian missionary activities), the *utenzi* poets recounted the struggles of the Islamic prophets, such as Abdurahman prevailing against an array of enemies, or parts of the Prophet Muhammad's life.[18]

---

[14] Randall Pouwels, 'The East African Coast, c. 780 to 1900 C.E.', in *The History of Islam in Africa*, ed. Nehemia Levtzion and Randall Pouwels (Athens: Ohio University Press, 2000), pp. 251–72, 261–6.

[15] Ibid., p. 270. See also Clarissa Vierke, 'From across the Ocean: Considering Travelling Literary Figurations as Part of Swahili Intellectual History', *Journal of African Cultural Studies*, vol. 28, no. 2 (2016): 225–40.

[16] Clarissa Vierke, *On the Poetics of the* Utendi: *A Critical Edition of the Nineteenth-Century Swahili Poem 'Utendi wa Haudaji' Together with a Stylistic Analysis* (Münster: Lit, 2011), pp. 51–3.

[17] *Utendi* is a dialect variation of *utenzi*. For an edition, see Jan Knappert, 'Het epos van Heraklios: Een proeve van Swahili poëzie', unpublished PhD thesis, Leiden University, 1958; Carl Meinhof, 'Chuo cha Herkal', *Zeitschrift für Kolonialsprachen*, vol. 2 (1911/12): 1–16, 108–36, 194–232, 261–96.

[18] For a synthetic overview, see Vierke, 'From across the Ocean'.

As the wave of Sufi reform spread southwards, *tenzi* manuscripts travelled with it: originally composed on the Lamu archipelago, a centre of textual production at the north of the coast (in present-day Kenya), *tenzi* soon reached Zanzibar, the leading hub under Omani rule, which attracted many Islamic scholars; via the Comoros, the *utenzi* continued travelling to Mozambique, including Angoche, which 'by the beginning of the twentieth century was a major center for Islamic activity' for the whole region.[19] In this context, Swahili became a language of poetic composition and was taught at newly founded Qur'anic schools.[20] This was not the first time Swahili had appeared on the Mozambican coast. While the larger Swahili world was important in the early history of the coastal towns – Angoche has its origin in the ancient city state of Kilwa – the arrival of the Portuguese in the fifteenth century disrupted broader coastal links. Like other so-called Swahili languages in the area, Ekoti, the language of Angoche, reflects this history: while Swahili left an early imprint on its basic vocabulary, its structure has largely been influenced by Emakhuwa, the major Bantu language of the area.[21] Ekoti is not mutually intelligible with Swahili (and Swahili needs to be translated in performances of the *Kaisa*). However, for many on the Mozambican coast (as well as on the Comoros and Madagascar) in the eighteenth and particularly the nineteenth century, Swahili was a second or third language, used for communication as well as a symbol of a translocal East African Muslim identity.

This kind of newly emerging common Muslim identity on the East African coast was also nurtured by *tenzi* narratives. Drawing on Ricci's study of Islamic texts in South and South-East India, one can conceive of *tenzi* as texts that formed a translocal 'literary network' or 'literary cosmopolis' that mirrored scholarly networks and 'connected Muslims across the boundaries of space and culture'.[22] This literary network gave a sense of belonging to the same translocal Muslim community, providing them with a set of shared

---

[19]Edward Alpers, 'A Complex Relationship: Mozambique and the Comoro Islands in the Nineteenth and Twentieth Centuries', *Cahiers d'Etudes Africaines*, vol. 41, no. 161 (2001): 85; Anne Bang, *Islamic Sufi Networks in the Western Indian Ocean (c. 1880–1940): Ripples of Reform* (Leiden: Brill, 2014), pp. 54, 55; Liazzat Bonate, 'Tradition and Transition: Islam and Chiefship in Northern Mozambique, ca. 1850–1975', unpublished PhD thesis, University of Cape Town, 2007.
[20]Alpers, 'A Complex Relationship', p. 85; Chapane Mutiua, 'O Islão e o Processo de Literacia no Norte de Moçambique entre os finais do século XIX e princípios do século XX', in *A Ciência ao Serviço do Desenvolvimento? Experiência de Países Africanos Falantes da Língua Oficial Portuguesa*, ed. Teresa Cruz e Silva and Isabel Maria Casimiro (Dakar: CODESRIA, 2015), pp. 205–19.
[21]Thilo Schadeberg and Francisco Mucanheia, *EKoti: The Maka or Swahili Language of Angoche* (Cologne: Köppe, 2000). On the nineteenth-century context and the spread of literacy, see Mutiua, 'O Islão', pp. 205–10.
[22]Ronit Ricci, *Islam Translated: Literature, Conversion, and the Arabic Cosmopolis of South and Southeast Asia* (Chicago: University of Chicago Press, 2011), p. 2.

stories, characters and historical and hagiographic accounts – sustaining or adding to existing networks of kinship or trade.[23] More specifically than Arabic referring to a larger Muslim world, the *tenzi* gave emphasis to a Swahili East African Muslim community.[24]

The colonizer did not merely change this world but profited from the Swahili networks and its use as a lingua franca throughout the Western Indian Ocean: after the Portuguese empire, which introduced it for official transoceanic correspondence,[25] German East Africa also adopted it as a language of the lower administration. Furthermore, the colonial administration in German and Portuguese East Africa in the late nineteenth century relied heavily on the same well-educated elite of Islamic scholars, versed in local law and Swahili writing, and trained them to serve in various positions in the colonial administration. The German colonial government emphasized German–Muslim solidarity. Besides hiring predominantly Muslim *askari* (soldiers) for the *Schutztruppe* (the German colonial defence force) and relying on Swahili and Arab traders' knowledge of the interior, they strategically stirred up anti-British sentiment. As the First World War approached – not only in Angoche, as the *Kaisa* shows us, but also in other colonies, like Sudan and East India, and fostered by the alliance of Germany and Austria with the Ottoman Empire on the eve of war – the German Kaiser became a symbolic cult figure of resistance in what was framed as a *jihad* against British and Portuguese imperialism.[26] However, while Islam prospered in German East Africa more than anywhere else, the relationship was not harmonious: much to the concern of the German colonial government, a large number of conversions to Islam among a variety of ethnic groups also happened very much in opposition to colonization, because of its secular education equated with Christianization, its increasing economic and political dominance and colonial violence.[27]

New *tenzi* emerged at that time, reflecting ambivalence about the new colonial world and providing new narratives to identify with. In German

---

[23] Ibid., p. 3.
[24] See Clarissa Vierke and Chapane Mutiua, 'The Poem about the Prophet's Death in Mozambique – Swahili as a Transregional Language of Islamic Poetry', *Journal for Islamic Studies*, vol. 38, no. 2 (2020): 44–74.
[25] Chapane Mutiua, 'Ajami Literacy, Class and Portuguese Precolonial Administration in northern Mozambique, 1861–1913', unpublished PhD thesis, University of Cape Town, 2014; Liazzat Bonate, 'Islam and Literacy in Northern Mozambique: Historical Records on the Secular Uses of Arabic Script', *Islamic Africa*, vol. 7 (2016): 60–80.
[26] On the anti-Portuguese and pro-German sentiment in northern Mozambique at the time and the growth of Islam, see Pesek, *Das Ende eines Kolonialreiches*, pp. 104, 112. Heike Liebau describes how the Kaiser became 'an important symbol of insurgency' among the Oroan communities in Chota Nagpur; see Heike Liebau, '*Kaiser Kii Jay* (Long Live the Kaiser)', in Liebau et al., *The World in Wars*, pp. 251–75.
[27] Pesek, *Das Ende eines Kolonialreiches*, pp. 107–12.

East Africa, a large corpus of historiographic Swahili *tenzi* was composed, partly on German commission, adapting the *utenzi* narrative of faraway Islamic battles to contemporary battles, particularly German military raids and anticolonial insurgencies between 1889 and 1907, like the Maji Maji Rebellion in the *utenzi* of the same name (*Utenzi wa Majimaji*), or the *Utenzi wa Wadachi Kutamalaki Mrima* ('Poem on the German Conquest of the Swahili Coast'), composed around 1889 by the renowned poet Hemedi bin Abdallah of Tanga. Unlike eulogies of the colonial government, both had a critical perspective on increasing colonial violence.[28] Poets in Angoche and Mozambique Island also increasingly explored the *utenzi* as a template for critically reflecting on their own experience of the so-called expansive phase of Portuguese colonization in Mozambique, characterized by brutal military raids in the north with the intention of 'pacifying' the Makhuwa.[29] The *Tambuka*, for instance, was adapted here not to narrate the war of the Prophet against the Byzantine emperor, as in the eighteenth-century *Utendi wa Tambuka*, but to recount, in a tone of parody, the military expeditions of notorious cavalry officer Mouzinho de Albuquerque, a Portuguese colonial hero.[30]

Although the Portuguese arrived in northern Mozambique as early as the fifteenth century, their influence remained restricted to some insular fortified hubs on the coast, nodes in the sea trade with little concern for or authority over the land. Until the late nineteenth century, most of the Muslim rulers of northern Mozambique cherished multidimensional relationships with Zanzibar and the sheikhs of the Comoros, while maintaining relative sovereignty and a vague form of vassalage to the Portuguese government. This is echoed in the scarcity of references to the Portuguese in the *Kaisa*. Only gradually did Portugal attempt to exert more control over the region, which was actually administered by the British Nyasa Company. The vacuum of political control stimulated what René Pelissièr terms the 'German appetite':[31] A German military attack on a border post in August 1914 was part of a strategy to push Portugal into war and profit from the fallout by taking over northern Mozambique. Thus, northern Mozambique suddenly became a contested map, with opposing colonial powers fighting over its shape. Among the *tenzi* recounting the colonial scramble, *Kaisa* became the most popular.

---

[28] All the poems can be found in Gudrun Miehe, Katrin Bromber, Said Khamis and Ralf Grosserhode (eds), *Kala Shairi: German East Africa in Swahili Poems* (Cologne: Köppe, 2002).
[29] See René Pelissiér, *História de Moçambique: Formação e oposição, 1854–1918*, vol. 2 (Lisbon: Editoria Estampa, 1994); J. M. De Albuquerque, *A Campanha contra os Namarrais. Relatórios* (Lisbon: Imprensa Nacional, 1897); Nancy J. Hafkin, 'Trade, Society, and Politics in Northern Mozambique, ca. 1753–1913', unpublished PhD thesis, Boston University, 1973.
[30] We are working on a text edition of the *Tambuka*.
[31] Pelissièr, *História de Moçambique*, pp. 394–5.

The battles taking place 'in the bush' in the last part of the poem seem to refer to the guerrilla war waged by the notorious German General Lettow-Vorbeck (Rito in the *Kaisa*), which largely devastated the area between 1916 and 1918. Escaping from the alliance of British, Belgian and later South African troops that outnumbered the Germans by far, he marched the *Schutztruppe* across the Ruvuma, the southern border of German East Africa.[32] Largely through a series of brief attacks and quick escapes ('tip-and-run'), he managed to outsmart his enemies until the end of the war, which left large parts of the area devastated and cost the lives of thousands of African soldiers and civilians: 'The death toll among African soldiers and military carriers recruited from British East Africa alone exceeded 45,000.'[33] More than machine guns,[34] hunger killed the inhabitants of the plundered villages.[35] The *Kaisa* recounts the forced recruitment of local ethnic groups as soldiers and *kariakoo* ('carrier corps'). From the start of the war to the end of 1917, more than a million Africans from the British colonies and German East Africa had been recruited for carrier duty with the British forces alone.[36] Some 14,600 African soldiers, the *askari*, fought in the German *Schutztruppe* alone.

Thus, the dynamic history and map of the Swahili coast and Angoche has been closely linked with the *utenzi* genre, which provided it with an equally dynamic template for narrating a changing world.

Narrating the First World War: How does *Kaisa* narrate *Dunia* ('the world')?

In the following, we want to explore how the poem narrates the 'world'. The *Kaisa* clearly considers itself a narrative of the world. Not only does the narrator claim to depict *urefu wa duniani* ('the extent of the world' or 'the world at large') (p. 4) but *dunia* ('the world', a well-established Arabic loanword in Swahili) recurs with unusual frequency throughout the *Kaisa*.

---

[32]Pesek, *Das Ende eines Kolonialreiches*, pp. 127–8; Tanja Bührer, *Die Kaiserliche Schutztruppe für Deutsch-Ostafrika: Koloniale Sicherheitspolitik und transkulturelle Kriegsführung 1885–1918* (Munich: Oldenbourg, 2011), p. 455.
[33]Edward Paice, *Tip and Run: The Untold Tragedy of the Great War in Africa* (London: Weidenfeld and Nicolson, 2007).
[34]Machine guns, which were first reserved for German soldiers and were a symbol of imperial superiority, were also given to *askari* in the later phase of the war, which afforded the *Schutztruppe* a decisive military advantage (Pesek, *Das Ende eines Kolonialreiches*, p. 70).
[35]For many in northern Mozambique and southern Tanzania, the war was merely a continuation of their experiences with the Maji Maji war (1905–7) or the military raids against the Makhuwa, which ended just two years earlier. See also Pesek, *Das Ende eines Kolonialreiches*, p. 128.
[36]Paice, *Tip and Run*, p. 346; Bührer, *Die Kaiserliche Schutztruppe für Deutsch-Ostafrika*, p. 442.

Dunia carries several shades of meaning that emerge variously in the poem. Like 'world' in the Germanic languages, it is both a spatial and temporal concept.[37] With regard to the former, unlike the sometimes synonymously used Bantu term *ulimwengu* ('universe'), which emphasizes the vertically layered 'cosmos', *dunia* refers more to the surface of the earth in its vast (global) extent, similar to the pictorial image of the world expressed in maps.

The *Kaisa* gives a wide-ranging account of the world. Soldiers come from Portuguese East Africa, British Central Africa, German East Africa, the Belgian Congo – places not only like Mururuli (probably the area of the Lurio river in Mozambique), Kasombe (in the Katanga area of the Congo), Bulantaya (Blantyre in present-day Malawi) and even Nosi Bé on Bukini (Madagascar) but also Poripo (Bordeaux), Marisea, Hambo and Mesheke – Europe is identified largely by its ports. Place names are legion in the *Kaisa* and the panorama constantly shifts: the battlefields rotate over a huge geographical plane between Europe and large parts of East Africa. There is an impression of depicting an entangled world in its widest extent. Hence, the *Kaisa* presents a perspective of what we have come to call a globalized modern world, defined by its connections and 'the intensification of world-wide social relations which link distant localities in such a way that local happenings are shaped by events occurring many miles away and vice versa'.[38]

Global connections also need to be fully delineated: on the one hand, the constant exchange of letters, telegraphed messages and messengers sent out to report on the other side of the world seems to reflect a modern world increasingly connected through media but, on the other, also build on the earlier phenomenon of letter exchange as found in Islamic *tenzi*, which has the benefit of creating a narrative link between the camps of the protagonists and antagonists.[39] The *Kaisa*, like other *tenzi*, narrates connections not only as chains of cause and effect (which, to echo Giddens again, 'link distant localities') but is most prominently concerned with depicting simultaneity, showing what happens at the same time in different parts of the world, relegating nothing to the background. The *Kaisa* hence constitutes what Hayot calls an 'ample' narrative. He introduces the notion of amplitude to define literary worlds by expanding on Auerbach's investigation of

---

[37] Ben Etherington and Jarad Zimbler, 'Introduction', in *The Cambridge Companion to World Literature*, ed. Ben Etherington and Jarad Zimbler (Cambridge: Cambridge University Press, 2018), pp. 1–20, 4; Robert Stockhammer, 'World Literature or Earth Literature? Remarks on a Distinction', in *Re-Mapping World Literature: Writing, Book Markets and Epistemologies between Latin America and the Global South / Escrituras, mercados y epistemologías entre América Latina y el Sur Global*, ed. G. Müller, J. J. Locane and B. Loy (Berlin: De Gruyter, 2018), pp. 211–24, 215.
[38] Anthony Giddens, *The Consequences of Modernity* (Stanford: Stanford University Press, 1990), p. 64.
[39] Vierke, *On the Poetics of the* Utendi, pp. 269–75.

realism in the Old Testament and Homer in terms of the foregrounding and backgrounding of aspects of narration.[40] The *Kaisa* is an ample narrative, because it foregrounds as much as possible: every place and all troops need to be listed, every confrontation is taken to the battlefield. This entails the narrator's constant change of perspective, jumping back and forth between antagonists and protagonists so that nothing remains in the background. After showing, for instance, how the British assemble new troops, the narrator jumps to the German camp, depicting their preparations for war before the two sides meet on the battleground and retreat again. This narrative technique is also found in many other *tenzi* and epic traditions and is a major way to not only build the *utenzi*'s tension but also for depicting the breadth of the connected world, surpassing individual perceptions tied to a smaller lived world.[41]

The *Kaisa* is not a chamber piece but depicts the 'world at large' (p. 4) in the form of a tension-driven grand narrative of enormous scope. It isn't long merely because the war is long, but because length is a prescribed feature of the genre: by definition, an *utenzi* cannot be pithy but presents, according to Shariff, a 'long explanation' (*maelezo marefu*) of historical importance.[42] In terms of its understanding of history, the *Kaisa* suggests a perspective on the world that 'is concerned with the total', to echo Etherington and Zimbler.[43] On the one hand, the poem reflects on historical events, such as the extended guerrilla war 'in the bush'. On the other, everything needs to be spelled out in superlatives that exceed the fuzziness and mediocrity of realism. In narrating the First World War, the *Kaisa* stages French–German confrontations not by depicting the front advancing westwards before becoming mired in disastrous trench battles (as in most European accounts) but by narrating sea battles between the Kaiser and Napoleon, the prototypical conqueror. In depicting the Kaiser as victorious, the *Kaisa* seems to evoke not the First World War but the Franco-Prussian War of the 1870s, including the siege of Paris (whose scenery the *Kaisa* develops in astonishing realism: burning houses, wounded people calling for doctors, overcrowded hospitals). Thus, the *Kaisa* blends several historical confrontations into *the* dramatic narrative of war, which has also been described as a narrative device of *utenzi* more generally.[44] The *Utendi wa Tambuka* made the battle of Tabuk, which probably never took place, seem like a major turning point

---

[40] Hayot, *On Literary Worlds*, p. 57.
[41] Vierke, *On the Poetics of the* Utendi, p. 271; Carol Clover, *The Medieval Saga* (Ithaca, NY: Cornell University Press, 2019), pp. 111–12.
[42] Ibrahim Noor Shariff, *Tungo zetu: Msingi wa mashairi na tungo nyinginezo* (Trenton: Red Sea Press, 1988), p. 94.
[43] Etherington and Zimbler, *Introduction*, p. 4. However, their notion of literary totality is different, namely referring to the totality of verbal art.
[44] Vierke, 'Ocean'.

in Islamic history.⁴⁵ Also the *Kaisa* strives to transcend the particular and the minute: the world and an eternal historic truth need to be narrated.

The *Kaisa* does not understand itself as depicting *a* narrative of a world war but *the* narrative of the world at war. Nothing less than the world at large, the course of history, the 'age of man' is at stake. In its temporal dimension, *dunia*, more generally speaking, refers, firstly, to the *maisha* (life) of an individual, as echoed in idiomatic expressions for 'to die', such as are also found in the *Kaisa*, like 'to lose the world' (*-pwetea dunia*) or 'to leave the world' (*-fariki dunia*, literally 'to die from the world'), for instance, in the verse *umefariki dunia na manuwari pamoya* ('He left the world together with the warships' (p. 123)). Secondly, not unlike the literal etymology of Germanic 'world' as 'age of man',⁴⁶ *dunia*, in a more eschatological Islamic sense, also refers to the destiny of humankind, which will come to an end on the *Siku ya Qiyama*, the Day of Final Judgement, which is also the subject of classical Islamic *tenzi* of the eighteenth and nineteenth centuries.⁴⁷

Though the *Kaisa*, like other colonial *tenzi*, seems to move away from an eschatological reading, defining a *dunia* in the here and now of East Africa in connection with the geographically broad world, it also does not merely leave behind an allegorical reading of the world (war). The many *tenzi* depicting the German incursions between 1889 and 1914 confirm the extent to which the *utenzi* became a template for narrating history, as has been variously shown, documenting new and increasing confrontations, like the gradual conquest of the Swahili coast, the Maji Maji uprising or the raids against the famous Hehe leader Mkwawa.⁴⁸ Colonial *tenzi* have been described as realist, since they document historical events with an astonishing level of historical detail: for instance, the *Utenzi wa Majimaji*'s narrative of the events of the large-scale Maji Maji uprising, which shook the whole south of Tanzania, runs largely parallel to the colonizer's record of events; the *Utenzi wa Vita Vya Wadachi Kutamalaki Mrima* ('The Utenzi of the German Conquest of the Mrima Coast'), by Hemedi bin Abdallah El-Buhry (1850–1928), depicts the resistance efforts on the Mrima coast in 1888 and 1889 under the leadership of the famous Abushiri bin Salim, in which the poet himself participated. Even so, both narratives also offer an allegorical history, continuing the narrative of the eternal struggle of Muslims against their opponents. As Katrin Bromber has shown, Hemedi El-Buhry, who also wrote Islamic *tenzi*, adapted the model of the struggle between Christians

---

⁴⁵Albert Gérard, 'Structure and Values in the Three Swahili Epics', *Research in African Literatures*, vol. 7 (1977): 7–22, 8.
⁴⁶Etherington and Zimbler, *Introduction*, p. 4; Stockhammer, 'World Literature', p. 215.
⁴⁷Like, for instance, the *Utenzi wa Qiyama*; see Roland Allen (ed.), '*Utenzi wa Kiyama (Siku ya Hukumu)* by Hemedi bin Abdallah bin Saidi el-Buhry: Text. With Introduction, Analysis, Translation and Notes', *Special Supplement to Tanganyika Notes and Records*, 1945.
⁴⁸For an overview, see Miehe et al., *Kala Shairi*.

and Muslims to narrate the resistance wars of colonial times:[49] for instance, the sultan is asked to protect local Muslims against the Germans, who are depicted primarily as Christian: 'Protect us in the war against your enemies, who reject your religion and prevent us from worshipping the mighty' (*Tunusuru waja wako / Vita vya adui zako / Wakataa dini yako / Tusiabudu Taaa*).[50] From this perspective, the historiography of war is always also a world history of *the* Islamic war – and hence echoes the allegorical dimension of *dunia*, as the secular or Christian world, encroaching on Islam.

The *Kaisa* itself does not claim to depict the First World War – though all the performers we interviewed insisted that the poem is about this war – but the 'war of the pagans' (*Vita zao makufari*). The way the *Kaisa* speaks of the Europeans is ambivalent, portraying them as great warriors, but also with utter contempt: with names, like *mayahudi* (Jews), *ahali Kuresih* ('the Kureish clan': the enemies of the Prophet during his lifetime) and *malauni* ('the cursed'), the *Kaisa* uses the same vocabulary as the *Utendi wa Tambuka*. Not only do all the fallen Western warriors go directly to hell, but in the parodic parts of the poem, they fill their bellies with pork and alcohol; the drunkard and the insatiable eater are stereotypical depictions of Christians found throughout Swahili anti-Christian pamphlets and booklets distributed by the Sufi brotherhoods at the time. The appearance of the sultan of Istanbul (*Rumu*), the absolute king of the world, receiving all the other kings of the world at the beginning of the *Kaisa*, is a striking parallel to the *Utendi wa Tambuka*, where the emperor of Byzantium is the major antagonist. Furthermore, besides creating an intertextual reference, it can be considered to refer to the historic alliance between the Ottoman Empire and the German Kaiser during the First World War. Narratively, the world and its history are based on an Islamic foundation:[51] war breaks out in Istanbul, yet Istanbul remains untouched by it. An allegorical history is also being narrated.

An account of timeless significance, the *Kaisa*'s tone is hyperbolic: from the very beginning, it is not just anybody inviting the *wafaume wa duniani* ('kings from all over the world', p. 36), but the *Sultani Imamu ya duniani* ('the sultan, the imam of the world', p. 36), the sultan of Istanbul. The poem favours large-scale battles, enlarging in scope throughout the narrative,

---

[49] Katrin Bromber, 'Ein Lied auf die hohen Herren: Die deutsche Kolonialherrschaft in der historiographischen Swahiliverskunst der Jahrhundertwende', in *Alles unter Kontrolle: Disziplinierungsprozesse im kolonialen Tansania (1850–1960)*, ed. Albert Wirz, Andreas Eckert and Katrin Bromber (Cologne: Köppe, 2003), pp. 73–5.
[50] Quoted in Anne Biersteker, *Kujibizana: Questions of Language and Power in Nineteenth- and Twentieth-Century Poetry in Kiswahili* (East Lansing: Michigan State University Press, 1996), p. 170.
[51] Much to the concern of the German colonial government, in East Africa, the sultan of the Ottoman Empire was considered the most powerful leader in the world (Pesek, *Das Ende eines Kolonialreiches*, p. 285).

fought by the greatest military leaders – *mashujaa wa dunia* (p. 72), 'the heroes of the world'. In seemingly endless lists of ships and troops – the classical epic catalogue found also in other *tenzi* – the sheer number of names conveys an impression of exhaustive totality. While in the *Utendi wa Tambuka*, an ever-increasing number of tens of thousands of soldiers appear on the battleground such that the earth trembles under the hooves of their horses, the *Kaisa* uses the same formula – the 'earth trembles day and night' (*Dunia wakatetema usiku wa leilia*, p. 140) – to describe guns and cannon-firing warships. Particularly in those parts where the *Kaisa* praises modern weapon technology (airplanes, torpedoes, machine guns) – *dunia* also doubles as a cabinet or inventory of wonders of the world. The most destructive military technology replaces the miraculous *jinns*, the many-headed monsters and angels of earlier Islamic *tenzi*.

The most revered of these objects are the warships (*manuwari*). Apart from their very restricted use in actual colonial warfare – most battles were fought on the East African mainland – *manuwari* were a leitmotif of the imperial imaginary of superiority and wonders of technology (next to the railway and the Zeppelin) in other colonial Swahili *tenzi*, travelogues and Swahili-language newspapers (e.g. *Kiongozi*) of the late nineteenth and early twentieth centuries.[52] Awestruck, the poet refers to the warships as *dunia manuwari* (literally 'world ships', p. 165), which, given the verses' grammatical ellipsis, can be read as 'a world of ships' (in the sense of 'many ships'); as referring to their massiveness ('ships as huge as the world'); or as a miniature world unto themselves ('ships as the world'). The sudden, almost miraculous appearance of these ships, like a 'thunderstorm' (*ghubari*), their deadly assaults and their dramatic sinking are an unfathomable wonder – if not a metaphor – of the world as a whole.

The metadiegesis of narrating the world

Most interestingly for discussions of world literature, the *Kaisa*, like many other *tenzi*, also reflects on how to narrate the world: it makes the act of narrating the world a subject of the poem. *Tenzi* typically start with a frame narrative, in which a narrator – the narrating 'I' of the poem's third-person narrative – declares his or her intention or motive to compose a poem: in the *Utendi wa Tambuka*, Bwana Mwengo bin Bakari explains that the sultan of Pate commissioned him to translate Arabic sources on Tambuka into Swahili;[53] in the *Utenzi wa Kutamalaki Mrima*, the narrator announces his account of 'the European' from the 'beginning to the end';[54] and in the

---

[52]Bromber, 'Ein Lied', pp. 73–98.
[53]Meinhof, 'Herkal', stz. pp. 7–9.
[54]Miehe et al., *Kala Shairi*, p. 119.

Kaisa, it is the very possibility of narrating the world that becomes an object of discussion between the narrator and his wife. The scene starts with the narrator telling her, 'Worries have troubled me' (*zimeniingia shughuli*, p. 4). After his wife encourages him to share his concerns, he tells her about his decision to compose a poem about the 'war of the pagans' (*Vita zao makufari*, p. 4). The metafictional frame narrative dramatizes the initial urge to compose the poem yet to take shape, thematizing both the initial creative spark – the sudden inspiration of the poet – as well as the possibility of failure: the narrator's fear of failing at his project or of getting lost in his or her own narrative is a recurring trope in *tenzi*, which the *Kaisa* acts out in the form of dialogue. The wife expresses doubt at her husband's capacity to narrate the 'world at large': 'How could you possibly narrate about overseas and the world at large, when you have never been there?' (*Mutaweza hali gani maneno ya baharini / Urefu wa duniani nawe hukuwasilia*, p. 4).

The dialogue emphasizes the relation between the narrative's here and now, anchored in the smaller world of Angoche, and the 'world at large' (literally 'the length of the world', *urefu wa duniani*, p. 4). The question of whether *dunia* can be narrated – and *if* it can be narrated from Angoche – is not a given in the poem; it also entails the question of *how* to narrate the 'world'. For the *Kaisa*, narrating the world is both an empirical question (how to narrate the experience of a large world outside one's limited perceptual reach) and a textual question (how to make the world emerge from an *utenzi* narrative). The wife's question seems to foreground the former, namely the lack of lived experience – her husband has not seen enough of the world. Her husband's solution is to pray for heavenly support, so that God may guide him through the narration: 'We will pray to God and his beloved Prophet' (*tunamuomba wahabu na mtumiwe habibu*, p. 5). After also receiving the blessing of his wife, the narrator feels relieved and inspired to start: 'On that day, you should know, I had joy in my heart: it is better to narrate the world' (*Na siku hiyo yuwani / furaha yangu moyoni / maneno ya duniani / afadhali kuhadithia*, p. 5). Thus, for him, inspiration – coming from God – and hence the narration, rather than experience of the world, is the crucial concern.[55] As the narrator's *maneno ya duniani* ('words of the world') in this verse suggest, reporting on the world is primarily a question of *maneno* ('words'). Again following a typical *utenzi* formula, the narrator then urges his wife to provide good 'paper from Mecca' (*barua ya kimaka*) and an 'exquisite pen' (*kalamu ya ajabu*, p. 5).

---

[55] This part links the poem with the prayer in the opening verses, the evocation of Allah's name, the *bismillah*; not only inspiration but also the successful completion of any creation, including poetry, depends on Allah. The narrator's concern about narrating the world suggests itself as a variation of the often-evoked motif of the world as God's narration, according to which God writes the world's destiny.

The *Kaisa*, with its metadiegetic reflections on how to narrate the world, highlights the constructed nature of this 'world'. The world does not exist; it needs to be written and performed. With an almost poststructuralist gesture, the *Kaisa* emphasizes its fictionality: the world is but the narrator's version of it. In this way, the *Kaisa* seems to suggest a theory of text that we consider important for discussions of world literature. It reminds us that the relationship between 'literature' and 'world' is not a given but should rather be a primary question in debates of world literature: what is the notion of world *in* and the narrated world *of* the text? The *Kaisa*, as we are attempting to show, offers a whole range of views on *dunia* and transforms experiences of war with the conceptual tools of the *utenzi*. Emphasizing narrated worlds in relation to locally prevailing concepts, genres (the *utenzi* in the case of the *Kaisa*) and notions of literature means going beyond reading literature to confirm preconceived, far-reaching historical, political and geographical realities, such that literature always seems to be secondary to a primarily defined cosmopolitan world (typically anchored in the West). It also means not judging potential candidates for world literature predominantly by their emergence from and circulation in a predefined 'global' field – an aspect that we highlight below.

Conclusion

The *Kaisa* seems to be an odd specimen of world literature: it has not been consecrated by the 'World Republic of Letters' nor by the book market; it has not even been printed. It does not travel – neither to the West nor in any other 'significant geography'[56] – and, to refer to Damrosch's notion of world literature as literature in translation, it 'gains in translation'[57] (into Ekoti) not a broader reach but a more local one. It also does not unequivocally speak back to power or emit an air of cosmopolitanism that transcends the nation; the latter is not a concern, because Angoche sits at the edge of the nation, the Swahili world, several empires and various ethnic communities.[58]

In thinking about 'world literature's other other' through the poetry of the Colombian poet León de Greiff, Héctor Hoyos proposes a strategic reconsideration of the much-despised category of the 'parochial', which, as he constructs it in contrast to the 'provincial' (as well as 'provincial cosmopolitanism'), avoids the dichotomy of a wider outlook versus a

---

[56] Orsini, 'The Multilingual Local in World Literature', pp. 345–6.
[57] David Damrosch, *What Is World Literature?* (Princeton, NJ: Princeton University Press, 2003).
[58] While Swahili poetry, particularly contemporary *tenzi* poetry, has been widely studied, the Mozambican Swahili literary tradition has received hardly any scholarly attention. The colonial heritage of the boundaries between the Portuguese and British spheres of influence appears to have had a lasting impact on research perspectives.

smaller perspective, defined by 'navel-gazing and glorified local colour'. He proposes the 'parish' as a flexible category, which

> partially overlaps with something as ethnic as the nation, as geographic as the region, or as small-minded as the province. It is neither circumscribed only ethnicity nor oblivious to it; parochialism acknowledges the power of place without being exhausted by it. More importantly, although opposed to cosmopolitanism – which forcibly happens at a bigger scale – parochialism is not inimical to cosmopolitanism: the good parishioner, so to speak, can also be a cosmopolitan.[59]

The *Kaisa* is a 'good parishioner' that speaks out against the narrowness of the local, necessarily concerned with the small worlds of smaller communities and typically also expressed in vernacular, in opposition to the globalized world, the habitat of the cosmopolitan. Narrating the First World War, the poem projects a broad vision of the world with regard to both time – writing a part of world history (and not just *any* history but the history of a *world* war) – and space, imagining a vast topography of the world, including Africa. The poem not only creates an imagination of the 'modern' world's wonders, envisioning one of the two *world* wars, a crucial event in Western modernity, but also makes the West an important setting. However – and central to our concern – neither is the West the only centre of the poem's narrative, nor can the poem be read as adapting Western narratives. Rather, it largely makes use of local and transregional literary and conceptual tools that had travelled widely beyond the 'parish', writing the First World War into the Swahili genre of the *utenzi*, in which large worlds and wars were recited all along the East African coast for at least two centuries. The transregional genre also cuts across boundaries of colonies and empires: worldliness did not come to East Africa with the West. Much earlier the *utenzi* became a travelling template for the production of a global history of war – from the early Muslim battles to colonial invasions in German East Africa – of which the *Kaisa* forms one instalment. The *utenzi* allows us an East African – not Western – vantage point on 'world' and 'literature' – and in this way, it is neither belated nor peripheral. The *utenzi* is linked to a different notion of literature and medium – handwritten manuscripts in Arabic script and oral recitation rather than print – but also does not preclude the topics of modernity, technology and media: it depicts twentieth-century East African experiences in engagement with the world. From such a perspective, what the 'world' is, how it changes and how it is narrated become a (comparative)

---

[59]Héctor Hoyos, 'Parochialism from Below: On World Literature's Other Other', in *World Literature, Cosmopolitanism, Globality: Beyond, Against, Post, Otherwise*, ed. Gesine Müller and Mariano Siskind (Berlin: De Gruyter, 2019), pp. 57–60.

question, not a given category, as we have sought to examine through the double optic of changing ecologies and the *Kaisa*'s narratives of *dunia*.

Bibliography

Allen, Roland (ed.) (1945), '*Utenzi wa Kiyama (Siku ya Hukumu)* by Hemedi bin Abdallah bin Saidi el-Buhry: Text. With Introduction, Analysis, Translation and Notes', *Special Supplement to Tanganyika Notes and Records*.

Alpers, Edward (2001), 'A Complex Relationship: Mozambique and the Comoro Islands in the Nineteenth and Twentieth Centuries', *Cahiers d'Etudes Africaines*, vol. 41, no. 161: 85.

Bang, Anne (2014), *Islamic Sufi Networks in the Western Indian Ocean (c. 1880–1940): Ripples of Reform*, Leiden: Brill.

Barber, Karin (1995), 'African-Language Literature and Postcolonial Criticism', *Research in African Literatures*, vol. 26, no. 4: 3–28.

Beecroft, Alexander (2015), *An Ecology of World Literature: From Antiquity to the Present Day*, New York: Verso.

Biersteker, Anne (1996), *Kujibizana: Questions of Language and Power in Nineteenth- and Twentieth-Century Poetry in Kiswahili*, East Lansing: Michigan State University Press.

Bonate, Liazzat (2007), 'Tradition and Transition: Islam and Chiefship in Northern Mozambique, ca. 1850–1975', unpublished PhD thesis, University of Cape Town.

Bonate, Liazzat (2016), 'Islam and Literacy in Northern Mozambique: Historical Records on the Secular Uses of Arabic Script', *Islamic Africa*, vol. 7: 60–80.

Bromber, Katrin (2003), 'Ein Lied auf die hohen Herren: Die deutsche Kolonialherrschaft in der historiographischen Swahiliverskunst der Jahrhundertwende', in *Alles unter Kontrolle: Disziplinierungsprozesse im kolonialen Tansania (1850–1960)*, ed. Albert Wirz, Andreas Eckert and Katrin Bromber, Cologne: Köppe.

Bührer, Tanja (2011), *Die Kaiserliche Schutztruppe für Deutsch-Ostafrika. Koloniale Sicherheitspolitik und transkulturelle Kriegsführung 1885–1918*, Munich: Oldenbourg.

Clover, Carol (2019), *The Medieval Saga*, Ithaca, NY: Cornell University Press.

Conrad, Sebastian, Andreas Eckert and Ulrike Freitag (eds) (2007), *Globalgeschichte. Theorien, Ansätze, Themen*, Frankfurt: Campus.

Cooper, Frederick (2005), *Colonialism in Question: Theory, Knowledge, History*, Berkeley: University of California Press.

Damrosch, David (2003), *What Is World Literature?* Princeton, NJ: Princeton University Press.

De Albuquerque, J. M. (1897), *A Campanha contra os Namarrais. Relatórios*, Lisbon: Imprensa Nacional.

Etherington, Ben, and Jarad Zimbler (2018), 'Introduction', in *The Cambridge Companion to World Literature*, ed. Ben Etherington and Jarad Zimbler, Cambridge: Cambridge University Press, pp. 1–20.

Gérard, Albert (1997), 'Structure and Values in the Three Swahili Epics', *Research in African Literatures*, vol. 7: 7–22.
Giddens, Anthony (1990), *The Consequences of Modernity*, Stanford: Stanford University Press.
Hafkin, Nancy J. (1973), 'Trade, Society, and Politics in Northern Mozambique, ca. 1753–1913', unpublished PhD thesis, Boston University.
Hayot, Eric (2012), *On Literary Worlds*, Oxford: Oxford University Press.
Hoyos, Héctor (2019), 'Parochialism from Below: On World Literature's Other Other', in *World Literature, Cosmopolitanism, Globality: Beyond, Against, Post, Otherwise*, ed. Gesine Müller and Mariano Siskind, Berlin: De Gruyter.
Knappert, Jan (1958), 'Het epos van Heraklios: Een proeve van Swahili poëzie', unpublished PhD thesis, Leiden University.
Liebau, Heike (2010), '*Kaiser Kii Jay* (Long Live the Kaiser)', in *The World in Wars: Experiences, Perceptions and Perspectives from Africa and Asia*, ed. Heike Liebau, Katrin Bromber, Katharina Lange, Dyala Hamzah and Ravi Ahuja, Leiden: Brill, pp. 251–75.
Liebau, Heike, Katrin Bromber, Katharina Lange, Dyala Hamzah and Ravi Ahuja (eds) (2010), *The World in Wars. Experiences, Perceptions and Perspectives from Africa and Asia*, Leiden: Brill.
Meinhof, Carl (1911/12), 'Chuo cha Herkal', *Zeitschrift für Kolonialsprachen*, vol. 2: 1–16, 108–36, 194–232, 261–96.
Miehe, Gudrun, Katrin Bromber, Said Khamis and Ralf Grosserhode (eds) (2002), *Kala Shairi: German East Africa in Swahili Poems*, Cologne: Köppe.
Mutiua, Chapane (2014), 'Ajami Literacy, Class and Portuguese Precolonial Administration in Northern Mozambique, 1861–1913', unpublished PhD thesis, University of Cape Town.
Mutiua, Chapane (2015), 'O Islão e o Processo de Literacia no Norte de Moçambique entre os finais do século XIX e princípios do século XX', in *A Ciência ao Serviço do Desenvolvimento? Experiência de Países Africanos Falantes da Língua Oficial Portuguesa*, ed. Teresa Cruz e Silva and Isabel Maria Casimiro, Dakar: CODESRIA, pp. 205–20.
Orsini, Francesca (2015), 'The Multilingual Local in World Literature', *Comparative Literature*, vols 6/7, no. 4: 345–74.
Paice, Edward (2007), *Tip and Run: The Untold Tragedy of the Great War in Africa*, London: Weidenfeld and Nicolson.
Pelissiér, René (1994), *História de Moçambique: Formação e oposição, 1854–1918*, vol. 2, Lisbon: Editoria Estampa.
Pesek, Michael (2010), *Das Ende eines Kolonialreiches: Ostafrika im Ersten Weltkrieg*, Frankfurt: Campus.
Pouwels, Randall (2000), 'The East African Coast, c. 780 to 1900 C.E.', in *The History of Islam in Africa*, ed. Nehemia Levtzion and Randall Pouwels, Athens: Ohio University Press, pp. 261–6.
Ricci, Ronit (2011), *Islam Translated: Literature, Conversion, and the Arabic Cosmopolis of South and Southeast Asia*, Chicago: University of Chicago Press.
Schadeberg, Thilo, and Francisco Mucanheia (2000), *EKoti: The Maka or Swahili Language of Angoche*, Cologne: Köppe.
Shariff, Ibrahim Noor (1988), *Tungo zetu: Msingi wa mashairi na tungo nyinginezo*, Trenton: Red Sea Press.

Stockhammer, Robert (2018), 'World Literature or Earth Literature? Remarks on a Distinction', in *Re-Mapping World Literature: Writing, Book Markets and Epistemologies between Latin America and the Global South / Escrituras, mercados y epistemologías entre América Latina y el Sur Global*, ed. G. Müller, J. J. Locane and B. Loy, Berlin: De Gruyter, pp. 211–24.

Vierke, Clarissa (2011), *On the Poetics of the* Utendi: *A Critical Edition of the Nineteenth-Century Swahili Poem 'Utendi wa Haudaji' Together with a Stylistic Analysis*, Münster: Lit.

Vierke, Clarissa (2016), 'From across the Ocean: Considering Travelling Literary Figurations as Part of Swahili Intellectual History', *Journal of African Cultural Studies*, vol. 28, no. 2: 225–40.

Vierke, Clarissa, and Chapane Mutiua (2020), 'The Poem about the Prophet's Death in Mozambique – Swahili as a Transregional Language of Islamic Poetry', *Journal for Islamic Studies*, vol. 38, no. 2: 44–74.

7

Early Sesotho, isiXhosa and isiZulu novels as world literature

Ashleigh Harris

In *An Ecology of World Literature: From Antiquity to the Present Day*, Alexander Beecroft elaborates six ecologies of literary circulation that range from the intensely local to the global. Each of these ecologies marks a centripetal movement outwards from the source of their emergence. The most contained scope of circulation is found in *epichoric* literatures tending to be orally 'transmitted over long periods of time', which are limited to a 'small-scale community' and geography.[1] This is followed by the *panchoric* mode, which operates 'in regions with small-scale polities ... where literary and other cultural artifacts circulate more broadly', requiring self-awareness of the space of circulation 'as some kind of cultural unity'.[2] A *cosmopolitan* ecology then opens out to a larger circumference of circulation. Here, we see 'a single literary language ... used over a large territorial range and through a long period of time'.[3] As *cosmopolitan* literature expands, so too does its assimilation into new spaces, which results in *vernacular* literatures, which emerge 'when sufficient cultural resources accumulate behind some version of a locally spoken language to allow for its use for literary purposes'.[4] A *national* literature, in Beecroft's model, marks a congealing of these *vernacular* literatures to mirror and reinforce the consolidation of a

---

[1]Alexander Beecroft, *An Ecology of World Literature: From Antiquity to the Present Day* (London: Verso, 2015), Kindle edition, loc. 667 of 7487.
[2]Ibid., loc. 675 of 7487.
[3]Ibid., loc. 684 of 7487.
[4]Ibid., loc. 692 of 7487.

national imaginary and identity.⁵ Finally, then, we enter a model of 'literary circulation that truly knows no borders', the *global*, which Beecroft explains as occurring when 'major languages (most obviously, of course, English) escape the bonds of the nation-state, and texts begin to circulate more rapidly around the planet'.⁶ Beecroft does not intend these ecologies to be understood along a linear and 'evolutionary' temporality.⁷ Nevertheless, the spatial implications of the model do plot out along a teleological temporality. Moreover, Beecroft's ecological system has formal implications in which the epichoric tends to be dominated by oral cultures, the panchoric opens up to manuscript circulation, the cosmopolitan and the vernacular are print-enabled, the national tends towards large-scale print and the global towards internet circulation.

The South African situation complicates the teleology and materiality of these ecologies in numerous ways. I have argued elsewhere that these different ecologies of literary circulation are compacted, overlapping and entangled in this context:

> In the early to mid-nineteenth century, one can see concurrent examples of at least four of Beecroft's stages: an epichoric oral literature in |Xam, a language that is now extinct, the panchoric traditions of isiXhosa and isiZulu praise poetry, cosmopolitan forms in English, such as accounts of the African interior that were enjoying global circulation in the metropolitan newspapers of Europe and America, and vernacular processes, such as the translation of John Bunyan's *The Pilgrim's Progress* into isiXhosa in 1866, as well as the [national] consolidation of the Afrikaans Language Movement in 1875, which aimed to have Afrikaans legitimated as a language.⁸

I extend this argument here to investigate what these compressed temporalities and materialities of literary circulation have meant for literatures in Sesotho, isiXhosa and isiZulu, both on the national and global levels.⁹ The chapter considers three texts that are widely accepted as being the first novels in these languages: Thomas Mofolo's *Moeti oa Bochabela* (1907) (Sesotho for

---

⁵Ibid., loc. 699 of 7487.
⁶Ibid., loc. 715 of 7487.
⁷Ibid., loc. 666 of 7487.
⁸Ashleigh Harris, 'The Locations and Orientations of South African Literature: From Sol Plaatje to Peter Abrahams', in *Claiming Space: Locations and Orientations in World Literatures*, ed. Bo G. Ekelund, Adnan Mahmutović and Helena Wulff (New York: Bloomsbury, 2021), p. 61.
⁹Thomas Mofolo is, strictly speaking, a Lesotho author, not a South African one. But the language of Sesotho traverses the colonial geographical imaginary. Even this complicates the idea of a *national* ecology of literary circulation. Also, Afrikaans literature is a well-formed vernacular and national literature, and through a robust translation industry circulates globally. However, Afrikaans literature is beyond the scope of this chapter.

Traveler of the East), S. E. K. Mqhayi's *Ityala lamawele* (1914) (isiXhosa for *The Lawsuit of the Twins*) and John Langalibalele Dube's *Insila ka Tshaka* (1930) (isiZulu for *Shaka's Body Servant*). Born within five years of each other (Dube in 1871, Mqhayi in 1875 and Mofolo in 1876), these writers give us a glimpse into a time at which cosmopolitan (mostly colonial English, French and Dutch) literatures were becoming simultaneously vernacularized within various different languages in Southern Africa. The mission presses and indigenous language newspapers were key to this early vernacularization, which explains the extensive involvement all three authors had with newsprint and the Christian press. Between 1904 and 1910 Thomas Mofolo was an editor, reporter and reviewer for the missionary-run Morija Press, which published the newspaper *Leselinyana La Le-Sotho* (The Little Light of Lesotho).[10] In 1897, S. E. K. Mqhayi was an early editor of the isiXhosa paper *Izwi Labantu* (The Voice of the People) and later also worked at *Imvo Zabantsundu* (The People's Opinion), and John Langalibalele Dube founded the isiZulu paper, *Ilange lase Natal* (The Natal Sun) in 1903.[11]

The nineteenth century saw vast and rapid growth of mission stations across the South African interior.[12] Yet, it was only in the latter part of the century, after the missions took on an educational role, that they made any real headway. As Franco Frescura writes,

> A change of heart appears to have occurred from the 1880s onwards when the initial success of the first trade schools at Morija in 1841 and Lovedale in 1857 spurred others to follow their example. By 1902 fifteen such institutions had opened their doors in southern Africa alone, and fifty-six throughout the African continent.[13]

---

[10]Thomas Jeffrey, 'A Hundred Years of Thomas Mofolo: A Tribute', *English in Africa*, vol. 37, no. 2 (October 2010): 39; Daniel Kunene, *Thomas Mofolo and the Emergence of Sesotho Prose* (Johannesburg: Ravan Press, 1989), p. 24.

[11]A major figure of Setswana literature, Sol T. Plaatje should be considered alongside these writers. Yet, in the interests of space and because Plaatje's first novel *Mhudi* (1930) was written in English, I have not included his work in this discussion. See Harris, 'Locations and Orientations' for a discussion of Plaatje's relationship to the national ecology of writing.

[12]Franco Frescura, who provides us with the most substantial mapping of the growth of mission stations to date, has listed '1030 mission stations established by some 60 missionary societies over a period of 125 years' (from 1800 to 1925), a list that is still incomplete. Franco Fresco, 'Missionary Settlement in Southern Africa 1800–1925', *South African History Online*. Available at https://www.sahistory.org.za/article/missionary-settlement-southern-africa-1800-1925. Accessed 23 May 2021.

[13]Franco Frescura, 'A Case of Hopeless Failure: The Role of Missionaries in the Transformation of Southern Africa's Indigenous Architecture', *Journal for the Study of Religion*, vol. 28, no. 2 (2015): 68–9.

These educational mission stations, where the first printing of books, pamphlets and translations of church materials into indigenous languages occurred, were cosmopolitan centres, with a significant number of people, literature and newsprint from all over the colonial world flowing through them. Mofolo, Mqhayi and Dube were all educated and employed at such mission stations, though these differed in that they were founded by congregations from different parts of the protestant world. Morija Mission in Lesotho, where Mofolo studied and worked, was founded by the French, Paris Evangelical Mission Society; the Lovedale Mission in the Eastern Cape, where Mqhayi was based, was founded by the Glasgow Missionary Society; and Dube was born at Inanda at the American Zulu Mission, where his father was an ordained minister.[14] Each of the missions had its own curriculum, and taught different languages and literary and church canons, even if some texts, like John Bunyan's *The Pilgrim's Progress*, were common across the region and circulated in translation in multiple European and indigenous languages.[15] These cosmopolitan variations aside, there was significant similarity in the experience of learning and working at these mission stations, which not only attracted visitors from various international and local backgrounds but also enabled an inward flow of international newspaper print that connected these locations more immediately with global questions and concerns.[16] Over time, even the exclusive faith-based material of the mission presses became more diverse. Daniel Kunene notes, for example, the development of the mission paper *Leselinyana la Le-Sotho* from entirely church and local concerns to 'the addition of new departments so that already quite early in its career it carried (albeit usually slightly out of date) summaries of international news and events'.[17]

---

[14]Nhlanhla Maake discusses similarities between Morija, Lovedale and the American Zulu Mission Press in 'A Survey of Trends in the Development of African Language Literatures in South Africa: With Specific Reference to Written Southern Sotho Literature c1900–1970s', *African Languages and Cultures*, vol. 5, no. 2 (1992): 159.

[15]For a full account of this text's circulation in Africa, see Isabel Hofmeyr, *The Portable Bunyan: A Transnational History of the Pilgrim's Progress* (Princeton, NJ: Princeton University Press, 2004).

[16]Stephen Gill, writing about Morija Mission, notes that

> Students came to Morija from many parts of Lesotho, the Free State, the Transvaal, Mozambique and Barotseland. Others, like D.D.T Jabavu, were from prominent families in the Eastern Cape. These came to Morija not simply because it was a Protestant school with ties to their home churches, but also because its results surpassed even those of Lovedale and Healdtown, renowned missionary centres whose educational products would also wield great influence in the decades to come. Thus, Morija was a cosmopolitan centre.

Stephen Gill, 'Thomas Mofolo: The Man, the Writer and His Contexts', *Tydskrif vir letterkunde*, vol. 53, no. 2 (2016): 27.

[17]Daniel Kunene, '*Leselinyana la Lesotho* and Sotho Historiography', *History in Africa*, vol. 4 (1977): 152.

While the secularization of these papers led the editorial boards of mission papers to react with increasingly strict censorship,[18] this also prompted the growth of the secular, independent, indigenous language press. The growth of the Black press, which played an important role in consolidating a political platform in the aftermath of the Native Lands Act of 1913, was the primary site through which Black literature emerged and circulated in the early twentieth century in South Africa. As scholars such as Tim Couzens argue, this makes it impossible to ignore the 'almost inseparable connections, between literature, journalism and politics' at this time.[19] In this chapter I argue that this triadic relationship of literature, journalism and politics ultimately contributed to the attrition of an already under-resourced and politically contested vernacular press in South Africa, as the imperatives for a pan-African language diluted the cultural politics of preserving local languages and traditions. Furthermore, by understanding how emergent indigenous language literature was articulated in relation to this triad, we nuance our formal definition of these books as simply novels.

The fact that the political situation prevented the consolidation of a vernacular literature in any indigenous language in Southern African set the stage for a national literature represented almost entirely by only English and Afrikaans. Moreover, it is that body of work that has come exclusively to represent South Africa in the world republic of letters, in Pascale Casanova's terminology. This post facto consecration of the novel form *as* national form par excellence is particularly problematic in South Africa, where the growth of the novel actively marginalized the potential of other vernacular forms. What this means for indigenous language literature is that scholars and commentators work to tether an account of this literature to the origins of the novel, hence the need to classify the three texts under discussion here today as foundational novels in each language. The novel and the colonial language of English and Afrikaans have set the terms of the national literature of South Africa and this, in turn, has created what Beecroft sees as a 'technique of literary history, uniquely emergent in the national literary ecology', which operates as 'a crucial device that at once legitimates a literature and the nation it embodies, integrates it into an existing system of national literatures, and reduces the quantity of information within the literary system'.[20] If world literature as a technique of literary history is to avoid reiterating an ecology that delegitimates and expels African-language literature from its system, then the very moment of the so-called emergence

---

[18]See Maake, 'A Survey of Trends in the Development of African Language Literatures in South Africa', 158; and Jeff Opland, 'The First Novel in Xhosa', *Research in African Literatures*, vol. 38, no. 4 (Winter 2007): 87.
[19]Tim Couzens, 'The Continuity of Black Literature in South Africa before 1950', *English in Africa*, vol. 1, no. 2 (September 1974): 11.
[20]Beecroft, *An Ecology of World Literature*, loc. 4258 of 7487.

of the African-language novel becomes a dense source of investigation. By considering the materiality and form, as well as the intended circulation, of these three Southern African texts, I hope to challenge a world literary historiography that tends to locate the origins of African literature in the English and French novel.

Thomas Mofolo: Newsprint, the novel and the entanglements of form

Thomas Mofolo's *Moeti oa Bochabela* (1907) is often credited as 'the first novel by an African to appear in Africa'[21] and, in an autobiographical sketch written in 1930, Mofolo himself describes *Moeti oa Bochabela* as his 'first novel'.[22] However, scholarly commentators do not always agree with this classification, finding the text too syncretic in form and function to comfortably fit the genre conventions of the novel. Nhlanhla Maake, for example, considers *Moeti oa Bochabela* and Mofolo's second longer work *Pitseng* (1910) as 'precursors of the novel in Sotho literature',[23] a statement that implies a kind of striving towards the achievement of the novel form. I would argue, rather, that the form of *Moeti oa Bochabela* is less conceptually linked to the novel than it is materially entangled in newsprint. The narrative first appeared serialized in the bimonthly *Leselinyana La Le-Sotho* (The Little Light of Lesotho), a newspaper run by the Morija mission where Mofolo was then working. The serialization began on 1 January 1907 and ran for seventeen editions until 1 September, when the story was published as a book by the Morija Book Depot. Like many other novels that originate in serialized form, the narrative shape of the story is episodic. That said, this episodic structure of each chapter was not always aligned with the serialization: the text was printed according to how much space the type-copyists had available in each edition.[24]

---

[21]Rosemary Moeketsi, 'Mofolo, Thomas Mokopu', in *The Routledge Encyclopedia of African Literature*, ed. Simon Gikandi (Oxford: Routledge, 2003), p. 341; Jeffrey, 'A Hundred Years of Thomas Mofolo', p. 37.
[22]Thomas Mofolo, 'Autobiographical Sketch', in *Traveller to the East*, trans. the Society for the Promotion of Christian Knowledge [1934], ed. Stephen Gray (Cape Town: Penguin Books, 2007), p. viii.
[23]Maake, 'A Survey of Trends in the Development of African Language Literatures in South Africa', p. 161.
[24]The penultimate episode of the story in the 15 August 1907 edition of *Leselinyana* begins in the middle of chapter ten, includes the entire chapter 11 and ends in the middle of the final chapter of the book. Thomas Mofolo, 'Moeti oa Bochabela', *Leselinyana la LeSotho*, 15 August 1907, pp. 3–4. This might suggest that the entire text was written in advance of the serialization.

Beyond the materiality of the serial form, the episodic structure of the text could also be the result of Mofolo's debt to *The Pilgrim's Progress*, as Tim Couzens and Isabel Hofmeyr have discussed in depth.[25] The overall plot structure of the book is, indeed, very similar to *The Pilgrim's Progress*: the protagonist Fekisi, like Bunyan's Christian, is prompted to leave the moral morass of the City of Destruction, here rendered as an Africa 'still clothed in great darkness, dreadful darkness, in which all the works of darkness were done'.[26] Fekisi sets out on a pilgrimage to seek, like Christian, the enlightenment and truth of the Celestial City (which in Mofolo's account is Ntsoanatsatsi, the mythical home of the Basotho people). Again like Christian, Fekisi must overcome various challenges and temptations and prove himself true in order to be delivered 'to the home of God'.[27] When his pilgrimage is over, Fekisi's story ends with his death: 'His spirit had gone to his Creator in glory, his body remained in the house of prayer.'[28] The imaginary of moving from a perceived dark and unenlightened past towards the glory of a Christian God is not only a religious allegory but one of colonization too. Fekisi's journey takes him away from Africa (he 'crosses the sea'),[29] where he arrives at an 'enlightened' place where 'the people were white in colour, with hair like the manes of horses'.[30] They are also, notably, literate: 'Fekisi was quick to observe that these people knew how to talk to each other although they were not together. One man makes little marks, they will arrive and speak where they go to. He asked and it was explained to him, and then he was taught to read and write.'[31] As Daniel Kunene puts it, Fekisi campaigns alone for a 'wholesale abandonment of Basotho institutions, traditions and values', he 'sees God's wrath coming to the Basotho because they live according to their traditions'.[32]

As the first African novel, then, this text has a compromising view of Basotho culture itself, promoting literate, Christian, European culture over oral, African culture and beliefs. Yet, unlike the protagonist Fekisi's

---

[25]Tim Couzens, *Murder at Morija* (Johannesburg: Random House, 2003); Hofmeyr, *The Portable Bunyan*.
[26]Mofolo, *Traveller to the East*, p. 1. This is not only an effect of translation, as readers of the original Sesotho version can ascertain: 'Litaba tsa motho eo re 'molelang, re itse ke tsa khale, tsa boholo-holo mehleng ea ha lefatše lena la Africa le ne le sa aparetsoe ke lefife le leholo, lefifi le tšabehang, leo tsohle tsa lefifi li etsoang ka lona'. Mofolo, 'Moeti oa Bochabela', p. 2.
[27]Mofolo, *Traveller to the East*, p. 85.
[28]Ibid., p. 88.
[29]Ibid., p. 74.
[30]Ibid., p. 75.
[31]Ibid., p. 79. Once again, in Sesotho: 'A phakisa a lemoha hore batho ban aba tseba ho buidana leha ba arohane. E mong a etse metakanyana a tla fihla e bua moo e eangteng. A botsa, 'me a hlalosetsoa, a ba a rutoa ho bala le ho ngola.' Mofolo, 'Moeti oa Bochabela', p. 2.
[32]Daniel Kunene, 'Ntsoanatsatsi/Eden: Superimposed Images in Thomas Mofolo's *Moeti oa Bochabela*', *English in Africa*, vol. 13, no. 1 (May 1986): 21.

betrayal of his culture, the text itself is ultimately not the 'wholesale abandonment' of Basotho culture that it at first appears to be: instead, as Kunene concludes, it 'vacillates between affirmation and rejection' of that culture.[33] Mofolo's vacillation can even be traced in the formal elements of the book, which illustrate an assortment of many different influences, both local and cosmopolitan. Isabel Hofmeyr argues that the 'book is very much a "parliament" of texts and a book of conspicuous quotation',[34] citing 'the literary forms of Protestantism like prayer, liturgy, and the "minidrama" of the catechism',[35] as well as 'writers like the colonial adventure novelist Henry Rider Haggard and the bestselling author Marie Corelli'.[36] But it is not only these liturgical and popular Western texts that make up the montage of *Moeti oa Bochabela*. Indeed, running throughout the book are the oral literary traditions of the Basotho that Fekisi, in his pilgrimage, attempts to disavow. Hofmeyr, again, points out the 'Sotho historical tropes and discourses' and the formal range that Mofolo draws on, such as 'poems, songs, passages, and oral narratives'.[37]

Mofolo's syncretism illustrates the tensions experienced by Black intellectuals and writers in starting to shape a unique writerly voice in their own languages at this time, a voice that would engage and continue the traditions of their cultural past at the same time as it could open up to the Christian world view of their mission education. Furthermore, the vacillation apparent in this syncretic mode also points to the inevitable balancing act Mofolo had to achieve in this work, given that he was reliant on the conservative mission press to publish his writing. He was also employed at Morija as a reviewer, reporter, editor and secretary to Reverend Casalis, as Thomas Jeffrey notes, indicating the extent to which Mofolo was materially dependent on the mission press.[38] Indeed, shortly after publishing *Moeti oa Bochabela*, Mofolo completed his much less ambivalent novel, *Chaka*, which although completed in 1909 was only published in 1925. Many critics agree that Morija's hesitance to publish the novel was because 'Mofolo's individual attitude to history and the plentiful supernatural imagery in *Chaka* were not pleasing to the Morija missionaries'.[39]

There is a further reason, I argue, for the syncretic style of the text, which is that it emulated the various styles and modes present in the newspaper

---

[33] From the outset, the narrator reveals this tension by telling us the 'Basuto of old ... truly believed that there is a living God, who has made all things' (Mofolo, *Traveller to the East*, p. 3). Kunene elaborates this point in more detail. Kunene, 'Ntsoanatsatsi/Eden', p. 21.
[34] Hofmeyr, *The Portable Bunyan*, p. 171.
[35] Ibid., pp. 171–2.
[36] Ibid., p. 172.
[37] Ibid., pp. 171–2.
[38] Jeffrey, 'A Hundred Years of Thomas Mofolo', p. 39.
[39] Ibid., p. 48.

in which it appeared. Long before trying his own hand at writing, Mofolo was familiar with the content of *Leselinyana* through his studies at the Bible School of the Morija mission, where he studied from 1894 to 1896.[40] Daniel Kunene writes that in the 1890s, *Leselinyana* saw the emergence of 'an entirely new breed of Mosotho, namely, the literary person, obsessed with an urge to make the paper speak and at the same time be a more reliable storehouse of the human memory'.[41] By 'memory', Kunene refers to the tendency in this, as in other papers, to use print media as a space to archive indigenous languages and their threatened oral cultures. Azariele Sekese 'contributed numerous articles on the traditions, legends and history of the Basotho, as well as other aspects of early Sesotho culture' during this time and '*Leselinyana* carried several instalments of his work on Sesotho proverbs, finally publishing them in book form in 1895'.[42] Indeed, just as we can see the influence of Bunyan in *Moeti oa Bochabela*, so too can we see the likely influence of an earlier piece published in *Leselinyana* on 1 January 1889 by Daniele Methusala. This was 'an account of [Methusala's] visit to *Ntsuanatsatsi, golimo e ntso* (Ntswanatsatsi, the black heaven), Ntswanatsatsi being, according to Basotho mythology, the place of origins where in the beginning all living things came out of a bubbling spring in the ground'.[43] The story's plot is very like Fekisi's pilgrimage to Ntsoanatsatsi, which also indicates a further aspect of the 'newspaper aesthetic' that we see in Mofolo's work in the blurring of fiction and non-fiction. This particular ease of movement between fiction and non-fiction, as we will see in the discussion of S. E. K. Mqhayi below, was not unusual in the Black press of the time because it continued an understanding of the social role of the literary arts from oral traditions: stories and poetry were not about creating fictional worlds, à la Rider Haggard and Marie Corelli, but fulfilled mnemonic and social functions that were very much about the lived world and real events.

With this in mind, it is not surprising that the blurring of genre and form was common to Mofolo's peers, too. Maake notes how 'Mofolo's contemporaries followed up [the serialisation of *Moeti oa Bochabela*] with a variety of genres', including

> Motsamai's *Mehla ea Malimo* [Days of the Cannibals] in 1912, an anthology of eighteen short stories based on the structure of folk tales; Mangoaela's *Har'a Libatana le Linyamatsana* [Among the Carnivores and the Herbivores] in 1913, a genre in many respects similar to Motsamai's collections, and *Lithoko tsa Marena a Basotho* [The

---

[40]Gill, 'Thomas Mofolo', p. 26.
[41]Kunene, '*Leselinyana la Lesotho* and Sotho Historiography', p. 156.
[42]Ibid.
[43]Ibid., p. 152.

Praises of the Chiefs of the Basotho] in 1921; [and] Segoete's *Monono ke Moholi ke Mouane* [Wealth is Mist, Vapour] in 1910, a picaresque autobiographical novel.[44]

The materiality of the newspaper clearly enabled and encouraged this fluidity of form, which was common for Basotho writers before, during and after Mofolo's publication of *Moeti oa Bochabela*. Yet, inevitably the text closest to the novel has been posited as foundational to the Sesotho canon. This privileging of the novel form, and post facto shoe-horning of certain texts into that classification, is complicit in the disavowal of oral cultures in these early literatures. Instead, the capacity of these writers to emulate the novel is the determining narrative in later reconstructions of the origins of African literature. Nowhere is this clearer than in Mofolo's later consolidation as a novelist through his globally successful book *Chaka*. As Maake notes, in its French translation (1940), *Chaka* was 'destined to influence writers of the négritude movement [including] Léopold Sedar Senghor's *Chaka* (1956), S. Badian's *La Mort de Chaka* (1961), ... Condetto Nenekhaly-Camara's *Amazoulou* (1970), and Djibril Niane's *Chaka* (1971), [who] adopted Mofolo's title hero as the symbol of African unity'.[45] As I argue below, the pan-Africanist potential of the novel form also contributed to the overshadowing of other genres in the narrative of the growth of African literature.

S. E. K. Mqhayi: Documenting precarious culture

Just as Thomas Mofolo's changing view of the writing of indigenous history in his novel *Chaka* coincided with his politicization and leaving his job at Morija Book Depot, so too did S. E. K. Mqhayi's increasing tensions with missionary ideology and censorship prompt him to seek independence as a writer beyond the mission press.[46] Nhlanha Maake notes that the

> conditions of missionary censorship at Lovedale seem to have been similar to Morija's, as Mqhayi explains in his autobiography that his first manuscript was kept at home for a long time. Eventually he had to

---

[44]Maake, 'A Survey of Trends in the Development of African Language Literatures in South Africa', p. 161.
[45]Ibid., p. 163.
[46]Parts of the section that follows on Mqhayi appear in 'Communal Intellection and Individualism in the African Novel', *Cambridge Journal of Postcolonial Literary Inquiry* (forthcoming).

leave Lovedale Press because of conflict with the missionaries, an incident which calls to mind Mofolo's departure from Morija.[47]

The year 1907, when Mofolo serialized and published *Moeti oa Bochabela*, was also the year of the first publication of a twenty-five-page isiXhosa text that has been called everything from a pamphlet and novelette to a novel.[48] This text was *USamson* by S. E. K. Mqhayi, who, as Jeff Opland notes, paid for the text's printing, distribution and marketing himself, possibly to avoid the censorship of the Lovedale editors.[49] From the outset, the dynamics of publishing and censorship cast a shadow over the creative expression of Black writers in Southern Africa.

Mqhayi's first isiXhosa 'fiction' (again, *USamson* is difficult to classify) was published as a book first, unlike Mofolo's serialized text above. Nevertheless, the text was still deeply imbricated in Mqhayi's work at Lovedale as an editor and his knowledge and strategic use of the newspaper *Izwi Labantu* in marketing his story. Opland writes that 'Mqhayi issued an advertisement [for *USamson*] in *Izwi labantu* on 30 July 1907 that appeared ten times, in each subsequent edition until 1 October 1907.'[50] Despite Mqhayi's efforts to market the text at the time, and perhaps because it did not enter the formal record of the Lovedale Press or appear in serialized form in *Izwi Labantu*, there are no surviving copies.

We have to rely, then, on the next 'novel' that Mqhayi wrote and published for an analysis of the origins of the isiXhosa South African novel. *Ityala lamawele* (The Lawsuit of Twins) was published by Lovedale Press, but their censorious involvement in its editing has left us with a somewhat fragmented book and a similarly fragmented book history to patch together. The original 1914 text 'consisted of 9 chapters and 19 pages',[51] extended in 1915 to '20 chapters and 66 pages', of which sixteen chapters focused on the story of the twins and four were historical accounts of Xhosa chiefs.[52] The fifth and fullest version of the isiXhosa text included a further four poems, and 'notes on various people and organisations introduced by a poem entitled "*Ibacu*" (Destitutes)'.[53] Today, only the abridged version, which covers the first sixteen fictional chapters, is available in print, leaving the contemporary reader with the impression that these chapters were imagined

---

[47]Maake, 'A Survey of Trends in the Development of African Language Literatures in South Africa', p. 166.
[48]Opland, 'The First Novel in Xhosa', p. 88.
[49]Ibid., p. 96.
[50]Ibid., p. 97.
[51]Jeff Opland, 'Introduction' to S. E. K. Mqhayi, in *Abantu Besizwe: Historical and Biographical Writings, 1902–1944*, ed. and trans. Jeff Opland (Johannesburg: Wits University Press, 2009), p. 18.
[52]Ibid.
[53]Ibid., p. 19.

as a self-contained novella, even though the material history of the text tells a more complex tale.

Not only the form of the novel but the very medium of written isiXhosa (and other indigenous languages, for that matter) was still fluid when Mqhayi wrote the text. IsiXhosa orthography underwent major shifts across the years in which the text was reissued. Mqhayi himself was actively involved in the isiXhosa subcommittee of the African Orthography Committee in 1929, which led to substantial revision of existing orthography.[54] As Jeffrey Peires summarizes, 'the awesome effect of the "New Orthography" was to turn every literate African into a functional illiterate. Even Mqhayi and Soga, who had sat on the Xhosa sub-committee, could not (or would not) write their manuscripts correctly in [it]'.[55] This would have even larger consequences for the material history of *Ityala lamawele*. Lovedale editor W. G. Bennie, who was 'an enthusiastic convert and propagandist of the New Orthography', abridged the text for schools, cutting out substantial historical chapters and censoring sections that included material the church looked down upon, including praise poems, 'witch-craft in the Old Testament' and critiques of the church.[56] In the process Mqhayi was lured into agreeing to publish the abridged edition, without knowing that

> Lovedale Press intended to drop the full edition in favor of the abridged version. On 28 September 1939 he wrote [Lovedale principal R.W] Shepherd an alarmed letter saying that he had heard that the last impression of the full edition (in the Old Orthography) was out of print, and adding that 'I do not want this edition to die away'.[57]

It is also important to note that Mqhayi was, first and foremost, an *imbongi*: a poet in the established oral Xhosa tradition. Poets in this tradition made extensive use of improvised and sometimes impromptu praise poems,

---

[54] At first, the Xhosa sub-committee agreed to only one change, the introduction of a new symbol to denote the implosive 'b', but gradually they succumbed to the blandishments of linguistic perfectionism. Far-reaching changes were adopted: the introduction of three new letters, the creation of a number of new didacts (two-letter consonants), the use of diacritic marks to indicate tone and stress, the practice of doubling vowels to indicate length, and new rules for the division of words.
Jeffrey Peires, 'The Lovedale Press: Literature for the Bantu Revisited', *History in Africa*, vol. 6 (1979): 155–75, 161. 'The grammars of isiXhosa, initially at least, was a model to benefit speakers of other languages and not native speakers.' Pamela Maseko, 'Exploring the History of the Writing of isiXhosa: An Organic or an Engineered Process?' *International Journal of African Renaissance Studies*, vol. 12, no. 2 (2017): 81–96, 84.
[55] Peires, 'The Lovedale Press', p. 161.
[56] Ibid., pp. 161, 165.
[57] Ibid., p. 166.

which are allegorical and symbolically dense and 'are not narrative: they do not tell a story'.[58] Karin Barber notes that

> the actions and events that gave rise to [such allusive poems] are not recuperable from the words themselves. They hint at narratives but do not tell them. ... The 'obscurity' of such epithets lies in the fact that the narrative expansion lies outside the text itself. The knowledgeable listener has to know the story in order to make full sense of the epithet.[59]

Xhosa oral tradition also covers a narrative tradition known as *amabali* (storytelling or historical stories), a form that also blurs Western generic conventions between imaginative stories and historical memory.[60] Moreover, praise poems (*izibongo*), while not narrative, are deeply entangled with the narrative form of *amabali*. These two traditions are, as Opland notes, 'learned and transmitted in parallel'.[61] Opland writes of the cultural and historical knowledge an *imbongi* must have to compose an improvised praise poem.[62] The praise poem, which makes meaning only in relation to an assumed shared knowledge held by poet and listeners, operates in a distinctly epichoric ecology, in Beecroft's terminology. This communal sense-making is taken for granted: one's belonging in and to the community (and its histories and stories) is a prerequisite for understanding. This is a form of community too intimate for print media, which addressed readers in a much larger, *panchoric* manner.

In this broader circulation, then, the social relevance of praise poetry is dislocated and what emerges instead in written forms is the metadescription of oral forms. This was apparent already in Mofolo's *Moeti oa Bochabela* through the account of Fekisi's talents as a herdboy. When Fekisi begins his pilgrimage, he offers a praise poem to his favourite cow before leaving. The poem is included in the text, with some of the imagery and themes already introduced by the preceding prose. This makes sense of the praise poem for non-local readers, even if its immediate improvised and epichoric quality is lost in the adaptation of the oral form to the page.[63] Proverbs are similarly

---

[58] Opland, 'Introduction', p. 10.
[59] Karin Barber, 'Text and Performance in Africa', *Bulletin of the School of African and Oriental Studies*, vol. 66 (2003): 328; cited in Opland, 'Introduction', p. 10.
[60] Opland's magisterial collection of Mqhayi's historical and biographical writings in *Abantu Besizwe* aims 'not only to restore Mqhayi's reputation as a historian, but to demonstrate that such narratives should be judged not only as history in the western conception of the word, but also as a major expression of Xhosa literature'. Ibid., p. 20.
[61] Ibid., p. 10.
[62] Jeff Opland, *Xhosa Poets and Poetry*, 2nd edn (Pietermaritzburg: University of Kwa-Zulu Natal Press, 2017), pp. 7–14.
[63] While talking about isiXhosa rather than Mofolo's Sesotho tradition, Opland notes that some of Mqhayi's earliest memories of composing *izibongo* were 'during the long hours spent herding livestock' as a boy. Opland, *Xhosa Poets and Poetry*, p. 15.

included, with descriptive frames such as 'as the Basuto say' or 'a saying has it', which has a similar distancing effect.[64] All three authors discussed here, by using indigenous languages, were addressing a particular linguistic and cultural group. Nevertheless, we can see how writing itself imposes this conceptual distancing from a shared experience of the world and adapts that experience for wider reception.

Mqhayi also uses the written form in *Ityala lamawele* to give wider reception to a particular social form: the Xhosa court. Here, we are not working at the intimate level of the epichoric; rather, Mqhayi wants to document a major tradition of the Xhosa people that was widely known and respected throughout their kingdom. At its most simple, *Ityala lamawele* is an adaptation of a biblical story, but this is all part of a device to document a dying tradition in a threatened culture. The story that frames the text is that of the birth of the twins Pharez and Zarah. During the birth, one twin's hand appears and a midwife ties a red thread around the baby's wrist to indicate that this is the firstborn. The baby then retracts his hand and is ultimately born second, creating uncertainty around primogeniture. Mqhayi adapts the story to Gcalekaland (present-day Eastern Cape) under the Xhosa king Hintsa (1789–1835). Here, the customary act of midwives cutting off the first joint of the smallest finger (*ingqithi*) replaces the thread, but in all other aspects the plot is the same and Mqhayi's twins end up in a conflict of inheritance and primogeniture after their father's death. *Ityala lamawele* moves through the workings of the Xhosa court in its deliberations and judgement on the case. After significant discussion with and advice from the community, Hintsa finally decides which of the brothers is to be considered heir and firstborn. This verdict is, however, rhetorically complex and leads both brothers to believe that the king has ruled against them. They accept the king's ruling and leave in a spirit of acceptance. This ultimately leads the brothers to resolve their differences and work together for the overall betterment of the homestead.

This privileging of social cohesion above legal absolutes has led *Ityala lamawele* to be commonly described as 'a defense of Xhosa law before European administration',[65] which Mqhayi's preface to the text of 1914 also loosely suggests. Yet, the idea that the text was directed at a European or world audience sits awkwardly with the fact that the text is written in isiXhosa and Mqhayi's preface is not consistent on this matter. He also states that he is not primarily addressing his text to what he tongue-in-cheek

---

[64]Mofolo, *Traveller to the East*, pp. 1, 9.
[65]'Ityala lamawele', *Encyclopedia Britannica Online*. Available at https://www.britannica.com/topic/Ityala-lamawele. Accessed 28 February 2021. See also Maseko, who sees it as a defence of 'the intricacies of African law and its similarities with Western law'. Pamela Maseko, 'Introduction' to S. E. K. Mqhayi, in *The Lawsuit of the Twins*, trans. Thokozile Mabeqa (Cape Town: Oxford University Press South Africa, 2018), p. vi.

refers to as 'the enlightened nations'.[66] Rather, his preface overtly addresses Xhosa youth. He writes,

> It is up to young Xhosa males and females to look carefully at precisely what will disappear when these wise and distinguished expressions and customs of their origin vanish completely. These are therefore deliberate endeavours to resist the wave that will demolish the whole nation. You, too, should strive to support these attempts. (p. 3)

Here, again, we see a type of vacillation between a defence of Xhosa culture for a cosmopolitan audience and a direct petition to young amaXhosa to sustain their culture against the onslaught of colonial deculturation. We have already seen that Black contributors to newspapers like *Leselinyana* made strategic use of that forum to archive proverbs, praise poetry, stories, histories and other previously oral forms. Newspapers and anthologies, unlike novels, enabled the transcription of these oral cultures into writing without narrative framing. Mqhayi's contemporary, mentor and colleague W. B. Rubusana[67] had self-published a substantial anthology of isiXhosa 'praise poems and material culled from newspapers'[68] under the title *Zemk'inkomo magwalandini* [There go the cattle, you cowards] in 1906, a work that Mqhayi would have known well. Opland writes that, in the year following the publication of Rubusana's anthology,

> his young protégé S. E. K. Mqhayi paid for the printing of *USamson* by the Lovedale Press. The fact that both Rubusana and Mqhayi themselves paid for the publication of their books probably stemmed from a desire for independence, free of mission control.[69]

Both Rubusana and Mqhayi were keen to use their writing to archive the cultural past.

This double-urge to retain independence from the censorial missions and to archive a threatened oral tradition resonates with broader political frustrations emerging at the time. It is perhaps unsurprising that all three of the authors I have chosen to discuss here, alongside many of their contemporary teachers, journalists, poets and writers across all indigenous languages in South Africa, began to mobilize politically at this particular historical juncture. Thomas Mofolo became 'a member of the *Lekhotla la*

---

[66] S. E. K. Mqhayi, '1914 Preface' to *The Lawsuit of the Twins*, trans. Thokozile Mabeqa (Cape Town: Oxford University Press South Africa, 2018), p. 3.
[67] 'In 1897 Mqhayi left Lovedale to assume a teaching position at a school in West Bank, East London, under the charge of Rubusana.' Opland, 'Introduction', p. 4.
[68] Ibid., pp. 24–5.
[69] Opland, 'The First Novel in Xhosa', p. 96.

Tsoelo-pele (Council of Progress) (given the English name of *Basutoland Progressive Association*)' in 1907,[70] a year after the founding of the South African Native National Congress (variously SANC and SANNC) which became the African National Congress (ANC) in 1923. W. B. Rubusana and my next case study, John Langalibalele Dube, were both founding members of the SANC. Mqhayi, too, was 'elected as a member of the Executive Council of *Inqungquthela*, [the SANC at its founding] in 1906'.[71] A perfect illustration of the extent to which newspapers, writing and politics are entangled can be found in the 25 August 1908 edition of *Izwi Labantu*, an East London paper also founded in 1906. Mqhayi, who was sub-editor of the paper at the time, included in that edition an advertisement 'announcing the availability of his book [*USamson*] at the forthcoming SANC Convention'.[72] Not only does this illustrate Tim Couzens's argument about the 'almost inseparable connections, between literature, journalism and politics' in Black intellectual life at this point in South African history,[73] but it also tells us something about the varied roles of literature at the time.

John Langalibalele Dube: The pan-African novel

Like Mofolo and Mqhayi, John Langalibalele Dube was professionally involved in education, creative and journalistic writing, editing and politics. Dube was also an ordained pastor in the Congregational Church of Inanda for eight years,[74] a position he left in 1908 after increasing political tensions in the church (much like Mofolo and Mqhayi).[75] Dube also founded the Zulu newspaper *Ilange lase Natal* in 1903. Of the three writers discussed in this chapter, Dube is the least 'literary' in the sense that he was neither a trained poet like Mqhayi, nor did he go on to write further fiction like Mofolo.[76] Despite being hailed as the first writer of an isiZulu novel, all his later writings were biographical, political or didactic. While *Insila*

---

[70] Daniel Kunene, 'Introduction' to Thomas Mofolo, *Chaka*, trans. Daniel Kunene (Harlow: Heinemann, 1981), p. xi.
[71] Opland, 'Introduction', p. 5.
[72] Opland, 'The First Novel in Xhosa', p. 97.
[73] Couzens, 'The Continuity of Black Literature in South Africa before 1950', p. 11.
[74] Robert M. Kavanagh, 'Introduction' to John Langalibalele Dube, in *Insila: The Eyes and Ears of the King*, trans. T. N. Nene and R. M. Kavanagh (Johannesburg: Themba Books, 2017), p. xiii.
[75] Heather Hughes, 'Doubly Elite: Exploring the Life of John Langalibalele Dube', *Journal of Southern African Studies*, vol. 27, no. 3 (2001): 445–8, 457.
[76] He did, however, also invest in an archiving of isiZulu culture, as Rubusana did for isiXhosa and Plaatje for Setswana, by collecting and transcribing, with his first wife Nokutela Dube, isiZulu songs in a songbook entitled *Amagama Abantu* (Songs of the People). See Tsitsi Jaji,

ka Tshaka (1930) is more substantial in length and more consistent in its narrative style and form than Mofolo's and Mqhayi's texts discussed above, it is nevertheless a difficult book to categorize. *Insila*'s most recent translator notes, for example, how the 'narrative style owes a lot more to the *inganekwane* [the isiZulu traditional story] than to the conventional novel'.[77]

Insila ka Tshaka is a historical fiction that tells the tale of Jeqe, who first earns the trust of King Shaka through his quick-wittedness, agile fighting and loyalty. He then betrays Shaka after a struggle of conscience over the violent and unmotivated attacks on innocent people that the king orders him to perform. When the conspirators of Shaka's half-brother Dingane kill the king, Jeqe – who by custom, as the *insila* (chief body guard) should be ritually executed and buried with the king – flees. During his travels, he falls ill in the land of the Thonga and, in the most remarkable chapter in the book, is saved by Sithela, the 'great instructress' of the Bathonga's physicians/healers and spiritual healers/guides.[78] Sithela takes Jeqe to her island and puts him in the care of an old man, Ngqelebani, an *inyanga* (physician/healer) whose 'duty was to attend to all the tokoloshe and matindane, the dwarves, sprites and familiars, and all the animals needed by the izinyanga on the island'.[79]

The spirits and spirit animals on the island disrupt what would have otherwise passed as an acceptable piece of historical fiction to the mission presses at the time. On Sithela's island, Jeqe becomes an *inyanga*, a skill that helps him find a home among the Swati after he leaves the land of the Thonga. Ultimately, he makes a happy marriage to a beautiful Thonga girl who bears him six children. The novel quite obviously follows a *Bildungsroman* structure, with Jeqe undergoing various trials of conscience and cunning, and ultimately finding himself employed and happily married with children. However, the chapter on Sithela's island, where Jeqe receives the education that will lead to his successes in life, unsettles the expectations of the novel considerably. Given how mission editors insisted on cutting material on indigenous belief systems, this chapter may be understood as a bold statement of resistance and independence. The chapter also functions as a record of the beliefs of the Bathonga, not dissimilar to Mqhayi's account of the practices of the isiXhosa court.

Insila ka Tshaka first appeared in 1930, just five years after Thomas Mofolo's novel *Chaka* was finally published. Not only can we consider the novel a response to Mofolo's text – a more critical historical perspective on King Shaka – but we can also take both novels as exemplary of how

---

'Re-collecting the Musical Politics of John and Nokutela Dube', *Safundi*, vol. 13, nos 3–4 (2012): 213–29.
[77]Kavanagh, 'Introduction', p. xxiii.
[78]Dube, *Insila*, p. 114.
[79]Ibid., p. 118.

the novel form was consolidating by the mid-1920s to early 1930s in Southern Africa. In the sixteen years between Mqhayi's *Ityala lamawele* and this novel, much had changed in publishing and politics in South Africa. That this consolidation was mirrored by increasingly strong transatlantic connections between the Black press and politics in Africa and those in the United States is well-illustrated through a closer look at Dube's biography.

John Dube was born and educated at the American Zulu Mission in Inanda. Through this association with the AZM, he came to attend the Oberlin Academy in Ohio, where he became an acolyte of Booker T. Washington. Back in South Africa, he established the Zulu Christian Industrial school in 1901, which was fashioned after Washington's Tuskegee Institute in Alabama. Thus, by the Native Lands Act of 1913, which notoriously prohibited Black South Africans from purchasing land anywhere outside of a set of reserves that constituted less than 10 per cent of the country, Dube's transatlantic links were well-established. The Native Lands Act galvanized political dissatisfaction and also prompted greater political outreach to garner international support (Solomon Plaatje and S. E. K. Mqhayi, for example, 'joined the SANNC leadership on a delegation to London in protest' at the Act).[80] It was also the Land Act that prompted Plaatje to write '*Native Life in South Africa* [which] almost failed to find a publisher before the printing of its first edition in London in 1916.'[81] As the politicization of Black writing consolidated, the censoriousness of South African publishers and presses became all the more apparent.

By the time Dube published *Insila ka Tshaka*, then, the field of publishing and politics had been utterly entangled in global and specifically pan-African politics. The second Pan-African Congress was held in 1921,[82] which was widely reported in the Black South African press. Multilingual newspapers of the 1920s, such as *Umtleli wa Bantu* (which included Sesotho, isiZulu, isiXhosa and English text), had a strong international focus and were, perhaps partially as a result of this, increasingly dominated by the English language.[83] Perhaps the most obvious success of English as the language of global and pan-African connection for Black intellectuals of this time is Sol Plaatje's English novel *Mhudi*, published the same year

---

[80] Jaji, 'Re-collecting the Musical Politics of John and Nokutela Dube', p. 214.
[81] Chris Holdridge, 'Sol Plaatje's Native Life in South Africa: Past and Present', *South African Historical Journal*, vol. 71, no. 2 (2019): 348–52, 348.
[82] Out of which came W. E. B. Du Bois's 'Manifesto to the League of Nations', published in the November 1921 edition of the African-American and pan-African interest paper, *The Crisis*, a paper cited in various Black South African newspapers at the time.
[83] By the early 1930s, Dube's isiZulu paper *Ilanga lase Natal* had merged with *The Bantu World*, thereby losing its Zulu language focus.

as *Insila* but enjoying far greater recognition in the subsequent South African canon (it is often hailed as the first English novel written by a Black South African).[84]

Plaatje used writing, in both Setswana and English, as a strategy to archive the threatened Sestwana oral culture that he was desperate to maintain. In his preface to *Mhudi* he stated that he hoped the novel would generate enough revenue for his real project: 'to collect and print (for Bantu schools) Sechuana folktales, which, with the spread of European ideas, are fast being forgotten. It is thus hoped to arrest this process by cultivating a love for art and literature in the vernacular.'[85] Plaatje had already started this project with the publication of *Sechuana Proverbs with Literal Translations and Their European Equivalents* (1916) and *A Sechuana Reader in International Phonetic Orthography with English Translations* (with Daniel Jones, 1916), but these publications are no longer in print and exist only in single copies at a handful of university libraries. While *Mhudi* is quite certainly a novel, it nevertheless has some unusual characteristics that show these oral influences, too.[86] Like *Insila*, *Mhudi* provides long historical or cultural chronicles that lose narrative pace. As Kavanagh notes, in *Insila*, the 'long interlude of repetitious and out of context information on the Swazis takes us away from the narrative' and 'describes an aspect of an Nguni culture which is in many ways the same as that of the Zulus – and this has already been quite comprehensively covered in the opening chapters'.[87] Dube's attention to detail here betrays the work of the archivist of culture that we are seeing as a point of similarity across all these literary figures in four of the major languages of Southern Africa. This would have been prompted by the disappearing specificity of individual cultures and languages under the increasing linguistic and cultural dominance of English, but it is also perhaps an acknowledgement of the shared cultural repertoires of Black South Africans as they strategically came together in political formations that crossed over local differences: the ANC or the Pan-African Congress.[88] That is to say, local languages and forms became increasingly precarious as Black South Africa was forced to seek international support and solidarity for the struggle against white rule. Each of the writers above was profoundly aware of this dynamic and found compromises to both record their cultures

---

[84] See, for example, Stephen Gray, 'Sources of the First Black South African Novel in English: Solomon Plaatje's Use of Shakespeare and Bunyan in *Mhudi*', *Munger Africana Library Notes*, no. 37 (December 1976): 6–28.
[85] Sol T. Plaatje, *Mhudi* (London: Penguin Modern Classics, [1930] 2006), p. xi.
[86] For a longer discussion, see Harris, 'The Locations and Orientations of South African Literature'.
[87] Kavanagh, 'Introduction', p. xxvii.
[88] While it is beyond the scope of this chapter, the increasing influence of the Ethiopianist movement at the time is also worth noting.

and articulate links with pan-African writing, education, Christianity and politics.

Conclusion

The novel form never became a major literary force in indigenous languages in South Africa, as we can see from sales of novels in that country: of the 1,008 South African published novels sold in 2020, 687 were in Afrikaans, 319 in English, two in isiZulu and none in the remaining eight national languages.[89] Perhaps this is the inevitable outcome of the historical moment in which novels in indigenous languages emerged in Southern Africa. At the very point at which vernacularization of the novel form in this context began, a number of factors interrupted its development. First, indigenous language orthographies had not yet been settled, which delayed the consolidation of these languages as literary media. Second, the colonial and historical weight of the established English literary canon and infrastructure quashed an emerging vernacular ecology. Third, writers felt ambivalent about the fact that writing was hastening the end of rich oral cultures. Finally, indigenous languages were de-prioritized by Black writers themselves with the increasing need for pan-African solidarity. This seems to be implicitly acknowledged by Plaatje when he decided to write his novel *Mhudi* in English, rather than in his mother tongue, Setswana, which he was at pains to preserve.

Contemporary world literary studies is left with two possible approaches to South African literature. The first option, which has thus far been the status quo, is to accept that South Africa's contribution to the world of letters is through its English (and to a far lesser extent Afrikaans) literature. The second, more challenging option, is to see the field of world literature as necessarily having a seventh ecology, which we might call a settler-colonial ecology.[90] Within the settler-colonial ecology, epichoric, panchoric, cosmopolitan, vernacular, national and global logics of circulation are intensely compressed and overlapping. Within this clamour for cultural capital, the dominant colonial language intervenes to 'reduce the quantity of information within the literary system',[91] by foreclosing the possibility of indigenous languages to vernacularize cosmopolitan forms. The settler-colonial ecology, then, misses a step in Beecroft's system. By denying vernacularization, literary production moves from epichoric or panchoric modes directly to national ones in the development of Black South African

---

[89]Statistics based on Nielsen BookScan point-of-sale data for South Africa, 2020. The other eight languages are isiXhosa, Sesotho, Sepedi, Setswana, Tshivenda, Xitsonga, siSwati and isiNdebele.
[90]I am grateful to David Watson for helping me articulate this idea.
[91]Beecroft, *An Ecology of World Literature*, loc. 4258 of 7487.

writing: a national literature that has become narrowly limited to English and Afrikaans. If we wish to decolonize our view of the contribution of African writing to world literature, we need to critically engage how this systematic investment in colonial languages over indigenous ones has formed the global field of letters and then recover those emergent texts in African languages for our historiography of Africa's contribution to world literature. To critically re-engage the settler-colonial ecology of the stages of literature's journey into the world would require a certain amount of book history and spadework, then – a recovery of forms and writings that became ephemeral by virtue of not conforming to publishing and linguistic standards of their time. This will also prompt us to engage with a richer material of African literary history, across a wider variety of modes, genres, languages and materialities, that have thus far not entered the world of letters.

Bibliography

Barber, Karin (2003), 'Text and Performance in Africa', *Bulletin of the School of African and Oriental Studies*, vol. 66: 324–33.
Beecroft, Alexander (2015), *An Ecology of World Literature: From Antiquity to the Present Day*, London: Verso.
Couzens, Tim (1974), 'The Continuity of Black Literature in South Africa before 1950'. *English in Africa*, vol. 1, no. 2: 11–23.
Couzens, Tim (2003), *Murder at Morija*, Johannesburg: Random House.
Dube, John Langalibalele (1930), *Insila ka Tshaka*, Marianhill: Marian Hill Mission Press.
Dube, John Langalibalele (1951), *Jeqe The Bodyservant of King Tshaka*, trans. J. Boxwell, Lovedale: Lovedale Press.
Dube, John Langalibalele (2017), *Insila: The Eyes and Ears of the King*, trans. T. N. Nene and R. M. Kavanagh, Johannesburg: Themba Books.
Fescura, Franco (2015), 'A Case of Hopeless Failure: The Role of Missionaries in the Transformation of Southern Africa's Indigenous Architecture', *Journal for the Study of Religion*, vol. 28, no. 2: 64–86.
Frescura, Franco, 'Missionary Settlement in Southern Africa 1800–1925' *South African History Online*. Available online https://www.sahistory.org.za/article/missionary-settlement-southern-africa-1800-1925. Accessed 23 May 2021.
Gill, Stephen (2016), 'Thomas Mofolo: The Man, the Writer and His Contexts', *Tydskrif vir letterkunde*, vol. 53, no. 2: 15–38.
Gray, Stephen (1976), 'Sources of the First Black South African Novel in English: Solomon Plaatje's Use of Shakespeare and Bunyan in *Mhudi*', *Munger Africana Library Notes*, vol. 37: 6–28.
Harris, Ashleigh (2021), 'The Locations and Orientations of South African Literature: From Sol Plaatje to Peter Abrahams', in *Claiming Space: Locations and Orientations in World Literatures*, ed. Bo G. Ekelund, Adnan Mahmutović and Helena Wulff, New York: Bloomsbury, pp. 59–84.

Harris, Ashleigh (forthcoming), 'Communal Intellection and Individualism in the African Novel', *Cambridge Journal of Postcolonial Literary Inquiry*.

Hofmeyr, Isabel (2004), *The Portable Bunyan: A Transnational History of the Pilgrim's Progress*, Princeton, NJ: Princeton University Press.

Holdridge, Chris (2019), 'Sol Plaatje's Native Life in South Africa: Past and Present', *South African Historical Journal*, vol. 71, no. 2: 348–52.

Hughes, Heather (2001), 'Doubly Elite: Exploring the Life of John Langalibalele Dube', *Journal of Southern African Studies*, vol. 27, no. 3: 445–58.

'Ityala lamawele', *Encyclopedia Britannica Online*. Available online: https://www.britannica.com/topic/Ityala-lamawele. Accessed 28 February 2021.

Jaji, Tsitsi (2012), 'Re-collecting the Musical Politics of John and Nokutela Dube', *Safundi*, vol. 13, nos 3–4: 213–29.

Jeffrey, Thomas (2010), 'A Hundred Years of Thomas Mofolo: A Tribute', *English in Africa*, vol. 37, no. 2: 37–55.

Kavanagh, Robert M. (2017), 'Introduction' to John Langalibalele Dube, in *Insila: The Eyes and Ears of the King*, trans. T. N. Nene and R. M. Kavanagh, Johannesburg: Themba Books, pp. v–xxxii.

Kunene, Daniel (1977), '*Leselinyana la Lesotho* and Sotho Historiography', *History in Africa*, vol. 4: 149–61.

Kunene, Daniel (1981), 'Introduction' to Thomas Mofolo, *Chaka*, trans. Daniel Kunene, Harlow: Heinemann, pp. xi–xxiii.

Kunene, Daniel (1986), 'Ntsoanatsatsi/Eden: Superimposed Images in Thomas Mofolo's *Moeti oa Bochabela*', *English in Africa*, vol. 13, no. 1: 13–39.

Kunene, Daniel (1989), *Thomas Mofolo and the Emergence of Sesotho Prose*, Johannesburg: Ravan Press.

Maake, Nhlanha P. (1992), 'A Survey of Trends in the Development of African Language Literatures in South Africa: With Specific Reference to Written Southern Sotho Literature c1900–1970s', *African Languages and Cultures*, vol. 5, no. 2: 157–88.

Maseko, Pamela (2017), 'Exploring the History of the Writing of isiXhosa: An Organic or an Engineered Process?' *International Journal of African Renaissance Studies*, vol. 12, no. 2: 81–96.

Maseko, Pamela (2018), 'Introduction' to S. E. K. Mqhayi, in *The Lawsuit of the Twins*, trans. Thokozile Mabeqa, Cape Town: Oxford University Press South Africa, pp. v–xii.

Moeketsi, Rosemary (2003), 'Mofolo, Thomas Mokopu', in *The Routledge Encyclopedia of African Literature*, ed. Simon Gikandi, Oxford: Routledge, p. 341.

Mofolo, Thomas (1 January 1907), 'Moeti oa Bochabela', *Leselinyana la LeSotho*, p. 2.

Mofolo, Thomas (1 August 1907), 'Moeti oa Bochabela', *Leselinyana la LeSotho*, p. 2.

Mofolo, Thomas (15 August 1907), 'Moeti oa Bochabela', *Leselinyana la LeSotho*, pp. 3–4.

Mofolo, Thomas (1907), *Moeti oa Bochabela*, Morija: Morija Press.

Mofolo, Thomas ([1934] 2007a), 'Autobiographical Sketch', in *Traveller to the East*, translated by the Society for the Promotion of Christian Knowledge, ed. Stephen Gray, Cape Town: Penguin Books, pp. vii–viii.

Mofolo, Thomas ([1934] 2007b), *Traveller to the East*, trans. the Society for the Promotion of Christian Knowledge, ed. Stephen Gray, Cape Town: Penguin Books.

Mqhayi, S. E. K.(1914), *Ityala lamawele*, Lovedale: Lovedale Press.

Mqhayi, S. E. K. (2018a), *The Lawsuit of the Twins*, trans. Thokozile Mabeqa, Cape Town: Oxford University Press South Africa.

Mqhayi, S. E. K. (2018b), '1914 Preface', in *The Lawsuit of the Twins*, trans. Thokozile Mabeqa, Cape Town: Oxford University Press South Africa, p. 3.

Opland, Jeff (2007), 'The First Novel in Xhosa', *Research in African Literatures*, vol. 38, no. 4: 87–110.

Opland, Jeff (2009), 'Introduction' to S. E. K. Mqhayi, in *Abantu Besizwe: Historical and Biographical Writings, 1902–1944*, ed. and trans. Jeff Opland, Johannesburg: Wits University Press, pp. 1–28.

Opland, Jeff (2017), *Xhosa Poets and Poetry*, 2nd edn, Pietermaritzburg: University of Kwa-Zulu Natal Press.

Peires, Jeffrey (1979), 'The Lovedale Press: Literature for the Bantu Revisited', *History in Africa*, vol. 6: 155–75.

Plaatje, Sol T. ([1930] 2006), *Mhudi*, London: Penguin Modern Classics.

Rubusana, Walter B. ([1911] 1906), *Zemk'inkomo magwalandini*, 2nd edn, London: The Editor.

Williams, Raymond (1977), *Marxism and Literature*, Oxford: Oxford University Press.

8

African multilingualism as an asset in world literature: A case against cultural conformity and uniformity

Munyao Kilolo

Introduction

In the last five years, I have been involved in various projects and conversations about African languages, and the works that are being produced in them. First, through the *Jalada* Africa translation project;[1] then, through the Mabati Cornell Kiswahili Prize;[2] and now, my work at the Ngũgĩ wa Thiong'o Foundation[3] and the Ituĩka publishing project.[4] Consequently, I wanted to engage with both activism and practical solutions to the various questions that affect African language literatures, but first, I felt the need to find all the material I could written in Kiikamba, my mother tongue. By reading such literary production in my own language, I could make a more meaningful contribution to pertinent discussions.

---

[1] https://jaladaafrica.org/2016/03/22/jalada-translation-issue-01-ngugi-wa-thiongo/. Accessed 1 February 2022.
[2] https://kiswahiliprize.cornell.edu/. Accessed 1 February 2022.
[3] https://www.ngugiwathiongofoundation.org/mission.html. Accessed 1 February 2022.
[4] https://www.ituika.org/. Accessed 1 February 2022.

Growing up, I was not exposed to a lot of written materials in Kiikamba, except perhaps for the Bible, which we studied at Sunday School, and Kiikamba text pamphlets here and there. The pamphlets were mostly instructional materials from NGOs and the government. Beyond that, literature in my mother tongue was impossible to find. In a detailed account of Kenyan-language publishing in Shiraz Durrani's book *Never Be Silent: Publishing and Imperialism 1884–1963*, it is clear that there was extensive publication of Kenyan-language materials before the string of bans in 1952. The Mau Mau struggle for independence was met by extreme measures from the colonial administration, most of which aimed to curtail the freedom struggle. Even before these bans during the 1952 State of Emergency, Durrani writes that the colonial administration set strict controls over all forms of publishing from the onset of colonial rule in Kenya.[5] Therefore, publications that seemed to endanger colonial rule were often banned. A penal code established in 1950 allowed colonial authorities to confiscate any material that was (by their definition) seditious.[6] Nonetheless, some of the publications that sprouted after 1945 in all manner of Kenyan languages persisted through to independence. Many of these publications have become extinct: it is hard to find one that is thriving today in Kenya. Additionally, the archives of those that existed once are not widely available to the public.

Even so, I had access to literature originating from all manner of places, the greatest percentage of which was in English and, occasionally, in Kiswahili. This reinforced in me not only the habit of reading in English and Kiswahili but also of thinking exclusively in those two languages as I grew up. There was, however, no literature originating in Kiikamba that I could find easily, even though, since the time of the missionaries, there has been an established tradition of Kiikamba writing. As Ngũgĩ wa Thiong'o details in *Decolonizing the Mind*, we were not allowed to read or speak our mother tongue in school. The natural language spoken at home and which I felt most comfortable speaking was erased from my learning experience. The cultural wealth of my people was not being deeply explored meaningfully or enjoyed at home through my language, even though thousands used that language every day to conduct business, adjudicate court proceedings and conduct important ceremonies.

Today, the situation has not changed significantly for the better. In my home library, I have a Kiikamba grammar book published locally by

---

[5]Shiraz Durrani, *Never Be Silent: Publishing and Imperialism 1884–1963* (Nairobi: Vita Books, 2006), p. 94.
[6]Bodil Folke Frederiksen, 'Print, Newspapers, and Audiences in Colonial Kenya: African and Indian Improvement, Protest, and Connections', *Journal of the International African Institute*, vol. 81, no. 1 (2011): 155–72, 166.

Twaweza Communications[7] and authored by Angelina Kioko.[8] The other Kamba book, beyond the Bible, is a collection of bilingual Kiikamba–Kiswahili stories titled *Vau Tene ... Hapo Zamani*. It is jointly authored by Angelina Kioko and Karsten Legere[9] and these are my prized possessions. My search hasn't located many more such books in my language, even though in literal sense they must exist somewhere. Bookstores in Nairobi rarely stock any works in Kenyan or African languages. Children's books in African languages are increasingly available, but they do not get the same attention as English books. Whether at home or at school, writings in these languages tend to be seen as a cultural artefact.

A big gap therefore exists. Literary production and consumption of our works in African languages is subject to deep systematic challenges. Adegbija rightly observes that across many African countries, African languages 'are designated to function only at the lower levels or during the first few years of primary school education'.[10] This inadequacy in the application of African languages, Adegbija adds, has given European languages the chance to fill the vacuum. The historical and contemporary violence against African languages often means that they do not thrive or contribute significantly to world literatures. As a result, a whole generation of Kenyan writers and intellectuals do not have the tools for effective writing in their mother tongue. There are also very few formal learning opportunities to enable them to do significant work in these languages. As Mbithi argues in her seminal article 'Multilingualism, language policy and creative writing in Kenya', there is an urgent need for organized systems of teaching and testing competence in these African languages.[11] If that happens, then the benefit will not only be for the native speakers who will then have an opportunity to release literary material but also for anyone willing to learn these languages. Unwilling to accept that my fate is to witness my mother tongue relegated to one of those languages whose existence is purely oral, and whose trajectory could be eventual extinction, I decided to get beyond thinking about and discussing these issues, to small but practical steps contributing to the visibility of African languages.

---

[7] Angelina Nduku Kioko, *A Grammar of Kĩĩkamba* (Nairobi: Twaweza Communications Limited, 2019).
[8] https://books.google.co.ke/books/about/A_Grammar_of_K%C4%A9%C4%A9kamba.html?id=irQ-zQEACAAJ&redir_esc=y. Accessed 1 February 2022.
[9] https://search.library.wisc.edu/catalog/9912412354202121. Accessed 1 February 2022.
[10] Efurosibina Adegbija, *Language Attitudes in Sub-Saharan Africa: A Sociolinguistic Overview* (Clevedon: Multilingual Matters), p. 4.
[11] Esther Mbithi, 'Multilingualism, Language Policy and Creative Writing in Kenya', *Multilingual Education*, vol. 4, no. 19 (2014), https://doi.org/10.1186/s13616-014-0019-9. Accessed 1 February 2022.

Language

Let me go back to the beginning of the problem. I, like millions of other Africans, grew up in a culturally rich African context. Our culture, for centuries embodied in a rich oral tradition, faces more challenges than we can enumerate. However, African languages are spoken every day, and orality is thriving. When I am in my hometown, my mother tongue is the default language of business. People in the markets, at home and in many social gatherings use Kiikamba to discuss important issues. Some of the most viewed music on YouTube and other social media is in local languages. This tells us that there is a significant following for this kind of creative expression in African languages. However, the same has not meaningfully translated into the written, literary production. While the oral tradition of African languages continues to thrive, little is visible in terms of writing. Many people of my generation struggle to read even simple paragraphs in their mother tongues. In a recent interview for The Conversation, Mūkoma wa Ngũgĩ argues that the inability to fully access African languages means that young people are limited in how much of their history and knowledge they can benefit from.[12] Without the production of work in African languages, a lot of history has been lost. Mūkoma further makes the point that our generation, stuck in the English metaphysical empire, is becoming alienated from their past, present and future. In a much earlier article by Bgoya, the Tanzanian publisher observed that this difficulty is sometimes extended to the artificially acquired European language, where students fail to master it. In many cases, and in addition to not acquiring proficiency in English and other European languages, they also lose the opportunity to become proficient in their own languages. He rightly observes that this linguistic dependency is costly to the progress of African nations.[13]

Indeed, when I go to the shopping centres back home and ask for a book in a Kenyan language, the merchants look at me as though I have asked a strange question. Others look offended or embarrassed that someone is seeking material in their mother tongue. Asking after a book in Kiikamba often makes me look like I am in the grip of an impossible dream. For instance, over the last year, I have been looking for a dictionary in Kiikamba[14] that was created by John Harun Mwau. Some Nairobi booksellers say that they once stocked it, but since it sold out, it has become a rare commodity that

---

[12] Mūkoma wa Ngũgĩ, 'New Kiswahili Science Fiction Award Charts a Path for African Languages', The Conversation, 7 July 2021, https://theconversation.com/new-kiswahili-science-fiction-award-charts-a-path-for-african-languages-163876/. Accessed 1 February 2022.
[13] Walter Bgoya, 'The Effect of Globalisation in Africa and the Choice of Language in Publishing', International Review of Education, vol. 47 no. 4 (2001): 283–92, 287.
[14] John Harun Mwau, *Kikamba Dictionary-osa Vinya Mukamba* (Nairobi: J. H. Mwau, 2006).

many other interested readers and researchers have failed to locate. Clearly, there is a widespread negative attitude towards not only creating but also making available literary material in Kenyan and African languages.

The task, therefore, is to change this attitude towards African language writing and reading. In writing about linguistic justice, Musau stated that this widespread negativity towards African languages is often propagated by its elite populations.[15] It is this attitude, often embraced by those with the power to make a change, that becomes a great obstacle in the implementation of justice for African languages. In a keynote address delivered at the XVII World Congress of the International Federation of Translators held at Tampere, Neville Alexander argued that

> unless the educational systems of the continent are based on the mother tongues of the people of Africa instead of on foreign languages as most of them are at present, all attempts at establishing a platform for improving the quality of education will in the final analysis benefit only the elite and its progeny. This fact is not yet openly acknowledged even by the most courageous of our intelligentsia.[16]

Ngũgĩ, on the other hand, noted that meaningful discussion of African literature would not be possible outside the context of the social forces that have made it a problem that calls for a resolution.[17] An impactful approach in changing attitudes towards literature in African languages calls for the positive participation of all stakeholders, especially the elite who have the power to administer policy changes. Government policy, mainstream publishing, book distribution and reading habits must all be re-examined as to how they influence and perpetuate these attitudes.

Scholars that study these languages also do not seem to be translating their research and academic interests into actual literary material. There are thousands of journal articles, conference papers and theses about writing in African languages. However, there are very few actual books that people can read and engage with. It makes me sad when I go looking for a book and cannot find it anywhere, even though in a literal sense it exists somewhere. Even the writings of people like John S. Mbiti, who committed a great deal of effort in creating materials in my mother tongue, are not widely available. Some of this material

---

[15]Paul Musau, 'Linguistic Human Rights in Africa: Challenges and Prospects for Indigenous Languages in Kenya', *Language, Culture and Curriculum*, vol. 16, no. 2 (2010): 155–64, 162.
[16]Neville Alexander, 'The Potential Role of Translation as Social Practice for the Intellectualisation of African Languages', *Marxists*, 2005, https://www.marxists.org/archive/alexander/2005-potential-role-of-translation.pdf. Accessed 1 February 2022.
[17]Ngũgĩ wa Thiong'o, *Decolonising the Mind: The Politics of Language in African Literature* (London: Heinemann, 1986), p. 4.

exists in libraries abroad: far-off places that neither I nor my people can reach. We, the people who need it the most, are unable to access this material. The inability to access material in our own languages is what drove my colleagues and I to start the *Jalada* Language and Translation Project. Enough discussions had been held on the concept of writing and publishing in African languages. It is the practical work we wanted to see happen. We invited people to write and translate material in their languages, and then we published these materials. The editorial process of publishing these stories and translations followed the same rigour we applied in our English anthologies. Editorial challenges were experienced and met in real time. For instance, we realized we could develop an editorial process that allowed a single anthology to be published in many languages. Multilingual publishing hence ceased to be a dual juxtaposition of one language with another, especially a 'validating' European language with an 'inferior' African language. We could publish each language as a stand-alone page on the website and ask people to find the translation on another. The reader then had the option of simply giving their full attention to the text that they were reading without having to look at the European language translation as a superior object.

Multilingualism and translation

Our strength in this project lies in the fact that we live in a deeply multilingual society. Roy-Campbell observes that this multiplicity of African languages is seen in many cases as a major constraint in the development of the African languages.[18] The author identifies this misconception as arising from the knowledge that, because there are many languages that often lack a written tradition, providing written material in each of them would be practically impossible. In the evidence- and practice-based policy advocacy brief by the UNESCO Institute for Lifelong Learning, the case for multilingualism is made with beautiful clarity:

> Africa's multilingualism and cultural diversity is an asset that must, at long last, be put to use. Multilingualism is normality in Africa. In fact, multilingualism is the norm everywhere. It is neither a threat nor a burden. It is not a problem that might isolate the continent from knowledge and the emergence of knowledge-based economies, conveyed through international languages of wider communication. Consequently, the choice of languages, their recognition and sequencing

---

[18]Zaline Makini Roy-Campbell, 'Revitalizing African Languages for Transformation', *Contemporary Journal of African Studies*, vol. 6, no. 1 (2019): 27–45.

in the education system, the development of their expressive potential, and their accessibility to a wider audience should not follow an either-or principle but should rather be a gradual, concentric and all-inclusive approach.[19]

There is no doubt that people are interacting with multiple languages daily. It is not unusual in Kenya to find people who speak up to five languages fluently, but this does not translate in literature. Not only is there very little written in local languages, but there is very little literary translation between Kenyan languages. The only way to achieve extensive material in African languages is through commitment to ensuring that translations aid the availability of our literature in African languages. This is in line with Ngũgĩ's argument that the possibilities of translation between African languages are massive. He writes that 'African languages have been and still are legitimate sources of knowledge; that thought can originate in any African language and spread to other African languages and to all the other languages of the world'.[20] The *Jalada* Translation Project is a perfect example of this, as a story moved from Gikuyu to a hundred other languages, most of which are African.

Examples of people doing incredible work in enriching African languages through translation are numerous. Jane Obuchi, a writer and translator working in the Ekegusii language, has translated *Romeo and Juliet* into her mother tongue as *Romeo na Churieti*. She has also translated Chinua Achebe's *Things Fall Apart* into Ekegusii as *Binto Mbisebererekani*. Her dream is to translate as many classics and African writers as possible into Ekegusii. Kọ́lá Túbọ̀sún from Nigeria translated *Childhood* (2014), a book of poetry by American poet Emily R. Grosholz, into his language Yoruba as *Ìgbà Èwe*. His commitment to develop literature in the Yoruba language is also supported by his wide-ranging research to examine and popularize the best aspects of the Yoruba language.

Of course, the most powerful demonstration of the possibilities in translation between African languages has been the *Jalada* Translation Project. I conceived the project in 2015 and oversaw the editorial coordination over the years. The difficult questions in translation between African languages were answered. Again, the project showed the importance of digital facilities in enabling the publication of literary work in multiple African languages. Since digital facilities allow easy collaboration, cheap publishing and constant innovation, many constraints and barriers were

---

[19] Adama Ouane and Christine Glanz, 'Why and How Africa Should Invest in African Languages and Multilingual Education: An Evidence- and Practice-Based Policy Advocacy Brief' (UNESCO Institute for Lifelong Learning, 2010), p. 6.
[20] Ngũgĩ wa Thiong'o, 'The Politics of Translation: Notes towards an African Language Policy', *Journal of African Cultural Studies*, vol. 30, no. 2 (2017): 124–32, 130.

done away with. In addition, the idea of hierarchy between languages was crushed. European languages did not take special precedence but were languages just like Gumbai from Chad and Igala from Nigeria. However, due to the historical subjugation of African languages there was no theoretical framework that we could use to enable translation between these languages. We had to use the regional *lingua Franca*, English, French or Arabic (among other widely spoken languages), as a bridge between African languages. For instance, translation into Somali relied more on the Arabic translation than the English. The Arabic had itself been translated from English, into which the original Gikuyu was translated. In this way, a story often moved from one language to another via bridge languages. While many translators tried to stay true to the original, often one would adopt the work into the context of their culture and the ways in which stories are told in their languages, without deviating much from the original.

Part of what *Jalada* did was to contribute to the availability of African languages in the online space. Already, there is a large audience for the African language materials. It does not make sense that such a big audience should completely lack access to materials in their own languages. If we continue to make available written texts in these African languages, they will meet that available audience and thrive. Translation such as that done by *Jalada* is essential in increasing the availability of African language material. However, we also need translation of literature from around the world into African languages to continue enriching them. A language like my own mother tongue, Kiikamba, would benefit immensely if there were translations of world classics such as Gabriel García Márquez's *A Hundred Years of Solitude* or Chinua Achebe's *Things Fall Apart*. Not only would there be more content, but many native speakers would have the chance to engage in their language while reading some of the world's finest literary books. Alexander maintains that African institutions of higher learning can be a fertile ground for this kind of work.[21] He challenges programmes in applied language studies across African universities to explore and use innovative ways that will both initiate and sustain the intellectualization of African languages. He gives the example of the Japanese intelligentsia who were required to invest in their language over several generations: 'Like the Japanese and the followers of Kemal Ata Türk in the 1920s and 1930s, we will have to find the most cost-efficient ways of increasing rapidly the corpus of great works of world literature and science in the relevant African languages.'[22]

---

[21]Alexander, 'The Potential Role', p. 6.
[22]Ibid., p. 9.

Circulation

Once material in African languages is made available, the question of getting these materials into the hands of readers is very important. We appreciate first that there is a challenge in publishing these materials and a bigger challenge in ensuring that the intended audience know about the existence of the work, cares enough about it and is willing to spend their often-limited resources in terms of money and time to engage with that literature in African languages. Already, most of the publishers working in many African countries are academically oriented: their focus is on school publishing, and we cannot blame them because their approach is also hinged on business sense. Ogechi and Bosire-Ogechi, writing about educational publishing in African languages, maintain that a published work makes a lot of sense if it can be read widely.[23] The implication is that books written in languages that are widely spoken will appeal more to publishers. These publishers then benefit from reduced production costs and significantly increase their target audience. There is a ready market for this work because it is required reading for millions of young people in schools. Bookstores across Kenya, for instance, will most definitely carry books required for the school curriculum. A selection of these books, especially grades 1 to 4, are often in the mother tongue. Today in Kenya, the government buys such books from the publishers and distributes them to schools across the country if they are required reading. Such arrangements make wide distribution of books published in African languages both possible and exciting.

Publishing literary books in African languages has no guarantees. In an interview with Nanda Dyssou, Ngũgĩ wa Thiong'o argued,

> The problem is, unfortunately, those that write in African languages remain invisible, their works are hardly ever reviewed or translated. Publishing venues are limited and getting published is one of the most infuriating challenges of writing in African languages. There are hardly any publishing houses devoted to African languages. So, writers in African languages are writing against great odds: no publishing houses, no state support, and with national and international forces aligned against them. Prizes are often given to promote African literature but on the condition that the writers don't write in African languages.[24]

---

[23]Nathan Oyori Ogechi and Emily Bosire-Ogechi, 'Educational Publishing in African Languages, with a Focus on Swahili in Kenya', *Nordic Journal of African Studies*, vol. 11, no. 2 (2002): 167–84, 168.
[24]Nanda Dyssou, 'An Interview with Ngũgĩ wa Thiong'o' (Los Angeles: Los Angeles Review of Books, 2017), https://lareviewofbooks.org/article/an-interview-with-ngugi-wa-thiongo/. Accessed 1 February 2022.

The odds are against publishing African literature in African languages. There is no requirement to read such literature beyond primary school. Zell (2018) agrees with the reasoning of most publishers, noting that 'publishing in African languages can only be financially viable if there is in fact a market for those books, either in the form of government guarantees or incentives, or other tangible support'.[25] With less incentive to publish from a business sense, there is no developed distribution system. However, for the few publishers who take up the challenge of bringing out books in African languages, it is essential to navigate these challenges and circulate their publications effectively. Books must be brought as close to the readers as possible. This includes marketing in areas where such languages are widely spoken. Local language radio stations can be used to spread the word. However, since broadcast marketing can be quite expensive, booksellers also need to send sales representatives to small towns and villages and sell these books directly to people. Due to the gap in publishing and distribution of African language books, publishers must adopt radical approaches.

Effective circulation and distribution of African language books has also to consider the power of the internet. Shringarpure notes that though we take for granted the massive role of the internet and digital technology in promoting African literature, including that in African languages, the ways in which we read have been substantially altered. She states that we

> read so much now on screens, circulate PDFs via email, follow famous writers online, write mini-reviews on Amazon and Goodreads, consume all kinds of viral book controversies, cry out on Twitter for more diversity in literature, and feverishly share listicles and book recommendations on our Facebook timelines.[26]

With all its fault lines, the internet has provided a powerful alternative to the publishing and distribution of African language materials. It can be used to widely market new publications and increase access, at minimal cost. Restrictions are minimized when writers put their work into cyberspace where communities continue to arise, and the use of the internet is increasing among Africans.[27] However, Bgoya and Jay warn that this

---

[25]https://www.readafricanbooks.com/opinion/publishing-in-african-languages/. Accessed 1 February 2022.
[26]Bhakti Shringarpure, 'African Literature and Digital Culture' (Los Angeles Review of Books, 2021), https://lareviewofbooks.org/article/african-literature-and-digital-culture/. Accessed 1 February 2022.
[27]Shola Adenekan, *African Literature in the Digital Age: Class and Sexual Politics in New Writing from Nigeria and Kenya* (Suffolk: Boydell and Brewer Limited, 2021).

celebration of the possibilities of empowering publishing that is inherent in the digital age should be approached with caution. Many Africans across the continent still live in what these authors call 'grinding poverty and staggering levels of unemployment'.[28] Only a small population have the purchasing power to afford the kind of gadgets required for reading and there are issues to do with the cost of internet connections, affordability of computers and their software, as well as the reliability of electricity. In many cases, these factors retard the gains of digital facilities. Despite the odds, many African language enthusiasts continue to use digital facilities to reap maximum benefits.

Jane Obuchi, Kọ́lá Túbọ̀sún, Maazi Ogbonnaya and John Mambambo are good examples of effective social media users in promoting African languages. They are a testament to the possibilities we create every day for getting the work seen, known and appreciated. When this kind of circulation is done on social media, the authors are not only seeking to sell the work but also to gradually change the minds of people. Seeing literary books in African languages being spoken about on social media contributes to normalizing such publications. Already, these books are rare and the more we can make them the object of people's social media consumption, the more this kind of work can become something that people care about. Sharing both African language materials and information on how they can be accessed is a transformative process. However, making the work available is not the same thing as making it accessible or affordable. If the sale price of an African literary book is more than $10, few people, whether in the big cities or in villages, will prioritize such a book. Without sacrificing the quality of the book as a product, publishers and booksellers must agree to ensure books are as affordable as possible. Thus, people will be encouraged to both read and invest in the process.

Publishing online solves some of these problems but creates another. It answers the problem of availability and access but leads to little or no financial reward. Blogging for individual writers and translators, all the way to fully commercialized websites, is an avenue to be explored. Commercializing the work is the trickiest part of the process. Access to most websites is free, and those that have paywalls rarely attract the kind of traffic to make it commercially viable. However, increased availability of African language material on websites and on blogs will create a devoted readership, more likely to purchase a book published in their language. We must find a way to create economic value for the work. Difficult, yes. But we must.

---

[28]Walter Bgoya and Mary Jay, 'Publishing in Africa from Independence to the Present Day', *Research in African Literatures*, vol. 44, no. 2 (2013): 17–34, 30.

Worldwide readership

Say that an economic model was created for books in African languages, and they flourished in the market. Even if these literatures were to find the same kind of success that their oral counterparts have, we would still need to answer some pertinent questions. Key, of course, is the widespread notion that African literary works are too ethnicity- and culture-specific.[29] How, then, would they appeal to a global audience? Mũkoma wa Ngũgĩ makes the case for worldwide readership by giving the example of early South African writing. He writes of Phaswane Mpe's criticism of South African language books as limited, in that they could only be easily accessed by Sesotho and Xhosa speakers, even though such writings were already translated into English. Mũkoma reasons that such criticism of South African writing in South African languages was emblematic of some of the problems that still face literature produced in African languages, and African literature in general.[30]

According to Marzagora, this problem is compounded by the fact that Afrophone literatures are 'rarely included in critical debates and remain a neglected component not only of comparative literature, postcolonial studies, and world literature, but also of African literary studies at large'. If anything, these literatures continue to be 'idealized, ignored, or misinterpreted'.[31] But writers in African languages continue to soldier on. Ngũgĩ wa Thiong'o remains one of the most iconic writers working in African languages and gaining global attention. Most of his novels, though originally written in Gikuyu and translated into English, have won awards, been required reading in classrooms around the world and made him a contender for the Nobel prize in literature. Not many that are writing in African languages will reach Ngũgĩ's status. However, he is an excellent example of the potential of literature in African languages and reminds writers in African languages not to create artificial barriers for themselves, 'from fears of being left out of the heaven promised by globalization. This arises from the earlier colonially rooted notion that African languages are not modern enough and that European ones are the only ladder to global heaven. If Africa promotes its languages, the continent will miss the train to Heaven.'[32]

Global recognition for literatures in African languages will call upon Africans themselves to take responsibility. From writing, editing, publishing and distribution, we cannot wait for an outsider to do the work for us.

---

[29] Sara Marzagora, 'Literatures in African Languages', *Journal of African Cultural Studies*, vol. 27, no. 1 (2015): 1–6, 1.
[30] Mũkoma wa Ngũgĩ, *The Rise of the African Novel: Politics of Language, Identity, and Ownership* (Ann Arbor: University of Michigan Press, 2018).
[31] Marzagora, 'Literatures in African Languages', p. 2.
[32] Ngũgĩ wa Thiong'o, 'The Politics of Translation', p. 126.

To control this process and bring its benefits to the people, Africans must own the process. By so doing, we are also taking control of the narrative, and ensuring that our literatures are valued by our fellow Africans. Books in African languages have the potential to offer essential and innovative contribution to world literature and literary theory (Marzagora 2015). By taking responsibility, African will reverse what Mbithi identified as an abnormality. This abnormality, Mbithi intimates, is where our literary tradition is shaped by European languages and no right or privilege is given to African languages.[33] With support for African language books, we can reclaim a high intellectual estimation for African languages and allow them to be significant contributors to world literature. We do not have to aspire and conform to European languages, the dominance of which is essentially creating some form of cultural uniformity, and we do not have to lose the diversity of African languages.

Conclusion

For African languages to fully contribute to literary production and become a solid part of world literature, we must first acknowledge the extreme challenges that face them. These range from attitudes to historical subjugation to supposed lack of economic viability and lack of worldwide appeal. The responsibility for meeting these challenges does not lie in any one person or institution; rather, it is a communal responsibility. African writers and scholars must do more to produce the content, and that content must be made visible to the world. Such visibility comes from the concerted efforts of writers, translators, publishers and book distributors. If everyone plays their part, Africans themselves will reject the cultural conformity that has come about due to the dominance of European languages.

Bibliography

Adegbija, Efurosibina (1994), *Language Attitudes in Sub-Saharan Africa: A Sociolinguistic Overview*, Clevedon: Multilingual Matters.

Adenekan, Shola (2021), *African Literature in the Digital Age: Class and Sexual Politics in New Writing from Nigeria and Kenya*, Suffolk: Boydell and Brewer.

Alexander, Neville (2005), 'The Potential Role of Translation as Social Practice for the Intellectualisation of African Languages', *Marxists*, https://www.marxists.org/archive/alexander/2005-potential-role-of-translation.pdf. Accessed 1 February 2022.

---

[33] Mbithi, 'Multilingualism, Language Policy and Creative Writing in Kenya'.

Bgoya, Walter (2001), 'The Effect of Globalisation in Africa and the Choice of Language in Publishing', *International Review of Education*, vol. 47, no. 4: 283–92.

Bgoya, Walter, and Mary Jay (2013), 'Publishing in Africa from Independence to the Present Day', *Research in African Literatures*, vol. 44, no. 2: 17–34.

Durrani, Shiraz (2006), *Never Be Silent: Publishing and Imperialism 1884–1963*, Nairobi: Vita Books.

Dyssou, Nanda (2017), 'An Interview with Ngũgĩ wa Thiong'o', Los Angeles: The Los Angeles Review of Books, https://lareviewofbooks.org/article/an-interview-with-ngugi-wa-thiongo/. Accessed 1 February 2022.

Frederiksen, Bodil Folke (2011), 'Print, Newspapers, and Audiences in Colonial Kenya: African and Indian Improvement, Protest, and Connections', *Journal of the International African Institute*, vol. 81, no. 1: 155–72.

Kioko, Angelina Nduku (2019), *A Grammar of Kĩĩkamba*, Nairobi: Twaweza Communications.

Marzagora, Sara (2015), 'Literatures in African Languages', *Journal of African Cultural Studies*, vol. 27, no. 1: 1–6.

Mbithi, Esther (2014), 'Multilingualism, Language Policy and Creative Writing in Kenya', *Multilingual Education*, vol. 4, no. 19, https://doi.org/10.1186/s13616-014-0019-9. Accessed 1 February 2022.

Mũkoma wa Ngũgĩ (2018), *The Rise of the African Novel: Politics of Language, Identity, and Ownership*, Ann Arbor: University of Michigan Press.

Mũkoma wa Ngũgĩ (7 July 2021), 'New Kiswahili Science Fiction Award Charts a Path for African Languages', The Conversation, https://theconversation.com/new-kiswahili-science-fiction-award-charts-a-path-for-african-languages-163876/. Accessed 1 February 2022.

Musau, Paul (2010), 'Linguistic Human Rights in Africa: Challenges and Prospects for Indigenous Languages in Kenya', *Language, Culture and Curriculum*, vol. 16, no. 2: 155–64.

Mwau, John Harun (2006), *Kikamba Dictionary-Osa Vinya Mukamba*, Nairobi: J. H. Mwau.

Ngũgĩ wa Thiong'o (1986), *Decolonising the Mind: The Politics of Language in African Literature*, London: Heinemann.

Ngũgĩ wa Thiong'o (2017), 'The Politics of Translation: Notes towards an African Language Policy', *Journal of African Cultural Studies*, vol. 30, no. 2: 124–32.

Ogechi, Nathan Oyori, and Emily Bosire-Ogechi (2002), 'Educational Publishing in African Languages, with a Focus on Swahili in Kenya', *Nordic Journal of African Studies*, vol. 11, no. 2: 167–84.

Ouane, Adama, and Christine Glanz (2010), 'Why and How Africa Should Invest in African Languages and Multilingual Education: An Evidence- and Practice-Based Policy Advocacy Brief', UNESCO Institute for Lifelong Learning.

Roy-Campbell, Zaline Makini (2019), 'Revitalizing African Languages for Transformation', *Contemporary Journal of African Studies*, vol. 6, no. 1: 27–45.

Shringarpure, Bhakti (4 January 2021), 'African Literature and Digital Culture', Los Angeles Review of Books, https://lareviewofbooks.org/article/african-literature-and-digital-culture/. Accessed 1 February 2022.

9

New cartographies for world literary space: Locating pan-African publishing and prizing

Zamda R. Geuza and Kate Wallis

On Saturday 16 February 2019, Samia Suluhu Hassan shared a photograph of herself on Instagram addressing those gathered for the award ceremony of the Mabati-Cornell Kiswahili Prize for African Literature, which had taken place the previous day at Mlimani City Hall in Dar es Salaam. Tanzania's first female president, Hassan was an invited guest at the prize's award celebration in her role as then vice president along with four other ministers. Images of Hassan presenting Zainab Alwi Baharoon with the fiction prize for *Mungu Hakopeshwi*,[1] a novel published by Dar es Salaam–based publisher Mkuki na Nyota (MNN), were widely circulated through the Tanzanian media,[2] as well as featuring on the Kenya-based leading African literature platform James Murua's Literature Blog.[3] This theatrical physical exchange between Hassan and Baharoon speaks to what James English in his influential study of prize culture describes as 'capital intraconversion', highlighting the ability of

---

[1] This title translates into English as 'God doesn't borrow time'.
[2] 'VP Awards Winners of African Literature', The Guardian, 16 February 2019, https://www.ippmedia.com/en/news/vp-awards-winners-african-literature; 'Makamu Wa Rais Akabidhi Tuzo Kwa Washindi Bora Wa Kiswahili'; Global Publishers, 15 February 2019, https://globalpublishers.co.tz/makamu-wa-rais-akabidhi-tuzo-za-washindi-bora-wa-kiswahili/.
[3] James Murua, 'Mabati-Cornell Kiswahili Prize for African Literature 2018 Winners Celebrated', James Murua Literature Blog, 18 February 2019, https://www.jamesmurua.com/mabati-cornell-kiswahili-prize-for-african-literature-2018-winners-celebrated/.

FIGURE 9.1 *Tweet from the Kiswahili Prize celebrating the 2018 award ceremony.*

literary prizes to enable multilayered transactions across spaces of cultural, economic, social and political power.[4] MNN's Director Mkuki Bgoya has emphasized the particular impact that seeing high-profile politicians talking about books has in terms of elevating and building audiences for books in Tanzania, noting the significance of MNN's publication of a series of high-profile political biographies and autobiographies for 'raising awareness of books'.[5] Strikingly, then, a tweet from the Mabati-Cornell Kiswahili Prize celebrating the award ceremony (see Figure 9.1) featured not only a staged photograph of Hassan and other political dignitaries with Abdilatif Abdalla, chair of the prize's board, and Mũkoma wa Ngũgĩ, co-founder, but also a

---

[4] James F. English, *The Economy of Prestige* (Cambridge, MA: Harvard University Press, 2005), p. 10.
[5] Mkuki Bgoya, interview by Zamda Geuza and Kate Wallis, 19 May 2021.

candid photograph of the pair browsing at MNN's bookstall, where copies of books by previous winners of the prize were available on sale together for the first time.

These exchanges provide a window onto the multifaceted processes and locations through which contemporary Swahili literature is produced, consecrated with prestige and circulated. As such, they offer a revealing entry point into this chapter, which examines the networks of cultural value and circulation that construct and are constructed by a collaboration between leading Tanzanian publisher MNN and the Mabati-Cornell Kiswahili Prize for African Literature. Through this, our intention is to explore the dynamics of capital intraconversion via which contemporary Swahili literature is positioned within world literary space.

MNN and the Mabati-Cornell Kiswahili Prize for African Literature

Independent publishing house MNN was founded in 1991 by Walter Bgoya. As A. K. Kaiza indicates, 'Mkuki na Nyota was conceived in crisis' after the Tanzania Publishing House (TPH), which Bgoya had run for the previous eighteen years, was decimated by the impact of IMF/World Bank structural adjustment programmes introduced in the late 1980s.[6] MNN could be described as a family business, with Walter Bgoya's wife Frida Mariki taking on the role of chief accountant and their son Mkuki Bgoya now a director. The company publishes books in English and Kiswahili across scholarly, educational and trade spaces, including vibrant lists of children's books and art books. However, fundamental to MNN's progressive publishing ethos has been the production of books in Kiswahili and building a critically acclaimed list of Swahili literature.[7] Notably, given this chapter's concern with the dynamics of world literary space, MNN has consistently positioned itself as a Tanzania-based publishing house that focuses on 'nurturing our indigenous literature' for a 'main market' of Tanzania, while simultaneously remaining committed to sharing Tanzanian and East African experiences, perspectives and books globally.[8] MNN's books are marketed and made available worldwide through African Books Collective (ABC), a non-profit African-owned distribution platform co-founded by Walter Bgoya in 1985 and which MNN has remained a 'key driver' of ever since.[9] In addition,

---

[6] A. K. Kaiza, 'A Luta Continua!', *New African*, no. 563 (July 2016): 74–8, 77.
[7] Kaiza, 'A Luta Continua!'; Mkuki Bgoya, interview by Zamda Geuza and Kate Wallis.
[8] Walter Bgoya, 'A Survey of Fourteen African Publishers', *Wasafiri*, vol. 31, no. 4 (1 October 2016b): 13–22, https://doi.org/10.1080/02690055.2016.1216272; 'About Us', 2021, https://mkukinanyota.com/about/; Mkuki Bgoya, interview by Zamda Geuza and Kate Wallis.
[9] Justin Cox, interview by Kate Wallis, 11 May 2021.

MNN has positioned itself through the widely circulated tagline 'Relevant Books, Books, Beautiful Books and Affordable Books'; as we examine here, an emphasis on the aesthetics of book production has been vital to shaping their collaboration with the Mabati-Cornell Kiswahili Prize for Literature.

The Mabati-Cornell Kiswahili Prize for African Literature (hereafter Kiswahili Prize) was founded in 2014 by Lizzy Attree, then director of the Caine Prize for African Writing, and Mūkoma wa Ngũgĩ, associate professor of Literatures in English at Cornell University known for his scholarly and creative writing, as well as for continuing the activist work of his father around literary production in African languages. As Doseline Kiguru has highlighted, the prize immediately 'gained from the symbolic capital' of both the Caine Prize and Ngũgĩ wa Thiong'o, 'who has tirelessly campaigned for African literatures written in African languages' and became an active member of the prize's board of trustees.[10] The Kiswahili Prize was established with two interlinked aims: firstly to 'promote writing in African languages' and secondly 'to encourage translation from, between and into African languages'.[11] With this in view, the prize awards up to US$15,000 annually to the best unpublished manuscript or recently published book in Kiswahili across the categories of fiction, memoir, poetry and graphic novels, with the first prize winner for fiction/non-fiction and poetry each receiving $5,000. The prize has established collaborations not only with MNN but also with East African Educational Publishers (EAEP) in Kenya, and the African Poetry Book Fund (APBF) in the United States, to facilitate the publication of winning titles in both Kiswahili and English.

The Kiswahili Prize has worked to differentiate itself from longer established prizes for Swahili literature – such as Kenya's Text Book Centre Jomo Kenyatta Prize for Literature or Tanzania's Ebrahim Hussein Poetry Prize – by moving beyond national boundaries and positioning itself as an international, pan-African literary award for writing in an African language. With this in view, the prize advocates for its 'contribution to the body of world literature',[12] pushing back at a conception of world literary space where the only international literary prizes for African writing focus on Europhone languages. In *The Rise of the African Novel*, Mūkoma makes a persuasive argument for the need to set up 'literary structures in African languages' in order to facilitate writers producing work in African languages.[13] His work with the Kiswahili Prize responds directly to this, and

---

[10]Doseline Kiguru, 'Language and Prizes: Exploring Literary and Cultural Boundaries', in *Routledge Handbook of African Literature*, ed. Moradewun Adejunmobi and Carli Coetzee (Abingdon: Routledge, 2019), pp. 399–412, 404.
[11]'About the Prize', https://kiswahiliprize.cornell.edu/about-the-prize/.
[12]Ibid.
[13]Mũkoma wa Ngũgĩ, *The Rise of the African Novel*, Politics of Language, Identity, and Ownership (Ann Arbor: University of Michigan Press, 2018), p. 70.

through this he places consistent emphasis on the prize as part of 'setting up a viable and thriving ecosystem for writing African languages' and, linked to that, the value of collaborating with MNN.[14] Notably, in interview, all those associated with the Kiswahili Prize – from Chair Abdilatif Abdalla to prize administrator Munyao Kilolo – shared a strong commitment to the prize, working to construct a model that could be used not just for Swahili literature but for 'prizes in African languages across the continent'.[15] One significant aspect of this 'model' is advocating for 'African philanthropy for African cultural production',[16] with the prize having been made possible through the ongoing support of its major funder, Kenyan steel roofing company Mabati Rolling Mills, as well as its parent company the Safal Group and sister company ALAF in Tanzania. However, this chapter argues that it is particularly through the Kiswahili Prize's collaboration with MNN that possibilities have been opened up for modelling new cartographies for African literary production and world literary space in both theoretical and practical terms. We begin by briefly situating this study in relation to existing scholarly debates around African literatures and world literary space, as well as previous interventions that have focused on East Africa's relationship with literary prize culture and the post-national circulations of Swahili literature. Building on this, the chapter goes on to explore in more detail the relationality between MNN and the Kiswahili Prize, arguing for the significance of MNN as an Africa-based publisher with a long-standing commitment to both the aesthetics of book production and a pan-African agenda in constructing new literary structures and global prestige for Swahili literature.

World literary space and Afrophone African literary production

Both MNN and the Kiswahili Prize are conscious of and committed to their work locating African literature in Kiswahili within world literary space. Stefan Helgesson has importantly highlighted that 'the remit of world literature studies should not be reduced to questions of international canonisation or global marketing' as this risks simply working to confirm existing geopolitical power structures. Instead, he argues for an idea of

---

[14]Mũkoma wa Ngũgĩ, interview by Kate Wallis, 18 May 2021; Lizzy Attree and Mũkoma wa Ngũgĩ, 'New Kiswahili Science Fiction Award Charts a Path for African Languages', The Conversation, 7 July 2021, http://theconversation.com/new-kiswahili-science-fiction-award-charts-a-path-for-african-languages-163876.
[15]Munyao Kilolo, interview by Zamda Geuza and Kate Wallis, 17 May 2021.
[16]wa Ngũgĩ, interview by Kate Wallis.

'conceptual worlding' that enables a consideration of the processes and locations through which 'transcultural' literary value is produced 'both within and in resistance to such power relations'.[17] While Helgesson reads this idea of 'conceptual worlding' through Ngũgĩ wa Thiong'o's critical writing, instead here we elucidate the ways in which MNN and the Kiswahili Prize as literary institutions engage in 'conceptual worlding' through their positionality and collaboration.

Pascale Casanova's conception of 'world literary space' as the transnational 'history and geography' through which the 'literary' is constituted[18] has been consistently complicated and expanded by scholars of African literary studies to better account for the value and relationality of non-European histories of literary production.[19] Particularly significant to the concerns of this chapter is Sara Marzagora's work, which advocates for increased engagement with Afrophone African literary production as enabling of new critical models for world literatures.[20] By foregrounding the relationality between Afrophone and Europhone African literary traditions, as well as between oral and written media, Marzagora pushes back at the idea of a single literary world and instead maps world literary space through a plural, polyglot framing of 'multilayered and intersecting literary systems'.[21] Building upon this, Marzagora's collaborative work with scholars working on Asian and Middle Eastern geographies powerfully articulates that 'world' is always necessarily a locally produced concept.[22] This resonates strongly with arguments put forward twenty-five years earlier by Ngũgĩ wa Thiong'o in his essay 'Moving the Centre'; here, Ngũgĩ is concerned to shift the idea

---

[17]Stefan Helgesson, 'Ngũgĩ wa Thiong'o and the Conceptual Worlding of Literature', *Anglia*, vol. 135, no. 1 (1 March 2017): 105–21, 119.
[18]Pascale Casanova, *The World Republic of Letters*, trans. M. B. DeBevoise (Cambridge, MA: Harvard University Press, 2004), pp. 3–4.
[19]Caroline Davis, *Creating Postcolonial Literature: African Writers and British Publishers* (Basingstoke: Palgrave Macmillan, 2013); Nathan Suhr-Sytsma, *Poetry, Print, and the Making of Postcolonial Literature* (Cambridge: Cambridge University Press, 2017); Stefan Helgesson, 'Postcolonialism and World Literature', *Interventions: International Journal of Postcolonial Studies*, vol. 16, no. 4 (2014): 483–500; Stefan Helgesson, 'Forum on World Literary Systems: Tayeb Salih, Sol Plaatje, and the Trajectories of World Literature', *Cambridge Journal of Postcolonial Literary Inquiry*, vol. 2, no. 2 (2015): 253–60; Sara Marzagora, 'African-Language Literatures and the "Transnational Turn" in Euro-American Humanities', *Journal of African Cultural Studies*, vol. 27, no. 1 (2015a): 40–55; Ruth Bush, *Publishing Africa in French: Literary Institutions and Decolonization 1945–1967* (Liverpool: Liverpool University Press, 2016).
[20]Marzagora, 'African-Language Literatures and the "Transnational Turn" in Euro-American Humanities'; Sara Marzagora, 'Literatures in African Languages', *Journal of African Cultural Studies*, vol. 27, no. 1 (2 January 2015b): 1–6.
[21]Ibid., p. 49.
[22]Karima Laachir, Sara Marzagora and Francesca Orsini, 'Multilingual Locals and Significant Geographies', *Modern Languages Open*, vol. 19, no. 1 (2018): 1–8.

that literature can be generalized from any one centre (and particularly from a 'narrow base in Europe'), instead making the case that 'different people in the world had their culture and environment at the centre'.[23] More recently in *Globalectics*, Ngũgĩ builds on this work to intervene explicitly in debates around world literature, setting out a model of reading that approaches the 'relationship between languages, cultures and literatures' as a network, emphasizing both translation and positionality as enabling conversations between texts within global space.[24] Responding to this shared call for located approaches to world literature, our work here and elsewhere[25] argues for the critical possibilities of mapping world literary space through the frame of Africa-based publishers. Across this chapter we are concerned, through a process of conceptual worlding, to ask: what worlds do MNN 'simultaneously *inhabit* and *create*'?[26] How is Afrophone African literature's relationality with world literary space defined and where from? What networks of production, cultural value and circulation are at stake in this process? How can scholarly work better foreground the significance of processes and locations of African literary production that 'directly benefit African economies'?[27]

Doseline Kiguru's work has been pioneering in recognizing and analysing the impact of literary prizes on the structures of African literary production, and the processes of capital intraconversion at stake here.[28] In ways that resonate strongly with the concerns of this chapter, Kiguru draws attention to the complex ways that literary prizes do more than respond to 'an already established literary culture'[29] but become actively engaged in building new literary structures.[30] Notably, Kiguru is the only scholar to date to have written about the Kiswahili Prize, looking at this alongside the Commonwealth Short Story Prize and the Tuzo ya Ubunifu Kiswahili Literary Award, to examine

---

[23]Ngũgĩ wa Thiong'o, *Moving the Centre: The Struggle for Cultural Freedoms* (Nairobi: East African Educational Publishers, 1993), pp. 6, 8–9.
[24]Ngũgĩ wa Thiong'o, *Globalectics* (New York: Columbia University Press, 2014), p. 61.
[25]Kate Wallis, 'Exchanges in Nairobi and Lagos: Mapping Literary Networks and World Literary Space', *Research in African Literatures*, vol. 49, no. 1 (2018): 163–86; Kate Wallis, 'Ngũgĩ wa Thiong'o: Networks, Literary Activism and the Production of World Literature', in *A Companion to World Literature*, ed. Ken Seigneurie (Chichester: Wiley-Blackwell, 2020), pp. 2721–32.
[26]Laachir et al., 'Multilingual Locals and Significant Geographies', p. 4.
[27]Walter Bgoya and Mary Jay, 'Publishing in Africa from Independence to the Present Day', *Research in African Literatures*, vol. 44, no. 2 (2013): 17–34, 31.
[28]Doseline Kiguru, 'Prizing African Literature: Creating a Literary Taste', *Social Dynamics*, vol. 42, no. 1 (2 January 2016): 161–74; Doseline Kiguru, 'Literary Prizes, Writers' Organisations and Canon Formation in Africa', *African Studies*, vol. 75, no. 2 (3 May 2016): 202–14; Kiguru, 'Language and Prizes'; Doseline Kiguru, 'Genre versus Prize: The Short Story Form and African Oral Traditions', *English in Africa*, vol. 47, no. 3 (10 February 2021): 37–54.
[29]Kiguru, 'Genre versus Prize', p. 51.
[30]Kiguru, 'Literary Prizes, Writers' Organisations and Canon Formation in Africa', p. 203.

the modes through which these awards 'claim a space for African literature in African languages on the global literary scene'.[31] Linked to this, she notes the significance of the Kiswahili Prize's agreements with partner publishers to its work 'enhancing literary networks', and that although through collaboration with EAEP novels by Anna Manyanza and Enock Margesi (awarded the inaugural 2015 prize) have been published, so far plans for translating the winning poetry titles into English for publication by APBF 'appear stalled'.[32] However, notably, the Kiswahili Prize's collaboration with MNN is not mentioned, Kiguru's piece being written just ahead of MNN also beginning to release and publicize a series of titles by winners of the prize at the end of 2018. Our own chapter is therefore able to build on Kiguru's work to show the significance of this more recent collaboration for the prize's evolving exchanges with local and transnational literary spaces.

While the Kiswahili Prize might intend to offer a 'model' for prizing Afrophone African literary production more broadly, the multidirectional geography and history of Swahili literature in particular bring with it its own positionality. Nathan Suhr-Sytsma has argued for the ongoing significance of a 'geography of prestige' to structures of literary prizing, showing how these geographies have the potential to be multidirectional and made up of 'circuits of exchange' that move across nations, regions and continents.[33] With over 150 million speakers, Kiswahili is notable for its 'cross-border relevance',[34] with Simon Gikandi observing that 'Swahili poetry and prose can be found along the East African coast from the Gulf of Oman to the Comoros and from the coast into the interior of Africa, in the Congo and the Zambian copper belt'.[35] While Lutz Diegner has highlighted, this 'resonates with Achille Mbembe's alternative forms of mapping, which characterize the African continent before and beyond colonialism',[36] as is the case with many Afrophone language literatures, the development of written Kiswahili remains deeply entangled with histories of colonialism.[37] Kiguru foregrounds the contradictions in the Kiswahili Prize's simultaneous

---

[31]Kiguru, 'Language and Prizes', p. 410.
[32]Ibid., p. 409.
[33]Nathan Suhr-Sytsma, 'The Geography of Prestige: Prizes, Nigerian Writers, and World Literature', *ELH*, vol. 85, no. 4 (2018): 1093–1122.
[34]Lutz Diegner, 'Postrealist, Postmodernist, Postnation? The Swahili Novel 1987–2010', *Research in African Literatures*, vol. 49, no. 1 (2018): 117–44, 126.
[35]Simon Gikandi, 'Introduction – Another Way in the World', *PMLA*, vol. 131, no. 5 (October 2016): 1193–1206, 1198.
[36]Diegner, 'Postrealist, Postmodernist, Postnation?', p. 127.
[37]Moradewun Adejunmobi, 'Routes: Language and the Identity of African Literature', *Journal of Modern African Studies*, vol. 37, no. 4 (1999): 581–96, 588; Ken Walibora Waliaula, 'The Afterlife of Oyono's "Houseboy" in the Swahili Schools Market: To Be or Not to Be Faithful to the Original', *PMLA*, vol. 128, no. 1 (2013): 178–84, 179; Xavier Garnier, *The Swahili Novel: Challenging the Idea of Minor Literature* (Suffolk: Boydell & Brewer, 2013), pp. 4–5.

positioning of Kiswahili as a 'world language' because of its expansive geographical reach, while expounding the principle that 'all languages are created equal'.[38] Linked to this, in interview, both prize administrator Kilolo and founder Mũkoma reflected on the risks of language hierarchies and the importance to the Kiswahili Prize of working in ways that allow Kiswahili to 'connect' and not 'dominate' other African languages.[39] Yet the significance of these tensions to literary structures and questions of capital intraconversion can't be ignored, particularly when within African literary studies Afrophone language literatures continue to be critically neglected, while Swahili literature works as an 'exception' with a well-established body of scholarship surrounding it.[40]

Significantly for this chapter then, there has been a variety of recent critical interventions that have explored Swahili literature's relationship with world literary space. For the most part this work has emphasized Swahili literature entering into dialogue with the world through its politics and through its choice of literary form.[41] Rémi Armand Tchokothe's innovations in close reading texts by Said A. Mohamed and Kyallo Wamitila through Ngũgĩ's conception of globalectics are notable in considering aesthetic decisions made by the publisher about cover design alongside literary form. Here, we build on Tchokothe's emphasis on the importance of book design to East African publishers and to Swahili literature's 'dominant global inclination',[42] but shift the emphasis to examining the ways in which MNN's cover designs for titles that have won the Kiswahili Prize directly enable processes of circulation and prestige.

Building publishing and prizing collaborations

While MNN and the Kiswahili Prize have been in dialogue since the prize's conception and launch, this relationship has evolved and shifted. When the Kiswahili Prize was launched in 2014 at Nigeria's Aké Arts and

---

[38]Kiguru, 'Language and Prizes', p. 40; 'About the Prize'.
[39]wa Ngũgĩ, interview by Kate Wallis; Kilolo, interview by Zamda Geuza and Kate Wallis.
[40]Flora Veit-Wild and Clarissa Vierke, 'Introduction: Digging into Language', *Research in African Literatures*, vol. 48, no. 1 (2017): ix–xviii, xii–xiii.
[41]Garnier, *The Swahili Novel*; Taylor A. Eggan, 'Regionalizing the Planet: Horizons of the Introverted Novel at World Literature's End', *PMLA*, vol. 131, no. 5 (October 2016): 1299–1315; Lutz Diegner, 'Leaving Parched Gardens and Discussing Narration with the Reader: Metatextualities in the Contemporary Swahili Novel', *Research in African Literatures*, vol. 48, no. 1 (2017): 24–43.
[42]Rémi Armand Tchokothe, 'Globalectical Swahili Literature', *Journal of African Cultural Studies*, vol. 27, no. 1 (March 2015): 30–9, 30.

Book Festival, Walter Bgoya was visible as one of the prize's eight trustees, yet EAEP were the only named publishing partner for winning titles in Kiswahili.[43] However, given the importance of publishing partnerships to building networks of prestige and circulation, and the impact of both the timing and quality of publication specifically, by 2017 the Kiswahili Prize had established a second publishing partnership with MNN.[44]

MNN has published four titles linked to the prize to date. Perhaps most notably, they published both the 2017 winners – Ali Hilal Ali's novel *Mmeza Fupa* and Dotto Rangimoto's poetry collection *Mwanangu Rudi Nyumbani* – making these titles available within a year of their win and, as we foregrounded in the opening to this chapter, ensuring these books were visible and available for purchase at the ceremony to award the 2018 prize. The Kiswahili Prize is open to unpublished manuscripts as well as books published within the last two years; fortuitously, then, MNN's 2017 publication of Baharoon's *Mungu Hakopeshwi* was selected in January 2019 as one of the 2018 winners, enabling MNN to make this title visible and available for purchase at the 2018 award ceremony as well. Finally, while EAEP published the two novels awarded the 2015 Kiswahili Prize, they did not release the winning poetry collection *N'na Kwetu*[45] by Mohammed Ghassani. Early in 2019, again in time for the 2018 award ceremony, MNN published another collection by Ghassani entitled *Machozi Yamenishiya*[46] and tenaciously promoted this as a title by a Mabati-Cornell Kiswahili Prize–winning author.

The Kiswahili Prize to date has not been able to make any financial investment in its publishing partnerships.[47] Given that translation is core to the prize's aims, there has been an ongoing commitment to raise funding for translation that would enable, among other things, collaboration with APBF to make the winning poetry titles available in English.[48] Mpale Yvonne Mwansasu Silkiluwasha, in her study of Tanzania's Burt Award, makes visible how this literary prize was able to work towards its objective to 'stimulate and support the African publishing industry and African literary production' by committing to a guaranteed purchase of 3,000 copies of each winning book.[49] By contrast, EAEP and MNN take on the publication of

---

[43] Cornell University, 'Major New Prize for African Literature Announced', 21 November 2014, https://web.archive.org/web/20141125080155/kiswahiliprize.cornell.edu/.
[44] Lizzy Attree, interview by Zamda Geuza and Kate Wallis, 18 May 2021; Abdilatif Abdalla, interview by Zamda Geuza and Kate Wallis, 7 June 2021; wa Ngũgĩ, interview by Kate Wallis.
[45] This title translates into English as 'I have a place I call home'.
[46] This title translates into English as 'No more tears'.
[47] Attree, interview by Zamda Geuza and Kate Wallis.
[48] Ibid.; wa Ngũgĩ, interview by Kate Wallis.
[49] Mpale Yvonne Mwansasu Silkiluwasha, 'Reflecting and Reflexing on Book Awards: A Case Study of the Burt Award', *Eastern African Literary and Cultural Studies*, vol. 7, nos 1–2 (3 April 2021): 116–32, 120.

Kiswahili Prize–winning titles entirely at their own financial risk, drawing on their own resources to invest in the cost of editing, production, marketing and distribution without any kind of guaranteed sales. However, while the collaboration between MNN and the Kiswahili Prize may not involve exchanges of financial capital, it is a relationship predicated on capital intraconversion that has brought reciprocal benefits to both.

Walter Bgoya has emphasized the important role that writing competitions play in MNN's work of supporting and developing writers.[50] Alongside this, we suggest this particular collaboration has enabled MNN to strengthen further the processes of commissioning and publishing that shape their market-leading list of Swahili literature. In interview, MNN staff reflected on the multiple ways that the Kiswahili Prize has directly impacted the quality of manuscripts they receive and publish.[51] Mkuki Bgoya spoke specifically about the prize working 'almost like a literary agent', helping to find talent and drawing MNN's attention to 'really good work',[52] work that, as editor Godance Andrew observed, has already been vetted by a professional judging team.[53] The Kiswahili Prize helps MNN find and retain writing talent, with several prize-winning authors returning to them to develop subsequent projects.[54] In addition, it also encourages a higher number of new submissions from writers who hope that MNN might take on their book and, having 'mastered the rules of the game',[55] put them in a stronger position when submitting work for the prize.[56]

By building this close publishing partnership with MNN and supporting their Swahili literary publishing, the Kiswahili Prize makes an important investment in literary structures that enable Afrophone African literary production. This publishing relationship is hugely significant in terms of signalling the prize's commitment to Africa-based institutions – and locating the dynamics of creation, production and circulation of 'African' texts from the African continent. However, given MNN's long-standing position as a leading publisher of Swahili literature in terms of both literary content and the aesthetics of the books themselves, arguably this relationship is one that brings even more literary value to the Kiswahili Prize itself. When asked about the prize's most significant achievements to date, founders Attree and Mũkoma, as well as prize administrator Kilolo, independently emphasized MNN's publication of the prize-winning titles and the global circulation this

---

[50] Bgoya, 'A Survey of Fourteen African Publishers', p. 18.
[51] Godance Andrew, interview by Zamda Geuza, 30 May 2021; Mkuki Bgoya, interview by Zamda Geuza and Kate Wallis.
[52] Mkuki Bgoya, interview by Zamda Geuza and Kate Wallis.
[53] Andrew, interview by Zamda Geuza.
[54] Ibid.
[55] Silkiluwasha, 'Reflecting and Reflexing on Book Awards', p. 130.
[56] Mkuki Bgoya, interview by Zamda Geuza and Kate Wallis.

enables.⁵⁷ For the Kiswahili Prize then, these books become calling cards that are immediately able to construct networks of prestige and engagement, and that have longevity; calling cards whose positionality is located in Tanzania but that can travel within the region, the African continent and beyond. As Kilolo commented,

> A few months after the ceremony it is forgotten. Once the book has been published, it stays and it is able to travel to readers almost anywhere that they want to read in Kiswahili.⁵⁸

Across the next two substantive sections of this chapter we show how the success of this collaborative relationship, and the ability of these Kiswahili Prize–winning books to circulate in ways that enable new cartographies of literary value, is rooted in MNN's long-standing commitment to both the book as an aesthetic object and pan-Africanism.

Making material: Producing 'beautiful books'

Reflecting on the Kiswahili Prize's collaboration with MNN, founders Attree and Mũkoma have placed particular emphasis on the quality and expertise in evidence in the physical books produced, commenting on their 'eye-catching covers'⁵⁹ and being books that 'you want to hold'.⁶⁰ Similarly, and again without being directly prompted, chair Abdalla observed that MNN produces 'very well designed books compared to other publishers even in Kenya'.⁶¹ Tchokothe has emphasized the 'iconographic power of cover pages' to 'act as entry as well as exit points … with regard to the question of writing the world'.⁶² Here we suggest that book design does not need to specifically evoke a global thematic in order to be significant to how literary texts become constituted within world literary space. As Kelvin Smith and Melanie Ramdarshan Bold argue, cover design is of 'great importance' to publisher, bookseller and reader alike in its ability to 'add value' by increasing books' visibility, accessibility and allure.⁶³

---

⁵⁷Attree, interview by Zamda Geuza and Kate Wallis; Kilolo, interview by Zamda Geuza and Kate Wallis; wa Ngũgĩ, interview by Kate Wallis.
⁵⁸Kilolo, interview by Zamda Geuza and Kate Wallis.
⁵⁹Attree, interview by Zamda Geuza and Kate Wallis.
⁶⁰wa Ngũgĩ, interview by Kate Wallis.
⁶¹Abdalla, interview by Zamda Geuza and Kate Wallis.
⁶²Tchokothe, 'Globalectical Swahili Literature', p. 33.
⁶³Kelvin Smith and Melanie Ramdarshan Bold, *The Publishing Business: A Guide to Starting Out and Getting On* (London: Bloomsbury, 2018), pp. 134–5.

MNN's attention to the aesthetics of cover design and commitment to producing 'beautiful' books has been consistently emphasized by founder Walter Bgoya[64] and critics.[65] More recently, this emphasis can be strongly linked to the influence of Walter Bgoya's son Mkuki Bgoya, who trained as a designer at Texas A&M University and founded his own Dar es Salaam–based branding agency Spearhead in 2009. His role at MNN involves overseeing the publishing house's creative direction, focusing on design, production and creative visioning. In interview, Mkuki Bgoya talked compellingly about the ways in which 'the content and the form' of the books MNN produces are consistently thought 'together'.[66] What this means in practice is that a book's 'visual language' and 'tactile context', as well as the impact of this on production decisions from cover design to page layout to paper choices, is considered from the outset alongside the editorial process.[67] This enables what Mkuki Bgoya described as a much more 'cohesive process', where a project is able to be conceived 'in its totality', bringing advantages to MNN in their collaborative work with writers while also positioning audiences at the core of their publishing processes.[68]

This attention to design and aesthetics is very much in evidence across MNN's publishing catalogue, with innovation visible in both their use of typographical designs and the ways their covers draw on photography. However, Mkuki Bgoya reflected on the specific opportunities opening up for creating covers in response to 'literary works', commenting that 'for a creative person you are inspired by other creatives as well'.[69] When approaching the design of their literary titles, MNN is concerned with creating cover artwork that both connects to the 'story' and that draws in readers both online and in bookshops.[70] The four titles MNN has published by Kiswahili Prize winners were all designed in-house and, for Mkuki Bgoya, designing covers that 'match the excitement of prize-winning works' is particularly 'inspiring' and 'challenges you to try to do even better'.[71] With this in view, we want to draw attention to the ways in which Ali Hilal Ali's *Mmeza Fupa* (Figure 9.2) and Dotto Rangimoto's *Mwanangu Rudi Nyumbani* (Figure 9.3), the two initial titles MNN produced as Kiswahili

---

[64]Walter Bgoya, 'The Endeavour of Publishing: Its Limits of Success with Swahili Readers', in *Beyond the Language Issue: The Production, Mediation and Reception of Creative Writing in African Languages*, ed. Anja Oed and Uta Reuster-Jahn (Köln: Köppe, 2008), p. 92; Kaiza, 'A Luta Continua!', p. 75.
[65]Tchokothe, 'Globalectical Swahili Literature'; Kaiza, 'A Luta Continua!'.
[66]Mkuki Bgoya, interview by Zamda Geuza and Kate Wallis.
[67]Ibid.
[68]Ibid.
[69]Ibid.
[70]Bgoya, 'The Endeavour of Publishing', p. 92; Mkuki Bgoya, interview by Zamda Geuza and Kate Wallis.
[71]Mkuki Bgoya, interview by Zamda Geuza and Kate Wallis.

FIGURE 9.2 Mmeza Fupa *by Ali Hilal Ali (Mkuki na Nyota, 2019).*

FIGURES 9.3 and 9.4 Mwanangu Rudi Nyumbani *by Dotto Rangimoto (Mkuki na Nyota, 2018).*

Prize winners following the 2017 awards, are particularly striking in their use of design.

Mmeza Fupa translates into English as 'The Secret Keeper' and is the story of Bi Msiri, a woman who has lived for over two centuries. She witnesses the killing of her father, a senior government official, and is forced to flee carrying that secret. While the story is set on an imaginary island, it is deeply concerned with political and social issues.[72] MNN's cover design evokes the story's fantastical element through its choice of surreal colours and imagery.[73] The eye is immediately drawn to the solitary woman, blocked out in purple, standing on a mountain-side ablaze in orange and yellow and looking down to a sea of human skulls. The orange and yellow typography used for the title and author name is arresting against the black background of the mountain-side that contains it. Mkuki Bgoya described how MNN, through this visual language, worked 'to capture the mood and theme of the book', playing to the 'loneliness' of the old lady who has 'lived all these years' and the novel's coastal setting, as well as to its magical and sci-fi qualities through the choice of colours (Figures 9.3 and 9.4).[74]

Mwanangu Rudi Nyumbani translates into English as 'Child Come Back Home' and is a collection of poetry notable for engaging with complex and hard-hitting issues of politics and family in a creative and accessible way. Rangimoto was praised by the prize judges for his 'seductive metaphors and imagery', with particular attention paid to his poetry drawing on deep Kiswahili poetic devices (often associated with coastal writing, while Rangimoto emanates from rural Tanzania mainland).[75] The cover design responds directly to the collection's title and the idea of a mother longing for her son to come home: the front cover represents a 'mother image' while the back cover represents her son.[76] Strikingly, when the book is opened, the two photographic profiles face away from each other. While the tone of both images has been darkened to blend into the black background of the cover design, the woman's image is more prominent and visible in its lighting and positioning. In this portrait of an older African woman, the eye is drawn to the detail of her patterned head-wrap and her earring, which are accented in pale blue, while the lines on her face are also clearly visible. Mkuki Bgoya explained how MNN took a deliberate decision to position the title of this poetry collection in a contrasting bright yellow running *down* rather than *across* the page, with the intention here to be 'more

---

[72] Ali Hilal Ali, interview by Zamda Geuza, 9 May 2021.
[73] Mkuki Bgoya, interview by Zamda Geuza and Kate Wallis.
[74] Ibid.
[75] '2017 Winners', 16 January 2018, https://kiswahiliprize.cornell.edu/2016-winners/.
[76] Mkuki Bgoya, interview by Zamda Geuza and Kate Wallis.

FIGURE 9.5 *Mkuki na Nyota's Kiswahili Prize–winning authors on the African Books Collective website.*

poetic' and to challenge readers' expectations by 'push[ing] the boundaries of interpretation'.[77]

Both *Mmeza Fupa* and *Mwanangu Rudi Nyumbani* feature the strapline 'Hii Imetunukiwa Tuzo ya Kiswahili ya Mabati-Cornell ya Fasihi ya Afrika, Mwaka 2017' prominently on their front covers, signalling these books as winners of Kiswahili Prize in 2017, while also including quotations from the judges on the back cover. Claire Squires, focusing on the Booker Prize, has argued for the importance of prize straplines in conferring cultural value and contributing to sales success, while also showing how these can take on a self-reflexive role in 'defining the Prize' itself.[78] The idea that, as material and aesthetic objects produced by MNN, the published books in turn directly reflect and construct the literary value of the Kiswahili Prize explains in part why the prize founders have placed such strong emphasis on their importance. We suggest that MNN is equally conscious of their role as partner publishers in building this visual identity for the Kiswahili Prize – and that this is very much in evidence in how the cover designs work in dialogue as a set a four (see Figure 9.5). The books MNN made available for sale in time for the 2018 award ceremony complement each other visually and draw on similar colour palettes, making strong use of yellow, orange and black. It is also notable that all four feature a woman on the front cover,

---

[77] Ibid.
[78] Claire Squires, 'Book Marketing and the Booker Prize', in *Judging a Book by Its Cover: Fans, Publishers, Designers, and the Marketing of Fiction*, ed. Nickianne Moody and Nicole Matthews (Abingdon: Routledge, 2007), pp. 81–2.

yet across very different forms and styles, taking on heightened significance given the male-dominated Swahili publishing space.

Our close readings show how, through MNN's commitment to the aesthetics of book production and Mkuki Bgoya's expertise in this area, each cover design is crafted out of a detailed and holistic engagement with these literary texts on their own creative terms. While as a result no uniform branding is created for the Kiswahili Prize–winning titles, a distinctive aesthetic in terms of colour palette, imagery and approach emerges, which speaks to what Zahrah Nesbitt-Ahmed has termed 'the power of effective cover design'.[79] This 'adds value' and recognition for both MNN and the Kiswahili Prize, becoming key to how these books are able to circulate in East Africa and beyond, and ultimately opening up an idea of Swahili literature that has a pan-African mobility and works against structural inequalities. In the final substantive section of this chapter, we build on this analysis to unpack how a pan-African ethos shapes the positionality and relationality of MNN's collaboration with the Kiswahili Prize and in turn the new cartographies for world literary space modelled through this.

Pan-Africanism and world literary space

Appositely described by Tsitsi Jaji as an 'eclectic set of ephemeral cultural movements and currents', pan-Africanism is a term with a long, varied and contested critical history.[80] Tracing a series of significant and interlinked interventions within this critical history, Albert Kasanda makes a persuasive case for pan-Africanism's relevance today and how it might be defined through an ongoing commitment to human dignity and global justice.[81] Kasanda's argument resonates strongly with Kenyan writer Binyavanga Wainaina's commitment to a pan-African vision that encompasses an African queer and liberatory politics, pushing back at 'multiple structures of domination and oppression'.[82] Coming back to the question of the worlds that MNN both '*inhabit* and *create*',[83] the publishing house's vision has consistently been to publish 'progressive' and 'liberating' content from Tanzania.[84] This

---

[79]Zahrah Nesbitt-Ahmed, 'Continuing to Judge Books by Their Covers', *Bookshy* (blog), http://www.bookshybooks.com/2019/07/continuing-to-judge-books-by-their.html.
[80]Tsitsi Ella Jaji, *Africa in Stereo: Modernism, Music, and Pan-African Solidarity* (New York: Oxford University Press, 2014), p. 3.
[81]Albert Kasanda, 'Exploring Pan-Africanism's Theories: From Race-Based Solidarity to Political Unity and Beyond', *Journal of African Cultural Studies*, vol. 28, no. 2 (3 May 2016): 179–95.
[82]Adriaan van Klinken, 'Queering Pan-Africanism', 30 January 2020, https://africasacountry.com/2020/01/queering-pan-africanism.
[83]Laachir et al., 'Multilingual Locals and Significant Geographies', p. 4.
[84]'About Us'.

vision has been defined and articulated by Walter Bgoya, building upon his work at TPH where he published a variety of books that aimed at political, economic and cultural liberation, including Walter Rodney's *How Europe Underdeveloped Africa* (1972) and Issa Shivji's *Class Struggles in Tanzania* (1976). In a recent interview, Walter Bgoya explained that his 'understanding of progressive' publishing is to have a 'world view' that is 'informed by literature that is basically liberating people'.[85] Throughout this conversation he consistently emphasizes the importance of 'indigenous generation of knowledge', and that for him 'liberation' is people having access to 'different sources of knowledge, of ideas'.[86] For Walter Bgoya, publishing in African languages is vital to this, with MNN publishing over 50 per cent of its content in Kiswahili (across genres as diverse as crime fiction, primary and secondary school textbooks, and literary translations) as part of a deliberate decision to 'strengthen the local base'.[87] As Kenyan literary scholar Tom Odhiambo has commented, Walter Bgoya is 'very much invested in pan-Africanism', but his investment in 'local knowledge' does not come with 'an essentialised idea of Africa'.[88]

Arguably, locating the 'world view' of the Kiswahili Prize is more complicated, given that the prize lacks the fixed local base that Tanzania provides for MNN; founders Mũkoma and Attree are based in the United States and UK, respectively; the prize's chair Abdalla in Germany; and the prize's administrator Kilolo in Kenya. As a result, Abu Amirah, founder of Hekaya Arts Initiative, has reflected on the positioning of the Kiswahili Prize as being that of 'outsiders looking in', while arguing that this 'gives them a better perspective than other prizes that are homegrown'.[89] As Kiguru foregrounds, the prize's 'collaboration between local and international institutional institutions and figures' brings with it both 'prestige and contradiction'.[90] Across this chapter, we have been concerned to show that through collaboration with Africa-based MNN the Kiswahili Prize has been able to expand literary cartographies for Swahili literature. Key to enabling this, we suggest, is a shared pan-African and progressive ethos that can be most strongly located through the interlinked political and publishing trajectories of Walter Bgoya and Abdilatif Abdalla.

---

[85] The Funambulist Podcast, 'Walter Bgoya: Pan-African Publishing and the Struggle for a Second Liberation', vol. 135, https://soundcloud.com/the-funambulist/walter-bgoya-panafrican-publishing-struggling-for-a-second-liberation.
[86] The Funambulist Podcast.
[87] Walter Bgoya, 'The Effect of Globalisation in Africa and the Choice of Language in Publishing', *International Review of Education*, vol. 47, no. 3 (1 July 2001): 283–92, 291; Bgoya, 'The Endeavour of Publishing', p. 94.
[88] Quoted in Kaiza, 'A Luta Continua!', p. 76.
[89] Abu Amirah, interview by Zamda Geuza and Kate Wallis, 23 May 2021.
[90] Kiguru, 'Language and Prizes', pp. 405, 408.

Born in Mombasa in 1946, Kenyan poet and political activist Abdilatif Abdalla could be defined as belonging to the same generation of East African progressive intellectuals as Walter Bgoya, who was born in Ngara in 1942. Kai Kresse has positioned Abdalla as a 'mobile, morally committed and globally connected and informed thinker' for whom Kiswahili has been 'a localizing feature'.[91] As a renowned Kiswahili poet, editor, translator and teacher, imprisoned for his writing by the Kenyan government and forced into exile, who over the last five decades has lived across Dar es Salaam, London and Leipzig, Abdalla's literary, intellectual and geographical trajectory brings vital networks of prestige to the Kiswahili Prize. Critical to this is his own family background, with Abdalla frequently referencing the impact of coming from a line of distinguished coastal Swahili poets, musicians, artists, scholars and oppositional politicians, as well as speaking multiple dialects of Kiswahili.[92] Part of a family of *wasomi*, Abdalla's roots are in deeply entrenched networks of cultural value that have existed on the Swahili coast for generations and that, as Kresse highlights, operate in ways that are simultaneously 'hierarchical, yet integrative'.[93]

Abdalla, as chair of the Prize, oversees the key decisions, including the annual appointment of the judges and the judging process itself.[94] As Attree explained, Abdalla's role is central: 'He is the main lead on everything. He is so wise and so calm and knows everyone who is worth knowing in the Swahili world.'[95] His role in the prize is particularly crucial given neither of the prize's founders are embedded in the Swahili world themselves in terms of their own language proficiency or creative practice. Arguably, then, by appointing Abdalla as the prize's permanent chair and connecting pivot, the Kiswahili Prize works to position the prize through him as rooted in a long and dynamic Swahili literary tradition, constructed from within East Africa yet with cultural value and connections that travel well beyond the region.

When asked about the Kiswahili Prize's 'geography of prestige',[96] Abdalla was keen to stress that what marks it out as different from previous Swahili literary prizes is its 'pan-African' positioning.[97] On the one hand, this brings the prize a broader global reach, with participation encouraged from across

---

[91] Kai Kresse, 'Kenya: Twendapi?: Re-reading Abdilatif Abdalla's Pamphlet Fifty Years after Independence', *Africa*, vol. 86, no. 1 (2016): 1–32, 2.
[92] Ibid., p. 6; Daniela Waldburger, 'A Conversation with Abdilatif Abdalla', *Stichproben – Vienna Journal of African Studies*, vol. 20 (2020): 105–17, 108.
[93] Kai Kresse, *Philosophising in Mombasa* (Edinburgh: Edinburgh University Press, 2007), p. 54.
[94] Abdalla, interview by Zamda Geuza and Kate Wallis; Attree, interview by Zamda Geuza and Kate Wallis; Kilolo, interview by Zamda Geuza and Kate Wallis.
[95] Attree, interview by Zamda Geuza and Kate Wallis.
[96] Suhr-Sytsma, 'The Geography of Prestige'.
[97] Abdalla, interview by Zamda Geuza and Kate Wallis.

and beyond the African continent; on the other, it speaks to a broader progressive ethos. Abdalla continued,

> Most of us on the board of trustees are pan-Africanists. We'd like to see Africa united and speak with one voice, and these geographical boundaries we have should be abolished.[98]

This pan-African 'world view' works against a positioning of 'insider' or 'outsider', locating the prize in its commitment to solidarity between African peoples – a commitment that is shared with Walter Bgoya and that has liberatory politics and global justice at its core. Maria Suriano has written about Bgoya and Abdalla's long-standing friendship forged in Dar es Salaam in the 1970s, making a powerful case through this for a shared pan-Africanism and world view as significant to the 'resilience of independent cultural producers and institutions' on the African continent.[99] Through this collaboration, we suggest, this collective ethos is able to open up Swahili literary space and make this more inclusive, breaking down problematic and entrenched geographical, generational and gender hierarchies that have come to define it. This is reflected in Abdalla's emphasis on carefully selecting judges to not only ensure they are 'prominent names' in Swahili literature but that there is an imperative to work towards both 'the gender balance and the territorial balance'.[100] While the Swahili writers who have traditionally had the most cultural value placed on them are older men, very often pursuing teaching careers alongside their writing, this collaboration has begun to 'flatten the landscape'[101] and to bring younger writers, including women, from more diverse geographies into the Swahili literary canon.

Diegner highlights that, while Swahili literature has its roots in the 'coastal strips' of present-day Kenya and Tanzania, this literature has developed in very different ways either side of the border and 'Kenyan readers seem to read Tanzanian novels to a considerably greater extent than Tanzanians read Kenyan novels'.[102] Arguably, then, while Swahili literature has been considered 'regional' or 'post-national',[103] Kenya and Tanzania have

---

[98] Ibid.
[99] Maria Suriano, 'Dreams and Constraints of an African Publisher: Walter Bgoya, Tanzania Publishing House and Mkuki Na Nyota, 1972–2020', *Africa: The Journal of the International African Institute*, vol. 91, no. 4 (2021): 575–601, 597.
[100] Abdalla, interview by Zamda Geuza and Kate Wallis.
[101] Attree, interview by Zamda Geuza and Kate Wallis.
[102] Diegner, 'Postrealist, Postmodernist, Postnation?', pp. 126–7, 135–6.
[103] Mikhail D. Gromov, 'Regional or Local? On "Literary Trajectories" in Recent Swahili Writing', in *Habari Ya English? What about Kiswahili? East Africa as a Literary and Linguistic Contact Zone*, ed. Lutz Diegner and Frank Schulze-Engler (Amsterdam: Brill, 2015), pp. 67–79; Diegner, 'Postrealist, Postmodernist, Postnation?'

each constructed their own 'intersecting literary systems'[104] with separate structures of cultural capital. The Kiswahili Prize's pan-African positioning and lack of fixed local base has created opportunities to build networks that can operate across these literary systems, putting writers into dialogue across national borders in ways that are non-hierarchical and outside existing structures of regional literary exchange. One significant example is the dialogue established between Hekaya Arts Initiative, the Kiswahili Prize and MNN. Hekaya is a Mombasa-based cultural production platform, established in 2017 with the aim of putting 'contemporary Swahili art and literary content back on the global map'.[105] Hekaya runs literary activities in schools, has launched a literary prize, set up a bookshop, published a collaboratively authored novel and founded the annual Swahili Literary Festival. Kiswahili Prize winners have featured prominently at the festival with 2018 poetry winner Jacob Ngumbau speaking at the inaugural edition and the 2021 festival, themed around 'Celebrating Women', showcasing Manyanza and Baharoon – the prize's two female winners – in conversation. Notably, founder Amirah has acknowledged the important role that Abdalla has played in both inspiring and supporting Hekaya.[106] When asked about this mentoring role, Abdalla made clear it was separate from his work with the Kiswahili Prize and that he had taken it on because of a personal connection he felt to Amirah's work, commenting, 'He really touched me. So I said I will render my support in whatever I can to help this thing succeed.'[107] Hekaya has also been in consistent conversation with MNN, and since 2019 has stocked MNN's Kiswahili Prize–winning titles in its bookshop and actively promoted these books in Mombasa.[108] However, while this certainly reflects the Kiswahili Prize enabling cross-border circulation and visibility for Swahili literature, these relationships are informal and logistical barriers to the wider circulation and distribution of MNN's publications in Kenya remain. These barriers are exemplified in Amirah's observation that not only has he not 'heard many people talk about the Kiswahili Prize-winners in Nairobi', he himself was first introduced to *Mungu Hakopeshwi* not via MNN but through *Aurélie Journo, a scholar of African literature based* at the University of Paris.[109]

---

[104]Marzagora, 'African-Language Literatures and the "Transnational Turn" in Euro-American Humanities', p. 49.
[105]Abdulrahman 'Abu Amirah' Ndegwa, 'Literary Activism in the Swahili Coast', *Eastern African Literary and Cultural Studies*, vol. 7, nos 1–2 (3 April 2021): 92–6, 92.
[106]Ndegwa, 'Literary Activism in the Swahili Coast'; Aurélie Journo, '"Heroes and Scholars Are Everywhere": Q&A with Abu Amirah, Founder of Hekaya', 10 February 2020, https://africainwords.com/2020/02/10/heroes-and-scholars-are-everywhere-qa-with-abu-amirah-founder-of-hekaya/.
[107]Abdalla, interview by Zamda Geuza and Kate Wallis.
[108]Amirah, interview by Zamda Geuza and Kate Wallis.
[109]Ibid.

Both Ali and Rangimoto reflected in interview on the importance of social media as a space for sharing and developing their writing, and the ways in which their first manuscripts were drawn together from Facebook posts.[110] Arguably then, the production of their prize-winning manuscripts as beautiful physical books by MNN is important principally because of the networks of prestige this opens up, rather than as a way to reach a larger audience.[111] While creative writing can be widely shared and responded to via the digital African literary space, the circulation of physical books on the African continent continues to be hampered by a lack of distribution structures, with the cost of transporting books, navigating customs processes and chasing payments quickly becoming prohibitive even across nearby borders. Yet 'print on demand' (POD) technology means these books have begun to travel globally in ways that are enabled by MNN's high production and design values, without books needing to be packaged and travel physically from Dar es Salaam. Through POD, ABC makes MNN's books available worldwide with a particular emphasis on reaching markets in the Global North. Reflecting on the motivations for setting up ABC, Walter Bgoya emphasized the importance of 'mak[ing] our own stories heard in the North as we as African publishers and African authors publish our own stories about our own realities'[112] and African-owned ABC could also be positioned through its pan-African commitment. In 2021 ABC made MNN's four books by Kiswahili Prize–winning authors available for the first time; as ABC's CEO Justin Cox commented in an interview, there was an immediate interest and energy via social media in response and ABC is currently seeing an expanding market for books in Kiswahili.[113] The Kiswahili Prize titles remain prominently featured on ABC's home page and are showcased as lead titles in ABC's new 2021 Swahili catalogue – their first non-English catalogue.[114] While we are interested in documenting the expanding cartographies for Swahili literature reflected here, again contradictions and entrenched barriers to the global circulation of Afrophone African language literature sit alongside this. While ABC has made the Kiswahili Prize books highly visible and available, their business model works through the long tail approach: ABC makes large numbers of books from Africa-based publishers available, but each sells in relatively low numbers. As Cox acknowledged, even with high levels of visibility and excitement, strong sales for these titles would be in the region of just a hundred copies annually.[115] A further

---

[110]Ali, interview by Zamda Geuza; Dotto Rangimoto, interview by Zamda Geuza, 11 May 2021.
[111]Ibid.
[112]Walter Bgoya, *The Academic Book in the South*, 2016a, https://www.youtube.com/watch?v=KibTWqMShvA&t=1501s.
[113]Cox, interview by Kate Wallis.
[114]Ibid.
[115]Ibid.

constraint is Amazon not being willing to support e-books in Kiswahili, given the dominance of this as a sales platform for books in the United States and Europe; ABC was even temporarily banned from the platform, with all their Kindle books removed for a week, for contravening Amazon's language policies by uploading Swahili books.[116]

For MNN and the Kiswahili Prize, the global circulation of these publications is about more than sales. MNN is fully cognizant that the market for Swahili literature titles beyond academia remains small, and of the need to work to expand and grow this.[117] However, the decision to invest in publishing in this area is not motivated by an immediate 'commercial or business decision' but by 'the philosophical position of the publishing house'.[118] For the Kiswahili Prize, even if the market and sales remain small, this doesn't impact the ability of these books to work as calling cards that bring longevity and profile, and enable the prize to expand geographically. Abdalla highlighted that one of the aspects of the prize that he has focused most energy on is expanding its geographical reach.[119] While in its first few years the majority of submissions came from Tanzania, increasingly the prize has attracted submissions from a wider and more diverse geography – including in 2021 from Burundi to Nigeria across sub-Saharan Africa, as well as from Austria, Canada, Egypt, Europe, North America and the Middle East.[120] In this way the prize works to bring together a wider Africa-based and diaspora community around Swahili literary production.

Conclusion

Alongside its successes, this collaboration between the Kiswahili Prize and MNN can be characterized through a series of contradictions and disjunctures. The prize has carved out a unique position of prestige in East Africa, continually able to draw in high-profile figures in Kenyan and Tanzanian politics to be part of the annual award ceremony – from Hassan to Willy Mutunga to Mama Salma Kikwete – and attracting significant regional media coverage. However, as co-founder Mũkoma commented, it is 'mind-boggling' that, given this unusual level of recognition, it remains hard for the prize to secure funding from institutions in the Global North and to get the financial support necessary for prize-winning titles to be translated into both Europhone or Afrophone languages.[121] Similarly, as we have

---

[116] Ibid.
[117] Walter Bgoya, 'The Effect of Globalisation in Africa and the Choice of Language in Publishing'; Mkuki Bgoya, interview by Zamda Geuza and Kate Wallis.
[118] Mkuki Bgoya, interview by Zamda Geuza and Kate Wallis.
[119] Abdalla, interview by Zamda Geuza and Kate Wallis.
[120] Ibid.; Kilolo, interview by Zamda Geuza and Kate Wallis.
[121] wa Ngũgĩ, interview by Kate Wallis.

shown, the Kiswahili Prize has worked through its collaboration with MNN to create a more inclusive Swahili literary space and a model that could be replicated to build new literary prizes for other African languages. Yet, as Silkiluwasha importantly exposes through her study of the Burt Award, there is a risk that the prestige associated with the Kiswahili Prize becomes so interlinked with MNN that this becomes a self-perpetuating cycle, with new titles produced by MNN perhaps having a stronger chance of winning future editions of the prize.[122] Even as the prize is intended to offer a model for other African languages, its networks of prestige and structures of literary circulation remain deeply embedded within the particularities of Kiswahili.

Mapping world literary space through a plural, polyglot framing of 'multilayered and intersecting literary systems'[123] necessarily involves building new critical models for world literatures that allow for contradictions and disjunctures. As Madhu Krishnan compellingly shows in her study of spatiality and the West African Europhone novel, the world in which these texts participate is 'entirely more complex than any singular mode of mapping might allow for'.[124] Krishnan's work continues to reflect a nuanced attentiveness to the complexities of 'positioning' in relation to 'African literature and literary production within a world literary landscape'.[125] We have similarly argued here for the significance of attending to both positionality and collaboration, suggesting that through this we can read MNN and the Kiswahili Prize as engaged in a significant process of 'conceptual worlding'[126] that has the potential to move beyond existing 'literary structures'[127] in both practical and theoretical terms.

In practical terms, this mutually beneficial collaboration has impacted the space of Swahili literary production across the lifecycle of writing and publishing, shaping MNN's submissions and commissioning processes, the construction of networks of prestige and cultural value, and the production, design and circulation of new books. While the Kiswahili Prize's lack of a fixed East African base opens opportunities for expanded cross-border and global dialogue and readership for Swahili literature, MNN's commitment to producing beautiful physical books from Dar es Salaam roots this literary production on the African continent and within Africa-owned economic structures. The decision that representatives of MNN and EAEP should

---

[122] Silkiluwasha, 'Reflecting and Reflexing on Book Awards'.
[123] Marzagora, 'African-Language Literatures and the "Transnational Turn" in Euro-American Humanities', p. 49.
[124] Madhu Krishnan, *Writing Spatiality in West Africa* (Suffolk: Boydell & Brewer, 2018b), p. 178.
[125] Madhu Krishnan, *Contingent Canons: African Literature and the Politics of Location* (Cambridge: Cambridge University Press, 2018a), p. 63.
[126] Helgesson, 'Ngũgĩ wa Thiong'o and the Conceptual Worlding of Literature', p. 119.
[127] wa Ngũgĩ, *The Rise of the African Novel*, p. 70.

be permanent members of the Kiswahili Prize's board of trustees signals a commitment to this collaboration that locates the prize's investment in Africa-based literary structures.[128]

In theoretical terms, this case study enables us to demonstrate the possibilities of tracing new cartographies for world literary space through the frame of Africa-based publishers and an attentiveness to modes of collaboration and relationality. What does it mean to bring a pan-African lens to mapping world literature? Here we see a pan-African ethos, defined in part through a commitment to Afrophone African languages, enabling collaborative relationships that can stretch across intersecting literary systems and cut through reductive hierarchies of global/local or insider/outsider. These are pan-African solidarities that 'conceptually' produce new literary worlds. From this, we argue for reading African literatures in world literary space through their publishing locations, and in particular through Africa-based publishers, as a model for 'escaping Euro chronology'.[129] Collaboration with Dar es Salaam–based MNN, and the publisher's long-standing commitment to both progressive publishing and to the book as an aesthetic object, is fundamental to how the Kiswahili Prize is able to build networks of prestige. While the physical books by Kiswahili Prize–winning authors produced by MNN are rooted in Tanzania and may not sell in large quantities outside this, they become a calling card for the prize that opens up Swahili literature to new modes of authorship, cultural value and circulation.

Bibliography

'2017 Winners'. 2018. 16 January, https://kiswahiliprize.cornell.edu/2016-winners/. Accessed 1 March 2022.

Abdalla, Abdilatif (7 June 2021), interview by Zamda Geuza and Kate Wallis.

'About the Prize'. 2021, https://kiswahiliprize.cornell.edu/about-the-prize/. Accessed 1 March 2022.

'About Us'. 2021, https://mkukinanyota.com/about/. Accessed 1 March 2022.

Adejunmobi, Moradewun (1999), 'Routes: Language and the Identity of African Literature', *Journal of Modern African Studies*, vol. 37, no. 4: 581–96.

Ali, Ali Hilal (9 May 2021), interview by Zamda Geuza.

Amirah, Abu (23 May 2021), interview by Zamda Geuza and Kate Wallis.

Andrew, Godance (30 May 2021), interview by Zamda Geuza.

Attree, Lizzy (18 May 2021), interview by Zamda Geuza and Kate Wallis.

Attree, Lizzy, and Mũkoma wa Ngũgĩ (7 July 2021), 'New Kiswahili Science Fiction Award Charts a Path for African Languages', The Conversation, http://

---

[128] Abdalla, interview by Zamda Geuza and Kate Wallis.
[129] Gikandi, 'Introduction – Another Way in the World', p. 1199.

theconversation.com/new-kiswahili-science-fiction-award-charts-a-path-for-african-languages-163876. Accessed 1 March 2022.
Bgoya, Mkuki (19 May 2021), interview by Zamda Geuza and Kate Wallis.
Bgoya, Walter (2001), 'The Effect of Globalisation in Africa and the Choice of Language in Publishing', *International Review of Education*, vol. 47, no. 3: 283–92.
Bgoya, Walter (2008), 'The Endeavour of Publishing: Its Limits of Success with Swahili Readers', in *Beyond the Language Issue: The Production, Mediation and Reception of Creative Writing in African Languages*, ed. Anja Oed and Uta Reuster-Jahn, Köln: Köppe, pp. 87–94.
Bgoya, Walter (2016a), *The Academic Book in the South*, https://www.youtube.com/watch?v=KibTWqMShvA&t=1501s. Accessed 1 March 2022.
Bgoya, Walter (2016b), 'A Survey of Fourteen African Publishers', *Wasafiri*, vol. 31, no. 4: 13–22.
Bgoya, Walter, and Mary Jay (2013), 'Publishing in Africa from Independence to the Present Day', *Research in African Literatures*, vol. 44, no. 2: 17–34.
Bush, Ruth (2016), *Publishing Africa in French: Literary Institutions and Decolonization 1945–1967*, Liverpool: Liverpool University Press.
Casanova, Pascale (2004), *The World Republic of Letters*, trans. M. B. DeBevoise, Cambridge, MA: Harvard University Press.
Cornell University (21 November 2014), 'Major New Prize for African Literature Announced', https://web.archive.org/web/20141125080155/kiswahiliprize.cornell.edu/. Accessed 1 March 2022.
Cox, Justin (11 May 2021), interview by Kate Wallis.
Davis, Caroline (2013), *Creating Postcolonial Literature: African Writers and British Publishers*, Basingstoke: Palgrave Macmillan.
Diegner, Lutz (2017), 'Leaving Parched Gardens and Discussing Narration with the Reader: Metatextualities in the Contemporary Swahili Novel', *Research in African Literatures*, vol. 48, no. 1: 24–43.
Diegner, Lutz (2018), 'Postrealist, Postmodernist, Postnation? The Swahili Novel 1987–2010', *Research in African Literatures*, vol. 49, no. 1: 117–44.
Eggan, Taylor A. (2016), 'Regionalizing the Planet: Horizons of the Introverted Novel at World Literature's End', *PMLA*, vol. 131, no. 5: 1299–1315.
English, James F. (2005), *The Economy of Prestige*, Cambridge, MA: Harvard University Press.
Garnier, Xavier (2013), *The Swahili Novel: Challenging the Idea of Minor Literature*, Suffolk: Boydell & Brewer.
Gikandi, Simon (2016), 'Introduction – Another Way in the World', *PMLA*, vol. 131, no. 5: 1193–1206.
Gromov, Mikhail D. (2015), 'Regional or Local? On "Literary Trajectories" in Recent Swahili Writing', in *Habari Ya English? What About Kiswahili? East Africa as a Literary and Linguistic Contact Zone*, ed. Lutz Diegner and Frank Schulze-Engler, Amsterdam: Brill, pp. 67–79.
Helgesson, Stefan (2014), 'Postcolonialism and World Literature', *Interventions: International Journal of Postcolonial Studies*, vol. 16, no. 4: 483–500.

Helgesson, Stefan (2015), 'Forum on World Literary Systems: Tayeb Salih, Sol Plaatje, and the Trajectories of World Literature', *Cambridge Journal of Postcolonial Literary Inquiry*, vol. 2, no. 2: 253–60.

Helgesson, Stefan (2017), 'Ngũgĩ wa Thiong'o and the Conceptual Worlding of Literature', *Anglia*, vol. 135, no. 1: 105–21.

Jaji, Tsitsi Ella (2014), *Africa in Stereo: Modernism, Music, and Pan-African Solidarity*, New York: Oxford University Press, https://oxford.universitypress scholarship.com/10.1093/acprof:oso/9780199936373.001.0001/acprof-9780199936373. Accessed 1 March 2022.

Journo, Aurélie (10 February 2020), '"Heroes and Scholars Are Everywhere": Q&A with Abu Amirah, Founder of Hekaya', https://africainwords.com/2020/02/10/heroes-and-scholars-are-everywhere-qa-with-abu-amirah-founder-of-hekaya/. Accessed 1 March 2022.

Kaiza, A. K. (2016), 'A Luta Continua!' *New African*, no. 563 (July): 74–8.

Kasanda, Albert (2016), 'Exploring Pan-Africanism's Theories: From Race-Based Solidarity to Political Unity and Beyond', *Journal of African Cultural Studies*, vol. 28, no. 2: 179–95.

Kiguru, Doseline (2016a), 'Prizing African Literature: Creating a Literary Taste', *Social Dynamics*, vol. 42, no. 1: 161–74.

Kiguru, Doseline (2016b), 'Literary Prizes, Writers' Organisations and Canon Formation in Africa', *African Studies*, vol. 75, no. 2: 202–14.

Kiguru, Doseline (2019), 'Language and Prizes: Exploring Literary and Cultural Boundaries', in *Routledge Handbook of African Literature*, ed. Moradewun Adejunmobi and Carli Coetzee. Abingdon: Routledge, pp. 399–412.

Kiguru, Doseline (2021), 'Genre versus Prize: The Short Story Form and African Oral Traditions', *English in Africa*, vol. 47, no. 3: 37–54.

Kilolo, Munyao (17 May 2021), interview by Zamda Geuza and Kate Wallis.

Kresse, Kai (2007), *Philosophising in Mombasa*, Edinburgh: Edinburgh University Press.

Kresse, Kai (2016), 'Kenya: Twendapi?: Re-Reading Abdilatif Abdalla's Pamphlet Fifty Years after Independence', *Africa*, vol. 86, no. 1: 1–32.

Krishnan, Madhu (2018a), *Contingent Canons: African Literature and the Politics of Location*, Cambridge: Cambridge University Press.

Krishnan, Madhu (2018b), *Writing Spatiality in West Africa*, Suffolk: Boydell & Brewer.

Laachir, Karima, Sara Marzagora and Francesca Orsini (2018), 'Multilingual Locals and Significant Geographies', *Modern Languages Open*, vol. 19, no. 1: 1–8.

'Makamu Wa Rais Akabidhi Tuzo Kwa Washindi Bora Wa Kiswahili' (2019), Global Publishers. 15 February 2019, https://globalpublishers.co.tz/makamu-wa-rais-akabidhi-tuzo-za-washindi-bora-wa-kiswahili/. Accessed 1 March 2022.

Marzagora, Sara (2015a), 'African-Language Literatures and the "Transnational Turn" in Euro-American Humanities', *Journal of African Cultural Studies*, vol. 27, no. 1: 40–55.

Marzagora, Sara (2015b), 'Literatures in African Languages', *Journal of African Cultural Studies*, vol. 27, no. 1: 1–6.

Murua, James (2019), 'Mabati-Cornell Kiswahili Prize for African Literature 2018 Winners Celebrated', James Murua Literary. 18 February 2019, https://www.

jamesmurua.com/mabati-cornell-kiswahili-prize-for-african-literature-2018-winners-celebrated/. Accessed 1 March 2022.

Ndegwa, Abdulrahman 'Abu Amirah' (2021), 'Literary Activism in the Swahili Coast', *Eastern African Literary and Cultural Studies*, vol. 7, nos 1–2: 92–6.

Nesbitt-Ahmed, Zahrah (2019), 'Continuing to Judge Books by Their Covers', *Bookshy* (blog), http://www.bookshybooks.com/2019/07/continuing-to-judge-books-by-their.html. Accessed 1 March 2022.

Ngũgĩ wa Thiong'o (1993), *Moving the Centre: The Struggle for Cultural Freedoms*, Nairobi: East African Educational Publishers.

Ngũgĩ wa Thiong'o (2014), *Globalectics*, New York: Columbia University Press.

Rangimoto, Dotto (2021), interview by Zamda Geuza, Dar es Salaam, 11 May.

Silkiluwasha, Mpale Yvonne Mwansasu (2021), 'Reflecting and Reflexing on Book Awards: A Case Study of the Burt Award', *Eastern African Literary and Cultural Studies*, vol. 7, nos 1–2: 116–32.

Smith, Kelvin, and Melanie Ramdarshan Bold (2018), *The Publishing Business: A Guide to Starting Out and Getting On*, London: Bloomsbury.

Squires, Claire (2007), 'Book Marketing and the Booker Prize', in *Judging a Book by Its Cover: Fans, Publishers, Designers, and the Marketing of Fiction*, ed. Nickianne Moody and Nicole Matthews, Abingdon: Routledge, pp. 71–82.

Suhr-Sytsma, Nathan (2017), *Poetry, Print, and the Making of Postcolonial Literature*, Cambridge: Cambridge University Press.

Suhr-Sytsma, Nathan (2018), 'The Geography of Prestige: Prizes, Nigerian Writers, and World Literature', *ELH*, vol. 85, no. 4: 1093–1122.

Suriano, Maria (2021), 'Dreams and Constraints of an African Publisher: Walter Bgoya, Tanzania Publishing House and Mkuki Na Nyota, 1972–2020', *Africa: Journal of the International African Institute*, vol. 91, no. 4: 575–601.

Tchokothe, Rémi Armand (2015), 'Globalectical Swahili Literature', *Journal of African Cultural Studies*, vol. 27, no. 1: 30–9.

The Funambulist Podcast (2020), 'Walter Bgoya: Pan-African Publishing and the Struggle for a Second Liberation', vol. 135, https://soundcloud.com/the-funambulist/walter-bgoya-panafrican-publishing-struggling-for-a-second-liberation. Accessed 1 March 2022.

van Klinken, Adriaan (30 January 2020), 'Queering Pan-Africanism', https://africasacountry.com/2020/01/queering-pan-africanism. Accessed 1 March 2022.

Veit-Wild, Flora, and Clarissa Vierke (2017), 'Introduction: Digging into Language', *Research in African Literatures*, vol. 48, no. 1: ix–xviii.

Vierke, Clarissa (2017), '"What Is There in My Speaking": Re-Explorations of Language in Abdilatif Abdalla's Anthology of Prison Poetry, Sauti Ya Dhiki', *Research in African Literatures*, vol. 48, no. 1: 135–57.

'VP Awards Winners of African Literature' (16 February 2019), *The Guardian*, https://www.ippmedia.com/en/news/vp-awards-winners-african-literature. Accessed 1 March 2022.

Waldburger, Daniela (2020), 'A Conversation with Abdilatif Abdalla', *Stichproben – Vienna Journal of African Studies*, vol. 20: 105–17.

Waliaula, Ken Walibora (2013), 'The Afterlife of Oyono's "Houseboy" in the Swahili Schools Market: To Be or Not to Be Faithful to the Original', *PMLA*, vol. 128, no. 1: 178–84.

Wallis, Kate (2018), 'Exchanges in Nairobi and Lagos: Mapping Literary Networks and World Literary Space', *Research in African Literatures*, vol. 49, no. 1: 163–86.

Wallis, Kate (2020), 'Ngũgĩ wa Thiong'o: Networks, Literary Activism and the Production of World Literature', in *A Companion to World Literature*, ed. Ken Seigneurie, Chichester: Wiley-Blackwell, pp. 2721–32.

10

Aké Festival and the African world stage

Lola Shoneyin

I think I should start with a little story.[1] When we were planning the first edition of Aké Arts and Book Festival in 2013, I decided to do something unusual with the way the books were displayed in the festival bookstore. Given that the festival primarily focuses on African creativity and embraces African writers, artists and poets, we created an 'African Literature' section for books by and about Africa, and a 'World Literature' section populated with books by non-African writers, labelling the shelves according to country. I imagined that this would generate a sense of pride in the African writers present. This was not a space where they would be othered; I wanted to show in a meaningful way that, while they were at Aké Festival, they were the central focus: the main dish, the reason for the existence of the festival. Some writers who, like me, had seen their work banished to the World Literature section of bookstore chains in the West found it quite amusing. Most people didn't understand the humour behind the categorization, but the curation made sense to them, for organizational purposes.

When I consider the term 'world literature' – and I'm looking at this from the perspective of a reader, a writer, a publisher, a bookstore owner and the festival organizer – it has unique resonance, depending on which hat I am wearing. The idea of world literature is one of the ways that the West has been able to categorize everything that is different from the West

---

[1] This chapter is based on an interview that the editors conducted with Lola Shoneyin. The interview was recorded, transcribed and some edits have been made for clarity.

and doesn't promote Western values. It points to the existence of a standard, and everything that fails to meet that standard is relegated to the World Literature section. I have seen instances where non-Western authors have made the transition from the World Literature section to the mainstream shelves where they enjoy more attention and legitimacy, making it seem as if stories can only be accepted into the mainstream when they are written in a voice that is melodious to the Western ear and establishment. How many of the books set in Africa or Asia that you'll find in those mainstream shelves were actually written by those who regard those continents as their home? Are these voices not trusted? Why do these works have to fight for space and credibility in bookstores? The exclusion implicit in 'world literature' seems to be rooted in race and language. Many writers do not think that that is helpful.

For many writers of African origins, the struggle begins on the African continent, where we still grapple with the vestiges of colonialism, which are unsurprisingly noticeable in the literary space. Ironically, those who created this categorization have contributed, in no small way, to the devastation of the worlds that one encounters in the World Literature section. On the African continent, for example, our literature is locked into Western languages, thereby eroding the development of indigenous language African literature. In Africa, there is so much disconnection along language lines, and more so along indigenous language lines, as a result of nation states that were cobbled together by the British, French, Portuguese, Belgians and Germans for their economic advantage. When promoting my work at literary festivals around the world, I have encountered Yoruba-speaking writers from Benin Republic. We converse in Yoruba because we speak the same indigenous language, but because Benin Republic was colonized by the French, accessing their creative work is a struggle. There is a language barrier that instantly limits creative connections. We have had to find other means of rekindling and re-establishing our links. This is one of the important roles that Aké Festival plays. The festival creates opportunities for networking, for exploring means of bridging language gaps, for ideas around the expansion of the reading population on the African continent. The process of achieving these ideals is not without problems, on a continent where education and literacy are not prioritized, and the publishing industry is not supported to thrive.

In 2014, the theme of the festival was Bridges and Pathways; we were very focused on getting Francophone and Anglophone Africa to speak to each other so that we could, from there, start talking seriously about closing the language gap and making translations more commonplace. *So Long a Letter*, the acclaimed novel by Mariama Bâ, was translated into English by Modupé Bodé-Thomas, a Nigerian translator. The only way anyone in Francophone Africa can access a copy of my novel *The Secret Lives of Baba Segi's Wives* is by ordering the French language edition published in France.

Many books written by English-speaking African writers have little or no chance of being translated by a French-speaking African who is more closely connected to the context. Instead, books are translated in France by French translators and shipped back to the African continent. That crazy journey should have been a straight line. This is the sort of infrastructure that must be in place if we are to have a functional African world stage.

There is no doubt that the West has put in the work required to develop the infrastructure that allows them to point to an established and ever-expanding literary canon. A big part of that involves building a strong literary eco-system that includes editors, publishers, writers, book promoters, distributors, etc. Many of the components of this eco-system have been lost in many countries in the Global South. A notable exception is India, which has a self-contained 'world' of Indian writers, many of whom write in indigenous languages. As such, when an Indian writer crosses over and is published in the West, it's just an added bonus. It is not the same for many writers on the African continent. Being published in the West is what writers aspire to and then they get stuck in the World Literature section!

The most egregious fall-out of 'world literature' is that it has resulted in the exclusion, perhaps even the erasure, of many writers of African descent. What we are trying to do with institutions like Aké Festival and Ouida Books is to rebuild the world of African literature where the development of African literature takes centre stage and we create a more enabling environment so that writers can produce, create and thrive. I am always interested in new ways to make access to books easier and more affordable. Widespread poverty and low literacy are huge obstacles, but I believe very strongly in the power of literature, and its capacity to teach empathy. It's important that Nigerians read Nigerian literature, but it's also important that they can access Malawian literature, South African literature, Senegalese literature. This way, we not only develop a deeper understanding of ourselves but also get insight into trends and common themes. History is often not taught in schools, so literary works across the continent are not only providing entertainment: they are also documenting history and the political landscape. In 2019, I attended the Abantu Book Festival in Soweto, South Africa, and met the distinguished author Zakes Mda. I had the good fortune of riding to the airport with him and he told me how the Black intellectual class in South Africa supported the Biafran army during the Nigerian Civil War, largely because they had all read Chinua Achebe's *Things Fall Apart* and so the Igbo world view felt familiar. A work of fiction achieved that.

When planning Aké Festival, the idea of African writers *competing* on a 'world stage' is not front and centre for me. If anything, I am interested in an 'African world stage' where themes that pertain to Africa and African writers are at the core of the discourse. This is not about excluding non-Africans but promoting the work of individuals who have been denied access to *any* platform. It is to make sure that people on the African continent can also access these writers and listen to them speak, which is so critical. Festivals that primarily look inwards have been few. Aké Festival attracts some of the finest writers on the African continent, but we also embrace writers in the African global diaspora. The festival is not only about creating space for connections, but it is also about listening to stories that reflect African and Black realities. For example, a good number of books coming out these days feature an LGBTQI character. Literature is an excellent vehicle for promoting representation and bringing to our consciousness stories often pushed to the fringes of African societies. It's cathartic to observe the commonalities and the peculiarities between Black stories. It's a privilege to be able to ask questions, to challenge one another and to celebrate our storytellers. There is still so much literary consolidation that still needs to take place. Aké Festival pushes this agenda forward.

It is called the Aké Arts *and Books* Festival because books are the main focus, but the truth is, people sometimes get turned off by books. They ask if all we do is talk about books all day. Right from the get-go, I thought very deeply about how we could make the festival more attractive to the average person, how we could draw the visitors in and then capture them with the buffet of art forms. So, we screen films and documentaries, we have an art exhibition, a poetry night, a concert, stage plays, book chats, engaging and provocative panel discussions. We are not just thinking of something for everyone, we want that something to be memorable. We also weave books into just about everything we do. Books don't always travel as swiftly or as effectively as other forms of the arts, like films for instance, so it is really important to us that people see the value of books. We do all sorts of things to get books into people's hands and encourage wider thinking about the issues that books raise.

Every year, Aké Festival publishes a literary journal called *Aké Review*. Every registered guest gets a free copy in their festival tote bag. The idea is for the words and the writing to travel beyond the physical space of the festival. Each edition contains a comprehensive interview with the headliner, who is always an African writer. This is our way of making sure that the younger generation is exposed to the work of the generations that paved the way for them. In forging a path to the future, it's important that they are aware of what has gone on in the past. *Aké Review* is our way of capturing and documenting the times. African literary publications remind us that we are here, that we are present, that Africans are writing, that Africa does not need to rely on the dictates of the Western literary establishment, that there is an enthusiastic audience that consumes these works.

Early in my writing career, there were several well-respected literary journals like *Okike, Glendora Review, Position,* and of course, with the emergence of the internet, many more have emerged: e-zines like *Saraba Magazine,* or more recently the *Lagos Review*. When we were planning the first Aké Festival in 2013, many of the journals I mentioned were no longer being published regularly. With so many African writers coming together for the festival, we thought it would be a lost opportunity if we did not capture something that visitors to the festival could take away. The *Aké Review* is different to many literary magazines today. It is multilingual and about 40 per cent of it is dedicated to Aké Festival guests. We generate ten questions every year that we send to all the invited guests. The questions are humorous, sometimes provocative. Each festival speaker gets their own page, which includes their answers to those questions, their photograph, photographs of their books, logos of their blogs and whatever. Apart from those ten questions, we do a call for submissions every year for new writing: poetry, art, short fiction, non-fiction. Out of about six hundred submissions, the editor selects fewer than sixty. Molara Wood has edited *Aké Review* for the last six years. She curates a wonderful collection of writing inspired by the festival theme. This year, the theme is Generational Discordance. In previous years, the themes have been 'The F Word', 'Beneath This Skin', 'Engaging the Fringe', 'Fantastical Futures' and 'The Shadow of Memory'.

Recently, Ouida Books – the publishing house that I founded in Nigeria – sold the rights of one of our novels to Rewayat, a publishing house in the UAE. This was a very significant moment for us because *An Abundance of Scorpions*, which was first published in Nigeria, is going to be available in Arabic. I like the idea that our authors will no longer need Western validation to achieve wider literary success, and that there are other avenues. Africa can now connect directly with other world markets without relying on the Western literary establishment. This idea of literary autonomy on the African continent is relevant to some of the other work that I do with One Read Africa, which is an application accessible on mobile devices. It was created last year and can only be accessed on the African continent. Every month, a new work of fiction or non-fiction by an African writer is made available for twenty-one days. We pay the authors, we push the book online, we put the book in our bookstores and in other bookstores. Again, this is an attempt to leapfrog some of the big obstacles, like distribution. In the second phase, we hope to have the content of the app available in French. One of the reasons the One Read application became necessary is that it has become almost impossible to acquire the rights of books written by African writers that were first published by Western publishers. When they deny African publishers access to the rights of books authored by African writers, it feels like literary colonization. We cannot let this continue. We are aware that this has to do with the breakdown of the literary eco-system on the African continent, so there is much rebuilding and reconstruction to be done, but this relationship has to be redefined. In Africa, we need to rethink the way that books are produced and books are distributed. With technology and the internet, the One Read app gives readers access to books for US$1 a month.

When African writers attend festivals in Europe and America, conveying the rhyme, reason and intelligence behind the decisions of a book's characters might come across as unconventional or disturbing. When writers talk to an African audience, the need to provide context is removed. So much is understood, so much is received whole because it resonates immediately. We need these spaces where the call and response happen organically. I am much more concerned about what Africans think about the works of other Africans than what Western readers think of books authored by Africans.

In terms of my own practice as a writer, when writing creatively, the audience I imagine before my eyes is African. I am one of those writers who *sees* scenes and then writes them. When I was writing *The Secret Lives of Baba Segi's Wives*, I would see the scenes play out in a particular theatre in Ibadan, which is where I grew up and where the book is set. I suppose this shows that my mind was working to feed the imagination of the people who were local to me, my constituency, the people that I could relate to, the people that I knew would understand my stories. My world has always been African. The world that I see, the world that I want to exist in has always been African. What else is it going to be? I lived in England for many years and was at school in England from the age of six, but what matters most is what feels like home. I hoped my book would start conversations among Africans. For me, it is very much about talking about those worlds, those stories, those experiences that are familiar, that are real, that are true, that are authentic. It is gratifying to be able to tell these stories with authority. It's worth noting that this world-making capacity is not unique to narrative literary forms. This is clear when you look at the work of a writer like Niyi Osundare. He, along with many other poets, explore our oral traditions in their poetry. They return to the source, to the very core of their creativity. For many writers in Africa, their inspiration is still rooted in African culture, in our proverbs, in our oral traditions, in our songs. We have so much by way of resources. We now need to master the ways of plumbing them.

11
Contemporary African literature and celebrity capital

Doseline Kiguru

Contemporary African literature is characterized by a growing number of different literary production platforms, including an increase in publishing avenues, growth of writers' collectives and organizations, access to digital literary platforms and the overall centrality of literary award bodies. Indeed, the African literary field has greatly been shaped by international literary awards such as the Booker Prize, the Commonwealth Prize, the AKO Caine Prize for African Writing, the Women's Prize for Fiction (formerly known as the Orange Broadband Prize for Fiction) and the Nobel Prize in Literature, among other prestigious awards. The result of the canonization mediated through the international award has meant that more African writers, and texts, continue to gain more visibility in the international literary marketplace and this high visibility has significantly influenced the creation of the celebrity author. Celebrity status generated by literary awards is especially foregrounded by the highly mediatized nature of literary awards, from their launch and shortlist announcements to the award ceremonies. Today, the figure of the celebrity African writer is a constant presence, with various celebrity authors occupying different levels of visibility and publicity.

Celebrity in the literary world means that 'the commodities to be sold – books – are marketed using the "personalities" directly connected to them'.[1] The marketing of 'personalities' alongside their work is what brings about

---

[1] Anders Ohlsson, T. Forslid and A. Steiner, 'Literary Celebrity Reconsidered', *Celebrity Studies*, vol. 5, nos 1–2 (2014): 32–44, 33.

the celebrity status and in a media-driven market that, by its nature, values high visibility, the writer also becomes marketed as a commodity. As Ohlsson et al. expound, as 'commodities, celebrities embody a certain abstract capital – "attention", i.e. "high public visibility and recognition" ... that in today's media-saturated society is in high demand'.[2] This chapter therefore is concerned with the commoditization and mediatization of contemporary African texts and their authors, exploring how celebrity status influences the production and circulation of value. It engages with the wider topic of African literature as world literature by focusing on the link between the local and the global literary fields, created through the personhood of the celebrity writer.

Olivier Driessens describes celebrity status as 'celebrity capital', which he defines as 'recognizability, or as accumulated media visibility that results from recurrent media representations'.[3] In this context, I use 'capital' in a broadly Bourdieusian sense that recognizes capital as existing beyond economic lenses and to include other aspects of social interaction. Pierre Bourdieu's work expands on Marxist analysis of society according to class divisions and foregrounds the idea of cultural capital, which he defines as the 'forms of cultural knowledge, competences or dispositions' that one acquires by virtue of being part of a particular social class and that ultimately contribute to one's economic and social standing.[4]

Introducing the idea of capital in the definition of celebrity status places the writer directly in the commodity market and forces an interrogation of the literary celebrity within the frameworks of production. Capital implies commercial value, and the concept of literary celebrity capital, therefore, points at the context of the commodification of both text and author. David Throsby affirms that 'cultural production and consumption can be situated within an industrial framework, and ... the goods and services produced and consumed can be regarded as commodities in the same terms as any other commodities produced within the economic system'.[5] However, as Joe Moran argues, the emergence of the celebrity author does not necessarily mean reducing authorship to mere consumerism. Writing in the context of American literature and readership, he challenges 'the way the emergence of literary celebrity is most commonly explained – in terms of the vulgarization of literary life by commercial mass media'.[6] This therefore calls for a deeper analysis of the complex relationship between the persona and the text as

---

[2] Ibid., p. 32.
[3] Olivier Driessens, 'The Celebritization of Society and Culture: Understanding the Structural', *International Journal of Cultural Studies*, vol. 16, no. 6 (2013): 641–57, 652.
[4] Pierre Bourdieu, *The Field of Cultural Production: Essays on Art and Literature* (Cambridge: Polity Press, 1993), p. 7.
[5] David Throsby, *Economics and Culture* (Cambridge: Cambridge University Press, 2001), p. 11.
[6] Joe Moran, *Star Authors: Literary Celebrity in America* (London: Pluto Press, 2000), p. 1.

commodities and beyond, acknowledging that 'celebrity is an unstable, multifaceted phenomenon – the product of a complex negotiation between cultural producers and audiences'.[7] A focus on literary celebrity cultures allows for a more sophisticated understanding of how contemporary African literature circulates across local and international markets, thereby contributing in converting the local to the global. The chapter achieves this by examining the value of celebrity status in literary markets over different mediums and platforms, and the effects of this on the literary text.

In Bourdieu's thesis on field theory, he equates capital to power and argues that the state as a field of power has accrued a meta-capital that enables it to wield authority 'over the different fields and over the various forms of capital that circulates in them'.[8] Nick Couldry furthers Bourdieu's argument on capital by introducing the concept of meta-capital within the media framework. He argues that the media has acquired a power similar to the state that allows it to circulate over different types of capital, a concept he names media meta-capital.[9] The argument in this chapter extends Bourdieu's and Couldry's ideas of meta-capital from the perspective of celebrity authorship in African literature. I discuss different ways in which celebrity capital circulates in African literature and the value it places on contemporary literary and cultural production networks. I argue from the perspective that celebrity status for writers comes as a result of accruing enough cultural and social capital within the wider global market for art and literature. Further, this capital can be, and is, intra-converted to other forms of capital necessary for the writers in their social-economic and political contexts, as well as for the networks within which these authors and their texts circulate.

Placing the study of celebrity cultures in contemporary African literature within the realms of capital allows for an evaluation of how capital intra-conversion continues to affect different aspects of literary and cultural production on the continent. Claire Squires explains that 'for the authors high in the hierarchy of marketability, the authorial role is expanded far beyond that of writer of the text'.[10] In the postcolonial cultural production industry, the writers' celebrity capital usually extends beyond literature. Ohlsson et al. affirm this position of writer and text within the global literary markers, arguing that celebrity theory 'provides tools and concepts

---

[7]Ibid., p. 3.
[8]Pierre Bourdieu and L. J. D. Wacquant, *An Invitation to Reflexive Sociology* (Chicago: University of Chicago Press, 1992), p. 114.
[9]Nick Couldry, 'Media Meta-Capital: Extending the Range of Bourdieu's Field Theory', in *After Bourdieu: Influence, Critique, Elaboration*, ed. D. L. Swartz and V. L. Zolberg (New York: Kluwer Academic, 2004), pp. 165–89.
[10]Claire Squires, *Marketing Literature: The Making of Contemporary Writing in Britain* (Basingstoke: Palgrave Macmillan, 2007), p. 37.

for a more thorough analysis of the commodification and mediatisation of the author'.[11]

Nigerian writer Chimamanda Ngozi Adichie is perhaps one of the most celebrated and commercially successful contemporary African writers and she continues to be highly visible in the media, both locally and globally. Adichie's popularity has particularly been foregrounded by literary awards that continue to contribute significantly to her consecration as an African literary celebrity. Indeed, the centrality of literary prizes in aiding the author to access different platforms cannot be underestimated. James English convincingly argues that awards are 'the single best instrument for negotiating transactions between cultural and economic, cultural and social, or cultural and political capital'.[12] Furthermore, Gillian Roberts affirms that

> one process of conversion effected by the literary prize is that of popularization, which might initially appear to be at odds with symbolic capital and the cultural respectability it entails. But the literary prize, operating within 'a broader range of motivations and implications,' engages not only in the celebration of literary excellence but also in the promotion of particular authors and texts, the attraction of media attention to literary production, and the 'support [of] the consumption of literature generally'.[13]

In the contemporary African literary marketplace, celebrity authorship is mainly produced through international prizes that serve the role of conferring not only the monetary award but also the literary prestige that later converts into celebrity status. English, in his analysis of literary prizes, defines celebrity as 'essentially fame subjected to the temporality of fashion', affirming that 'there is no question that prizes have become the dominant apparatus of star production in virtually every field of culture'.[14] Adichie has published the novels *Purple Hibiscus* (2004), which won the Commonwealth Writers' Prize and the Hurston/Wright Legacy Award; *Half of a Yellow Sun* (2006), which won the Orange Prize (Baileys Women's Prize for Fiction) and was a National Book Critics Circle Award Finalist and a *New York Times* Notable Book; and *Americanah* (2013), which won the National Book Critics Circle Award and was named one of *The New York Times'* Top Ten Best Books of 2013. Adichie has also

---

[11]Ohlsson, Forslid and Steiner, 'Literary Celebrity Reconsidered', p. 41.
[12]James English, *The Economy of Prestige: Prizes, Awards and the Circulation of Cultural Values* (Cambridge, MA: Harvard University Press, 2005), p. 10.
[13]Gillian Roberts, *Prizing Literature: The Celebration and Circulation of National Culture* (Toronto: University of Toronto Press, 2011), p. 19.
[14]English, *The Economy of Prestige*, pp. 77–8.

published numerous short stories, available both in print and online. She was shortlisted for the AKO Caine Prize for African Writing in 2002 with the short story 'You in America' and was runner-up in the Commonwealth Short Story Competition the same year for 'The Tree in Grandma's Garden'. Besides these creative texts, Adichie has also published several essays and is a well-known figure in contemporary African literature, both as a writer and as a creative writing trainer, especially at the Farafina Creative Writing Workshop, which continues to attract a huge number of interested candidates each year. Apart from the popularity that comes from winning or being shortlisted for major awards, much of the publicity and public attention that Adichie and her work receive comes from her large media presence. This includes both social and traditional media platforms.

In September 2016, Adichie featured in the Dior catwalk show at Paris Fashion Week. Previously, the writer had also been included in the *Vanity Fair* international Best Dressed list. Indeed, throughout her writing career, she has been widely featured in fashion magazines, including *Vogue*, as a fashion model. Matthew Lecznar provides intriguing insights on the significance of Adichie's transmedia presence, focusing on both the increase in her celebrity capital through the fashion industry and how this capital is channelled into different aspects of her creative work. Lecznar especially foregrounds Adichie's fashion politics and explains that, because fashion functions on different material, modal and discursive levels, Adichie has successfully deployed fashion's 'transformative significance to forge an intersectional and transmedia discursive space: one that enables her to speak in registers at once popular and literary, and to engage diverse audiences with her feminist politics'.[15] For Adichie, her presence in the fashion industry both as a model and as inspirational figure provides an entry point into a wider discussion on the circulation of literary and other cultural artefacts across genres and boundaries. As a celebrity author, her work effortless flows through the different media and material channels, extending from the literary to the textile, and to the visual industries, thereby exposing the transient nature of boundaries in creative production.

Indeed, as Lecznar explains, 'transmedia adaptation destabilises sociocultural meanings and economic hierarchies that underpin cultural artefacts'.[16] Adichie's 2012 TEDxEuston talk 'We Should All Be Feminists'[17] has had more than 6.8 million views on YouTube and was later published in book form under the same title. During the 2016 Dior fashion fair, the words 'We Should All Be Feminists' were emblazoned on a T-shirt that one of the models wore. Further, words from this talk were sampled by pop music icon

---

[15]M. Lecznar, 'Texts, Talks and Tailoring: Chimamanda Ngozi Adichie's Fashion Politics', *Celebrity Studies*, vol. 8, no. 1 (2017): 167–71, 167.
[16]Ibid., p. 168.
[17]https://www.youtube.com/watch?v=hg3umXU_qWc. Accessed 1 January 2022.

Beyoncé Knowles in her hit song 'Flawless',[18] expanding Adichie's capital to pop culture. Further extending her celebrity capital beyond the writing scene, Adichie's second novel *Half of a Yellow Sun* (2006) was adapted into a film, premiered at the 2013 Toronto International Film Festival. She has also notably made a guest entry into the popular American animation series *The Simpsons*, where the characters refer to one of her texts in one of the episodes.[19] Notably, the fictional blog that starts in Adichie's third novel, *Americanah* (2013), titled *Raceteenth or Various Observations about American Blacks (Those Formerly Known as Negroes) by a Non-American Black*, was further extended beyond the fictional realm when she created a real blog under the title *The Small Redemptions of Lagos* where Adichie blogs as the character Ifemelu. This real blog appears to pick up from where the fictional blog in *Americanah* (2013) leaves off, in a move that seems to blur the line between fiction and reality. These different networks and platforms within which Adichie and her work continue to circulate are both a result of her celebrity status and an ongoing process of building further on this capital. The examples above map the circulation of the text 'We Should All Be Feminists' through different media spaces and mediums where the text merges with image, textile, body and voice, thereby demonstrating the power of celebrity capital across literary, intellectual and popular forms. This power across genres and boundaries has enabled Adichie to 'reach culturally and geographically diverse audiences while at the same time increasing her celebrity capital'.[20]

On the same note, the figure of the celebrity writer can also be converted and used as cultural capital relevant beyond the writer's own work. Kate Wallis (2018) presents an extensive exploration of the complex dynamics of production in African literature by focusing on the networks and linkages created and maintained between different literary platforms, which can be traced back to personal connections between specific individuals. Relying on the professional and social relationship between the celebrity writers Binyavanga Wainaina (*Kwani?* Trust) and Chimamanda Ngozi Adichie (*Farafina*), Wallis conceptualizes and characterizes the literary networks associated with these individuals and the organizations they represent(ed), demonstrating how their sociocultural capital forms 'the foundations of an overlapping pan-African literary network with the power not only to nurture

---

[18] https://www.youtube.com/watch?v=IyuUWOnS9BY. Accessed 1 January 2022.
[19] In episode 15 of Season 26 of *The Simpsons* titled 'The Princess Guide', Adichie is mentioned, together with Ben Okri and Chinua Achebe. Towards the end of the episode, an African princess gives Moe three African literary titles to thank him for showing her around Springfield: Ben Okri's *The Famished Road* (1991), Chinua Achebe's *Things Fall Apart* (1958) and Adichie's *The Thing Around Your Neck* (2009).
[20] Sandra Mayer, 'Introduction: Art and Action: Authorship, Politics and Celebrity', *Celebrity Studies*, vol. 8, no. 1 (2017): 152–6, 154.

and bring literary value to individual writers, but to inspire and validate new literary institutions'.[21] Both Wainaina and Adichie were involved in the much-publicized book launches of the novels *Fine Boys* (2011) by Nigerian author Eghosa Imasuen in 2012, and *Dust* (2013) by Kenyan writer Yvonne Adhiambo Owuor in 2013. These novels were launched through the *Farafina* and *Kwani?* Platforms, respectively. The introduction of these texts to the market through these official launches where the two celebrity writers played hosts and discussants served to elevate the social capital of the authors and the new texts in the literary market. These platforms employed the cultural and social capital of the celebrity authors to promote the new novels in the market. As Wallis explains, the celebrity writers 'therefore not only brought cultural value to the novel[s] by direct association with ... their own literary prestige, but drew attention to ... the equivalent author relationship and publishing history'.[22] The active role played by the celebrity writers in these launches acted as a stamp of authority on the new novels and their writers, positively shaping their market reception.

Expanding authorial role beyond the text

The concept of literary celebrity status is directly linked to the persona of the writer, where the biographical information of the writer becomes a text read and consumed alongside the literary text. This perspective recalls Roland Barthes's thesis on the 'Death of the Author' (1967), where biographical information of the author was forced to take a backseat based on the argument that literary criticism should not rely on details about the author's biography and should instead focus on the text itself. It advanced the idea that the author has no influence on how readers interpret their work. However, in celebrity theory, the author, through media visibility, is packaged (or packages themself) as a cultural commodity. Ohlsson et al. argue that today, the anti-biographical position taken by poststructuralists such as Barthes and Michel Foucault is untenable:

> To ignore the importance of authors of different kinds of witness literature – gender oppression, colonialism, or the Holocaust – is problematic both from an academic and moral perspective, since the authenticity of these texts, which is crucial, is closely connected to the figure of the author.[23]

---

[21]Kate Wallis, 'Exchanges in Nairobi and Lagos: Mapping Literary Networks and World Literary Space', *Research in African Literatures*, vol. 49, no. 1 (2018): 163–86, 182.
[22]Ibid., p. 171.
[23]Ohlsson, Forslid and Steiner, 'Literary Celebrity Reconsidered', p. 34.

Indeed, Sarah Brouillette notes that, when it comes to postcolonial writers, the author is not dead: they are a marketing tool, because the 'separation between any text's meaning and the circumstances of its existence as a marketed commodity is largely incomplete'.[24]

As expounded earlier, Adichie is only one of several celebrity authors on the continent whose persona has become a cultural commodity relevant not only to their literary outputs but also to the various literary platforms they become associated with. Sometimes, this celebrity capital is converted beyond the literary margins to include the socio-political influence of the celebrity author. When Wole Soyinka won the 1986 Nobel Prize in Literature, he used his prize lecture to speak against apartheid in South Africa. Karin Berkman analyses Soyinka's role as a celebrity author in voicing different political concerns, such as brutality and corruption both in Nigeria and abroad over different historical periods. She notes that 'directed towards the political rather than the personal, celebrity becomes a means to endorse a substantive, ethical activism'.[25] The way in which celebrity capital intraconverts in complex ways across the literary field is not unique to African literatures. An example from the Indian subcontinent is Arundhati Roy, whose literary celebrity status has converted into economic and symbolic capital to lend legitimacy to her social and political activism. Roy came to prominence after winning the Booker Prize in 1997 and has since become a 'writer-activist' who has mainly turned to non-fiction to comment on the environment, human rights, power and domination.[26]

Similarly, on the African continent, the late Kenyan author Binyavanga Wainaina, winner of the AKO Caine Prize for African Writing in 2002 for the short story 'Discovering Home', immediately rose to fame and celebrity status and was one of the founding members of the Kenyan publishing platform *Kwani?* He became the first editor of *Kwani?* in 2003. Furthermore, the award, which was the first step towards fame and celebrity status, afforded him the authority to comment on different social and political issues currently affecting the African continent, from sexual orientation and discrimination to representations and misrepresentations of Africa in the literary and political fields.[27] Wainaina's memoir *One Day I Will Write about This Place* (2011) received critical acclaim both at home and internationally, cementing his role as a major voice in African

---

[24] Sarah Brouillette, *Postcolonial Writers in the Global Literary Marketplace* (London: Palgrave Macmillan, 2007), p. 12.
[25] Karin Berkman, 'Literary Celebrity and Political Activism: Wole Soyinka's Nobel Prize Lecture and the Anti-Apartheid Struggle', *Critical Arts*, vol. 34, no. 1 (2020): 73–86, 85.
[26] A. Adesokan, *Postcolonial Artists and Global Aesthetics* (Bloomington: Indiana University Press, 2011), p. 156.
[27] See Binyavanga Wainaina, 'How to Write about Africa', *Granta*, vol. 92 (2005): 91–5.

narratives of representation. However, it was the publication of the piece 'I Am a Homosexual, Mum' that played the biggest single role in promoting his celebrity status. The piece, stylized as a lost chapter from his memoir, was first published online on the *Africa Is a Country* and the *Chimurenga Chronic* websites and continued to spread through social media sites. While the reception of his 'coming out' through this article was both positive and negative in equal measure, the ultra-visibility that came with it continued to foreground him in both mainstream and social media spaces, building further on his celebrity status. His public coming out was especially significant in the political and social context of a country and continent with oppressive laws on homosexuality as well as a conservative society that promotes homophobia. This public announcement ensured his continued hypervisibility in the media.

Despite the fact that he initially came to the limelight through the Caine Prize, Wainaina was especially vocal in his dismissal of prizes managed and awarded from and by former colonial powers. To this end, he was instrumental in establishing and foregrounding local literary organizations, magazines, journals and awards that consecrate value on contemporary African literature. Wainaina called for the need to provide alternative literary structures for writers in order to counter the material and symbolic capital that foreign legitimating bodies possess. Following his Caine win and his subsequent essays on leadership and democracy, Wainaina was in 2007 nominated, alongside 250 other 'Young Global Leaders', by the World Economic Forum – an award that he declined. The Young Global Leader award recognizes young leaders from around the world for their professional accomplishments, commitment to society and potential to contribute to shaping the future of the world. In a letter to the award organization following the nomination, Wainaina wrote,

> The problem here is that I am a writer. And although, like many, I go to sleep at night fantasizing about fame, fortune and credibility, the thing that is most valuable in my trade is to try, all the time, to keep myself loose, independent and creative ... it would be an act of great fraudulence for me to accept the trite idea that I am going to significantly impact world affairs.[28]

The refusal of this cultural prize demonstrated Wainaina's discomfort with foreign legitimating bodies; his awareness of the value of celebrity capital across fields and genres; and served to expose his uneasiness with the figure of the celebrity author becoming a representative.

---

[28] https://muse.union.edu/newsarchives/2007/01/31/visiting-writer-wainaina-winning-worldwide-accolades/. Accessed 1 January 2022.

Borrowing celebrity capital from television, media and film

While a focus on literary celebrity provides a link for analysing the text within its sociocultural and political field, it is important to note here that the field of celebrity culture is wide and expands beyond the literary arena to include personalities whose fame is drawn from various other cultural fields. The development from 'ordinary' to 'celebrity' figure is fuelled not only by achievements of individuals but also by their visibility through the media. Olivier Driessens refers to celebrity as wide recognition and argues that celebrity capital 'is conceptualized as accumulated media visibility that results from recurrent media representation'.[29] Using this analogy, the artistic fields of music, television and film therefore represent major avenues for the production of celebrity capital and explains the huge number of celebrity figures drawn from this field. Increasingly, these celebrity figures in fields such as pop music, film, the television industry and comedy are being commissioned to create literary texts. These texts are, however, mainly limited to autobiographies and children's books and include texts such as Hollywood star Lupita Nyong'o's storybook *Sulwe* (2019) and South African stand-up comedian Trevor Noah's autobiography *Born a Crime* (2016). However, different literary platforms in Africa are increasingly reliant on the capital of celebrity figures from different fields in order to draw more visibility to local texts and publishers. A discussion of celebrity status and literature also needs to acknowledge the growing field of celebrity capital from other artistic fields lending its capital to local literary production. This is especially relevant to new and upcoming literary platforms.

Moradewun Adejumobi, writing on the publicness of African letters from the perspective of Abiola Irele's work, notes that for Irele it was 'not enough to facilitate the publishing of a creative text. In addition to being published, the creative work had to become part of an ongoing critical discourse.'[30] She argues that, for a text to move from just being published and read to being part of ongoing critical discourse, there is need for intermediaries, and notes that academia acts as a major intermediary, providing a space for the text to be 'cited and citable'.[31] Adejunmobi states that 'many though not all instances of recognition depend on the direct intervention of cultural intermediaries such as academic and professional critics with expertise in ascribing value to creative works'.[32] In the same vein, therefore, celebrity

---

[29] Driessens, 'The Celebritization of Society and Culture', p. 543.
[30] Moradewun Adejunmobi, 'Abiola Irele and the Publicness of African Letters', *Journal of the African Literature Association*, vol. 14, no. 1 (2020): 77.
[31] Ibid.
[32] Ibid., p. 81.

capital in this context also plays the role of an intermediary, adding value not only to creative texts but also to the platforms associated with them. In contemporary African print cultures, facing many hurdles, including poor visibility in both the local and international literary platforms, celebrity culture helps to promote both the writer's own work and networks with which the celebrity may be associated. Through their celebrity capital, the celebrity becomes key in influencing literary taste beyond the literary field. The celebrity figures are therefore much-needed intermediaries, bringing visibility to contemporary African writing and literary platforms.

The Southern African literary collective LongStorySHORT, and the Kenyan writers' platform *Mbogi ya Mawriters* are contemporary literary and cultural producers that have invested in general celebrity capital to promote contemporary African literature. Banking on the culture of orality, LongStorySHORT relies mainly on celebrity figures from theatre, film and television industries reading literary pieces and excerpts at community libraries. *Mbogi ya Mawriters*, on the other hand, relies on a celebrity artist from theatre and broadcasting fields to lead literary discussions and draw more attention to new Kenyan literary works. These platforms work at bringing local writers, and literature, to a wider visibility by relying on the cultural and symbolic capital of celebrity figures from outside of the literary field. Their literary projects are pegged to using celebrity capital to promote a literary reading culture. By relying on established celebrity figures to promote their work, literature and literary events become fashionable and exciting because of the association with the celebrities, creating a certain kind of popular prestige. This approach is used to draw more audience to new works, writers and literary platforms, therefore contributing to a growing literary tradition. Sandwith et al. explain that this approach to literature by LongStorySHORT 'emphasizes the entertainment value of literature and seeks to encourage young people to read as widely as possible'.[33]

Banking on the culture of orality, LongStorySHORT relies mainly on celebrity figures from the media industries in South Africa reading literary pieces and excerpts at community libraries. The readings are then packaged into literary podcasts for mobile phones and online platforms such as YouTube. LongStorySHORT is a project of a Pretoria-based arts consultancy, Kajeno Media, led by Kgauhelo Dube, and the stories are curated by Nigerian writer Yewande Omotoso. The readings take place in community libraries and are usually followed by discussion with the audience. Since its launch in 2015, the project has featured various short stories by African writers, with each oral performance being led by a South African media celebrity artist.

---

[33] Corine Sandwith, C., K. Soldati-Kahimbaara and R. Fasselt, 'Decolonizing the Reading Landscape: A Conversation with Kgauhelo Dube', *Journal of Commonwealth Literature*, vol. 55, no. 1 (2020): 121–35, 122.

While the celebrity figures are drawn from the South African media scene, the stories featured are by writers from all over the continent. Texts also include older stories that are brought to light through the community readings and the repackaging into other media formats such as podcasts. The short story 'Tropical Fish' by Doreen Baingana was read by theatre artist Lindiwe Matshikiza at the Afro-Zwanaka Book Cafe in Soshanguve, Pretoria.[34] The story was first published in 2003 by *African American Review* and shortlisted for the AKO Caine Prize for African Writing in 2005. It was later included in Baingana's short story collection *Tropical Fish: Stories Out of Entebbe* (2005). The collection brings together eight linked stories of three sisters in Uganda navigating the world of growing up, and it won the Commonwealth Prize for Best First Book, Africa Region in 2006. 'Tropical Fish' explores themes of sexuality, interracial relations, exploitation and exoticism, among others. The inclusion of this story at the LongStorySHORT's readings in 2015 was an acknowledgement of the universality and timelessness of such themes, aiding in provoking contemporary debates on the topic, especially in a post-apartheid society.

Zukiswa Wanner's short story 'The F Word' was read by actress Renate Stuurman at the Sunnyside Community library.[35] The story explores same-sex relationships and the socialization of homophobia. It features child characters, starting with their excitement at American pop music celebrities Bow Wow, Omarion and Lil' Romeo whose images and music the children consume through the television. The children want to be associated with these celebrity figures and one of the boys, Zuko, wants to braid his hair like them. The braiding of the little boy's hair triggers homophobic reactions from some adults and the mother takes this as a teaching opportunity around respect and rights. The story uses the shock effect of the curse words to draw attention to the theme and hopefully to invite conversations on uncomfortable topics that may otherwise not be addressed in such platforms, thereby fulfilling the project's goals – to provoke discussion. In conversation with the project's director, Sandwith et al. affirm this goal, adding that the project has also further invested in opening the conversation to other digital media platforms such as Facebook and Twitter 'through associated hashtags such as #FortheLoveofAfrikanLiterature and #OneStoryAtATime' so that in this way, 'the reading of stories facilitates a wider political discussion'.[36]

Other stories that have been featured in this project include 'Under The Bridge' by Uchechukwu Peter Umezurike, read by film and theatre star Quanita Adams; 'Tender' by Nozizwe Cynthia Jele, read by TV actress and social activist Hlubi Mboya; and short fiction by A. Igoni Barrett, read and

---

[34] https://www.youtube.com/watch?v=ej2oqZGSsbY&t=6s. Accessed 1 January 2022.
[35] https://www.youtube.com/watch?v=RCBSC1VJTOA. Accessed 1 January 2022.
[36] Sandwith, Soldati-Kahimbaara and Fasselt, 'Decolonizing the Reading Landscape', p. 123.

performed by Nigerian hip-hop group Fokn Bois, among others. Writing about this project in 'Decolonizing the Reading Landscape', Sandwith et al. argue that 'LongStorySHORT uses digital technology to make books more widely available and to circumvent a publishing context which is skewed towards writers in the US and the UK.'[37] The project acknowledges the gap created between texts and audience as a result of lack of economic empowerment and hence its investment in free digital audiovisual formats of texts that might otherwise be unaffordable and inaccessible. As Lee Erikson notes, 'the history of literary forms demonstrates that literature is materially and economically embedded in the reality of the publishing market'.[38] Therefore, while Tinashe Mushakavanhu talks of the popularity of short story as being derived 'from the fact that the form has been adopted as an economic publishing strategy', the argument could be furthered to note that the digital format of the short story is slowly gaining prominence not only because of the low cost of production and packaging but also because of its accessibility.[39] When celebrity figures lend their capital to these texts, the popularity of the text in all its formats is boosted.

As a local literary platform, LongStorySHORT has heavily invested in the role of the audience in literature, with the interaction between the celebrity figures and audience carefully mediated through the text in the context of discussions and communal readings. It relies on celebrity capital intra-conversion to lend prestige and value to local platforms and texts. Through the focus on local celebrities for local literary texts and platforms, spaces such as LongStorySHORT are further exposing 'the myth of the mediated centre', which Couldry identifies as one of the major misrecognitions involved in media rituals.[40] This myth is 'the assumption that the media are the privileged gatekeepers and access points to the imagined social center'.[41] In this context, these new literary outfits are engaged in multiple disruptions of the hierarchical power relations within literary and cultural production. This media visibility drawing from celebrity capital in different fields has contributed immensely to bringing global visibility to contemporary African literature and at the same time functioning to complicate the supposedly smooth circulation of the literary field from local to global ecologies and scales.

Similar to the LongStorySHORT project, *Mbogi ya Mawriters* is a series of literature discussion fora run by Writers Guild Kenya, Prestige Books and

---

[37]Ibid., p. 122.
[38]Lee Erikson, *The Economy of the Literary Form: English Literature and the Industrialization of Publishing* (Baltimore, MD: Johns Hopkins University Press, 1996), p. 8.
[39]Tinashe Mushakavanhu, 'Locating a Genre: Is Zimbabwe a Short Story Country?' *African Literature Today*, vol. 31 (2013): 127–34.
[40]Nick Couldry, *Media Rituals: A Critical Approach* (London: Routledge, 2003).
[41]Driessens, 'The Celebritization of Society and Culture', p. 543.

the Alliance Française de Nairobi. The discussion sessions are led by John Sibi Okumu, the Kenyan actor, broadcaster, playwright, writer, teacher and journalist. *Mbogi ya Mawriters* draws its name from the Sheng language to refer to a crew of writers. The use of both English and Sheng – a hybrid language spoken in most of urban Kenya – points to the new platform's linguistic and cultural self-positioning. The project seeks the attention of literature enthusiasts across different socio-economic and age groups. The word *mbogi* was popularized in Kenya by the hip-hop group Mbogi Genje, whose name directly translates to 'a crew of troublemakers'. This group is popular with youth and mostly from Nairobi's poor neighbourhoods. The group is locally known as 'the Sheng masters' and has popularized new Sheng words through their music.

By positioning this new literary platform within these linguistic and social cultural settings, *Mbogi ya Mawriters* positions itself as inclusive in both socio-economic and cultural representations. However, while the literary sessions include both upcoming and well-known Kenyan writers and also give space to self-published texts, language diversification is lacking. Launched in 2019, the monthly sessions, which have been heavily affected by the Covid-19 regulations in Kenya, have featured writers such as the AKO Caine Prize for African Writing winner Makena Onjerika, with her edited short story collection *Digital Bedbugs*; Ciku Kimani Mwaniki, with *Cocktail from the Savannah*; and Kinyanjui Kombani, who has won numerous literary awards including the Jomo Kenyatta Prize for Literature, the Wahome Mutahi Literary Prize and the Burt Africa Literary Awards. These texts are written in English and the discussion fora are also held in English, thereby excluding a wide audience for whom English serves as a language barrier. The forum has therefore been viewed as elitist. Despite the language barrier, however, this forum has continued to serve as a platform from which to launch new creative texts by Kenyan writers. Just as with the style of LongStorySHORT, the sessions are also packaged into accessible digital formats. The celebrity capital of Okumu is harnessed in this platform to draw more physical audience members to the reading and discussion fora, as well as in the accessibility of the packaged digital formats where the celebrity name is used to generate more clicks and to direct traffic to the website.

The significant link between these two platforms based in East and Southern Africa is their acknowledgement of the power of media visibility, and especially of television. The celebrity figures charged with lending their social and cultural capital to literature have mostly been affirmed and consecrated through the visual media. Nick Couldry convincingly argues for the need to accept and acknowledge 'the concentration in media institutions of the power to define reality'.[42] This power is channelled towards new texts, authors and literary platforms such as publishers when television,

---

[42] Couldry, *Media Rituals*, p. 19.

film and theatre celebrities becomes ambassadors for literature. Borrowing from Arjun Appadurai's concept of 'mediascapes' within the context of understanding the complex, fragmented and multidirectional nature of global cultural flow, I analyse how the foregrounding of the media and media personalities as literary ambassadors disrupts the power relations in African literary and cultural production. Appadurai uses the concept of mediascapes to refer both to 'the distribution of electronic capabilities to produce and disseminate information … and to the images of the world created by these media'.[43]

While literary celebrity figures are mostly consecrated through literary prizes, their celebrity status and fame continue to point to the unequal power relations in the world literary marketplace. This is especially significant when the link between the celebrity author and the literary prize is connected to the unequal access to the global literary canon that exists between writers in the Global North and those in the South. The significance of literary prizes, and especially international awards, has directly influenced the production and distribution of contemporary African literature. Increasingly, new texts that become accepted as African literature and are widely circulated and consumed through different platforms continue to be popularized, especially by international literary awards and publishing bodies. These texts that are slowly forming the contemporary African literary canon have also tended to foreground diasporic African writers, who are then viewed as representatives of the continent. However, as John Guillory argues, the process of canonization is directly influenced by the distribution of, or access to, the means of literary production.[44] From this perspective, therefore, a discussion of the value of literary celebrity in the contemporary African literary field also necessitates a discussion about the unequal distribution of the means of cultural and literary production. The figure of the literary celebrity, therefore, becomes linked to the distribution of and access to different means of literary and cultural production on the continent.

Over the last two decades, a record number of African writers, mainly writing and publishing in English and French, have successfully gained and maintained visibility and celebrity status after being awarded major international prizes. These writers have subsequently maintained their position as public figures that expand beyond the literary borders and include Chimamanda Ngozi Adichie, Binyavanga Wainaina, Alain Mabanckou, Ben Okri, Nadifa Mohamed, Helon Habila, Maaza Mengiste and Teju Cole, among others. Of note is the increasing popularity and celebrity status of African writers based mainly in the diaspora and whose works were originally

---

[43] Arjun Appadurai, *Modernity at Large: Cultural Dimensions of Globalization* (Minneapolis: University of Minnesota Press, 1996), p. 35.
[44] John Guillory, *Cultural Capital: The Problem of Literary Canon Formation* (Chicago: University of Chicago Press, 1993).

published and awarded prizes outside the continent. Milly Williamson argues that celebrity 'is a symbol of ongoing zeitgeist'.[45] Using this analogy, a reading of celebrity in contemporary African writing exposes the unequal power relations in literary publishing between Africa and the Global North. However, it also offers an avenue for exploring how the celebrity capital created and circulated through diasporic publishing platforms, awards, texts and writers translates into local contexts. For instance, Sandra Ponzanesi condemns the Nobel Prize in Literature as a Eurocentric prize 'which has been slow to recognise the talents and literary worth of authors from former European colonies, and writing in the language of their former masters'.[46] Therefore, for the African writers who become global literary celebrities, their lending of cultural capital to local texts, writers, ideas or organizations is perceived as an extension of the unequal power relation in literary and cultural production where power is concentrated in the Global North.

On the other hand, the local television, film and theatre celebrities lending their capital to literary platforms such as *Mbogi ya MaWriters* and LongStorySHORT present an opportunity to disrupt the unequal power relations in global literary production, while at the same time providing an alternative literary geography that is mainly driven by the local informing the global. These celebrity figures derive their cultural capital mainly through local cultural production such as local television and theatre programmes, and then lend that capital to local literary platforms, such as is the case with *Mbogi ya MaWriters* and LongStorySHORT.

Literary celebrity as a double-edged sword

The increasing significance of the power of celebrity figures from different fields lending their capital to both a text and the networks within which it circulates foregrounds the connection between celebrities and advocacy. This is what Liza Tsaliki terms the 'celebvocate', where celebrity capital allows the person to become an advocate in different fields owing to the power of their image.[47] However, Madhu Krishnan (2014) warns against 'the neoliberal impulse to telescope context into slogan' explaining that in the African literary scene, increasingly 'one-liners easily retweeted and production-laden, feel good moments of reflection which draw comfortable

---

[45] Milly Williamson, *Celebrity: Capitalism and the Making of Fame* (Cambridge: Polity Press, 2016), p. 3.
[46] Sandra Ponzanesi, *The Postcolonial Cultural Industry: Icons, Markets, Mythologies* (London: Palgrave Macmillan, 2014), p. 74.
[47] Liza Tsaliki, '"Tweeting the Good Causes": Social Networking and Celebrity Activism', in *A Companion to Celebrity*, ed. P. D. Marshall and S. Redmond (Cambridge, MA: Wiley Blackwell, 2015), pp. 235–57.

conclusions in eighteen minutes or less have taken prevalence in the shaping of a collective vision of Africa and the delimitations of the African writer's position' (p. 134).[48] In this context, while the presence of the 'celebvocate' has led to celebrity figures converting their capital into wider discussions on power across different fields and into political influence, the limitation of this capital to an individual exposes its subjectivity. Indeed, it becomes important to foreground the fact that 'authorial agency is always in close dialogue with its structural frameworks and therefore has its limitations'.[49]

Lorraine York explains the concept of celebrity in the arts through a focus on subjectivity. She argues that if 'the struggle to claim and bestow celebrity is, as Bourdieu says, nothing less than a struggle over what gets defined as human accomplishment, then celebrity is fully implicated in theoretical discussions about subjectivity itself'.[50] In a discussion on celebrity and subjectivity, therefore, the significant point to consider is 'the way in which celebrity, with its attendant discourses of authenticity or inauthenticity, is crucially related to the social and historical construction of the self'.[51] When engaging with the wider discussion of literary celebrity, the body, or the persona of the author, takes as much prominence as the text. Ainehi Edoro, the editor of the literary blog *Brittle Paper*, writes about African literature and literary paparazzi. Her blog post 'Literary Paparazzi – Soyinka's House and The Lives of Famous African Authors' starts as an analysis of Teju Cole's *New Yorker* piece on Soyinka and his work in literature and activism – 'Letter from Lagos: Madmen and Specialists.' Edoro focuses on the significance of authorial celebrity and why more critics need to pay attention to African literature from this perspective:

> An artist's body – and all the things clustered around it – is always implicated in [a] lot more things than we imagine it to be. The road from an artist's body to the body of his work is a very short one. Both bodies are legitimate machineries of meaning and do some of the most beautiful kinds of literary work when we place them in relation.
>
> It is a shame that the literary world, especial in Africa, has chosen to define itself against a celebrity culture it sees as commodifying and base, as something that should be left to lesser art-worlds of pop-musicians and movie stars or to Kim Kardashian. We are not supposed to be intrigued by the lives our favorite authors live behind the books they write for us. That is why we are forever doomed to waiting for memoirs – such

---

[48] Madhu Krishnan, *Contemporary African Literature in English: Global Locations, Postcolonial Identifications* (London: Palgrave Macmillan, 2014), p. 134.
[49] Mayer, 'Introduction', p. 153.
[50] Lorraine York, *Literary Celebrity in Canada* (Toronto: University of Toronto Press, 2016), p. 16.
[51] Ibid.

pretentious things – to learn the filtered and stilted versions of the lives of these famous men and women.

Alternatively, maybe we are long overdue for a literary paparazzi industrial complex.[52]

Edoro here echoes Ohlsson et al. calling for the foregrounding of the author alongside the text in literary criticism. A focus on the writer's life provides a different layer of meaning and interpretation of their work. In contemporary times, the avenues through which the audience consumes both the text and the author's personal life as different layers of the same narrative are ever increasing, with social media and literary blogs especially contributing greatly to this. Echoing the editor's sentiments in 2013, *Brittle Paper* is today one of the few contemporary literary platforms with a dedicated section on 'Lifestyle', covering various African writers. This includes congratulatory messages on engagements, weddings and births, birthdays and holidays, new books and other information on the social life of writers. This provides a space where the author gradually gains the media capital necessary for celebrity status. However, because celebrity capital is involved with the persona of the writer or the literary promoter, it is therefore always precarious and can easily be negatively affected if the public status of the celebrity changes. Looking at structures like the media industry that support celebrity culture and capital shows that celebrity capital is a double-edged sword. As Sandra Ponzanesi notes,

> What characterizes consumption as a mode of signification is that commodities no longer exist in and of themselves, but circulate as signs within a system of differences. ... The commodity in question, in this case the author or the book, gets its meaning only within a certain sign system. Therefore, cultural artefacts come to embody and signify meanings in the course of their circulation and consumption.[53]

Clearly this has historical precedent. One of the earliest writers considered a literary celebrity, Jean-Jacques Rousseau, was sceptical about celebrity status and often viewed his fame as a burden. Antoine Lilti, writing about Rousseau's paranoia as a result of his celebrity status, argues that 'the problem of Rousseau's paranoia is not a biographical one, and still less a psychopathological one. It is a problem of social history, which puts celebrity, as a particular form of consecration, into question.'[54] More recently, other

---

[52]Ainehi Edoro, 'Literary Paparazzi – Soyinka's House and the Lives of Famous African Authors', https://brittlepaper.com/2013/08/soyinkas-house-lives-famous-african-authors/. Accessed 1 January 2022.
[53]Ponzanesi, *The Postcolonial Cultural Industry*, p. 77.
[54]Antoine Lilti, 'The Writing of Paranoia: Jean-Jacques Rousseau and the Paradoxes of Celebrity', *Representations*, vol. 103, no. 1 (2008): 55.

writers have struggled to create a balance between the desire for popularity on the one hand and the need to maintain credibility on the other. Indeed, Mayer notes that 'celebrity authors engaging in political activism potentially face loss of prestige, charges of dilettantism and a precarious balancing act between artistic autonomy and meeting the demands of media, industries, institutions and audiences'.[55] For instance, Adichie has recently been in the spotlight in both local and international media as well as social media platforms for her comments on transgender identity, where she has been accused of fuelling hate and transphobia against transgender women in Africa.[56] There have been calls for her to be de-platformed through 'cancel culture', with the argument that, because of the power of her position as a celebrity, her stand on transgender rights and identities could result in hate crimes against transgender people. This scandal carries the potential for diminished prestige in the literary marketplace.

In addition, despite the success that comes with the capital intra-conversion of celebrity capital, there is always the danger of the author-turned-celebrity becoming an unwilling spokesperson and sometimes even going further, to speak instead of, rather than on behalf of. As Ponzanesi illustrates in her reading of award-winning literary celebrity Salman Rushdie,

> Long before the nefarious effect of the fatwa, which catapulted him from just a talented new author in the English language into the most hunted world writer, Rushdie had skilfully played the game of the cultural industry. By carving out for himself the role of the migrant author hovering between two cultures, Rushdie managed to become the leading spokesperson in the literary and personal terms of a whole new generation of diasporic writers from former colonies, especially India.[57]

In this regard, it becomes important to ask questions around the impact on the literary product when the author is marketed as a commodity, sometimes exclusively of the literary text, even with the understanding that 'one motivation for the study of postcolonial print culture is a sense that the internal dynamics of the postcolonial literary text are never quite separable from the ostensibly external world of commodity production and market relations'.[58] Adichie's profile, for instance, has led to ultra-visibility and continuous media presence for the writer. Her media presence extends to TV screens by way of news features, documentaries and interviews, where

---

[55] Mayer, 'Introduction', p. 153.
[56] https://www.theguardian.com/books/2017/mar/13/chimamanda-ngozi-adichie-clarifies-transgender-comments. Accessed 1 January 2022.
[57] Ponzanesi, *The Postcolonial Cultural Industry*, pp. 72–3.
[58] Sarah Brouillette and David Finkelstein, 'Postcolonial Print Cultures', *Journal of Commonwealth Literature*, vol. 48, no. 1 (2013): 3–7, 4.

she has continued to feature frequently in both local and international presses. She has appeared in several TV interviews speaking about, among other topics, race, feminism, human rights and African identities. However, this media visibility has resulted in her being elevated to the position of spokesperson in almost all areas of 'African' affairs. In 2013, Adichie's comments on her creative writing workshop series with Farafina as the yardstick for excellence in creative writing was interpreted as her gatekeeping contemporary African writing, patronizing former workshop participants. Adichie claimed that the AKO Caine Prize for African Writing shortlist did not represent quality work from the continent, pointing to the alumni of her writing workshops as a more honest representation of good writing. In an interview, Adichie replied as follows to a question on the significance of the high number of Nigerian writers on that year's Caine Prize shortlist:

> Elnathan [John] was one of my *boys* in my workshop. But what's all this over-privileging of the Caine Prize, anyway? I don't want to talk about the Caine Prize, really. I suppose it's a good thing, but for me it's not the arbiter of the best fiction in Africa. It's never been. I know that Chinelo [Okparanta] is on the short list, too. But I haven't even read the stories – I'm just not very interested. I don't go the Caine Prize to look for the best in African fiction. ... I go to my mailbox, where my workshop people send me their stories.[59]

With these comments came a media furore, with writers and other literary stakeholders on the continent questioning the limitations of celebrity capital and as the price of unfavourable and negative celebrity capital on the literary networks connected to them. Adichie's comments were interpreted as condescending and disrespectful. Many writers, such as Elnathan John, publicly distanced themselves from Adichie and severed ties and networks with her.

In conclusion, therefore, focusing on celebrity status helps to read the intersections between literary celebrity capital and politics, exposing how this influences the literary production and consumption of contemporary African literature. Adichie as an author has embraced this celebrity status and the social and cultural capital that comes with it, to draw attention to specific socio-political and cultural issues and concerns such as human rights, gender equality, the fight against racism and neocolonialism. It is therefore interesting to look at how a celebrity writer, packaged as commodity, influences the consumption of their literary products and, in

---

[59] https://www.salon.com/2013/07/14/chimamanda_ngozi_adichie_race_doesnt_occur_to_me_partner/. Accessed 1 January 2022.

extension, influences the perception of contemporary African literature. This reveals that the 'manner in which these texts reach audiences involves complex negotiations of political, commercial, and cultural boundaries and sensibilities'.[60]

This chapter argues that celebrity culture facilitates and maintains a literary network of value that is simultaneously local and global. Within the wider African literary and cultural production scene, the image and the persona of the celebrity has become an important investment, especially for new texts and for upcoming platforms, which extend from literary publishers to small magazines, creative writing workshops, literary festivals and even literary awards. Adichie and Wainaina, for instance, are perfect examples of successful capital intra-conversion processes that rely on the prestige of the writer to confer power and visibility on local literary projects. As mentioned, both Adichie and Wainaina have been heavily invested in creative writing on the continent, with Adichie heading the annual Farafina Creative Writing Workshop (Wainaina took part as a trainer). Wainaina was also a founding member of *Kwani?*, providing links with internationally recognized awards and publishing organizations.

Further, celebrity capital is malleable and this allows for the conversion of one capital to another, therefore making it possible for literature to benefit from celebrity capital drawn from other artistic fields such as music, television and theatre. The argument made in this chapter is that this circulation of value and the blurring of lines between genres and different artistic fronts is significant in drawing attention to contemporary African literature, as it goes directly to placing art as an important aspect of any cultural, political or economic life. In this context, the work of the celebrity extends beyond the text (whether their own or not) to focus attention on the literary and cultural production mechanisms that support the development of literature on the continent. This is especially relevant considering that, for a writer, being talked about does not necessarily translate to being read. However, the ultra-visibility of celebrity figures helps to drive more traffic towards the literary networks and platforms that they are associated with. The idea is to harvest the cultural and social capital of the celebrity figure for the expansion of local literary networks and platforms in the hope that more focus and attention on these spaces will translate to higher literary and cultural production on the continent. In the end, celebrity capital is used to increase visibility and output for contemporary African literature. By focusing on the networks that build upon, and which are a result of, literary celebrity culture, the work offers a reading of the process of transforming the local to the global.

---

[60] Brouillette and Finkelstein, 'Postcolonial Print Cultures', p. 3.

Bibliography

Adejunmobi, M. (2020), 'Abiola Irele and the Publicness of African Letters', *Journal of the African Literature Association*, vol. 14, no. 1: 72–89.

Adesokan, A. (2011), *Postcolonial Artists and Global Aesthetics*, Bloomington: Indiana University Press.

Anthony, A. (23 November 2014), 'Arundhati Roy: Goddess of Big Ideas', *The Guardian*, https://www.theguardian.com/books/2014/nov/23/arundhati-roy-interview-goddess-of-big-ideas. Accessed 23 March 2021.

Appadurai, A. (1996), *Modernity at Large: Cultural Dimensions of Globalization*, Minneapolis: University of Minnesota Press.

Bady, A. (14 July 2013), 'Chimamanda Ngozi Adichie: "Race Doesn't Occur to Me"', *Salon*, https://www.salon.com/2013/07/14/chimamanda_ngozi_adichie_race_doesnt_occur. Accessed 27 July 2021.

Baingana, D. (2005), *Tropical Fish: Stories Out of Entebbe*, Amherst: University of Massachusetts Press.

Barthes, R. (1977), *Image, Music, Text*, trans. S. Heath, London: Fontana.

Berkman, K. (2020), 'Literary Celebrity and Political Activism: Wole Soyinka's Nobel Prize Lecture and the Anti-Apartheid Struggle', *Critical Arts*, vol. 34, no. 1: 73–86.

Bourdieu, P. (1993), *The Field of Cultural Production: Essays on Art and Literature*, Cambridge: Polity Press.

Bourdieu, P., and L. J. D. Wacquant (1992), *An Invitation to Reflexive Sociology*, Chicago: University of Chicago Press.

Brouillette, S. (2007), *Postcolonial Writers in the Global Literary Marketplace*, London: Palgrave Macmillan.

Brouillette, S., and D. Finkelstein (2013), 'Postcolonial Print Cultures'. *Journal of Commonwealth Literature*, vol. 48, no. 1: 3–7.

Couldry, N. (2003), *Media Rituals: A Critical Approach*, London: Routledge.

Couldry, N. (2004), 'Media Meta-Capital: Extending the Range of Bourdieu's Field Theory', in *After Bourdieu: Influence, Critique, Elaboration*, ed. D. L. Swartz and V. L. Zolberg, New York: Kluwer Academic, pp. 165–89.

Driessens, O. (2013), 'The Celebritization of Society and Culture: Understanding the Structural', *International Journal of Cultural Studies*, vol. 16, no. 6: 641–57.

Edoro, A. (29 August 2013), 'Literary Paparazzi – Soyinka's House and the Lives of Famous African Authors', *Brittle Paper*, https://brittlepaper.com/2013/08/soyinkas-house-lives-famous-african-authors/. Accessed 2 September 2020.

English, J. F. (2005), *The Economy of Prestige: Prizes, Awards and the Circulation of Cultural Values*, Cambridge, MA: Harvard University Press.

Erikson, L. (1996), *The Economy of the Literary Form: English Literature and the Industrialization of Publishing*, Baltimore, MD: Johns Hopkins University Press.

Flood, A. (7 October 2014), 'Nobel Judge Fears for the Future of Western Literature', *The Guardian*, https://www.theguardian.com/books/2014/oct/07/creative-writing-killing-western-literature-nobel-judge-horace-engdahl. Accessed 23 March 2021.

Guillory, J. (1993), *Cultural Capital: The Problem of Literary Canon Formation*, Chicago: University of Chicago Press.

Kean, D. (13 March 2017), 'Chimamanda Ngozi Adichie Clarifies Transgender Comments as Backlash Grows', *The Guardian*, https://www.theguardian.com/books/2017/mar/13/chimamanda-ngozi-adichie-clarifies-transgender-comments. Accessed 28 July 2021.

Krishnan, M. (2014), *Contemporary African Literature in English: Global Locations, Postcolonial Identifications*, London: Palgrave Macmillan.

Lecznar, M. (2017), 'Texts, Talks and Tailoring: Chimamanda Ngozi Adichie's Fashion Politics', *Celebrity Studies*, vol. 8, no. 1: 167–71.

Lilti, A. (2008), 'The Writing of Paranoia: Jean-Jacques Rousseau and the Paradoxes of Celebrity', *Representations*, vol. 103, no. 1: 53–83.

Mayer, S. (2017), 'Introduction: Art and Action: Authorship, Politics and Celebrity', *Celebrity Studies*, vol. 8, no. 1: 152–6.

Moran, J. (2000), *Star Authors: Literary Celebrity in America*, London: Pluto Press.

Mushakavanhu, T. (2013), 'Locating a Genre: Is Zimbabwe a Short Story Country?' *African Literature Today*, vol. 31: 127–34.

Ohlsson, A., T. Forslid and A. Steiner (2014), 'Literary Celebrity Reconsidered', *Celebrity Studies*, vol. 5, nos 1–2: 32–44.

Ponzanesi, S. (2014), *The Postcolonial Cultural Industry: Icons, Markets, Mythologies*, London: Palgrave Macmillan.

Roberts, G. (2011), *Prizing Literature: The Celebration and Circulation of National Culture*, Toronto: University of Toronto Press.

Sandwith, C., K. Soldati-Kahimbaara and R. Fasselt (2020), 'Decolonizing the Reading Landscape: A Conversation with Kgauhelo Dube', *Journal of Commonwealth Literature*, vol. 55, no. 1: 121–35.

Squires, C. (2007), *Marketing Literature: The Making of Contemporary Writing in Britain*, Basingstoke: Palgrave Macmillan.

Throsby, D. (2001), *Economics and Culture*, Cambridge: Cambridge University Press.

Tsaliki, L. (2015), '"Tweeting the Good Causes": Social Networking and Celebrity Activism', in *A Companion to Celebrity*, ed. P. D. Marshall and S. Redmond, Cambridge, MA: Wiley Blackwell, pp. 235–57.

Wainaina, B. (2005), 'How to Write about Africa', *Granta*, vol. 92: 91–5.

Wallis, K. (2018), 'Exchanges in Nairobi and Lagos: Mapping Literary Networks and World Literary Space', *Research in African Literatures*, vol. 49, no. 1: 163–86.

Williamson, M. (2016), *Celebrity: Capitalism and the Making of Fame*, Cambridge: Polity Press.

York, L. (2016), *Literary Celebrity in Canada*, Toronto: University of Toronto Press.

12

Reversing the global media lens: Colonial spectacularization in the writing of Binyavanga Wainaina

Penny Cartwright

Afropolitanism and decoloniality: Situating Wainaina's worldliness

In 'Modern African Literary History', Ato Quayson relays an oft-observed feature of post-millennium African literatures: that they are principally produced by Africans living in the diaspora and published by Western presses with little of their predecessors' infrastructural and commercial connections to the continent.[1] For Quayson – as in numerous analyses of this kind – this

---

[1] Ato Quayson, 'Modern African Literary History: Nation and-Narration, Orality, and Diaspora', *Journal of the African Literature Association*, vol. 13, no. 1 (2019): 131–52. Detailed analyses of the origins of canonical Anglophone African literature within British publishing circuits (particularly Heinemann's foundational African Writers Series) can be found in Caroline Davies, *Creating Postcolonial Literature: African Writers and British Publishers* (New York: Palgrave Macmillan, 2013); James Currey, *Africa Writes Back: The African Writers Series & the Launch of African Literature* (Oxford: James Currey, 2008). For discussion of more recent developments in diasporic publishing centres see Pius Adesanmi and Chris Dunton, 'Nigeria's Third Generation Writing: Historiography and Preliminary Theoretical Considerations', *English in Africa*, vol. 32, no. 1 (2005): 7–19.

diasporic production context is mirrored in the thematic preoccupations of the works, which bear a decided 'impulse toward distinguishing their place in relation to the racial economy of the West, a racial economy that denominates differential locations for Asians, Africans, Hispanics, Filipinos, etc. in relation to the hegemonic order of white privilege'.[2] It is a literary landscape that focalizes the makings of identity within and against Western epistemic orders, rather than on the experiences of the postcolony per se: 'what happens to the African resident in London, New York, Edinburgh, Berlin, or Rome who keeps dreaming nostalgically of Africa.'[3] Quayson's analysis (others suggest 'diagnosis') is a now well-established position, thanks to the sustained scholarship on 'Afropolitanism' that followed the major commercial successes of self-consciously migratory-themed works by writers such as Taiye Selasi and NoViolet Bulawayo.[4] Prominent among these critical voices was the late Kenyan writer and *Kwani?* editor, Binyavanga Wainaina.

A declared 'Pan-Africanist' rather than an 'Afropolitan' (as announced in his keynote for the 2012 ASAUK (African Studies Association UK) conference),[5] Wainaina presents an interesting deviation from critical accounts (as in Quayson's above) that equate interest in the 'racial economy of the West' with diasporic settings and preoccupations. Though supporting his writing through an array of fellowships, including in the United States, Wainaina's creative output, both with *Kwani?* and independently, rigorously centres continental, particularly Kenyan-based, experience. Published from Nairobi, *Kwani?* has sought to act as a counterpoint to Kenyan national media – against 'our defining text … the politician's voice on the 9 o'clock news'[6] – with local features on Maasai land grabs, 'Silicon Nairobi' and a special double edition dedicated to violence in the aftermath of the 2007/8 Kenyan elections.[7] Wainaina's 2011 literary memoir *One Day I Will Write about This Place* roams in exuberant cosmopolitan fashion. Its waypoints

---

[2]Quayson, 'Modern African Literary History', p. 148.
[3]Ibid., pp. 148–9.
[4]See, for instance, *Afropolitanism: Reboot,* ed. Carli Coetzee (London: Routledge, 2017); Grace A. Musila, 'Part-Time Africans, Europolitans and "Africa Lite"', *Journal of African Cultural Studies*, vol. 28, no. 1 (2016): 109–13; Amatoritsero Ede, 'The Politics of Afropolitanism', *Journal of African Cultural Studies*, vol. 28, no. 1 (2016): 88–100.
[5]Stephanie Bosch-Santana, 'Exorcizing Afropolitanism: Binyavanga Wainaina Explains Why "I Am a Pan-Africanist, Not an Afropolitan" at ASAUK 2012', *Africa in Words* (blog), 8 February 2013, https://africainwords.com/2013/02/08/exorcizing-afropolitanism-binyavanga-wainaina-explains-why-i-am-a-pan-africanist-not-an-afropolitan-at-asauk-2012/. Accessed 1 March 2022.
[6]Billy Kahora, 'An Apprenticeship in Ethnicity: A Time beyond the Writer', *Kwani?*, vol. 5, no. 1 (2008): 8–12.
[7]For a sustained analysis on the position of *Kwani?* within the landscape of continent-based presses, see Kate Wallis, 'How Books Matter: Kwani Trust, Farafina, Cassava Republic Press and the Medium of Print', *Wasafiri*, vol. 31, no. 4 (2016): 39–46.

are not London and New York, but Nakuru, Nairobi, Lagos, Kampala and Johannesburg. Nonetheless, continental experiences are deeply infused, in Wainaina's writing, by the awareness of a globalized 'racial economy':[8] indeed, his apprehension of the possibilities of situated African lifeworlds is intricately bound up in the global structuration of 'differential locations for Asians, Africans, Hispanics, Filipinos, etc.'. Wainaina is deeply attuned, in other words, to encounters with 'the hegemonic order of white privilege' that continually occur *outside* Western capitals – confrontations, assimilations and negotiations that might not entail 'affluent mobility [within] the global north'.[9]

Colonial spectacularization

In his attention to Global South experiences of 'the racial economy of the West', Wainaina's interests are clearly aligned with the growing discourse on 'what decolonial theory has called "coloniality", meaning the transhistoric expansion of colonial domination and the perpetuation of its effects in contemporary times'[10] – a framework that is inherently globally oriented. Far from formal decolonization heralding a 'retreat' into, and immunity within, the national, persistent forms of coloniality[11] – the 'perpetuation of effects' stemming from colonial differentiation force attention back towards global epistemic orders and the uneven global structuration of rights and resources. A profound example of such unevenness, this chapter argues, can be found in the structuration of the 'global media' and its production of what I call here 'colonial spectacularization': a dominating mode of looking that claims as exclusive both the right *to look* – and so to act – upon others, and the relationship between one's look and reality as such. As Nicholas Mirzoeff has it, colonial modes of looking emerge in the 'surveillance of the overseer',[12] who alone may claim the proper 'visualisation of history', the 'nomination of the visible' and hence of the ontological 'real' itself.[13]

As Mirzoeff indicates, colonial spectacularization is deeply embedded in wider practices of world-formation. Lilie Chouliaraki and Debjani Ganguly further this notion with specific reference to the global media.

---

[8]Quayson, 'Modern African Literary History', p. 146.
[9]Grace Musila, 'Part-Time Africans, Europolitans and "Africa Lite"', *Journal of African Cultural Studies*, vol. 28, no. 1 (2016): 109–13, 111.
[10]Nicholas Mirzoeff, *The Right to Look: A Counterhistory of Visuality* (Durham, NC: Duke University of Press, 2011), p. 5.
[11]See Adesanmi and Dunton for a clear, literary-focused description of this idea of decolonization.
[12]Mirzoeff, *The Right to Look*, p. 2.
[13]Ibid., pp. 2–3.

Drawing on the Habermasian notion of media-instantiated publics, they describe the formation of a putative 'global public' and civil society through transnationalized media communications[14] – a public implicitly located primarily in Euro-America. Crucially, media communications do not merely reflect a pre-existing public but call it into being: Chouliaraki writes of their 'performative power ... *to constitute* the [global] public, as a collectivity with a will to act, at the very moment that they claim to address it'.[15] By thus constituting the 'global public' 'as a collectivity' with implicit contours – and, moreover, as the collectivity with *the* privileged 'will to act' – the media intensively shape processes of world-formation. Namely, they engender a distinctive cartography of the world as divided along lines of agents/non-agents, participants/non-participants, proximity/distance. As Ganguly vividly frames it, this is a conception of world (and worldliness) that revolves around the discomfiting 'phenomenological intimacy' between 'the global publics' and the 'remaindered zones of otherness' that they spectate.[16]

This chapter reads Wainaina's 2004 *Kwani*-published short story 'Ships in High Transit' ('SHiT') and *Beyond River Yei*, his 2006 investigation of Sudanese sleeping sickness, as two opposing interventions into the problem of colonial spectacularization and the kinds of world-formation it instantiates. While 'Ships in High Transit' (as its sly scatological acronym suggests) is an excoriating satire of colonial spectacularization – a diagnosis of the problem, as it were – *Beyond River Yei*, I argue, is an attempt at *prescription*: a formal experiment in how to look without dominating, taking the right of others to look, or claiming exclusive authority to the real. This chapter explores 'SHiT' and its depictions of piracy and direct, personal violation against foreign correspondents as metaphor for the hijacking of global media infrastructures and the dominating mode of looking they enable. Moreover, it elucidates *Beyond River Yei* and its idiosyncratic narrative strategies for constructing a non-dominating gaze, above all through the ambivalent device of Wainaina's metafictional informant, the poet Ajo Diktor. Both readings reveal how Wainaina reframes experiences of colonial spectacularization around African actors and their strategies, thereby pointedly intervening into dominant imaginings of world per se.

---

[14]Jürgen Habermas, *The Structural Transformation of the Public Sphere: Inquiry into a Category of Bourgeois Society* (Cambridge: Polity Press, 1992).
[15]Lilie Chouliaraki, *The Ironic Spectator: Solidarity in the Age of Post-Humanitarianism* (Cambridge: Polity Press, 2013), p. 142.
[16]Debjani Ganguly, *This Thing Called the World: The Contemporary Novel as Global Form* (Durham, NC: Duke University Press, 2016), p. 34.

'Flies on the eyelids and pot bellies': Wainaina and the global media

As countless media commentators attest, the distributive reach and resources of media producers worldwide is extremely asymmetrical, especially at the level of news agencies, such as 'Reuters or AP or Agence France', responsible for selling the raw footage and 'data' of news.[17] Thus one can speak, as Ella Shohat and Robert Stam do, of a principally Anglophone 'global media', whose ownership interests are based in Euro-America but whose circulation and dominance of news markets are effectively global.[18] This institutional conception of the 'global' media – which Chouliaraki and Ganguly identify as instrumental, in turn, to 'global public'-formation – has proved exceptionally fertile in Wainaina's imagination. Western foreign correspondent characters appear in 'SHiT' and in his 2007 short story 'All Things Remaining Equal', in which the protagonist's mother pursues an ambivalent relationship with an American cameraman. *One Day* scathingly depicts 'international correspondents with their long Dictaphones, and dirty jeans', rapaciously scouting for 'The Most Authentic Real Black Africanest Story they can find'.[19] While the exact forms of colonial spectacularization engendered by the global media necessarily differ across and within regions, within Africa arguably the dominant paradigm of the past few decades – and that with which Wainaina is most preoccupied – is that of humanitarian aid.[20]

Robert DeChaine charts the emergence of iconic humanitarian imagery of Africa in the increased practice of media organizations embedding with NGOs, a type of actor that rose to spectacular prominence on the continent in the wake of wholesale rearrangements of political economy produced

---

[17]See, for example, David Machin and Theo van Leeuwen, *Global Media Discourse: A Critical Introduction* (Oxford: Routledge, 2007); Edward S. Herman and Robert McChesney, *The Global Media: The New Missionaries of Corporate Capitalism* (London: Cassell, 1997).

[18]Ella Shohat and Robert Stam, 'From the Imperial Family to the Transnational Imaginary: Media Spectatorship in the Age of Globalization', in *Global/Local: Cultural Production and the Transnational Imaginary*, ed. Rob Wilson and Wimal Dissanayake (Durham, NC: Duke University Press, 1996), pp. 145–70. Alternative definitions of the 'global media', centred around 'global orientation' (or worldliness) are offered in Ulrika Olaussen, 'Theorizing Global Media as Global Discourse', *International Journal of Communication*, vol. 7 (2013): 1281–97. *Kwani?* might itself fit nicely into such a revised definition.

[19]Binyavanga Wainaina, *One Day I Will Write about This Place* (London: Granta, 2011b), p. 233.

[20]See, for instance, McKenzie Wark, *Virtual Geography: Living with Global Media Events, Arts and Politics of the Everyday* (Bloomington: Indiana University Press, 1994). A considerable portion of scholarly attention on this topic is dedicated to depictions of the Gulf region, including Shohat's work and Nicholas Mirzoeff, *Watching Babylon: The War in Iraq and Global Visual Culture* (Hoboken: Taylor & Francis Group, 2012).

by the 1980s IMF Structural Adjustment Programmes.[21] Following the SAPs, privately run NGOs have increasingly taken responsibility for a range of state functions and, according to DeChaine, operate frequently in co-dependent symbiosis with global media, brokering media access to the continent in exchange for vital publicity. (We might think of the strikingly candid admission by *Médecins Sans Frontières* founder Bernard Kouchner that 'wthout the media, there is no humanitarian action, and this in turn, feeds the papers'.)[22] Such a situation then encourages forms of political activism centred on *making suffering visible*, or on mobilizing what Ganguly calls 'an amplified global infrastructure of sympathy and witnessing'.[23]

Emblematized by the 1980s Ethiopian famine coverage and spectacular 'Band Aid' appeals, this humanitarian paradigm has been charged with presenting Africans as poverty-stricken, physically conspicuous victims of disaster: 'an AK-47, prominent ribs, naked breasts', 'flies on the eyelids and pot bellies'.[24] As Tiziana Morosetti writes, this is a question of marginalization not by invisibility but *hypervisibility*, in which certain images gain an iconicity that precludes multiple or oppositional ways of imagining the continent.[25] This next reading draws on this humanitarian context, particularly its hypervisible representations of the African body, to elucidate how the characters in 'SHiT' reverse the gaze of colonial spectacularization in a violent tale of global media retribution.

'Ships in High Transit': Reversing the colonial gaze

'Ships in High Transit' begins with the strange, striking image of a Japanese tourist watching the baboons that gather on his hotel terrace in Lake Nakuru National Park:

---

[21]Robert DeChaine, 'Humanitarian Space and the Social Imaginary: Médecins Sans Frontières/Doctors without Borders and the Rhetoric of Global Community', *Journal of Communication Inquiry*, vol. 26, no. 4 (2002): 354–69. As Achille Mbembe articulates, it is a common consensus that a major consequence of Structural Adjustment measures was to displace the site 'where political, regulatory, and technical choices are made' from the state to 'international trustees', who 'are different from those who must answer for their consequences to the people'. *On the Postcolony* (Berkeley: University of California Press, 2001), p. 75.
[22]Quoted in Ilan Kapoor, *Celebrity Humanitarianism: The Ideology of Global Charity* (London: Routledge, 2013), p. 85.
[23]Ganguly, *This Thing Called the World*, p. 34. Emphasis mine.
[24]Binyavanga Wainaina, *How to Write about Africa* (Nairobi: Kwani Trust, 2006), pp. 5–6, 8.
[25]Tiziana Morosetti, 'Black on Black: (In)Visibility in African Literary Heterotopias', *Research in African Literatures*, vol. 44, no. 2 (2013): 48–61.

Here is an aspect of reality as consensus: the man has spent his entire life watching nature documentaries. He said this to Matano [the tour guide], with much excitement, over and over again, on the van to Nakuru last week. How can he remind his adrenalin that these beasts can kill, when he knows them only as television actors? ... So, he hid a crust of bread, and when everybody was done with breakfast, threw it at a group of baboons outside, and aimed his camera at them. The larger male came for the bread, and then attacked the man, leaving with a chunk of his finger, and decapitating the green crocodile on his shirt. The baboon was shot that afternoon. A second green crocodile replaced the first.[26]

With its voyeuristic gesturing ('Here is an aspect') and sudden, climactic violence, the passage encapsulates the principal themes around which the story revolves: the dominating power of televisual media and the capacity of the spectated to retaliate and harm. It is the baboons' apparent familiarity as 'television actors' that renders them paradoxically invisible in their true, dangerous form: their very hypervisibility prompts their misrecognition. And yet, when the 'aim[ing]' of the camera occasions an attack, the tourist is forced to recognize the baboons as unpredictable, possessing an expressive capacity beyond that which he desires them to perform. The camera thus becomes the focal point for a series of acts of rebalancing violence, which crucially clarify the violence at the heart of the tourist encounter: the missed photo shoot is revenged in the fatal shooting of the animal, the easy replacement of the Lacoste crocodile logo staging the tourist as ultimate victor in a 'jungle' confrontation.

In opening the story in a tourist safari park, Wainaina immediately signals a far wider matrix of colonial spectacularization, beyond the global media.[27] Notably, the protagonist of 'SHiT', Matano, is a tour operator for 'WylDe AFreaka' tours, a venture that commodifies Maasai culture for international touristic consumption. Into this milieu enter the foreign correspondents, Prescott Sinclair, American presenter of 'something hard-hitting, like Sixty Minutes', and her cameraman, the 'Swedish Nature-lover, Jean Paul'.[28] Purveyors of 'Human Interest Stories', the pair have been seconded to Nakuru to profile Matano's 'boss/business partner, Armitage Shanks', heir to the eponymous 'toilet fortune'.[29] Shanks, an evident satire of Bob Geldof, whose previous achievements include 'sav[ing] the highland Samburu with his MTV song, Feed the Maa', has invested his inheritance

---

[26]Binyavanga Wainaina, 'Ships in High Transit', *Kwani?*, vol. 2 (2004): 60.
[27]For a detailed discussion of tourism and the colonial gaze, see Morgan Ndlovu, *Performing Indigeneity: Spectacles of Culture and Identity in Coloniality*, Decolonial Studies, Postcolonial Horizons (London: Pluto Press, 2019).
[28]Wainaina, 'Ships in High Transit', pp. 66, 69.
[29]Ibid., pp. 67, 60.

in a number of operations peddling African heritage and bodies, from 'the Nuba Tattoo Bar he started in London' to the 'Nairobi coffee shop … decorated with grainy black-and-white pictures of whichever Africans happened to be starving at the time'.[30] This distorted 'Africanness' is something the correspondents are only too willing to perceive and to circulate: 'Tonight, [Jean-Paul] will only see … reality through a camera, for their programme "A World of Cultures".'[31]

Wainaina persistently foregrounds the technical language of the camera, often presenting the narrative voice as director ('Same scene through Matano's eyes'),[32] outlining the uneven dynamics of spectacularization between the African characters and their observers. An erotic magazine that Matano produces as a side venture depicts his friend

> Otieno on the cover, body silvery, courtesy of Photodraw, kneeling naked facing the mud wall of the manyatta. Everything in the shot is variations of this silvery black, his red Maasai shawl, the only colour, spread on the ground. Two old white hands run along his buttocks, their owner invisible. It must be near sunset: his shadow is long and watery, a long wobbly silhouette of cock reaches out to touch his red shuka.[33]

Depicted prostrate, 'keeling naked', his body open to visual consumption, but his face (and hence his own possible 'right to look') averted, Otieno represents a parody of spectacularized prostration. Wainaina juxtaposes the sovereign invisibility of the hands' owner with Otieno's visual exposure, his shawl, like his shadow, 'spread' along the ground, thus posing 'African' versus 'white' identities in the dichotomous terms of dominating gaze and submitting spectacle. These positions hinge, moreover, on the uneven control of media technologies: hence the 'primitive' aesthetic of Otieno's mud wall is juxtaposed with the futuristic 'silvery' technology of Photodraw and the controlling, technical vocabulary of 'the shot'. It is the televisual gaze of the global media – figured here as erotically dominating – that underpins Wainaina's imagining of colonial spectacularization.

Significantly, this results in a politics that revolves around the *hijacking* of the dominating gaze, including the technologies that enable it. This is foreshadowed in Matano's very first glimpse of Prescott: 'those eyes, her skin

---

[30]Ibid., pp. 61, 62, 68. Geldof is something of a *bête noire* figure for Wainaina, appearing multiple times in the memoir, including the following: 'Every news broadcast, every song in the whole world. Bob Geldof. Wherever he is people fall, twist, writhe, lose language skills, accumulate insects around their eyes, and then die on BBC [sic].' Wainaina, *One Day I Will Write about This Place*, p. 86.
[31]Wainaina, 'Ships in High Transit', p. 81.
[32]Ibid., p. 63.
[33]Ibid., p. 74.

so white, made him shiver. He has in his mind the constant idea that white women are naked, people with skin peeled like baby rabbits, squirming with pain and pleasure in the heat.'[34] As Matano's menacing imagining of the 'peeled skin' suggests, the story takes the spectating position as inherently dominating: to look is to render the seen object vulnerable. If Prescott's eyes initially make Matano 'shiver', his own continued gaze succeeds in exerting an imagined dominance over her, fixing her 'squirming' in his mind's eye. This fantasy is then made disturbingly literal, when Matano arranges with Nigerian accomplices to trick the foreign correspondents into featuring in secretly recorded pornographic films:

> Reality TV Nigerian-style has hit the streets of Mombasa. Every fortnight, a new tape is released countrywide. Secret cameras are set up, for days sometimes, in different places. The first video showed a well-known councillor visiting a brothel; the next one showed clerks in the Ministry of Lands sharing their spoils after a busy day at the deed market.[35]

The Nigerians persuade Matano to get them into sites of white tourism – those 'strange hotel tribes'[36] – where they will play on the white tourists' sexual entitlement to African bodies in order to dupe them into 'performing' before the unseen cameras. Seizing televisual media technologies through which African characters have previously been focalized, Matano and the Nigerians dramatically reverse the direction of the exploitative gaze.

Framed in terms of advertising, distribution and image rights, the Nigerians' pornographic venture is a dark parody of the infrastructures of the mainstream global media itself. Here, African characters gain control of the cameras, the 'closed loop system the Nigerians have devised to reduce piracy' and 'the FM stations that have taken to advertising in the videos'.[37] It is the Nigerians who will distribute and profit from the images of white bodies, 'for 5,000 shillings per tape ... Fock the copyright, we're Nigerian'.[38] In seizing the mediating technologies, and hence the exploitative gaze, the heart of the story, Wainaina presents a highly cynical view of colonial spectacularization. Just as Brian Larkin defines 'piracy [as] nonideological in that it does not represent a self-conscious political project in opposition to capitalism', so Wainaina's piratical characters do not present a self-conscious political project in opposition to this gaze.[39] Rather than seeking to look

---

[34]Ibid., p. 78.
[35]Ibid., p. 69.
[36]Ibid., p. 80.
[37]Ibid.
[38]Ibid., p. 82.
[39]Brian Larkin, *Signal and Noise: Media, Infrastructure, and Urban Culture in Nigeria* (Durham, NC: Duke University Press, 2008), p. 226.

differently to the white antagonists, they seek only to plunder the rights to this gaze: a straightforward reversal of the cameras and their dominating effects.

The limitations of such a politics are underscored by the story's narrative voice, which continually vacillates in focalization between the foreign correspondents and the Nakuru residents, thus gradually revealing their backstories and the varied social rifts within their seemingly reified binary. In casual narrative digressions, Wainaina reveals, for instance, that the fake 'Maasai' female performers, none of whom 'know a word of what they are singing', will later hide the proceeds of the pornography trap from their husbands: 'the rest will go to their communal slush fund. Things will appear in the household. Conveniences explained away.'[40] He notes Matano's pleasure in humiliating Abdullahi, once 'a son of one the Coast's oldest Swahili families', now reduced to tourist ferry driver, as well as Prescott's disdain for the 'coward' Jean-Paul, who will not address their mutual knowledge of Prescott's affair with a co-worker.[41] The narrative asides thus reveal to us what the characters will not perceive: their internal divisions, their sexual- and class-based conflicts, their distinctive personalities, their shared, fractious humanity. Instead, 'SHiT's' protagonists continue to perpetuate a mutually violent experience of colonial spectacularization, in which to look *is* to exploit.

That the violence that underpins SHiT's narrative world goes unrecognised by the white characters is highly significant. In a 2013 AlJazeera interview, 'Rewriting Africa', Wainaina describes the imbrication of global media and aid agencies as 'the PR game', 'the happy face of the same PR machine'.[42] Much like the ambivalent slash describing Armitage Shanks's relationship to Matano as 'boss/business partner', or the telltale 'Freak' smuggled in the orthography of 'WylDe AFreaka's' branding, contemporary relations of spectacularization manifest, for Wainaina, in 'bad terms of engagement'[43] – encounters that hide their true intentions and propose as equivalence what is really hierarchy. Thus, the global media and the tourist venture express their coloniality in the 'happy face' of cultural curiosity and humanitarian intention, denying realities of looking as uneven rights and potentially exploitative acts. There is an evasion of the question, as Morgan Ndlovu puts it, 'about who gazes on whom and for what purposes'.[44] It is the prerogative of 'SHiT' to uncover

---

[40] Wainaina, 'Ships in High Transit', pp. 78, 81.
[41] Ibid., pp. 63, 71.
[42] Binyavanga Wainaina, 'Rewriting Africa', Talk to AlJazeera, 13 April 2013, https://www.youtube.com/watch?v=qMODRFS2Pbc. Accessed 1 March 2022.
[43] Ibid.
[44] Ndlovu, *Performing Indigeneity*, p. 94.

the fundamental violence entailed in colonial spectacularization and to dramatize its reversal: its strategic deployment by African characters who see the world quite differently.

Beyond River Yei: Dissolving the colonial gaze

If the characters of 'Ships in High Transit' find no way of dissolving the relations of colonial spectacularization, this second part of the chapter argues that this is precisely what Wainaina himself pursues in the complex – and sometimes perplexing – form of *Beyond River Yei*. Specifically, I suggest that the text's narrative destabilizations, most especially its deployment of metafictional intertexts, produce an aesthetics of unclear, accumulative and constantly revising sight. A longform literary-journalism investigation into the Sudanese sleeping sickness (locally known as Pongi), *River Yei* represents a somewhat ironic text in light of my previous argument, being a commission by the German NGO Malteser. Indeed, Wainaina's self-consciousness about his role is registered in the introduction, where he assesses the project as 'a bold move by Malteser and Echo, and ... *one that requires some defending*'.[45] The opening chapter revolves around a series of binaries, reminiscent of 'Ships in High Transit', between Wainaina in his 'foreign correspondent' role and the mediatized Sudanese subjects. Wainaina's entry into County Yei is surveilled by a 'lean, jaw-knotted teenag[e]' sentry who mans the road, and who, upon seeing Wainaina 'scar free ... fat, sleek, eyes unable to keep the pity out', brands him a 'Kawaja' (white man):[46] 'I am a white man in a black skin.'[47] Racially transformed (*à la* Fanon), Wainaina here takes on the *dominating* position in a relation of colonial spectacularization, 'pity[ing]' eyes turned upon a Sudanese subject who is rendered drastically, biologically Other.

Likewise, refuting the assumption 'that a war-torn place is aware of the abnormality of its situation', Wainaina dismisses the notion that Sudan will 'for your own modesty, hide the graves, the torn clothes, the guns slung over shoulders, the hostilities'.[48] The evocation of torn clothes, of hiding, modesty and immodesty, is redolent of the images of bodily exposure and prostration found in 'SHiT'. Wainaina conjures the African body as open, hypervisible

---

[45]Binyavanga Wainaina, *Beyond River Yei: A Journey into Sudan* (Nairobi: Kwani Trust, 2006), p. 4. Emphasis mine. ECHO is the acronym of the EU's European Civil Protection and Humanitarian Aid Operations programme.
[46]Ibid., pp. 8, 7.
[47]Ibid., p. 8. Wainaina appears to be referencing Frantz Fanon's classic study on the psychology of race, *Black Skin, White Masks* (1952).
[48]Ibid., p. 7.

to the gaze of the humanitarian, outside spectator – a kind of exceptional visibility that may even prompt prurience in the viewer. Moreover, unlike the enlightened spectator, the Sudanese are suspected of being unaware of their 'abnormality': the right to visualize Sudan's 'real' historical meaning – its position in a normative, universal history – is again the sole privilege of the outside spectator.

This impression of a binary colonial spectacularization between foreign correspondent and local, focalized subject is, however, complicated in Wainaina's inclusion of intertextual poems by the Sudanese doctor and former SPLA (Sudanese People's Liberation Army) fighter Ajo Diktor. Described by Wainaina as excerpts from the collection 'Lies and Eyes', picked up 'in a dusty bookshop in Eastleigh, Nairobi a year ago', the poems are interspersed throughout the narrative, including one on the blurb jacket of the *Kwani?* pocket edition, initially encouraging us to read them as intertextual counterfoil to Wainaina's narrative voice.[49] Diktor seems to represent the unmediated voice of the people whom Wainaina is there to investigate, continually offering world-weary correctives to Wainaina's perspective. Thus, where Wainaina vacillates between shock, paralysis and idealism over Pongi, Diktor is cynical and pragmatic: 'It will make no difference which fine or unfine/feeling brought you here./ Just do your job.'[50] Diktor's poems – fractious political tirades against those who come 'to test yourself in the heart of darkness'[51] – are initially presented as the testimony of a 'native informant', working against the main narrative voice and thus defying the gaze of foreign correspondents like Wainaina.

However, as *River Yei* unfolds it becomes apparent that Diktor's function is less to harden the dichotomies of colonial spectacularization and more to allow Wainaina to interrogate the possibilities of his own mode of looking. As the text progresses, Wainaina enacts a series of narrative destabilizations of sight, of which, as the next section shows, the narrative status of Diktor is the most dramatic. Chapter two, for instance, begins with the invitation 'Come My Friend, Come to Maridi Road', a flamboyant rhetorical gesture that seems to herald touristic display – the welcoming opening of Sudan to our readerly gaze.[52] However, the chapter later reveals that the expression 'Come My Friend' is a translation of 'Pojulio', the military force from which the Pojulu people of Yei county derive their name. The line comes to signal the closed-off, esoteric nature of local histories, as well as the deceptiveness of the surface glance: the 'Come My Friend' is ironically a reference to

---

[49]Ibid., p. 18.
[50]Ibid., p. 15.
[51]Ibid., p. 14.
[52]Ibid., p. 32.

warfare, but to discover this means dwelling longer in the myths of Yei county.

Such stalling, disordered revealing of information is typical of *River Yei's* narrative, disturbing our sense of being able to visualize subjects clearly. The text is replete with ellipsis and abrupt temporal shifts, creating a sense of discontinuity, missing information and unfinished storylines. A journey to Ado, site of the Pongi testing centre, is characteristically described:

> We drive past a giant church. The first stone-built church we have seen outside Yei. It stands, imposing and forlorn, a woman stands in front of it.
>
> Half an hour later, we park the car in Ado Village Square.[53]

The evocative impressions of the church as 'giant', 'imposing' and yet 'forlorn', the 'first stone buil[ding]' outside Yei, invite questions, as does the mysterious female figure outside its doors (waiting? guarding?). And yet these questions are met with only the pointed aporia of the line break that marks the passage of time. Wainaina depicts subjects passing across the field of vision as he drives but yielding no legibility to him. Registering but not visualizing, Wainaina's 'nomination of the visible' appears as a contingent and passive process.

Likewise, in chapter three we are introduced to a young woman, a Pisak resident who appears suddenly and anonymously:

> Pisak ... She stands at the doorway to her family house, her baby leaning away from one hip. She doesn't have the curiosity or the fluttering anxiety other women have shown when we have come to visit. We sit in the spear grass thatched homestead and watch her mother roasting coffee beans in an old tin pot. Her mother, Mrs M is telling us about manners.[54]

Moving elusively, via the ellipsis, from the place to the unnamed subject, Wainaina creates the impression of the woman 'breaking in' upon his sight, catching his eye unawares. Once again, however, this appearance fails to disclose any narratively salient information, raising more questions and emphasizing her non-transparency (unlike, for instance, the 'peeling' gaze that Matano turns upon Prescott). Notably, the daughter remains anonymous, even while her mother, defined in relation to her, is given a moniker of sorts: 'Her mother, Mrs M.' The girl remains the subject of the sentence, indicating her charismatic presence for Wainaina, yet his looking gains us no further access to her.

---

[53]Ibid., p. 60.
[54]Ibid., pp. 32–3.

'The complete fulfilment of my fancies': Reading Ajo Diktor

Such narrative techniques for troubling sight culminate in chapter four, following a campfire drinking session at which Wainaina observes Diktor 'quiet, his face made fierce by the flames ... lost in some internal place'.[55] As with Mrs. M's daughter, Wainaina registers the unknowability of the 'quiet' subject, the recognition that the 'internal place' is not visible to him. Startlingly, therefore, chapter four immediately begins in the narrative voice of Diktor himself, transforming his narrative function from intertextual critic of Wainaina's dominant narrative voice – an effect heightened by the paratextual use of his poems on the cover – to *explicitly fictional* construct.[56] This conceit is further amplified by Wainaina's decision not to develop a distinctively different voice for the doctor. Thus, Diktor reproduces Wainaina's idiosyncratically spatialized descriptions, wherein time and bodily sensation are designated as forms of place in themselves: where Wainaina writes of living 'in a happy bubble', for instance, or being 'held in this grip of a narrative that unfolds as we move', Diktor in turn describes the aftermath of his mother's death from Pongi as 'mov[ing] about in a bewildered now', 'cut ... loose like a helium balloon' until the family 'broke open my bubble'.[57] Likewise, Wainaina's distinctively unconventional grammar and syntax, and sensuous alliterations ('My eyes are half-lidded with languor')[58] rebound in the doctor's expressions of 'flowers-in-my-hand solemnity' or 'from my far frothy place of grotesque things made normal'.[59] Rendering Diktor's narrative voice indistinguishable from his own, Wainaina underscores our 'native informant's' fictionality, with drastic implications for the text's interrogations of sight and epistemic access.[60]

---

[55] Ibid., p. 43.

[56] An early hint at the blurring of Wainaina's and Diktor's narrative voices is found at the start of chapter two, in which Diktor's opening poem includes the word 'Kawaja', recalling Wainaina's encounter with the sentry in chapter one. The uncanny resonance creates a sense of voyeurism, almost as though Diktor – who is introduced through this poem – has been invisibly watching the scenes we have just witnessed: watching Wainaina who has himself come to look. In *One Day I Will Write about This Place*, Wainaina explains the fictionalization directly: 'I met a South Sudanese doctor who worked for the SPLA ... I decide to make him a poet. It is the first poetry I have written.' Wainaina, *One Day I Will Write about This Place*, p. 190. However, within *Beyond River Yei*, the fictionalization is made only gradually apparent.

[57] Wainaina, *Beyond River Yei*, pp. 9, 43, 56, 57, 54.

[58] Ibid., p. 15.

[59] Ibid., pp. 56, 57.

[60] Again, reading the text alongside *One Day* reveals more conspicuous overlaps. Notably, Diktor recalls, as a child, that

> one day, I set off on a journey; I walked as far as I could, trying to find the horizon. I wanted to find entry to another place – a soft-lit place, a far place, where life would not have stark

Crucially, where earlier portions of the text seemingly stage the Diktor intertexts as points of opening – a 'native informant's' supplementing perspective, offering vantages beyond Wainaina – Diktor now becomes something of a self-cipher, a device for Wainaina to introspect. Diktor's childhood recollections are abruptly curtailed with the statement:

> I would let myself stretch; and stretch, and stretch; until I was contorted into an asymmetric, illogical giant – comprising nothing but the complete fulfilment of my fancies.
> This, of course, never happened. *Not in this country*.[61]

In its sharp negation of the previous sentences, the passage reveals itself as, effectively, a commentary on the real author, Wainaina, who (it is implied), being actually 'not in this country', *is* able to grow, uncircumscribed, into the imagined 'asymmetric, illogical giant'. Rather than providing an 'insider's' glimpse into Sudan, as first appears, Diktor becomes a means for Wainaina to self-examine, for the gaze to retreat inwards. Under the pressures of colonial spectacularization, the text thus seems to collapse in self-doubt, despairing the formal possibility of creating a non-dominating focalization of others and instead turning the lens back on itself in its revelation of metafictional conceit. *River Yei* concludes again in Wainaina's first-person narrative voice, with Ajo 'turn[ing] to me, his face blank, "Lets [*sic*] go back to Yei. I feel like a beer"'.[62] Redelivered into 'blankness', his fictional status now confirmed, Diktor comes to stand not for privileged insight but for unknowability and the resolute resistance of the Sudan to be straightforwardly seen.

If 'SHiT' offers its characters no way of looking, outside the dominating relations of colonial spectacularization (the only possibilities for change inhering in the *direction* of that gaze), *River Yei* arguably encapsulates the failure of form to do likewise. In belatedly subverting the poems' apparent textual function, Wainaina highlights his subject's resistance to easy focalization – but he also complicates the ability to look productively at anything bar the self. The text's form might thus seem to encapsulate, in disturbingly direct manner, Lilie Chouliaraki's assertion that efforts to

---

realities. I was disappointed that the distant scenery became more and real [*sic*] as I came closer. There was no vague magical place, where reality blurred and I could slip through to elsewhere.

Wainaina, *Beyond River Yei*, p. 51. In *One Day I Will Write about This Place*, Wainaina's childhood self likewise dreams of the 'vague and blurred and pretty' world of the horizon: 'I am disappointed that all the distant scenery, blue and misty, becomes more and more real as I come closer: there is no vague place, where clarity blurs, where certainty has no force, and dreams are real.' Wainaina, *One Day I Will Write about This Place*, pp. 7–8.

[61] Wainaina, *Beyond River Yei*, p. 52. Emphasis mine.
[62] Ibid., p. 65.

supersede colonial spectacularization via self-awareness and 'emotional introspection' risk instead merely producing 'narcissistic public[s]', capable of construing the other only 'as a quasi-fictional figure – an individual inhabiting what [Richard] Rorty calls "the world of literary culture" (1989: 80)'.[63] In his play with narrative voice, and with the fictionality of voices besides his own, Wainaina raises the uncomfortable question of whether the alternative to colonial spectacularization is only solipsism, the inability to look meaningfully outwards whatsoever.

Second take: The unsolicited encounter

Yet, I argue that the gradual, percolating quality of *River Yei's* digressive narrative structure *does* offer a formal solution of sorts, revolving around processes of double-take and re-vision. Returning to the figure of Mrs M's daughter, Wainaina elaborates his initial impressions of her – 'stand[ing] at the doorway to the family house, not eighteen years old, her eyes sombre, then wistful, then just distant. / She is beautiful'[64] – before immediately cutting to a scene describing the makeshift testing lab and stamp card health pass devised for Pongi. As with the earlier depiction of the church en route to Ado, the change in time and setting is marked simply and elliptically with a line break. Mrs M's daughter is thus dismissed as an apparently dislocated moment of lyricism: a plangent appreciation of 'wistful' beauty that has no bearing on the narrative 'main event', on the visualization of history proper.

Several pages later at a campfire dance, in which people sing civil war songs – 'Elena, you are the beautiful lady / It would be better if my leg was amputated / So the recruitment won't take me away, / So I can stay with you' – Wainaina notices the girl again, and this time dwells upon her:

> One person is not dancing: Mrs. M's beautiful daughter, she is standing amongst a group of women who are cooking, but her face is so held in she could be alone in the world. I wonder, for a moment, what dreams she has, what legs have not been amputated for her, what legs have, who died and made her so sad.[65]

In this belated reflection, Wainaina is compelled to look beyond the daughter's attractive sadness and to wonder, more disconcertingly, about the particulars that might have produced her expression, particulars suggested in the song lyrics. In so doing, his sense both of the girl's relationship to

---

[63]Chouliaraki, *The Ironic Spectator*, p. 186.
[64]Wainaina, *Beyond River Yei*, p. 34.
[65]Ibid., p. 47.

her environment and of the story of Pongi itself recalibrates, prompting him to appreciate the civil war as central to Pongi's effects and meaning in the region. From his initial 'dislocating' surface gaze (one in which the girl seems to offer no narratively relevant 'information'), Wainaina is exposed to a second, *unsolicited* encounter, which transforms his visualization of the entire history at stake and draws him into plausible speculation (albeit speculation still) about the girl's life. Crucially, a happenstance encounter, the campfire scene is – unlike the work of Prescott and Jean-Paul – not an encounter of Wainaina's seeking, not engineered on his own terms. Wainaina does not come to look but chances to notice – and only then does the configuration yield a possible legibility to him, however unconfirmed. The narrative structure implies, in other words, that simply waiting, without demanding – allowing sights to gather and transform themselves into motifs – may enable meaningful understanding that does not depend on colonial modes of looking. Hence, the campfire songs provide plausible, specific context for what earlier seemed an abstract ideal of wistful feminine beauty, and ask Wainaina to reassess what the main and subordinate narrative images of the story really are.

An anecdote at the beginning of *Beyond River Yei* offers a telling glimpse into how else Wainaina might have constructed his text. Recalling a 'much-loved' childhood atlas that depicted the 'NATURAL RESOURCES OF AFRICA', Wainaina recounts days spent calculating 'what African had to mine, grow and sell to stop being poor'.[66] He 'needed those results', he explains, because 'I could not find a way to digest what leaked to me in the newspapers, in weekly news programmes like Dunia Wiki Hii (The World This Week)'.[67] The anecdote traces Wainaina's nascent encounters with the configuration of world instantiated by news media; significantly, it also offers a particular claim to narrative authority – which the text goes on, however, to refute – positioning Wainaina's relationship to his Sudanese subject matter as being that of a fellow 'African', fraternally implicated in what he is reporting. Yet, as we have seen, Wainaina quickly abandons this identification, accepting his designation as 'Kawaja' and establishing Diktor as textual counterfoil.

In making this decision, the text reveals its ambitions to explore beyond the issue of *who* looks (an issue dramatized fully in 'SHiT'), to interrogate instead the issue of *how* one looks. Acknowledging the possibility of colonial spectacularization to occur in any unequal encounter between spectator and spectated – not merely between territorially reified 'global publics' and 'zones of otherness' – the text subverts the dominant cartography established by global media and asks how a non-dominating mode of looking might be

---

[66]Ibid., p. 8.
[67]Ibid., p. 9.

formally exemplified. Likewise, 'SHiT' invites us to consider the strategies of characters subject to colonial spectacularization, who assert their very different vision of the world by hijacking and reversing that gaze and the apparatuses that support it. Together, then, the texts reveal the importance, to Wainaina's imagination, of the global media and of the kinds of looking and thus of world-formation such media entail. They represent efforts to intervene in world-formation, from an African perspective, inverting or dissolving dominant cartographies of world, and in *Beyond River Yei*, tentatively gesturing towards the shapes of a world as seen through a decolonial lens.

Bibliography

Adesanmi, Pius, and Chris Dunton (2005), 'Nigeria's Third Generation Writing: Historiography and Preliminary Theoretical Considerations', *English in Africa*, vol. 32, no. 1: 7–19.

Bosch-Santana, Stephanie (8 February 2013), 'Exorcizing Afropolitanism: Binyavanga Wainaina Explains Why "I Am a Pan-Africanist, Not an Afropolitan" at ASAUK 2012', *Africa in Words* (blog), https://africainwords.com/2013/02/08/exorcizing-afropolitanism-binyavanga-wainaina-explains-why-i-am-a-pan-africanist-not-an-afropolitan-at-asauk-2012/. Accessed 1 March 2022.

Chouliaraki, Lilie (2013), *The Ironic Spectator: Solidarity in the Age of Post-Humanitarianism*, Cambridge: Polity Press.

Coetzee, Carli (ed.) (2017), *Afropolitanism: Reboot*, London: Routledge.

Currey, James (2008), *Africa Writes Back: The African Writers Series & the Launch of African Literature*, Oxford: James Currey.

Davies, Caroline (2013), *Creating Postcolonial Literature: African Writers and British Publishers*, New York: Palgrave Macmillan.

DeChaine, Robert (2002), 'Humanitarian Space and the Social Imaginary: Médecins Sans Frontières/Doctors without Borders and the Rhetoric of Global Community', *Journal of Communication Inquiry*, vol. 26, no. 4: 354–69, https://doi.org/doi:10.1177/019685902236896. Accessed 1 March 2022.

Ede, Amatoritsero (2016), 'The Politics of Afropolitanism', *Journal of African Cultural Studies*, vol. 28, no. 1: 88–100.

Ganguly, Debjani (2016), *This Thing Called the World: The Contemporary Novel as Global Form*, Durham, NC: Duke University Press.

Habermas, Jürgen (1992), *The Structural Transformation of the Public Sphere: Inquiry into a Category of Bourgeois Society*, Cambridge: Polity Press.

Herman, Edward S., and Robert McChesney (1997), *The Global Media: The New Missionaries of Corporate Capitalism*, London: Cassell.

Kahora, Billy (2008), 'An Apprenticeship in Ethnicity: A Time beyond the Writer', *Kwani?*, Part 5, vol. 2.

Kapoor, Ilan (2013), *Celebrity Humanitarianism: The Ideology of Global Charity*, London: Routledge.

Larkin, Brian (2008), *Signal and Noise: Media, Infrastructure, and Urban Culture in Nigeria*, Durham, NC: Duke University Press.

Machin, David, and Theo van Leeuwen (2007), *Global Media Discourse: A Critical Introduction*, Oxford: Routledge.

Mbembe, Achille (2001), *On the Postcolony*, Berkeley: University of California Press.

Mirzoeff, Nicholas (2011), *The Right to Look: A Counterhistory of Visuality*, Durham, NC: Duke University Press.

Mirzoeff, Nicholas (2012), *Watching Babylon: The War in Iraq and Global Visual Culture*, Hoboken: Taylor & Francis Group.

Morosetti, Tiziana (2013), 'Black on Black: (In)Visibility in African Literary Heterotopias', *Research in African Literatures*, vol. 44, no. 2: 48–61.

Musila, Grace A (2016), 'Part-Time Africans, Europolitans and "Africa Lite"', *Journal of African Cultural Studies*, vol. 28, no. 1: 109–13, https://doi.org/doi:10.1080/13696815.2015.1099424. Accessed 1 March 2022.

Ndlovu, Morgan (2019), *Performing Indigeneity: Spectacles of Culture and Identity in Coloniality*, London: Pluto Press.

Olaussen, Ulrika (2013), 'Theorizing Global Media as Global Discourse', *International Journal of Communication*, vol. 7: 1281–97.

Quayson, Ato (2019), 'Modern African Literary History: Nation and Narration, Orality, and Diaspora', *Journal of the African Literature Association*, vol. 13, no. 1: 131–52.

Shohat, Ella, and Robert Stam (1996), 'From the Imperial Family to the Transnational Imaginary: Media Spectatorship in the Age of Globalization', in *Global/Local: Cultural Production and the Transnational Imaginary*, ed. Rob Wilson and Wimal Dissanayake. Durham, NC: Duke University Press, pp. 145–70.

Wainaina, Binyavanga (2004), 'Ships in High Transit', in *Kwani 02*, ed. Binyavanga Wainaina and Ebba Kalondo Nairobi: Kwani Trust.

Wainaina, Binyavanga (2006), *Beyond River Yei: A Journey into Sudan*, Nairobi: Kwani Trust.

Wainaina, Binyavanga (2011a), *How to Write about Africa*, Nairobi: Kwani Trust.

Wainaina, Binyavanga (2011b), *One Day I Will Write about This Place*, London: Granta.

Wainaina, Binyavanga (13 April 2013), Rewriting Africa. Talk to AlJazeera, https://www.youtube.com/watch?v=qMODRFS2Pbc. Accessed 1 March 2022.

Wallis, Kate (2016), 'How Books Matter: Kwani Trust, Farafina, Cassava Republic Press and the Medium of Print', *Wasafiri*, vol. 31, no. 4: 39–46.

Wark, McKenzie (1994), *Virtual Geography: Living with Global Media Events, Arts and Politics of the Everyday*, Bloomington: Indiana University Press.

13

The facts at the heart of the matter: Character and objectivity in the making of the Fante Intelligentsia

Jeanne-Marie Jackson

From 1868 to 1874, in and around the humid, bustling city of Cape Coast, self-determination got ahead of what we now know as Africa's anticolonial history. What had been a loosely allied group of Fante kingdoms along the Gold Coast took on official administrative form as the Fante Confederation, what Kwaku Larbi Korang calls a 'protonationalist' state possessing a constitution, judiciary and small army.[1] Though short-lived in its efforts to thwart the consolidation of British rule, it bore intellectual fruit across a century at least. The succeeding generation of Fante leaders – including J. E. Casely Hayford, John Mensah Sarbah, S. R. B. Attoh Ahuma and J. W. de Graft Johnson – wove a powerful intelligentsia in its image from a small canon of legal and humanistic essays and treatises, *systematizing* custom and *characterizing* culture in equal parts. However, while Korang and others have paved the way for a richer exploration of these intellectuals' role beyond being 'some other era's prehistory' (in particular, that of independence-era Ghanaian nationalism),[2] there have been few efforts to

---

[1] Kwaku Larbi Korang, *Writing Ghana, Imagining Africa: Nation and African Modernity* (Rochester: University of Rochester Press, 2003), p. 16.
[2] Ibid., p. 20.

untangle their epistemological and generic challenges and innovations on a broad conceptual scale.

To this end, this chapter contends that post-Confederation, pre-nationalist Fante intellectual life around the turn of the twentieth century is best seen as a textual moment determined to present *objectivity* as an African virtue; as a moral good, that is, with a distinctly emplaced characterological mandate. In so doing, it marks what David Scott might call a 'problem space' that is at once pro-imperial and anticolonial, eschewing the familiar opposition of empire and self-rule to apprehend what was then an 'ongoing moral argument' over the most useful and righteous synthesis of available positions and ideals.[3] The collectively authored figure of the 'literate African',[4] to use de Graft Johnson's term, in this context represents the championing of both knowledge standardization and cultural uniqueness. One promotes a posture of neutrality vis-à-vis facts, and the other claims the capacity to *see* facts as the product of a specific cultural location.

The kind of world-making at stake for the Fante intelligentsia, then, is not primarily translational or oppositional but righteous and even messianic. Rather than just moving between the metropole and colony to translate one world to the other or opposing the so-called periphery to the centre, the 'character' type of the literate African becomes lived evidence for 'character', conceived of as a situated but universalizing moral epistemology. That is to say, while the British late-imperial ideal of objectivity is not on the face of it misguided, only the 'literate African' is equipped to see it through. The project of Fante self-explication thus aims to one-up, so to speak, the British imperial confluence of facts and fate, scientific 'rigor' and foreordained progress. By pinpointing what London fails to see about its colonies, Gold Coast intellectuals fulfil their proclaimed destiny of *situating* the view from nowhere as uniquely theirs. Objectivity thus appears as a posture of due self-interest instead of dishonest self-effacement. This Fante textual tradition claims 'worldliness' because it imagines itself to be leading the *whole* world to moral rectitude, by carefully codifying the customary minutiae of its own.

The Gold Coast intellectual situation

This chapter's primary archive will be two treatises and two essay collections – all of which balance customary and/or legal expertise with an interest in character exposition – first published between 1903 and 1928: *Gold Coast Native Institutions* by J. E. Casely Hayford (1903);

---

[3]David Scott, *Refashioning Futures: Criticism after Postcoloniality* (Princeton, NJ: Princeton University Press, 1999), p. 7.
[4]J. W. de Graft Johnson, *Towards Nationhood in West Africa: Thoughts of Young Africa Addressed to Young Britain* (London: Routledge, [1928] 2014), p. 8.

Fante Customary Laws by John Mensah Sarbah (1904); *The Gold Coast Nation and National Consciousness* by S. R. B. Attoh Ahuma (1911); and *Towards Nationhood in West Africa: Thoughts of Young Africa Addressed to Young Britain* by J. W. de Graft Johnson (1928). The subtitle of the last text identifies the audience for all, which was split between the ruling class of (post-)Edwardian Britain and, through practices of mutual citation, the Fante intellectual milieu that was also their subject. Some historical background is essential to appreciate the seemingly incommensurable investments driving this flourishing era of print. First, the Fante intelligentsia have long been identified as cultural 'middlemen', or what Korang describes as 'an African middle class discovering, relative to its own native sphere of belonging, its alienated messenger status'.[5] As a sub-group of the larger Akan ethnicity, the Fantes broadly assumed a collective identity between the fifteenth and nineteenth centuries as they brokered between the rival Asante Empire to their north and a fluctuating balance of European powers (mainly Portuguese, Dutch and English) in their coastal terrain around the traditional headquarters of Mankessim. A loose alliance of Fante states predates the formation of an official Confederation in 1868, led by a group of kings, chiefs and merchants that also included the foundational Krio intellectual and surgeon Africanus Horton. Following Dennis Laumann in his overview of the Confederation's historiography, its immediate cause was a Dutch-British agreement to swap several forts, expanding the British presence in Fante-led areas.[6] This in turn threatened to upset the Fantes' role in negotiating between the Asante (with whom they had frequently been at war) and the Europeans. Laumann contends that Casely Hayford later exaggerated the extent to which the Confederation sought to rebuff British expansionism *in general* and for reasons of nationalist ideology, as opposed to confederating mainly in order to maintain a profitable balance of power. For my purposes here, it does not matter much whether this criticism holds; it is the Confederation's role in later, collective projects of self-authorship that interests me.[7]

When Korang turns to Casely Hayford's non-fiction writing in English, he describes the Fantes' mediating role and its language of expression in Faustian terms as that which 'bears the uneasy symbolism of fatal compromise'.[8] The common idea that Casely Hayford and his British-educated ilk were at once European and 'native' can thus easily be turned

---

[5] Korang, *Writing Ghana, Imagining Africa*, p. 178.
[6] Dennis Heinz Laumann, 'Compradore-in-Arms: The Fante Confederation Project (1868–1872)', *Ufahamu: A Journal of African Studies*, vol. 21, nos 1–2 (1993): 120–36, 126.
[7] On the Confederation's often-fuzzy history, see Francis Agbodeka's essay 'The Fanti Confederacy 1865–69: An Enquiry into the Origins, Nature and Extent of an Early West African Protest Movement', *Transactions of the Historical Society of Ghana*, vol. 7 (1964): 82–123.
[8] Korang, *Writing Ghana, Imagining Africa*, p. 179.

on its head, a both/and cultural situation cast pejoratively as neither/nor. The Ghanaian political scientist F. K. Drah, in his 1971 introduction to the second edition of de Graft Johnson's *Toward Nationhood in West Africa*, remarks as much, berating 'accusations, often made with an inflated sense of self-importance by some latter-day nationalists against the earlier generations of western-educated West African leaders ... that nearly all the pre-World War II educated leaders were "colonial stooges" who did not want self-rule for Africans'.[9] By now, this rush within later African decolonial movements to condemn their forebears' too-assimilationist politics has received serious attention in historical studies of particular colonial African communities. Philip S. Zachernuk's 2000 study of the southern Nigerian colonial intelligentsia, *Colonial Subjects*, arrives, for example, at a notably similar formulation to Scott's 'problem space' in describing the Saro [Creole] population: 'The educated community was not moving from the African to the European,' Zachernuk writes, 'but rather was seeking to define itself within an emergent Nigerian society. This was not an unstable transitional society waiting to find order by absorbing Western norms but an admittedly changeable society engaged in an ongoing – and unending – process of living through problems as it met them.'[10] Such thinking rightly suggests that understanding the more prominent movements to national independence of the twentieth century should entail an attempt to imagine our way back to a time and place in which they were all but inconceivable.

As Drah indicates, the salient challenge in addressing turn-of-the-century Gold Coast intellectual life is rather *how* an ideal of self-determination worked within the constraints of its moment. 'They were constrained to be reformist in outlook and conduct,' he reasons, 'partly because they were confronted by adamant, technologically superior alien rulers',[11] and, as Korang notes, partly because the group 'had an interest in maintaining and preserving the hegemony of the modern in the particularly British [liberal-constitutionalist] institutional form – albeit not its specific colonial political form – that it had come to the Gold Coast'.[12] It is important, too, to see the intellectual leaders of this era as strategic and thus shifting in their institutional aims and affiliations. Even the brief historical background guiding Drah's remarks evinces just how fluid the relationship was between 'self-determination' as an overarching goal and the *particular* political alliances of a career like Sarbah's or Casely Hayford's. Throughout the Canada-born Gordon Guggisberg's 'progressive' tenure as governor of the Gold Coast from 1919 to 1928 (during which time he founded the

---

[9]Drah, Introduction to de Graft Johnson, *Towards Nationhood in West Africa*, p. ix.
[10]Philip S. Zachernuk, *Colonial Subjects: An African Intelligentsia and Atlantic Ideas* (Charlottesville: University Press of Virginia, 2000), pp. 32–3.
[11]Drah, Introduction to de Graft Johnson, *Towards Nationhood in West Africa*, p. xi.
[12]Korang, *Writing Ghana, Imagining Africa*, p. 206.

illustrious Achimota College), the educated Fante leadership was beset by internal disagreement over their own rightful place in working towards self-governance versus that of the so-called paramount chiefs (chiefs, that is, who were appointed by the colonial government to provincial councils, and in much smaller number than elected to the colony's Legislative Council). In Drah's vibrant telling, the two major African independence organizations at the time – the National Congress of British West Africa (mostly opposed to the chiefs) and the Aborigines' Rights Protection Society (allied with the chiefs and against the more zealously nationalist NCBWA) – ultimately assumed inverted historical roles. Casely Hayford eventually supported the Provincial Council system when dispatched to London under the auspices of the ARPS, thus securing some degree of African representation in the colonial government but inflaming nationalist sentiments among the Society's younger membership, including the well-known writer Kobina Sekyi.[13]

This is not in the main an historical piece (as I am not an historian) but one about how best to interpret a pair of Afro-cosmopolitan print genres – what I have called the legal-humanistic treatise and essay collection – in a context that is difficult to categorize. My aim, then, is to recapture some of that context's open-endedness, amid debates over what might now seem like fine points of an ineluctable movement towards Ghana's birth as a nation state. These surrounded, for example, the question of the Gold Coast's status as a British colony, as opposed to a protectorate; going back before the fateful Land Bills of 1894 and 1897 (in which British authorities encroached on native land rights beyond the limits of their forts), it also recalls the then-widespread view of the Gold Coast as a willing 'host' to the British as a military and trading partner with strictly delineated occupational privileges. (I have already noted that the Fante elite were 'middlemen' not only in a transcultural sense of negotiating between metropole and colony but in a mercantile one of moving trade between Europeans and the Asantes.) As Frederick Cooper has written elegantly, 'what gets lost in narrating history as the triumph of freedom by failure to use that freedom is a sense of *process*. If we can, from our present-day vantage point, put ourselves in the position of different historical actors ... we see moments of divergent possibilities, or different configurations of power, that open up and shut down'.[14] When this attunement to process inflects critical treatments of the Gold Coast, often considered unique within the British sphere of power due to its degree of cooperation between African and colonial leadership, anticolonial and pro-imperial politics seem less opposed than they might now. As Cooper notes

---

[13] Drah, Introduction to de Graft Johnson, *Towards Nationhood in West Africa*, p. xxi.
[14] Frederick Cooper, 'Possibility and Constraint: African Independence in Historical Perspective', *Journal of African History*, vol. 49, no. 2 (2008): 167–96, 169.

even of colonies with far less 'native' participation in governance, 'our gaze backward from the era of independence fails to appreciate – or belittles – ... another form of politics in Africa in the 1940s and 1950s: an effort not to escape empire, but to transform it'.[15] This is truer still of the located turn-of-the-century period at issue here, occurring, as it does, on the heels of the Fante Confederation experiment in actual, intra-imperial African self-rule. To have imagined themselves as real partners, then, in advancing what Attoh Ahuma in 1911 refers to as the British imperial cause of 'justice, freedom, and fairplay' in 'the bond of peace [under] one paramount emperor' may not have been as naïve as it rings to a twenty-first-century ear.[16]

At the very least, it was a combination of sentiments that proved as intellectually generative and as under-theorized as it was politically ill-fated. A number of postcolonial scholars have sought to revisit the curious conjuncture of imperial pride and commitment to African self-determination. As Simon Gikandi acknowledged, for many nationalist intellectuals,

> This was not a contradiction: the reason they were fighting colonial rule was not because they wanted to return to a precolonial past (in spite of the nationalist rhetoric gesturing that way) but because they wanted to access the privileges of colonial culture to be spread more equitably, without regard to race and creed.[17]

In the colonial as opposed to transitional or independence periods, this also bears the more specific imprint of Victorian affective and intellectual affiliations. Victoria J. Collis-Buthelezi, for example, in her work on Cape Town as a site of Black Victorian modernity, finds the history of radical mid-twentieth-century African social movements in a (lost) faith in earlier liberal imperial reforms. 'Many leading figures on both sides of the Atlantic saw the vote and education as the way into freedom for the black race',[18] she reminds the reader more attuned to postcolonial norms. 'Black Victorians did not envision independent nation-states; instead many hoped for the end of racial and colonial oppression through *empire*.'[19] Similarly, in her response to Chris Taylor's book about Caribbean imperial liberalism, Adom Getachew invokes the common occlusions of a broader British post-imperial framework. 'It is tempting to narrate these declarations of imperial fidelity

---

[15] Ibid., p. 174.
[16] S. R. B. Attoh Ahuma, *The Gold Coast Nation and National Consciousness* (London: Routledge, [1911] 2006), p. 7.
[17] Simon Gikandi, *Maps of Englishness: Writing Identity in the Culture of Colonialism* (New York: Columbia University Press, 1996), p. xix.
[18] Victoria J. Collis-Buthelezi, 'Under the Aegis of Empire: Cape Town, Victorianism, and Early-Twentieth-Century Black Thought', *Callaloo*, vol. 39, no. 1 (2016): 115–32, 121.
[19] Ibid., p. 127.

and fraternity by figures so deeply associated with the age of decolonization as mere preludes to the triumphal rise of an anticolonial nationalism that birthed the postcolonial nation-state', she writes, in reference to C. L. R. James. 'In doing so, we rehearse a familiar story in which the counterpoint to empire is necessarily sovereign statehood.'[20]

And yet the case of the Fante intelligentsia around the turn of the twentieth century complicates even this more generous, historically robust critical impulse. Put simply, the very fact of the Fante Confederation's existence in the mid-nineteenth century means that Fante intellectual leaders in the succeeding generation were not just 'imagining' possible ways to make the round peg of self-determination fit into the square hole of empire but also *remembering* one. While Taylor's account of West Indian imperial attachments emphasizes their reliance on fictionality – as 'a fantasy that madly conjures a responsible empire that never in fact had a presence' – a figure like J. E. Casely Hayford had at least *some* basis for believing that a reciprocity of African self-governance and imperial common cause might be possible.[21] In the first chapter of *Gold Coast Native Institutions* from 1903, in which he censures the British for what is 'in some cases, an insane thirst for territorial acquisition',[22] Casely Hayford nonetheless upholds that 'the Aborigines of the Gold Coast triumph in the wave of imperialism which at present sways the public sentiment of Great Britain'.[23] Later, in offering a detailed criticism of the Gold Coast's governance structure as it mediates between the British-appointed governor, king and insufficient native representation (two out of five) among its Legislative Council's unofficial (or mainly advisory) membership, he admits that he 'can understand why, for example, you will rightly or wrongly refuse full representative government, say, to Jamaica or Trinidad' on account of their not having 'an indigenous people' with a history of representative institutions.[24] Casely Hayford views his own milieu, however, as offering a *true* possibility for cooperation in the name of civilizational advancement. With their demonstrated indigenous capacity for representative government, 'the Gold Coast is perfectly unique,' he writes, 'among all the other so-called Dependencies of Great Britain'.[25]

His tone as regards British leadership is one of forthright and even patronizing correction, a far cry from the emphases on trauma and subversion that characterize much of African postcolonial studies rooted

---

[20]Adom Getachew, 'The Problem of Liberal Empire Reconsidered', *Small Axe*, vol. 60 (2019): 167–77, 168.
[21]Christopher Taylor, *Empire of Neglect: The West Indies in the Wake of British Liberalism* (Durham, NC: Duke University Press, 2018), p. 143.
[22]J. E. Casely Hayford, *Gold Coast Native Institutions* (London: Sweet and Maxwell, 1903), p. 5.
[23]Ibid., p. 6.
[24]Ibid., p. 128.
[25]Ibid., p. 129.

in the independence era.²⁶ I am not suggesting that Casely Hayford and his milieu actually *were* on equal political or economic footing with London; rather, they make no bones about presenting themselves in writing at least as equals, and often as superiors. The Fante Confederation stands here as a key point of evidence for what Casely Hayford views as the right (and ultimately, reclaimable) course of imperial affairs. Directing his British readers to the Confederation's constitution (also called the Mankessim Constitution), he concludes that it is 'harmful' and 'useless ... for a Government to attempt to set back the onward tide in the progress of a nation under its protection'.²⁷ The British, then, have not forsaken a romantic past horizon of mutuality so much as foolishly deviated from a practical arrangement that served all parties well. Far from waxing poetic about a shared imperial bond, Casely Hayford extols the Confederation's logistical foresight. 'Fancy the Aborigines of the Gold Coast, thirty-two years ago, thinking of the necessity of good roads, fifteen feet wide, connecting the principal producing districts with the sea coast!'²⁸ he muses. And whereas the Fante Confederation set itself to concrete kinds of progress, British leadership in the decades that follow was mired in 'stupid officialism and red tape'.²⁹ The Confederation's plans for education, likewise, in its 'special provision for female education, and provision for meeting the expense of school building, and ensuring the attendance of all children between the ages of eight and fourteen' meant 'the emergence of the country in two or three generations from a lower to a higher order of civilization'.³⁰ Now, to summarize Casely Hayford's complaint, all of this ground will have to be re-covered, when it had been in line with the *supposed* and rightful goals of British imperial modernity all along.

If there is one epistemological motif that captures this confidence in a past now marshalled as a *tone* to direct the future, it is that of the fact. Casely Hayford sanctifies the factual episteme, along with its close cousin 'evidence', in a familiar nineteenth-century recourse to 'history' and 'science', which he believes will naturally guide colonial administrators in the process of re-finding the path set by the bygone Fante Confederation. 'Science will tell you that there can be no healthy growth except from within,' he reminds them, 'and the history of the Gold Coast will disclose to you the facts and circumstances which must guide such internal growth'.³¹ References

---

[26]For a broader overview of African and Caribbean intellectuals' position *within* London in the first few decades of the twentieth century, see Marc Matera's essay 'Colonial Subjects: Black Intellectuals and the Development of Colonial Studies in Britain', *Journal of British Studies*, vol. 49, no. 2 (2010): 388–418.
[27]Hayford, *Gold Coast*, p. 132.
[28]Ibid., p. 186.
[29]Ibid., p. 187.
[30]Ibid.
[31]Ibid., p. 8.

to history as the domain of facts, unmarred by any particular historical institution (but particularly that of early British colonial ethnography), abound. 'The reader must be prepared to disabuse his mind of all prejudice in this matter', Casely Hayford writes later:

> If you once start with the premises that the Ashantis are a barbarous, bloodthirsty people ... you naturally take a different standpoint from the historian, whose object is the ascertainment of truth from facts as they are, and not as they are supposed or wished to be for purposes of argument or invective.[32]

In a chapter called 'The Conflict of Systems' that posits a long tradition of representative government among the Akan, he again carves out space for the Gold Coast's unique and verifiable role in the British Empire. Anticipating 'the criticism that self-government is reserved by Great Britain for those English-speaking Colonies whose populations are nearly or wholly white', Casely Hayford offers an alternative standard to a racial one that is both more universal and less generalizable. 'I am inclined to think that it is not so much a question of the particular people inhabiting a particular Dependency, as yielding to the logic of facts in the given circumstances', he writes. And, to make things abundantly clear, 'In the case of the Gold Coast we shall appeal to the logic of facts, and shall not appeal in vain.'[33]

The next section of this chapter will delve deeper into the conceptual stakes, among the Fante intelligentsia, of this hallmark British linking of facts to destiny. First, though, I want to lay a foundation for seeing facts as indicative of character, as revealing not just an objective historical reality but an unevenly distributed ability to *see* that it contradicts the structure of political power in which it is enmeshed. The 'real' essence of history, in other words – the facts of who and what the Gold Coast is – exists apart from the history that shapes even the impulse to get these facts on record. Another way of putting this is that Casely Hayford, in the passages above, calls on the self-evident nature of facts to make Akan traditions *into* facts in the act of their written systematization. He shares this goal with John Mensah Sarbah, a fellow lawyer and co-founder of the Aborigines' Rights Protection Society, as evidenced by the latter's *Fanti Customary Laws*. In both cases, an air of unassailable objectivity surrounds the task of individual curation that is nonetheless essential to this process. In his preface, addressed to family friend and senior Gold Coast jurist George Eminsang, Sarbah confesses that this is 'my first attempt in the thorny paths of literature'.[34] While he clearly

---

[32] Ibid., p. 26.
[33] Ibid., p. 127.
[34] John Mensah Sarbah, *Fanti Customary Laws* (London: William Clowes, 1904), p. xi.

intends 'literature' here to mean written texts as such, this description nonetheless asks what might be 'literary' about Sarbah's work in a more delimited sense.

On the one hand, Sarbah's reference to a 'thorny path' invokes the messiness of the Akan lived experiences on which *Fanti Customary Laws* draws and, on the other, adheres to a notion of accuracy in their print rendition. 'I know that you have often given the first *correct* idea on Customary Laws to newly arrived European officials,' he praises Eminsang,[35] and later remarks on the failure, before his own text, 'to test [Customary Laws'] accuracy by comparison with similar cases in other districts affecting the same class of persons.'[36] The 'literary' work, then, done by both *Fanti Customary Laws* and *Gold Coast Native Institutions* is in their dual claim to creation (of bringing an archive of laws, beliefs and traditions into 'official' existence), and to be merely recording what is already there. A virtuosic cultural vision is harnessed to a more prosaic kind of documentary responsibility. Extrapolating from this to provisionally define the literary as a category in and for this milieu, Sarbah's thorniness suggests that literary authorship is marked by sheer will to disciplined observation (staying *out* of the thorns, one might say). Such a premium on ideological *suspension* in the name of political self-determination diverges crucially from the long tradition of identifying African literature with its professed ideological credentials, typically departing from struggles for national independence in the mid- to late twentieth century.

To some degree this recalls the central argument of Mary Poovey's monumental *A History of the Modern Fact*, which charts the means by which the fact, over the eighteenth and early-nineteenth centuries in Britain, came to '[sustain] the illusion that numbers are somehow *epistemologically* different from figurative language, that the former are somehow value-free whereas the excesses of the latter disqualify it from all but the most recreational or idealist knowledge-producing projects'.[37] Being able to look back at the Fante Confederation as evidence of a self-determined people, rather than just forward to what new forms this goal might take, imbues 'history', in Casely Hayford's use of the term, with something like this same neutral valence. While there is a principle of selection in play that elevates Fante modernity above not just its close Asante counterpart but indeed above its British one, the Confederation is also seen to provide clear-cut insight into Fante cultural uniqueness. As Poovey summarizes in her introductory discussion of Lorraine Daston's work in historical epistemology (i.e. the history of the terms and categories by which knowledge is organized), 'facts

---

[35] Ibid., p. ix, emphasis mine.
[36] Ibid., p. x.
[37] Mary Poovey, *A History of the Modern Fact: Problems of Knowledge in the Sciences of Wealth and Society* (Chicago: University of Chicago Press, 1998), p. 6.

seem (and can be said) to exist as identifiable units only when they constitute evidence for some theory – only, that is, when there is a theoretical reason to notice these particulars and name them as facts'.[38] The literary, in Sarbah's terms, might thus also be said to consist in what and *how* he and his peers perform this act of 'notice', in service of the idea that the Fante past provides plain evidence for the British Empire's best line of advancement. As Casely Hayford puts it in *Gold Coast Native Institutions*, Akan self-governance is a matter of 'ordinary common sense' that nonetheless demands hundreds of pages of detailed explanation.[39]

While it must be said that *Fanti Customary Laws* is hardly gripping on the order of well-plotted fiction, neither is it only an ordered list of cases tried in the Supreme Court of the Gold Coast Colony (though it is an impressive feat on this basis alone). Sarbah's introduction lays out a clear orientation towards a

> vain dream to hope a time is coming when the several [Akan] nationalities, united under a beneficent and enlightened Government, will develop and foster the clan feeling and instincts, which in times past have been as free from the impulses, which have degraded the African nature, as great in the qualities, which have ever graced manhood in all ages and under all climes.[40]

In addition to once more upholding an evidentiary, historical basis for Fante leadership and universalism, Sarbah raises the promise of Fante character in his turn to 'nature' and 'qualities'. In this light, it becomes possible to read these treatises, and by extension their intellectual context, through a claim to objectivity as what I have called a distinctly African virtue. This also shifts the weight of argument from the status or legitimacy of objectivity as such – in Poovey's terms, the evolution of the fact from the Enlightenment to the nineteenth century – to the role of a particular Fante character type in advancing its aims.[41] A better Victorian touchstone, then, for understanding the significance of Gold Coast intellectual history to broader questions

---

[38] Ibid., p. 9.
[39] Hayford, *Gold Coast*, p. 99.
[40] Sarbah, *Fanti Customary Laws*, p. 5.
[41] This is as good a place as any to note the obvious masculinity of the character type in question. For a detailed discussion of male-genderedness in the broader diasporic intellectual constellation of which Casely Hayford and to some degree Sarbah are part, including its reliance on Victorian conceptions of 'gentlemanliness', see Michelle Ann Stephens's *Black Empire: The Masculine Global Imaginary of Caribbean Intellectuals in the United States, 1914–1962* (Durham, NC: Duke University Press, 2005). For a feminist rendition of the period in question and a view from the other side of an elite Gold Coast marriage, see Adelaide M. Cromwell's iconic *An African Victorian Feminist: The Life and Times of Adelaide Smith Casely Hayford 1868–1960* (London: Frank Cass, 1986).

of African colonial 'worlding' through print might be George Levine's *Dying to Know*, which takes up objectivity as a moral quest as well as an epistemological commitment. In an effort to salvage objectivity from its sundry uses by false universalisms, Levine revisits as flawed but noble the turn in nineteenth-century England to 'moralized objectivity' as expressed in philosophy and scientific thought by 'a surrender of the self to the thing studied'.[42] As the force of religious belief wanes, this story goes, faith in science – broadly conceived – fills the historical and moral void. Instead of a self that faces God, the self is suppressed or transcended in order to seek what Richard Rorty has referred to as an intrinsically flawed 'Gods-eye view'.[43]

A historical explanation for the cachet of the scientific posture that is rooted in secularization falls short in the face of Gold Coast intellectual history, for the simple reason that the intellectuals in question here are, for the most part, enthusiastic Christians: Attoh Ahuma, whose work I will address in this chapter's second half, was a Methodist minister. Even aside from this, however, Levine's vision of the pursuit of objectivity as a force for shaping narrative has both points of relevance to and points of divergence from the post-Confederation Fante context; each of them is illuminating. In the first camp, Levine links science to Victorian literature by means of 'the language of impartiality' and a 'determination to thwart desire and preconceptions' in pursuit of truth.[44] On this score, at least, *Gold Coast Native Institutions* shares a self-transcending moral vocabulary with a writer like George Eliot. But whereas *Dying to Know* seeks to take a step back from the view that 'the self-abnegation that is part of the history of scientific epistemology must disguise some kind of interest'[45] – that is, it entertains the idea of a sincere investment in seeing the world from outside one's own situation – Casely Hayford and Sarbah make no attempt to conceal their investment in the 'facts' they present about Gold Coast political systems. Their critique of the British is that they are *less objective than the Fantes*; they do not see the writing on their own imperial walls. Levine contends persuasively that 'the critique of an objectivity that turns out in fact to be a disguise of interest undercuts its own objectives if after the exposure of particular interests, it goes on to argue – or imply – that the very act of seeking objectivity is invalid'.[46] This is a useful formulation because it clarifies how the Fante

---

[42]George Levine, *Dying to Know: Scientific Epistemology and Narrative in Victorian England* (Chicago: University of Chicago Press, 2002), p. 3.
[43]Richard Rorty, *Objectivity, Relativism, and Truth* (Cambridge: Cambridge University Press, 1991), p. 7.
[44]Levine, *Dying to Know*, p. 7.
[45]Ibid., p. 5.
[46]Ibid., p. 18.

writers I have cited do precisely the inverse: they 'expose' the absence of facts as a means of *advancing* objectivity in the name of shared imperial goals.

The 'worldly African' as moral character

Perhaps counterintuitively, all the texts treated here espouse objectivity through focused characterological exposition as well as casual invocation. Objectivity, one could say, is not just asserted or tonally performed but represented in and as the figure of the post-Confederation Fante intellectual. In other words, it is embodied as a distilled version of the writers at the heart of this chapter. S. R. B. Attoh Ahuma, in *The Gold Coast Nation and National Consciousness* (a series of essays from the *Gold Coast Leader* newspaper reprinted together in 1911), bemoans the fact that the Gold Coast's progress towards its national-cum-imperial destiny has stagnated due to insufficient rigour of thought among even its educated populace. 'Thinking is an Art' he writes: 'it is the greatest blessing in the gift of Heaven and may not even be found in some talented men who could box the compass of the whole circle of academical education'.[47] The easy elitism of this assessment gives way to a more artful directive as to where a model of serious thought should be found. Pivoting from the metaphor of nation-builders as ingenious architects – a task likened to the '*debris* [covering] a marble out of which Michael Angelo liberated an imprisoned seraph'[48] – Attoh Ahuma looks back to his forebearers. Rather than fetishize empire as decreed by London and its 'melancholy spectacle of a huge Baboon in an irreproachable evening dress suit sporting the latest vogue in silk hats',[49] he urges that 'the easiest way to become civilized, refined and enlightened is to endeavour at all times, in all places and circumstances, to remain a true-born West African – nothing more, nothing less; and that Grand Reformation, which is after all an intelligent backward movement, should begin here and now'.[50] The 'true-born West African' here does a good deal of conceptual work: it is a 'type' that has already come to fruition in the Confederation era, now self-consciously re-engineered by Attoh Ahuma to recover and advance the very empire it challenges.

In this merging of past and future in a timely social role, Attoh Ahuma also manages both to valorize the individual intellectual and typify him on a limited scale. The Fante Confederation as touchstone serves a curatorial role even as it is presented in the name of proto-national unity, redemption and regeneration.[51] A few brief passages from *The Gold Coast Nation*

---

[47] Ahuma, *The Gold Coast Nation and National Consciousness*, p. 6.
[48] Ibid., p. 10.
[49] Ibid.
[50] Ibid., p. 11.
[51] Ibid., p. 12.

and National Consciousness evince objectivity, and its tonal corollary of restraint, as the product of a tense union between insistent individuality and collective destiny. Taken together, they suggest that moral education (a key term for Attoh Ahuma) among the Fante intelligentsia entails a correspondence between how individual and class uniqueness is adduced. He presents the cultivation of character in the name of national progress *back* to a (supposedly) objectively sound model of empire – that is, one of incipient partnership between the British and the Akan – as a re-mapping of the process whereby systematizing Fante contributions 'creates' what was already there. In one essay, called fittingly 'I Am: I Can', Attoh Ahuma remarks that 'having a full and complete sense and cognizance of the supreme value of our respective individualities, and living, thinking, speaking, and doing as if alone in the wide, wide world' serves as the 'fundamental principle upon which States are constituted'.[52] There is clearly a divine mission at stake here, with each man containing some essence of God. More to my point, however, is the fact that Attoh Ahuma sees individuality and destiny as mutually reinforcing; as each upholding the other's self-evident rightness and yet 'right' because they achieve this mutual upholding.

In the essay that follows 'I Am: I Can', titled 'I Ought: I Will', he entreats the next generation of Gold Coast leaders to move 'higher and higher at all times … as long as we understand ourselves, and our actions spring from pure motives, guided by the instincts of our enlightened consciences, and in full sight of the goal to which the inexorable finger of destiny points, we should go FULL STEAM AHEAD'.[53] Together, the capacities for supreme individualism (which would seem to imply agency) and adherence to progress's foreordained course (which would seem to constrain it) add up to a character sketch. The ideal Gold Coast leader is, above all, 'wise and prudent', Attoh Ahuma stipulates, someone who 'knows that he knows what are the dangers and perils, pitfalls and temptations, gins and snares that would impede his progress or retard his advancement in the path of duty'.[54] The meta-reflexive priority displayed here – not just knowing but *knowing* about knowing – speaks to the broader goal of 'objective' self-analysis that he shares with Casely Hayford and Sarbah. A particular brand of post-Confederation Fante intellectual is brought into being in part by standardizing himself. 'By exercise of the faculties with which we are endowed,' Attoh Ahuma continues,

> we should be able to differentiate in all our acquisitions what is essential from non-essentials, we should know HOW and WHEN and WHERE to

---

[52] Ibid., p. 22.
[53] Ibid., p. 27.
[54] Ibid., p. 30.

skip what may militate against our onward and upward flight, we should recognise and mark out our limitations, and endeavour to be independent of foreign fads and fashions, and to correspond to our surroundings.[55]

This last point marks *this* chapter's main concern: the ability to make determinations of proportion, limitation and the sorts of cultural 'facts' of which Casely Hayford writes is bound to the Gold Coast location.

Turning back to *Gold Coast Native Institutions* in this light reveals an even more explicit connection than Attoh Ahuma's between emplaced sensibility and place-transcendent perspective. A section called 'The People' describes the 'Gold Coast man' as intrinsically equipped with 'the force of a logic which no decent British Cabinet can withstand',[56] and free to adopt 'European comforts and amenities' without assimilationist peril due to 'the resourcefulness, tact, and practical common sense of his nature'.[57] Later, in the section 'The Fetish System', Casely Hayford flips the script on British condescension to native spirituality to make *theirs* seem like the unsubstantiated view. While certain forms of direct spirit-communion 'to the unscientific mind seem barbarous,' he responds that 'when critically examined, [they] cover a mine of truth and inspiration'.[58] The English espouse objectivity but fall short of achieving it, so that their superior affect is out of sync with Casely Hayford's oft-cited 'evidence' and thus ill-suited to imperial flourishing. 'Your matter-of-fact Englishman is too prosaic for the average native intelligence',[59] he writes bluntly. From this view, the Gold Coast governor is not helped in his myopia by being in service to 'an overtaxed official [the Colonial Secretary], some 3,000 miles away, who may or may not be a capable man, and who gleans his information as to the local conditions from his obedient servant, the Governor!'[60] The tactical concern here is readily apparent: a closed informational loop of British leadership that excludes Gold Coast leaders from influence is 'against true imperialism and the expansion of British influence and prestige'.[61] However, this is also a point on which Casely Hayford epitomizes the connection between analytic distance and cultural and geographical intimacy. Levine wonders poignantly whether 'the primary values of localism and particularism [have] done what good work [they] can, and are now ... playing into the obsessive individualism of contemporary social and economic structures'.[62]

---

[55] Ibid.
[56] Hayford, *Gold Coast*, p. 80.
[57] Ibid., p. 81.
[58] Ibid., p. 101.
[59] Ibid., p. 118.
[60] Ibid., p. 125.
[61] Ibid.
[62] Ibid., p. 14.

In contrast, the Fante intelligentsia seems to declare that it is only by seeing from within that one can productively labour towards glimpsing truth from without.

Certainly, some of what these Fante intellectuals espouse is absorbed from different phases of Victorian discourse; as Collis-Buthelezi reminds us, liberalism is 'in the air' all around the British Empire. Lauren Goodlad pinpoints a shift from an early- and mid-Victorian emphasis on 'prescriptive character' to a late-Victorian narrowing to 'descriptive character', with the first valuing 'the elasticity of character' in a way that 'gave rise to ambitious schemes of moral perfectability'.[63] Drawing heavily on Mill, Goodlad argues that a prescriptive emphasis on character-building is ultimately about the second part of that term; its precise contents are 'infinitely plastic', configured variably to abet an engaged citizenry and institutions meant to link individual growth to 'a holist social ontology'.[64] In this way, the dominant Victorian notion of character might be seen as both liberal and socialist, a pairing that also aptly describes the delicate merger of valiant post-Confederation Fante intellectual and the larger project of Akan, African and indeed racial uplift at whose helm he stands. 'Character-building' so imagined is a metonymic enterprise, valuable for its ability to link developing human parts with a developmentally minded institutional apparatus. By the dawn of the twentieth century, however, Goodlad suggests that a more punitive notion of character has come to the fore. 'Fuelled by the globalization of capital, the quest for dominion over world markets, and the growing competition among European powers for far-flung empires,' she writes, 'these social and geopolitical factors were integral to the increasing rejection of an Enlightenment discourse that held human character to be fundamentally equal and perfectible across geographic, racial, and cultural boundaries.'[65] Accompanied by the consolidation of racial pseudo-science beginning in the 1880s in all its profane confusion of biological and social factors, 'colonized people were conceived at best to be lagging in a temporal cultural trajectory that would eventually resemble England's, and at worst to differ incorrigibly from the normative qualities of Anglo-Saxon character'.[66] *This* version of the link between character and objectivity is precisely the one Casely Hayford rejects, so that looking back to the Fante Confederation overlaps neatly, for him and his peers, with recapturing a more open-ended notion of character in Victorian intellectual life.

---

[63]Collis-Buthelezi, 'Under the Aegis of Empire', p. 132.
[64]Lauren Goodlad, 'Moral Character', in *Historicism and the Human Sciences in Victorian Britain*, ed. Mark Bevir (Cambridge: Cambridge University Press, 2017), pp. 128–53, 141.
[65]Ibid., pp. 141–2.
[66]Ibid., p. 146.

Perhaps the most salient dimension of Victorian ideas on character, however, in terms of how they permeate Gold Coast thought is an emphasis on the moral value of *constraint*. As Stefan Collini has noted,

> the blurring of the distinction between [explanatory and evaluative senses of character] was facilitated by the assumption that the possession of settled dispositions indicated a certain habit of restraining one's impulses. The contrast was with behaviour which was random, impulsive, feckless; and where the impulses were identified ... with the 'lower self' ... then a positive connotation was conferred on the habit of restraint itself.[67]

Beyond its explanatory force for the proposed Fante intelligentsia relationship between one's moral standing and capacity to be objective – to see 'just the facts' even where one's own culture is concerned – this summary is helpful for understanding the link between these intellectuals' investment in self-representation and their valorization of their decidedly *un*-representative milieu. The project of self-determination at this juncture, which I have described as pro-imperial but anticolonial, is as much about understanding the limitations of agency as it is about having more. Collini's assessment that mid-nineteenth-century English liberalism was motivated less by the commonly cited priorities of liberty or individual rights and more by a 'fundamental emotional dynamic' that he describes as 'hostility to unreflective and unjustified privilege and a related hatred of being patronized' also rings true in this context.[68] From the perspective of Casely Hayford or Sarbah, British imperialists have erred by overstepping the *bounds* of their knowledge, rather than by fundamentally misunderstanding what knowledge is. Imperial flourishing is thus best imagined not as top-down epistemological diffusion but as collating different scales of self-representation in the pursuit of a common truth. Facts can then be brought into view by the part, for the whole; marking clear limits allows for their transcendence.

Though it is far from the Gold Coast situation, Kunal Parker's work on nineteenth-century American law offers an illuminating discussion of how constraint as an ideal bridges moral, characterological and political registers. 'The ideational world of the nineteenth century was a world in which the notion of *given* constraints was very real indeed', he writes. 'In other words, this was not a world in which the subject – whether an individual, a group, or a society – ordinarily deemed itself free to act entirely as it pleased, to reimagine the world in a thoroughgoing way.'[69] If the British

---

[67] Stefan Collini, 'The Idea of "Character" in Victorian Political Thought', *Transactions of the Royal Historical Society*, vol. 35 (1985): 29–50, 34.
[68] Ibid., p. 44.
[69] Kunal M. Parker, 'Law "in" and "as" History: The Common Law in the American Polity, 1790–1900', *UC Irvine Law Review*, vol. 1, no. 3 (2011): 587–609, 596.

Empire is envisioned as bearing some *intrinsic* relation to the highest ideals of civilizational advancement, then African self-determination becomes a matter of internal reconfiguration within a predetermined shape. (For this reason, too, the Fante Confederation proves a generative reference point.) Attoh Ahuma refers to an arrangement of '*imperium in imperio*', or a state within a state, as 'the highest organized form of government in creation'.[70] Imperial symbols in this vision serve as the 'true' form of what is to some degree historically variable content. 'We are being welded together under one umbrageous Flag,' he continues, 'a Flag that is the symbol of justice, freedom, and fairplay; … The Gold Coast under the *aegis* of the Union Jack is the unanswerable argument to all who may incontinently withhold from us the common rights, privileges, and status of nationality'.[71] The political constraint of empire here expresses the ultimate constraint of values that are imagined, as Parker notes, to be 'given' and immutable, a way of seeing the world as derived from first principles that predates more recent understandings of it as 'the product of nothing but history, as one historically locatable phenomenon giving way to another'.[72] Like the American nineteenth-century legal theorists whose perspective Parker wants to inhabit, the Gold Coast intellectuals here see politics as a means to an historical end that is already known. 'In other words,' Parker writes, 'political decision making, which took place in historical time, was constrained by a law that unfolded outside historical time. To many, this was not the contradiction that it appears to be to us.'[73]

It is far from incidental that so many members of the Fante intelligentsia in this period, including Casely Hayford and Sarbah, are also lawyers trained in the Common Law tradition of which Parker writes, and that it is legal discussion (namely, of the supposedly progressive 1925 Guggisberg Constitution) whereby their nationalist leanings grow sharper. Locating the capacity for objectivity within an appreciation of constraint – that is, the British are not objective because they fail to perceive their own epistemological limitations – also introduces a 'natural' way to limit democracy while advancing the goal of Gold Coast self-determination. Parker here again offers an eloquent summary of how law can be viewed as expressing a truth *beyond* history even as it is commanded to work for a timely historical cause. 'Even as many in the nineteenth century saw democracy as furnishing the logic of history,' he argues, 'to the extent that history was imagined to possess an underlying logic and meaning and direction, it could equally serve as a check on democracy.'[74] Casely Hayford's commitment, for example,

---

[70] Ahuma, *The Gold Coast Nation and National Consciousness*, p. 2.
[71] Ibid.
[72] Parker, 'Law "in" and "as" History', p. 603.
[73] Ibid., p. 602.
[74] Ibid., p. 603.

to 'carving the happy destiny of the Fanti as the predominant partner in the coming Imperial West Africa' rests on the value of his own ability to represent in print the traditions *of* representative government among the Akan,[75] as Sarbah likewise represents their laws. Self-determination within empire is essentially delegated to what Casely Hayford envisions as 'a small syndicate of independent men of means with patriotic fire in their hearts, [who] would endeavour to deserve the confidence and support of the community'.[76] Regardless of how one might weigh the legitimacy of this boldly minoritarian form of African leadership, the hybrid textual genre of the treatise is essential to its justification. In order to assume its key role in advancing imperial destiny, the Gold Coast requires a perspective that can split the difference between neutral observation and vigorous moral assertion. By moving easily between long, even tedious customary systematization and exposition of the type of character who can do this (i.e. themselves), *Gold Coast Native Institutions* and *Fanti Customary Laws* announce their authors' cultural uniqueness and their traditions' universal necessity in one fell swoop.

This way of thinking comes to a head in J. W. de Graft Johnson's 1928 collection of lectures, in whose first pages he declares that 'it is necessary to clear our minds of hazy notions and ideas in order to arrive at the truth about Africa. Facts, it is said, are stubborn things, and the truth is often unpalatable.'[77] He is chiefly concerned with revealing 'the facts constituting the truth about the African' to a British audience, thereby using knowledge as a tool for restoring England to its Victorian glory 'with its high standard of justice and deep sense of humanity'.[78] Notably, his alertness to this task is also evidence for why 'the educated African, who thoroughly understands his people to a degree nobody else can' should now 'take the lead in the forward march of progress'.[79] For de Graft Johnson, this motivates strong refutation of a policy of one man, one vote – at that point a hot topic of metropolitan debate – as he endorses the British policy of granting greater representation to graduates. Presenting what he claims is the real story of his character type, as one of its chief representatives abroad, allows him to not just *be* 'objective' but to moralize and mobilize objectivity. Among other traits, de Graft Johnson describes the 'radical simplicity and directness of [the educated African's] character',[80] before declaring that 'it is the grand and solemn duty of the intelligent members of the community to work for the uplift, advancement, and progress of the people'.[81] In naming the tone

---

[75]Hayford, *Gold Coast*, p. 263.
[76]Ibid., p. 180.
[77]de Graft Johnson, *Towards Nationhood in West Africa*, p. 6.
[78]Ibid., p. 49.
[79]Ibid., p. 50.
[80]Ibid., p. 49.
[81]Ibid., p. 50.

that he sees himself as performing (he repeats the word 'solemn' again in the next paragraph), he also in effect explains his choice of the outward-facing lecture form. Like the treatises of his immediate successors Casely Hayford and John Mensah Sarbah, the lecture reprinted as essay permits de Graft Johnson to self-invent as an ostensibly simple matter of observation.

These texts have value today to theorizations of world literature because they speak to the incredible variability of writing with conjoined African self- and world-making at its centre. More pointedly, they raise the bygone and now, counter-intuitive prospect of a British Empire – and by ambitious extension, world civilization – led by Africans. During this early-twentieth-century period of suspension between the short-lived Fante Confederation and the Ghanaian nationalist narrative into which it is later absorbed, the Gold Coast intelligentsia also ask far-reaching questions about how standardizing a local character type might relate to grand political change. Within a more limited frame, the Cape Coast–centred intellectual tradition surveyed here presents an alternative to Africa's uptake into discussions of worldliness via only a handful of 'global' capitals. A focus on treatises and essays, finally, and the centrality of such forms to the development of a regional print culture with aspirations to a world stage suggests non-fiction as a key source of 'literary' and imaginative history. Most significant of all, however, may be that these Fante intellectuals' textually manifest concern with the thread connecting self-description to *imperial* epistemological rejuvenation; they seek to create a new world order within the one they already inhabit. By espousing objectivity as a uniquely African moral and political credential, they make seeing *right* a matter of being good, and of building well.

Bibliography

Agbodeka, Francis (1964), 'The Fanti Confederacy 1865–69: An Enquiry into the Origins, Nature and Extent of an Early West African Protest Movement', *Transactions of the Historical Society of Ghana*, vol. 7: 82–123.

Attoh Ahuma, S. R. B. ([1911] 2006), *The Gold Coast Nation and National Consciousness*, London: Routledge.

Casely Hayford, J. E. (1903), *Gold Coast Native Institutions*, London: Sweet and Maxwell.

Collini, Stefan (1985), 'The Idea of "Character" in Victorian Political Thought', *Transactions of the Royal Historical Society*, vol. 35: 29–50.

Collis-Buthelezi, Victoria J. (2016), 'Under the Aegis of Empire: Cape Town, Victorianism, and Early-Twentieth-Century Black Thought', *Callaloo*, vol. 39, no. 1: 115–32.

Cooper, Frederick (2008), 'Possibility and Constraint: African Independence in Historical Perspective', *Journal of African History*, vol. 49, no. 2: 167–96.

Cromwell, Adelaide M. (1986), *An African Victorian Feminist: The Life and Times of Adelaide Smith Casely Hayford 1868–1960*, London: Frank Cass.

de Graft Johnson, J. W. ([1928] 2014), *Towards Nationhood in West Africa: Thoughts of Young Africa Addressed to Young Britain*, London: Routledge.

Getachew, Adom (2019), 'The Problem of Liberal Empire Reconsidered', *Small Axe*, vol. 60: 167–77.

Gikandi, Simon (1996), *Maps of Englishness: Writing Identity in the Culture of Colonialism*, New York: Columbia University Press, p. xix.

Goodlad, Lauren (2017), 'Moral Character', in *Historicism and the Human Sciences in Victorian Britain*, ed. Mark Bevir, Cambridge: Cambridge University Press, pp. 128–53.

Korang, Kwaku Larbi (2003), *Writing Ghana, Imagining Africa: Nation and African Modernity*, Rochester: University of Rochester Press.

Laumann, Dennis Heinz (1993), 'Compradore-in-Arms: The Fante Confederation Project (1868–1872)', *Ufahamu: A Journal of African Studies*, vol. 21, nos 1–2: 120–36.

Levine, George (2002), *Dying to Know: Scientific Epistemology and Narrative in Victorian England*, Chicago: University of Chicago Press.

Matera, Marc (2010), 'Colonial Subjects: Black Intellectuals and the Development of Colonial Studies in Britain', *Journal of British Studies*, vol. 49, no. 2: 388–418.

Parker, Kunal M. (2011), 'Law "in" and "as" History: The Common Law in the American Polity, 1790–1900', *UC Irvine Law Review*, vol. 1, no. 3: 587–609.

Poovey, Mary (1998), *A History of the Modern Fact: Problems of Knowledge in the Sciences of Wealth and Society*, Chicago: University of Chicago Press.

Rorty, Richard (1991), *Objectivity, Relativism, and Truth*, Cambridge: Cambridge University Press.

Sarbah, John Mensah (1904), *Fanti Customary Laws*, London: William Clowes.

Scott, David Scott (1999), *Refashioning Futures: Criticism after Postcoloniality*, Princeton, NJ: Princeton University Press.

Stephens, Michelle Ann (2005), *The Masculine Global Imaginary of Caribbean Intellectuals in the United States, 1914–1962*, Durham, NC: Duke University Press.

Taylor, Christopher (2018), *Empire of Neglect: The West Indies in the Wake of British Liberalism*, Durham, NC: Duke University Press.

Zachernuk, Philip S. (2000), *Colonial Subjects: An African Intelligentsia and Atlantic Ideas*, Charlottesville: University Press of Virginia.

INDEX

Please note that page numbers in *italics* refer the reader to images.

Abdalla, Abdilatif 154, *155*, 157, 164, 171–6
Achebe, Chinua, *Things Fall Apart* 2, 42, 145–6, 185
Adams, Quanita 200
Addonis, Sulaiman 40
Adegbija, Efurosibina 141
Adejunmobi, Moradewun 5, 198
Adesanmi, Pius, *You're Not A Country, Africa* 1
Adichie, Chimamanda Ngozi 13, 192–6, 203, 207–9
  Americanah 25, 192–4
  Half of a Yellow Sun 192–4
  Purple Hibiscus 192
  'The Tree in Grandma's Garden' 193
  'We Should All Be Feminists' 193–4
  'You in America' 193
Africa
  Afrocentrism 14
  Afrofuturism 27
  Afropessimism 28
  Afropolitanism 4, 18, 23, 213–14
  Akan people 235, 241–3, 246, 251
  Asante people (Ashanti) 235–7, 241–2
  Basotho people 121–4
  borders, unnaturalness of 17–33, 38, 173
  diasporas of 25–7, 59, 176, 203, 213–14
    writing 7, 41, 49 n.8, 186, 203
  Fante people
    Fante Confederation 14, 233–5, 238–52
    Fante intelligentsia 233–52
    Mankessim Constitution 240
  Igbo people 185
  Krio people 235
  languages of *see* languages
  'literate' African, the 14, 123, 234, 251
  literature *see* literature, African
  localism 64–5, 82–7, 92–3, 115, 122, 247 *see also* 'global', the
  Makhuwa people
  Maasai people 214, 219–22
  Mongo people 53
  national independence 50, 59, 66, 93, 140, 233, 236–9, 242 *see also* nationalism
    Aborigines' Rights Protection Society 237, 241
    National Congress of British West Africa 237
  Négritude *see* Négritude
  Nguni people 133
  pan-Africanism 24, 27–9, 130–4, 156–7, 170–8
    ideology 1, 13, 164, 214
    writing 38–9, 124, 194
  Pojulu people 224
  pre-colonial 3
  railways of 27, 107
  'Scramble' for 60–1
  self-determination 233, 236–9, 242, 249–51
  Swahili coast 19, 222
  Swahili people 92, 100, 222
  Swazi people 133

Thonga people 131
Vili people 59
Xhosa people 125, 129
'worldly' African *see* literature, world and 'worlding'
Zulu people 133
Alexander, Neville 143, 146
Ali, Ali Hilal 175
  Mmeza Fupa 162, 165–9, *166*
Amirah, Abu 171, 174
Andrew, Godance 163
Angola 30
Ansatzphänomen 21
anticolonialism 3, 101, 233, 239
  and pro-imperialism 234, 237–8, 249
anti-intellectualism 58, 64
Appadurai, Arjun 203
Arendt, Hannah 52
Arens, Sarah 8–10, 47–67
Asamoah, Sarpong Osei 28
Attoh Ahuma, S.R.B. 233–5, 238, 244
  The Gold Coast Nation and National Consciousness 235, 245–7, 250
Attree, Lizzie 156, 163–4, 171–2
Auerbach, Erich 20–1, 31, 103–4
Austria 94, 97, 100, 176

Bâ, Mariama, *So Long a Letter* 184
Baharaoon, Zainab Alwi, *Mungu Hakopeshwi* 153, 162, 174
Baingana, Doreen, 'Tropical Fish' 200
Baldwin, James 55
Balogun, Taye 28
Baraka, Carey 24
Barber, Karin 91, 127
Barrett, A. Igoni 200–1
Barthes, Roland 195
Baykädañ, Gäbrä-Həywät, *Aṭe Mənilǝkǝnna Ityopya* 80
Beecroft, Alexander 93, 115–16, 119, 127, 134
Belgium 50, 94
  Belgian imperialism 48, 63, 66, 94, 184
Ben Jellou, Tahar 48
Benin Republic 184

Bennie, W. G. 126
Berkman, Karin 196
Bgoya, Mkuki 154–5, 163–70
Bgoya, Walter 142, 155, 162–5, 171–5
Bildungsroman 53–5, 63, 66, 131
bin Abdallah bin Saidi El-Bhury, Hemedi 101, 105–6
bin Bakari, Bwana Mwengo 107
bin Salim, Abushiri 105
Bofane, In Koli Jean 10
  Congo Inc. : Le Testament de Bismarck 47, 50–3, 60–6
Bold, Melanie Ramdarshan 164
Bosire-Ogechi, Emily 147
Botswana 26, 38
Bourdieu, Pierre 190–1, 205
Braudel, Fernand 51
Bromby, Katrin 105–6
Brouillette, Sarah 11–12, 195
Bulawayo, NoViolet 214
Bulgaria 94
Bunyan, John, *The Pilgrim's Progress* 116–18, 121–3
Burundi 176
Busa, Roberto 31

Canada 28, 176
  Toronto International Film Festival 194
capital
  celebrity 13, 189–209
  cultural 190–2
  economic 192
  media 206
  political 192
  social 191–2
  symbolic 192
capitalism 37, 53
  digital 61–4
  global *see* 'global', the, globalization
Caribbean, the 59, 238–9
cartographies 11, 87, 157, 164, 170–1, 178, 216, 229–30
Cartwright, Penelope 13, 213–30
Casanova, Pascale 10, 51, 82, 119, 158
Casely Hayford, Adelaide 243 n.41

INDEX

Casely Hayford, J. E. 233–52
   Gold Coast Native Institutions 234, 239–44, 247, 250–1
Castro-Gomez, Santiago 87
Chad 146
Cheah, Pheng 11, 22, 39, 52, 61
China (PRC) 51–3, 63–7 *see also* neocolonialism
Chouliariki, Lilie 215–17, 227–8
Cole, Teju 203–5
   Open City 25
Collini, Stefan 249
Collis-Buthelezi, Victoria J. 238, 248
colonialism 3, 19, 25–8, 37, 183, 197, 238
   ahistoricity, imposition of 65
   'civilizing' mission of 56, 66, 245
   coloniality 215
   colonial gaze 218–23
   colonial spectacularization 13, 215–24, 227
   standardised time, imposition of 52, 61
Coly, Ayo A. 54
Comoros, the 99–101, 160
Congo 38–40, 51–2, 55–8, 160
   Belgian Congo 94, 103
   Congo Free State 60, 65
   Congolese Movement for Democracy and Integral Development 56
   Democratic Republic of Congo (DRC, formerly Zaire) 49 n.8, 60–6
      Kinshasa 53, 62–3
      Mobutu regime 57
      Katanga 103
      Nguesso regime 56
      People's Republic of Congo 55
   Republic of the Congo
      Loango 56, 59
      Pointe-Noire 52, 56–7
Condé, Maryse 48
Conrad, Joseph, *Heart of Darkness* 56
Cooper, Frederick 19, 93, 237–8
cosmopolitanism 2, 7, 22–3, 27 *see also* 'global', the

Afropolitanism *see* Africa, Afropolitanism
   cosmopolitan ethos 31
   ecology of literary circulation 115–18, 129, 134, 190
   'parochial', the 109–10
   'provincial' 109–10
Couldry, Nick 191, 201
Couzens, Tim 119, 130
covid-19 pandemic 29, 32, 202
Cox, Justin 175

Damrosch, David 51, 109
Daston, Lorraine 242–3
de Certeau, Michel 54
DeChaine, Robert 217–18
decolonialism and decolonisation 6, 14, 135, 213–15
   ideology 1, 230, 236
de Graft Johnson, J. W. 233–4
   Towards Nationhood in West Africa 235–6, 251
Derrida, Jacques 52
Diegner, Lutz 160
Djibouti 40, 77
Drah, F. K. 236–7
Driessens, Olivier 13, 190, 198
Dube, John Langalibalele, 130–2
   Insila ka Tshaka 117, 130–3
Dube, Kgauhelo 199
Dube, Nokutela 130 n.76
Du Bois, W. E. B. 132 n.82
Durrani, Shiraz, *Never Be Silent: Publishing and Imperialism* 140

Edoro, Ainehi 205–6
Egypt 176
   Nile Valley 57
   Suez Canal 78
El-Rufai, Hadiza, *An Abundance of Scorpions* 187
Eminsang, George 241–2
English, James 153, 192
Enlightenment, the 66, 243
epistemology 75, 88, 214–15, 226, 240–6, 249 *see also* war and violence, epistemological
Erikson, Lee 201

Eritrea
  Asmara 80
Ethiopia 10, 38–40, 71–88
  Addis Abäba 78
  Adwa 78
  constitution of 77–8
  Emperor Haylä Səllase 77
  Emperor Mənilək 73–4, 77–80
  Empress Taytu 78
  Emperor Tewodros 73
  Emperor Yohannəs 73
  establishment of 73
  Ethiopian empire 73
  famine 218
  Marxist junta 83
  occupation of 80
  Zäge 78
  Zämänä Mäsafənt (1769–1855) 73
ethnography 241

Fanon, Franz 223
Fasseltt, R. 199–210
feminism 207–8, 243 n.41
Fikre, Tolossa 83–7
Fokn Bois 201
Forsdick, Charles 48–9, 54
Forslid, T. 190–1, 195, 206
Foucault, Michel 195
France 59
  Bordeaux (Poripo) 94, 103
  Brittany 59
  Francocentrism 49
  Francophonie, la (OIF) 8–10, 48–9 see also languages, Europhone, French
  French imperialism 9, 48, 66, 184
  'greater' 8
  Hexagon, the 9, 48
  leaders of
    Macron, Emmanuel 48
    Napoleon (Lapuliyao) 94–5, 104
    Sarkozy, Nicolas 65
  Marseille (Marisea) 94–6, 103
  Paris 49, 95, 104, 174
Frescura, Franco 117

Gäbrä-Iyäsus, Afäwärq
  Dagmawi Mənilək Nəgusä Nägäst Zältyopya 73–4, 78–80
  Ləbb Wälläd Tarik (Tobbya) 10, 71–88
  publication of 72–3, 78
Gachagua, Clifton 38
Gakuru, Wanjeri 26–7
Gallina, Francesco 78
Ganguly, Debjani 22–3, 30, 38–40, 215–18
Gazemba, Stanley, *Stone Hills of the Maragoli* 43
Geldof, Bob 219
Germany 171
  Bildungsroman see Bildungsroman
  German imperialism 90, 103–5, 184
  German East Africa 100–3
  Hamburg (Hambo) 94, 97, 103
  Kaiser of 94–7, 100, 104–6 see also literature, African, poetry, *Kaisa*, the
  Kaiser's wife (Lihuwara) 97
  Leipzig 172
  Lettow-Vorbeck, General (Rito) 97, 102
  solidarity with Muslims 100
  unification of 61
  von Bismarck, Otto 60–1 see also Bofane, In Koli Jean, *Congo, Inc.*
Getachew, Adom 238–9
Ghana (formerly the Gold Coast) 233–52 see also Africa, Fante people
  Achimota College 237
  Cape Coast 233
  Guggisberg, Gordon 236, 250
  Land Bills (1894, 1897) 237
Ghassani, Mohammed, *Machozi Yamenishiya and N'na Kwetu* 162
Gicheru, Mwangi 42
Gikandi, Simon 6, 160, 238
Gila-Maryam, Gäbrä-Əgziabher 76–7
Gilroy, Paul 55
Goodland, Lauren 248
Guinea-Bissau 30

INDEX

'global', the 22, 31, 59 *see also* cosmopolitanism
   Anglophone emphasis of 49
   conflation with 'the world' 4, 7, 14
   definitions of 50
   ecology of literary circulation 115–16, 134
   global history 51–2
   global media 217–18, 222, 230
   Global North, the 13, 203–4, 215
   'global public' 216–17
   Global South, the 203, 215
   globalization 19, 51–4, 65–7, 71, 77, 92, 103, 248 *see also* capitalism
   as opposed to local 92, 110, 178, 190–1, 201, 209
Goethe, Johann Wolfgang von 20, 66
Gohil, Mehul 38
Grosholz, Emily R. 145
Gueza, Zamda R. 12, 153–78
Guillory, John 203
Gyasi, Yaa, *Homegoing* 25

Habermas, Jürgen 216
Habila, Helon 203
Halide, Fundi 92–4, 96
Haraway, Donna 30–1
Hargreaves, Alec 48
Harris, Ashleigh 11–12
Harrison, Olivia 60–1
Hartman, Saidiya, *Lose Your Mother* 25
Hayot, Eric 6, 93, 103
Heidegger, Martin 6, 52
Helgesson, Stefan 5, 157–8
Hiddleston, Jane 51, 67
Hofmeyr, Isabel 122
Horton, Africanus 235
Hoyos, Héctor 109
humanitarianism and non-governmental organisations (NGOs) 217–19, 222–4
human rights 207–8
hypervisibility 218–19, 223–4

Imasuen, Eghosa, *Fine Boys* 195
imprisonment 52–3, 72, 172
India 100, 185, 196, 207

International Monetary Fund (IMF) 65, 155, 218
internet, the *see* capitalism, digital
Irele, Abiola 198
Italy 78–80

Jackson, Jeanne-Marie 14, 233–52
Jaji, Tsitsi 170
James, C. L. R. 239
Japan 94, 146, 218–19
Jele, Nozizwe Cynthia, 'Tender' 200
John, Elnathan 208
Journo, Aurélie 174
Julien, Eileen 3–4

Kahora, Billy 4–5, 24, 37–45
Kaiza, A. K. 155
Kavanagh, R. M. 133
Kenya (formerly British East Africa) 26, 30, 98–9, 102, 140, 147, 156, 171–6, 202
   Dadaab 17, 29, 40
   Emergency 140
   'Great Kenyan Novel', the 4, 38, 42–5
   INGOs 17, 23, 28–9, 38–40 *see also* humanitarianism and NGOs
   Kakuma 17, 29, 40
   Kenyatta regime 44 n.4
   Lagos 215
   Mabati Rolling Mills 157
   Mau Mua 140
   Moi regime, the 42–3
   Mombasa 172–4, 221
   Nairobi 4, 17–33, 37–45, 141, 174, 202, 214–15
   Nakuru 215, 218–19, 222
   'silicon savannah' 23, 38–41, 214
Kiguru, Doseline 13, 156, 159, 171, 189–209
Kilolo, Moses 27
Kilolo, Munyao 12, 139–51, 157, 161–3, 171
Kimani, Peter 43
   Nairobi Noir 24–6
Kiriamiti, John 42
Kombani, Kinyanjui 43, 202
Korang, Kwaku Larbi 233–6
Kresse, Kai 172

Krishnan, Madhu 177, 204
Krishnan, Sanjay 50
Kunene, Daniel 118, 121–3

Laachir, Karima 4, 66
languages
  Afrophone 118–20, 128–9, 134, 141–51, 156–60, 175–8
  Amharic 10, 71–88
  Arabic 97–8, 107, 146, 187
  Bantu 103
  Ekegusii 145
  Ekoti 94, 99, 109
  Emakhuwa 99
  Gikuyu 145–6, 150
  Gumbai 146
  Igala 146
  intellectualisation of 146, 163, 171
  isiZulu 116–17, 130–4
  Kenyan 140–5
  Kiikamba 12, 139–42, 146
  Kikongo 51, 57
  Lingala 51, 57
  local language radio 148
  Luo 27
  oral ('traditional') 91–2, 141, 150
  preservation of 123, 133, 184
  Sesotho 2 n.3, 117, 123, 132, 150
  Setswana 133–4
  Sheng 202Somali 146
  Swahili (Kiswahili) 10, 13, 93–4, 97–101, 106–7, 110, 140–1, 168, 170–8, 222 *see also* prizes and prize culture, Kiswahili prize
  translation between 140–1, 145–6, 156, 176 *see also* translation
  Xhosa (isiXhosa), 116–17, 125–8, 132, 150
  Yoruba 145, 184
  |Xam 116
Amazon, policy on 176
bridge 146
Europhone 21, 116–20, 156–8, 176, 204
  Afrikaans 12, 116, 119, 134
  Dutch 117
  English 30, 51, 97, 132–5, 155–6, 202–3, 241
  French 8–10, 47–67, 120, 124, 146, 184–7, 203 *see also* France, *La Francophonie*
  German 97, 103–4
  Latin 31, 64
  Portuguese 4, 30, 97
  hierarchy of 135, 141–6, 151, 161, 184
  Indian 185
  language barriers 202
  linguistic injustice 143, 147
  Mandarin 51
  multilingualism 144, 172, 202
  orthography 126, 133–4, 222
Larkin, Brian 221
Laumann, Dennis 235
Lecznar, Matthew 193
Lesotho 117–18
Levine, George 244, 247
Lilti, Antoine 206
Linyekula, Faustin 40
literature, African
  as world literature *see* literature, world and 'worlding'
  autobiography 124, 154
  biography 154
  Black Atlantic *see* Négritude, Black Atlantic
  circulation of 12–13, 115, 147–9, 191
  collectives and organisations 189
    Afro-Asian Writer's Association 32
    Alliance Française de Nairobi 201–2
    CARROT Co., the 28–9
    Circle Art Gallery 29
    Enkare Review 44
    Farafina Creative Writing Workshop 193–4, 208–9
    GoDown Arts Centre 23–4
    Hekaya Arts Initiative 171, 174
    Jalada 38–9, 42–4
    Kwani? 4, 23–4, 27–9, 38–45, 194–6, 209, 214, 224

INDEX

LongStorySHORT 13, 199–201, 204
Mbogi ya Mawriters 13, 199–204
Writers Guild Kenya 201
commoditisation of 149, 190
essays and non-fiction 23, 43, 171, 187, 193, 237
festivals and events 27–31, 43–4
　Abantu Book Festival 185
　Afrolit Sans Frontières 24, 30
　Aké Arts and Book Festival 13, 161–2, 183–8
　Artists for Refugees 30
　Freedom|Flight|Refuge 29–30
　Jalada Mobile Literary and Arts Festival 27, 39
　Macondo Literary Festival 24, 30
　Nairobi: Maps or Exile 24
　Pawa 254 24, 29, 40
　Storymoja 44
　Swahili Literary Festival 174
folktales 133
historical 125–31
inganekwane 131
legal-humanistic treatise 237
literary magazines, journals and digital platforms 4, 23, 31–3, 40–1, 148–9, 189, 201–3 *see also* newspapers and magazines
　Africa is a Country 197
　Aké Review 186–7
　A Long House 24–5, 28
　Brittle Paper 205–6
　Chimurenga Chronic 197
　Glendora Review 186
　Jalada Africa 24–7
　James Murua's African Literature Blog 24–5, 153
　Lagos Review 186
　Lolwe magazine 24, 27
　Lotus 32
　Okike 186
　Position 186
　Saraba Magazine 186
　The Crisis 133 n.82
　The Small Redemptions Of Lagos 194
　Ushahidi 41

memoir 156, 196, 206
newspapers *see* newspapers
novels 4–6, 37, 43–5, 67, 156
　as currency of world literature 38–43, 91, 119, 124
　'dictatorship' 67
　definitions of 75–82, 85–7, 119–20, 123–5, 131, 134
　extroverted 3–5
　graphic 156
　'Great Kenyan' *see* Kenya, 'Great Kenyan Novel'
One Read Africa 187
oral and epichoric 42, 91, 94, 115, 121–3, 126–9, 133–4, *see also* languages, Afrophone, oral
panchoric 115, 127, 134
plays 186
poetry 125, 160–2, 168, 172–4, 187, 224, 226 n.56
　African Poetry Book Fund (APBF) 156, 162
　imbongi 126
　praise poetry 126–9
　tenzi 93, 97–111
　epistolatory 103
　Kaisa, the 10–11, 94–8, 95, 97–111
　Utenzi wa Majimaji 101, 105
　Utenzi wa Qiyama 105 n.47
　Utendi wa Tambuka 98, 101, 104–7
　Utenzi wa Wadachi (Vita Vya) Kutamalaki Mrima 101, 105–7
prizes for *see* prizes and prize culture
proverbs 129
publication of *see* publishing
readers of 11–12, 79–80, 86, 127–9, 146, 154
short stories 23, 43–4, 123, 129, 187, 193, 201
songs 130 n.76, 188, 228
tarik see Gäbrä-Iyäsus, Afäwärq, Ləbb Wälläd Tarik
travelogues 4, 107
vernacular 115, 134 *see also* languages, Afrophone

literature, world and 'worlding' 30, 37–45, 72, 92, 158–9
  cosmopolitanism *see* cosmopolitanism
  definitions of 5–6, 20, 109, 183–5, 190
  dunia (the world) 102–11
  emergence of 71, 81
  Eurocentrism of 18, 22, 204
    see also postcolonialism, Eurocentrism of
  French literature *see* France, French literature
  objectives of 72, 88
  objectivity 14, 234, 241–52
  'global', *the* see 'global', the
  methodologies of 71–2, 88
  novels, as currency of *see* literature, African, novels
  ulimwengu (universe) 103
  worldliness 51–2, 65–7, 91, 110, 234, 252
  world-making 7, 10, 14, 22, 32, 52, 110, 234, 252
  'worldly' African' 2–3, 183, 245–52
  'world novel', the 22
  world-projection 2, 5, 8–10

Maake, Nhlanhla 120, 123–4
Mabanckou, Alain 9–10, 48–56, 203
  African Psycho 55
  Le Sanglot de l'homme noir 59
  Lettre à Jimmy 55
  Petit Piment 50–4, 67
  Verre Casseé 54
Madagascar 94, 98
  Nosi Bé 103
Maillu, Davis 42
Makumbi, Jennifer Nansubuga 18
Malawi (formerly Nyasaland, British Central Africa) 93, 96, 103, 185
  British Nyasa Company 101
  Bulantaya (Blantyre) 103
Mangua, Charles, *Kanina and I* 42
Manyanza, Anna 160, 174
Mariki, Frida 155
Márquez, Gabriel Garcia 30, 146

Marxism 11, 83, 190
  Marxist-Leninism 55–7
Marzagora, Sara 4, 10–11, 66, 71–88, 150–1, 158
Matshikisa, Lindiwe 200
Mattana, Alessio 88
Mayer, Sandra 207
Mayrargue, Cédric 58
Mbembe, Achille 48, 51, 160, 218 n.21
Mbithi, Esther 141, 151
Mbiti, John S. 143
Mbogi Genje 202
Mboya, Hlubi 200
Mboya, Joy 23–4
Mda, Zakes 185
Megiste, Maaza 40, 203
Methusala, Daniele 123
metropolitanism 49–50, 251
migration and mobility 17–33, 50
  exile 18–20, 23–31, 57
  intra-African 18–20, 25, 37–8
  refugees and migrants
    art by 29–30, 40
    camps for 17, 29, 40
    as characters 37
    Chinese 53, 63–5
    drowning of 25
    rights of 29, 54
    Rwandan 25–6, 37
    Somali 26–8
  slavery *see* slavery
Miller, Christopher 49
Mirzoeff, Nicholas 215
modernism 3, 10, 32
modernity and modernisation 62–3, 72–7, 81–6, 103, 242
  as European 87, 91, 110, 240
  as opposed to tradition 92
  transnational 87–8, 158
Mofolo, Thomas 118, 129–30
  Chaka 2 n.3, 122–4, 131
  Moeti oa Bochabela 116–17, 120–7
  Pitseng 120
Mohamed, Nadifa 203
Moretti, Franco 21–2, 32, 71, 81–4, 87
Morosetti, Tiziana 218
Moudileno, Lydie 49

Mozambique (formerly Portuguese East Africa) 10, 30, 91–111
  Angoche 94, 97–102, 108
  Mozambique Island 94, 100
  Sofala 97
Mqhayi, S. E. K. 118, 124–6, 130–2
  Ityala lamawele 117, 125–8, 132
  USamson 125, 129–30
Mükoma wa Ngũgĩ, 24, 142, 150, 154–6, 155, 161–4, 171, 176
  Black Star Nairobi 26
  Nairobi Heat 26
Murphy, David 48
Murua, James 14, 31
Musau, Paul 143
Mushakavanhu, Tinashe 201
Mutahi, Wahome 42
Mutiua, Chapane 91–111
Mutiua, Chapane 10–11
Mwangi, Boniface 40
Mwangi, Meja
  Going Down River Road 37, 42
  The Bushtrackers 42
  The Cockroach Dance 42
Mwaniki, Ciku Kimani, Cocktail from the Savannah 202
Mwau, John Harun 142

Najjar, Alexandre 9
Namwalie, Stiawa 29–30
nationalism 1, 6, 233–4, 238 see also Africa, national independence
neo-nationalism 24, 29
Ndlovu, Morgan 222
Négritude 1–3, 124
  Black Atlantic, the 50, 54–5, 58–60, 132
  Global Blackness 25
neocolonialism 14, 48, 51, 66–7, 208 see also colonialism
neoliberalism 40
Netherlands, the
  Dutch see languages, Europhone, Dutch
  Dutch imperialism 235
newspapers and magazines
  Afrophone 119
    awaj, relationship with 76–7

Ilange lase Natal 117, 130, 133 n.83
Imvo Zabantsundu 117
Izwi Labantu 117, 125, 130
Kiongozi 107
Leselinyana La Le-Sotho 117, 120, 123, 129
literary see literature, African, literary magazines, journals and digital platforms
materiality of 124
style of 122–3
The Bantu World 133 n.83
erotic (fictional) 220
Europhone 116–18
  African American Review 200
  Gold Coast Leader 245
  New York Times 192
  Vanity Fair 193
  Vogue 193
multilingual
  Umtleli wa Bantu 132
Ngang'a, Mbugua 43
Ngũgĩ wa Thiong'o 26, 39, 145–7, 150, 156–8
  A Grain of Wheat 42
  Decolonizing the Mind 140, 143
  foundation 139
  Globalectics 159–61
  Petals of Blood 42
  Wizard of the Crow 42
Ngumbau, Jacob 174
Nigeria 26, 29–30, 38, 145–6, 185–7, 196, 236
  Biafra 185
  Ibadan 188
Noah, Trevor, Born a Crime 198
Nyong'o, Lupita, Sulwe 198
Nzekwu, Onuora, Wand of Noble Wood 2

Obuchi, Jane 145
Odhiambo, Tom 171
Oduor, Richard Okwiri 27, 38
Ogechi, Nathan Oyori 147
Ogolla, Margaret, The River and Source 42
Ogot, Bethuel 44 n.4

Ohlsson, Anders 190–1, 195, 206
Okparanta, Chinelo 208
Okri, Ben 203
Okumu, John Sibi 202
Oman 98, 160
Omotoso, Yewande 199
Onjerika, Makena, *Digital Bedbugs* 202
Onyango, Troy 27
Opland, Jeff 129
Orsini, Francesca 4, 7, 66
Osundare, Niyi 188
Ottoman empire (Byzantine empire) 100–1, 106
  Emperor Heraklios 98
  'sultan of Istanbul' (Rumu) 94, 106
Owuor, Yvonne Adhiambo 18, 24, 29–32
  Dust 43, 195
  The Dragonfly Sea 19, 26
  The Weight of Whispers 25, 37

Parker, Kunal 249–50
Pelissièr, René 101
Plaatje, Sol T. 132
  Mhudi 117 n.11, 132–4
  Native Life in South Africa 132
  Sechuana Proverbs with Literal Translations and their European Equivalents 133
  Sechuana Reader in International Phonetic Orthography with English Translations 133
Ponzanesi, Sandra 204–7
Poovey, Mary 242–3
pornography 221–2
Portugal
  Portuguese *see* languages, Europhone, Portuguese
  Portuguese East Africa *see* Mozambique
  Portuguese imperialism 93–4, 99–101, 184, 235
postcolonialism
  centre vs. periphery 8–11, 21–22, 50, 53, 59, 71–2, 81–6, 234, 237
  'dictatorship novel' 67
  diffusionism 81–6
  'distant reading' 21

Eurocentrism of 81, 84–7, 216
retribution 63, 221–2
settle-colonial ecology 134
'writing back' 86
poverty 26, 218 *see also* humanitarianism and NGOs
prizes and prize culture 8, 24, 27, 49 n.8, 147, 153–4, 157–9, 192, 203
  AKO Caine Prize for African Writing 25, 43, 156, 189, 193, 196–7, 200–1, 208
  Booker Prize 42, 169, 189, 196
  Burt Africa Literary Award 162, 177, 201
  Commonwealth Prize, Best First Book 200
  Commonwealth Short Story Prize 159, 189, 193
  Commonwealth Writers' Prize 192
  dismissal of 197
  Ebrahim Hussein Poetry Prize 156
  Hurston/Wright Legacy Award 192
  Jomo Kenyatta Prize for Literature 156, 201
  Kwani? Manuscript Prize 43
  Mabati Cornell Kiswahili Prize for African Literature 13, 139, 153–65, 155, 160–3, 169–78, 169
  Miles Morland scholarship 42
  National Book Critics Circle Award 192
  New York Times Notable Book 192
  Nobel Prize for Literature 150, 189, 196, 204
  Prince Claus Prize 43
  Tuzo ya Ubunifu Kiswahili Literary Award 159
  Young Global Leader Award 197
  Wahome Mutahi Literary Prize 201
  Women's Prize for Fiction (formerly Orange Prize, Bailey's Prize) 189, 192
publishing
  agents 12, 163
  celebrity capital *see* capital, celebrity
  copyright 12

cover art 156, 161, 164–70, *166, 167, 169*, 175–7
digital 41 *see also* literature, African, magazines, journals and digital platforms
distribution 143, 151, 175, 185–7, 203
African Books Collective (ABC) 155, 175–6
editors 12, 172, 185
multilingual 144
print on demand (POD) 175
publishers 7, 12–13, 132, 135, 147–8, 151, 159–61, 183–5 *see also* literature, African, collectives and organisations
censorship 122–5, 129, 132
East African Educational Publishers (EAEP) 156, 160–3, 177–8
Ituĩka 139
mission presses 117–19, 122–6, 129 *see also* newspapers and journals
Mkuki na Nyota (MNN) 12–13, 153–78, *166, 167, 169*
Ouida Books 185–7
Prestige Books 201
Rewayat 187
Tanzania Publishing House (TPH) 155, 171
Twaweza Communications 140
readers *see* Africa, literature of, readers
Western 41

Quayson, Ato 213–14
queerness 170, 186, 196–7, 200, 207

racism 25, 28, 74, 208, 238
racial pseudo-science 248
white privilege 214–15
Rangimoto, Dotto 175
Mwanangu Rudi Nyumbani 162, 165–9, *167*
realism, literary 82–7, 104
refugees *see* migration and mobility, refugees

religion
banned 58
Christians and Christianity 106, 134
allegory *see* Bunyan, John
Biblical stories 128, 140
Christian worldview 74
ecumenicalism 74
Methodists and Methodism 244
missionaries 2, 57–8, 78, 98
American Zulu Mission 118, 132
Glasgow Missionary Society 118
Lovedale 117–18, 125–6, 129
mission presses *see* publishing, publishers, mission presses
Morija 117–22
Paris Evangelical Mission Society 118
schools 118, 122
moral principles of 2, 73–5
Pentacostalism 58, 64
pre-colonial 58, 238
rulers 72
'truth' of 76, 86
dogma 64
conversion 75, 100
'infidels' and 'pagans' 72–3, 83–5, 94, 106–8
Jews (*mayahudi*) and Judaism 106
Muslims and Islam 19, 26, 83, 100–1
Allah 108 n.55
fatwa 207
history of 104–6
Mecca 108
poetry 98
Prophet, the 98–100, 108
scholarship 98–100
solidarity with Germany 100
Sufism 98–9, 106
religious networks 19
religious tolerance 75
secularism 74, 100, 106, 244
Ricci, Lanfranco 84
Ricci, Ronit 99
Roberts, Gillian 192
Rodney, Walter, *How Europe Underdeveloped Africa* 171
Rorty, Richard 228

Rosendahl Thomsen, Mads 5
Rousseau, Jean-Jacques 206
Roy, Arundhati 196
Rubusana, W. B. 130
  Zemk'inkomo magwalandini (1906) 129
Ruheni, Mwangi 42
Rushdie, Salman 207
Rwanda 25–6, 29, 37–8

Sandwith, Corine 199–201
Santur, Hassan Ghedi 28
Sarbah, John Mensah 233–5, 241–6, 249–52
  Fante Customary Laws 235, 241–4, 251
Schiller, Daniel 61
Scott, David 234
Sekyi, Kobina 237
Selasi, Taiye 214
Senegal 185
  Dakar 65
Shariff, Ibrahim Noor 104
Shire, Warsan 40
Shivji, Isssa, *Class Struggles in Tanzania* 171
Shohat, Ella 217
Shoneyin, Lola 13, 183, 188
  The Secret Lives of Baba Segi's Wives 184, 188
Shringarpure, Bhakti 4, 17–33, 38–40, 44–5, 148
Silkiluwasha, Mpale Yvonne Mwansasu 162, 177
Slaughter, Joseph R. 30, 53–5, 66
slavery 73
  transatlantic 19, 25–8, 54, 59
sleeping sickness (Pongi) 216, 223–9
Smith, Kelvin 164
social media 53, 142, 149, 197, 204–7 *see also* capital, social; capital, media
  Facebook 148, 175, 200
  Instagram 31, 153
  Twitter 65, 148, 154, *154*, 200, 204
Soldati-Kahimbaara, C. K. 199–201
Somalia 17, 26–9, 38–40
  Barawa 97

South Africa 12, 26, 30, 116–17, 125, 134, 150, 185, 199–200
  Afrikaans Language Movement 116
  apartheid 38, 196, 200
  Inanda 118, 132
  Johannesburg 215
  Lekhotla la Tsoelo-pele 130
  Native Lands Act (1913) 119, 132
  Pretoria 200
  South African Native National Congress (*Inqungquthela*, SANNC, later ANC) 130–3
  Soweto 185
  Zulu Christian Industrial School 132
South Sudan 17, 226 n.56
Soyinka, Wole 2–3, 196, 205
Squires, Claire 169, 191
Stam, Robert 217
Steiner, A. 190–1, 195, 206
Sudan 17, 29, 38, 100, 216, 223–4, 227–9
  Ado 224, 228
  Pisak 225
Suhr-Sytsma, Nathan 160
Suriano, Maria 173
Swamy, Vinay 9
Stuurman, Renate 200
Switzerland (Swisi) 78, 94

Taddesse, Tamrat 72
Tanganyika 97
Tansi, Sony Labou, *La Vie et demie [Life and a Half]* 56
Tanzania 12, 105, 142, 153–5, 162–4, 168, 171–8
  ALAF 157
  Dar es Salaam 153, 165, 172–8
  Hassan, Samia Suluhu 153–4, 176
  Ngara 172
  Tanga 101
Taye, Assefa 72, 83–7
Taylor, Chris 239
Tchokothe, Rémi Armand 161, 164
Thomas, Dominic 61
Throsby, David 190
transcolonialism 60–1

translation 4–7, 55–7, 144–6, 150–1, 159, 162, 172 *see also* languages
  creative 98
  difficulty of 53–4, 63, 72, 184
  'gains in' 109
  impossibilities of 11
  Jalada Translation Project 12, 39, 139, 144–6
  oral 92, 99
  translators
    African 107, 184–5
    Bodé-Thomas, Modupé 184
    French 185
    World Congress of the International Federation of Translators 143
    Tsaliki, Liza 204
    Túbọsún, Kọ́lá 145

Uganda 17, 26, 38
  Kampala 215
Umezurike, Uchechukwu Peter, 'Under the Bridge' 200
unheimlich, the 21
United Arab Emirates (UAE) 187
United Kingdom 29, 171, 201
  African Studies Association UK 214
  British Council 41
  British imperialism 14, 94, 100, 184, 234–4, 247–9, 252
  British missionaries 58
  king of (Kingi) 94–7, 239
  London 172, 237
  Manchester (Mesheke) 97, 103
United Nations
  Artists for Refugees *see* migration and mobility, refugees
  resolutions of 65
  UNESCO 12, 144
  UNHCR 30
United States 26, 29, 61, 94, 156, 171, 176, 201 *see also* neocolonialsm
  American law 250
  American literature 50, 55, 190
  American missionaries 58, 64
  Black Atlantic *see* Négritude, Black Atlantic
  Congress for Cultural Freedom 31
  Oberlin Academy (OH) 132

USSR 32, 56, 94

Vierke, Clarissa 10–11, 91–111

Wainaina, Binyavanga 5, 23, 42, 170, 194, 196, 203, 209, 213–30
  'All Things Remaining Equal' 217
  as a *kawaja* (white man) 223, 226 n.56, 229
  Beyond River Yei 13, 216, 223–30
  'I Am A Homosexual, Mum' 197
  Kwani? see literature, African, collectives and organisations, *Kwani?*
  One Day I Will Write About This Place 196, 214–17, 226 n.56, 226 n.60
  'Ships in High Transit (SHiT)' 13, 216–23, 227–30
Wäldä-Sǝlasse, Hǝruy 77
Wallis, Kate 12, 24, 153–78, 194–5
Wanner, Zukiswa 31
  'The F Word' 200
war and violence 219, 223, 235
  battle of Tabuk 104
  civil war, Mozambique 92–3
  civil war, Nigeria 185
  civil war, Somalia 28–9
  civil war, Sudan 224, 228–9
  Cold War 22–3, 32, 38, 42, 56, 61
  Ethiopia, to establish (fictionalised) 73
  epistemological 61–5
  First World War 11, 60, 92, 100, 106 *see also* literature, Africa, poetry, *tenzi*
  Franco-Prussian war 104
  graphic (fictional) 67
  guerrilla 102–4
  Italo-Ethiopian 78–80
  Maji Maji Rebellion 101, 105 *see also* literature, Africa, poetry, tenzi
  post-election, Kenya 40, 44, 214
  reproduction of 65
  Second World War 20, 31, 60
  soldiers 83, 93–4, 97, 102–4, 107
    kariakoo 102

Pojulio 224
Schutztruppe 100–2
Sudanese People's Liberation
    Army 224
war crimes 65
weapons and warships (*manuwari*)
    94–5, 105–7
Washington, Booker T. 132
West-Pavlov, Russell 64
Williamson, Milly 204
Wood, Molara 187
World Economic Forum 197
WReC (Warwick Research
    Collective) 21

Yemen 19, 98
Yonas, Admassu 72, 75, 83–7
Yoon, Duncan M. 66–7
York, Lorraine 205

Zachernuk, Philip S. 236
Zambia 160
Zanzibar 97–101
Zecchini, Laetitia 7
Zimbabwe 26, 38

www.ingramcontent.com/pod-product-compliance
Lightning Source LLC
Chambersburg PA
CBHW052218300426
44115CB00011B/1736